NBER Macroeconomics Annual 2023

NBER Macroeconomics Annual 2023

Edited by
Martin Eichenbaum, Erik Hurst, and Valerie Ramey

The University of Chicago Press
Chicago and London

NBER Macroeconomics Annual 2023, Number 38

Published annually by The University of Chicago Press.
www.journals.uchicago.edu/MA/

Subscriptions: For individual and institutional subscription rates, visit www.journals .uchicago.edu, email subscriptions@press.uchicago.edu, or call (877) 705-1878 (US) or (773) 753-3347 (international). Free or deeply discounted institutional access is available in most developing nations through the Chicago Emerging Nations Initiative (www.journals .uchicago.edu/inst/ceni).

Please direct subscription inquiries to Subscription Fulfillment, 1427 E. 60th Street, Chicago, IL 60637-2902. Telephone: (773) 753-3347 or toll free in the United States and Canada (877) 705-1878. Fax: (773) 753-0811 or toll-free (877) 705-1879. E-mail: subscriptions @press.uchicago.edu.

Standing orders: To place a standing order for this book series, please address your request to The University of Chicago Press, Chicago Distribution Center, Attn. Standing Orders/Customer Service, 11030 S. Langley Avenue, Chicago, IL 60628. Telephone toll free in the U.S. and Canada: 1-800-621-2736; or 1-773-702-7000. Fax toll free in the U.S. and Canada: 1-800-621-8476; or 1-773-702-7212.

Single-copy orders: In the U.S., Canada, and the rest of the world, order from your local bookseller or direct from The University of Chicago Press, Chicago Distribution Center, 11030 S. Langley Avenue, Chicago, IL 60628. Telephone toll free in the U.S. and Canada: 1-800-621-2736; or 1-773-702-7000. Fax toll free in the U.S. and Canada: 1-800-621-8476; or 1-773-702-7212. In the U.K. and Europe, order from your local bookseller or direct from The University of Chicago Press, c/o John Wiley Ltd. Distribution Center, 1 Oldlands Way, Bognor Regis, West Sussex PO22 9SA, UK. Telephone 01243 779777 or Fax 01243 820250. E-mail: cs-books@wiley.co.uk.

The University of Chicago Press offers bulk discounts on individual titles to Corporate, Premium and Gift accounts. For information, please write to Sales Department—Special Sales, The University of Chicago Press, 1427 E. 60th Street, Chicago, IL 60637 USA or telephone 1-773-702-7723.

This book was printed and bound in the United States of America.

ISSN: 0889-3365
E-ISSN: 1537-2642
ISBN: 978-0-226-83568-6 (pb.:alk.paper)
eISBN: 978-0-226-83569-3 (e-book)

Relation of the Directors to the Work and Publications of the NBER

1. The object of the NBER is to ascertain and present to the economics profession, and to the public more generally, important economic facts and their interpretation in a scientific manner without policy recommendations. The Board of Directors is charged with the responsibility of ensuring that the work of the NBER is carried on in strict conformity with this object.

2. The President shall establish an internal review process to ensure that book manuscripts proposed for publication DO NOT contain policy recommendations. This shall apply both to the proceedings of conferences and to manuscripts by a single author or by one or more coauthors but shall not apply to authors of comments at NBER conferences who are not NBER affiliates.

3. No book manuscript reporting research shall be published by the NBER until the President has sent to each member of the Board a notice that a manuscript is recommended for publication and that in the President's opinion it is suitable for publication in accordance with the above principles of the NBER. Such notification will include a table of contents and an abstract or summary of the manuscript's content, a list of contributors if applicable, and a response form for use by Directors who desire a copy of the manuscript for review. Each manuscript shall contain a summary drawing attention to the nature and treatment of the problem studied and the main conclusions reached.

4. No volume shall be published until forty-five days have elapsed from the above notification of intention to publish it. During this period a copy shall be sent to any Director requesting it, and if any Director objects to publication on the grounds that the manuscript contains policy recommendations, the objection will be presented to the author(s) or editor(s). In case of dispute, all members of the Board shall be notified, and the President shall appoint an ad hoc committee of the Board to decide the matter; thirty days additional shall be granted for this purpose.

5. The President shall present annually to the Board a report describing the internal manuscript review process, any objections made by Directors before publication or by anyone after publication, any disputes about such matters, and how they were handled.

6. Publications of the NBER issued for informational purposes concerning the work of the Bureau, or issued to inform the public of the activities at the Bureau, including but not limited to the NBER Digest and Reporter, shall be consistent with the object stated in paragraph 1. They shall contain a specific disclaimer noting that they have not passed through the review procedures required in this resolution. The Executive Committee of the Board is charged with the review of all such publications from time to time.

7. NBER working papers and manuscripts distributed on the Bureau's web site are not deemed to be publications for the purpose of this resolution, but they shall be consistent with the object stated in paragraph 1. Working papers shall contain a specific disclaimer noting that they have not passed through the review procedures required in this resolution. The NBER's web site shall contain a similar disclaimer. The President shall establish an internal review process to ensure that the working papers and the web site do not contain policy recommendations, and shall report annually to the Board on this process and any concerns raised in connection with it.

8. Unless otherwise determined by the Board or exempted by the terms of paragraphs 6 and 7, a copy of this resolution shall be printed in each NBER publication as described in paragraph 2 above.

Contents

Editorial

Martin Eichenbaum, *Northwestern University and NBER,* United States of America
Erik Hurst, *University of Chicago and NBER,* United States of America
Valerie Ramey, *Stanford University and NBER,* United States of America

The NBER's 38th Annual Conference on Macroeconomics brought together leading scholars to present, discuss, and debate five research papers on central issues in contemporary macroeconomics. In addition, it included a panel discussion on "The Return of Inflation: Why and What to Do About It." Kristin Forbes moderated the panel, which included Jason Furman, Ricardo Reis, and Silvana Tenreyro.

This conference volume contains edited versions of the five papers presented at the conference, each followed by two written discussions by leading scholars and a summary of the debates that followed each paper.

During the last few decades, aggregate real wage growth has stagnated despite growing aggregate productivity growth. Given this, there has been a renewed interest by both labor and macroeconomists in exploring whether changes in firm market power can explain why real wages have not kept up with productivity growth. In their paper, "An Anatomy of Monopsony: Search Frictions, Amenities, and Bargaining in Concentrated Markets," David Berger, Kyle Herkenhoff, Andreas Kostøl, and Simon Mongey develop a model to highlight and estimate the importance of three separate channels that can explain why workers are paid less than their marginal product. The first channel centers on workers' idiosyncratic preferences for firms generating an upward-sloping firm-specific labor supply curve. Second, some labor markets only have a small number of firms, which gives those firms market power over the workers in the labor market. The first two forces limit workers' ability to substitute across firms when market conditions change. Finally, workers can be paid less than

NBER Macroeconomics Annual, volume 38, 2024.
© 2024 National Bureau of Economic Research. All rights reserved. Published by The University of Chicago Press for the National Bureau of Economic Research. https://doi .org/10.1086/729193

their marginal product due to search frictions in the labor market. The framework highlights how these forces act in isolation and in combination to explain the extent to which worker wages can deviate from worker marginal product. Using detailed Norwegian data, the authors estimate that the average wage markdown in Norway in recent years is 21%. Using their structural model, they find evidence for all three forces in explaining wage markdowns.

Both discussants praise the paper for tackling the relatively unexplored question of what determines monopsony power in the labor market. Both discussants also note that the framework created by the authors is a nice starting point for such an analysis in that it combines many features from the literature into one model. However, both discussants noted features that are missing from the model that could affect the paper's quantitative inference. For example, in his comments, Giuseppe Moscarini pointed out that additional aspects of firm heterogeneity are not included, which could result in an upward bias in the estimated importance of labor market frictions. Katarína Borovičková, in her comments, noted how both heterogeneity across workers and heterogeneity in the distribution of firms across space can result in a different sort of bias with respect to the authors' decomposition of the relative importance of the different forces in their counterfactuals. Both discussants remark that additional data can be brought into the analysis to better distinguish the causes of the wage markdown.

The significant rise in inflation during 2021 and 2022 led to questions about its sources and why central banks failed to contain it. In "Inflation Strikes Back: The Role of Import Competition and the Labor Market," Mary Amiti, Sebastian Heise, Fatih Karahan, and Ayşegül Şahin set out to study which factors were the most important in leading the run-up in prices and to assess the Fed's response was suboptimal. The main part of the paper models the leading factors in a two-sector New Keynesian model. In particular, the model allows for supply chain disruptions, shocks to import prices, shifts in demand from one sector to another (in particular from services to goods), shocks to the disutility of labor (to capture the effects of COVID-19 on labor supply), variable markups, and accommodative monetary policy. The authors calibrate their model and analyze the impact of the various shocks on inflation. They find that their model can explain the entire rise in core inflation in 2021. Two of the findings are particularly noteworthy. First, the aggregate effect of the shocks is greater than the sum of the individual effects because of nonlinearities in the effects. In particular, the simultaneous occurrence of the supply chain shocks and the labor disutility shock raises inflation by 0.7 percentage points more than if they had hit separately. Second, they simulate a counterfactual path of the economy under the assumption that the Fed was more aggressive against inflation than it was. They find the surprising result that the more aggressive policy would have led to sharp declines in real activity without much effect on inflation.

The discussants, Şebnem Kalemli-Özcan and Matthias Trabandt, note the importance of the question addressed by the paper but raise questions about the features of the model that deliver the results. For example, Kalemli-Özcan notes that the large stimulus payments adopted simultaneously across multiple countries created a huge positive shock to demand. However, the authors model these demand shocks and the implied movements along a fixed supply curve instead of as supply shocks. Kalemli-Özcan and Trabandt point out that this modeling choice stacks the deck against the possibility that the Fed could have contained inflation without big output losses. Trabandt points out that the literature on optimal monetary policy shows that if inflation is demand driven, aggressive monetary policy can contain inflation without inducing a recession. Both discussants also call into question various other important modeling choices, such as the assumption that the United States is a small open economy, and compare the suitability of the authors' model with the ones used by other papers in the open economy literature that analyze the causes of the run-up in inflation.

In the recovery from the COVID-19 lockdowns, bottlenecks in supply chains received considerable attention as a source of constraints on production. In their paper, "Bottlenecks: Sectoral Imbalances and the US Productivity Slowdown," Daron Acemoglu, David Autor, and Christina Patterson take the idea of bottlenecks to a new level by offering the novel hypothesis that aggregate total factor productivity (TFP) growth can be slowed by bottlenecks in innovation along a supply chain. In particular, higher cross-sectional variance in innovation activity can reduce aggregate TFP because slow innovation by upstream suppliers can choke off growth of innovative downstream firms, resulting in lower aggregate TFP growth.

The authors motivate their hypothesis with leading historical examples of bottlenecks, such as batteries and transistors, as well as with a stylized theoretical model that develops the economic intuition. The main part of the paper consists of a statistical analysis of detailed industry data. The regressions using their main data set—the National Bureau of Economic Research (NBER) and U.S. Census Bureau's Center for Economic Studies

(CES) manufacturing data—show that higher variance of TFP across upstream industry suppliers results in slower productivity growth of the downstream industry, even after controlling for the mean. The authors conduct several robustness checks and explorations of alternative explanations, which tend to confirm or even strengthen the results. They also use an auxiliary data set on patent citations to show that the variance of patent citations across upstream industries also has a negative effect on downstream industry patenting. They document that the variance of TFP growth has risen over time and use their estimates to conclude that this rise was a major source of the productivity slowdown from 1997 to 2007.

Both discussant teams praise the authors' intriguing hypothesis but question whether the data support it. John Fernald and Eugenio Piga note that conventional wisdom and official US government data show that productivity growth accelerated from 1997 to 2005 in contrast to the slowdown in the authors' data. Fernald and Piga compare the NBER-CES data set used by the authors with the Bureau of Labor Statistics–Bureau of Economic Analysis (BLS-BEA) integrated accounts and find significantly different paths of productivity implied by each one. Attempts to reconcile the two data sets come up short. When Fernald and Piga reproduce the authors' analysis on the BLS-BEA data set, they find that increases in variance appear to raise rather than lower aggregate TFP. The second discussant team, Jennifer La'O and Eugenio Piga, offers an alternative explanation for the authors' empirical findings. La'O and Piga consider the possibility that TFP is mismeasured because none of the data sets account for variation in capital utilization. They present a neoclassical model in which variations in factor prices and mismeasurement of TFP can lead to the pattern of results found by the authors. However, these results reflect movements along a production function, not bottlenecks. La'O and Piga reestimate the authors' model, including controls suggested by their neoclassical theory. They find that the coefficient on the variance of TFP falls by two-thirds and becomes statistically insignificant. Thus, they concur with Fernald and Piga that further tests of the authors' very interesting hypothesis are warranted.

Since the financial crisis of 2008, macroeconomists have paid increasing attention to the role of the financial sector in aggregate fluctuations. A central question in the literature is how lending responds to macroeconomic and financial shocks. In their paper, "Aggregate Lending and Modern Financial Intermediation: Why Bank Balance Sheet Models Are Miscalibrated," Greg Buchak, Gregor Matvos, Tomasz Piskorski, and Amit Seru argue that existing models give misleading answers to this question.

The reason is that the models do not account for two key features of the industrial organization of the financial industry. First, shadow banks account for a substantial share of lending in many markets. Second, banks sell a significant fraction of the loans that they originate through securitization.

The authors focus on the origination of residential mortgages in the United States, highlighting the growth in nonbanks' share of these originations. They argue that using bank data to measure lending can lead to erroneous conclusions about how lending responds to economic or policy shocks.

The authors develop a dynamic quantitative model of lending that includes banks and shadow banks. They use the model to argue that calibration exercises must consider the financial industry's two features discussed above to provide empirically plausible characterizations of how shocks amplify through financial intermediaries. The authors' findings highlight the limitations of bank balance sheets as a source of data on lending in empirical exercises and the need to include lending by shadow banks.

The first discussant, Jeremy Stein, praised the authors for their thought-provoking paper. In his view, the most interesting interpretation of their results is that shocks to the capital of the entire sector would not have as significant on an impact on activity as they would in an all-bank economy.

This interpretation reflects an assumption that there is something special about nonbank lending that makes it either less capital-reliant or more resilient to capital shocks than bank lending. Stein argues this assumption may be incorrect. First, even nonbanks that primarily originate loans to distribute may require meaningful amounts of equity capital. Second, an increasing fraction of loans are sold off in the securitization market. So, to assess the financial system's stability, it becomes very important to ask what type of intermediary is buying these loans and what their capital structures and associated vulnerabilities are.

Stein's analysis suggests that perhaps one should not focus on the type of intermediary making a given type of loan. Instead, one should focus on the underlying lending technology for a given type of loan. That technology is likely similar across different intermediaries.

Stein concludes with the observation that shadow banking may have grown after the financial crisis because regulation drove lending activity into more lightly regulated shadows. But if that is true, it could be that the financial system is more vulnerable to shocks rather than less vulnerable, as in the authors' model.

The second discussant, Itamar Dreschler, focused his comment on the question of who are the ultimate buyers of mortgages originated by nonbanks. He argues that this question, rather than who originates the mortgages, is the key to understanding the supply of mortgage credit. In the end, it is the buyers that supply the capital that finances the mortgages. This perspective matters in analyzing the effects of shocks on the economy and providing guidance to regulators who want to influence the supply of credit.

Dreschler analyzes the composition of mortgage investors over time and shows that the share of residential mortgages owned by traditional banks has been between 40% and 50% since around 1990. The reason is that banks ultimately buy many nonbank mortgage originations in the form of agency-backed mortgage-backed securities.

Dreschler provides an interesting analysis of why banks want to hold so many long-duration mortgages. The basic idea is that banks' deposit franchise makes them natural buyers of long-term fixed-rate assets. That franchise allows them to pay deposit rates with a low sensitivity ("beta") to the short-term interest rate. So banks can hold long-term fixed-rate assets whose cash flows also have low sensitivity to the short rate, without being exposed to fluctuations in the short rate.

Academic macroeconomists typically attribute business cycles to the rational response of firms and households to persistent "fundamental" shocks—for example, technology or aggregate demand. In principle, such shocks should also explain stock market volatility. In practice, they do not, unless one allows for variation in investors' subjective discount rates. Unfortunately, the implied variation in expected returns is inconsistent with the properties of survey-based measures of those returns.

In their paper, "Long-Term Expectations and Aggregate Fluctuations," Pedro Bordalo, Nicola Gennaioli, Rafael La Porta, Matthew O'Brien, and Andrei Shleifer model volatility in financial assets and aggregate quantities. They assume investors are risk neutral but allow expectations to be nonrational. Critically, they measure expectations using stock analysts' consensus expectations of the earnings growth of S&P 500 firms.

The authors show that expectations of long-term earnings growth (LTG) for individual US-listed firms account for the volatility of equities as well as safe and risky bonds. Moreover, variations in LTG explain boom-bust cycles in economic activity.

Consistent with Keynes's view, an increase in LTG fuels an investment boom. That boom sharply reverses 2 years later in a way that is fully explained by predictable overoptimism in the initial expectations of LTG.

The results in the paper pose an important challenge to mainstream approaches to modeling business cycles.

The first discussant, George-Marios Angeletos, argues that the paper makes three important contributions. First, it provides a quantitatively potent proxy for subjective expectations. The apparent disconnect between asset prices and fundamentals largely disappears once we measure "fundamentals" by subjective expectations of earnings. Second, it identifies a rich set of novel empirical regularities. Third, it advances the authors' agenda about diagnostic expectations and overextrapolation.

Angeletos agrees that changes in subjective expectations, as measured by expectations in LTG, help account for fluctuations in asset prices and investment both in the aggregate and in the cross section.

In his view, expectations in LTG are a proxy for at least three different forces: overextrapolation of innovations in actual earning, which is the authors' main hypothesis; news about future TFP; and extrinsic sentiments or animal spirits. He argued that future research should aim to disentangle the quantitative role of these forces.

The next discussant, Venky Venkateswaran, summarizes the paper's primary contribution as making the case that equity analysts' forecasts of LTG are key to understanding movements in financial market variables and macro aggregates.

Venkateswaran raises an important caveat to the authors' conclusions. It may be that movements in the LTG are primarily the result of analysts mechanically revising their forecasts to rationalize observed price changes. He reviews the evidence in favor of and against this interpretation and argues that more work is needed to dismiss this possibility.

This point aside, Venkateswaran agrees with the authors that movements in expectations of LTG do remarkably well in matching observed stock price fluctuations. He also notes the striking relationship between LTG and investment, gross domestic product, consumption, employment, wages, and inflation. An upward revision to LTG acts like a "positive" business cycle shock in the short run, which largely reverses itself over a longer horizon.

Like Angeletos, Venkateswaran concludes that the key challenge is distinguishing changes in expectations of LTG from marginal efficiency of investment shocks, risk shocks, and confidence shocks.

The authors and the editors would like to take this opportunity to thank Jim Poterba and the National Bureau of Economic Research for their continued support for the *NBER Macroeconomics Annual* and the associated conference. We would also like to thank the NBER conference staff, particularly Rob Shannon for his continued excellent organization and support. Financial assistance from the National Science Foundation is gratefully acknowledged. We also thank the rapporteurs, Andrea Ferrara and Ali Uppal, who provided invaluable help in preparing the summaries of the discussions. Last but far from least, we are grateful to Helena Fitz-Patrick for her invaluable assistance in editing and publishing the volume.

Endnote

For acknowledgments, sources of research support, and disclosure of the authors' material financial relationships, if any, please see https://www.nber.org/books-and-chapters/nber-macroeconomics-annual-2023-volume-38/editorial-nber-macroeconomics-annual-2023-volume-38.

Abstracts

An Anatomy of Monopsony: Search Frictions, Amenities, and Bargaining in Concentrated Markets

David Berger, Kyle Herkenhoff, Andreas R. Kostøl, and Simon Mongey

We contribute a theory in which three channels interact to determine the degree of monopsony power and therefore the markdown of a worker's spot wage relative to her marginal product: (1) heterogeneity in worker-firm-specific preferences (nonwage amenities), (2) firm granularity, and (3) off- and on-the-job search frictions. We use Norwegian data to discipline each channel and then reproduce new reduced-form empirical relationships between market concentration, job flows, wages and wage inequality. In doing so we provide a novel method for clustering occupations into local labor markets. Our main exercise quantifies the contribution of each channel to income inequality and wage markdowns. The average markdown is 21 percent in our baseline estimation. Removing nonwage amenity dispersion narrows them by a third. Giving the next-lowest-ranked competitor a seat at the bargaining table narrows them by half, suggesting that granularity and strategic interactions in the bargaining process is an important source of markdowns. Removing search frictions narrows them by two-thirds. Each counterfactual reduces wage inequality and increases welfare.

NBER Macroeconomics Annual, volume 38, 2024.

Inflation Strikes Back: The Role of Import Competition and the Labor Market

Mary Amiti, Sebastian Heise, Fatih Karahan, and Ayşegül Şahin

U.S. inflation has recently surged, with inflation reaching its highest readings since the early 1980s. We examine the drivers of the rise in inflation, focusing on supply chain disruptions, labor supply constraints, and the shift of consumption from services to goods in the presence of accommodative monetary policy. Using a calibrated two-sector New Keynesian DSGE model with multiple factors of production, foreign competition, and endogenous markups, we find that the shocks account for all of the 4 percentage point rise in core inflation in 2021. We then show that the interaction of supply chain disruptions and the labor disutility shock increased price inflation in the model by 0.7 percentage point more than it would have risen if the shocks had hit separately. This amplification arises because the joint shock to labor and imported input prices makes substituting between labor and intermediates less effective for domestic firms. Moreover, the simultaneous foreign competition shock allows domestic producers to increase their pass-through into prices without losing market share. The simultaneous shift of demand towards goods further amplified inflation. While by itself the shift from services to goods would have caused a relatively muted inflationary effect of 0.5 percentage point, its inflationary effects were amplified to nearly 1 percentage point because of the simultaneous supply-side shocks. Intuitively, consumption of goods increased precisely when their production costs were already under pressure. We then show in the model that it would have required a very aggressive monetary policy to contain the inflation surge in 2021 since inflation was largely driven by supply-side factors and such a policy would have had a large negative effect on the labor market. We use aggregate and industry-level data on producer prices, wages, and input prices to provide corroborating evidence for the key amplification channels in the model.

Bottlenecks: Sectoral Imbalances and the US Productivity Slowdown

Daron Acemoglu, David Autor, and Christina Patterson

Despite the rapid pace of innovation in information and communications technologies (ICT) and electronics, aggregate US productivity growth has been disappointing since the 1970s. We propose and empirically explore the hypothesis that slow growth stems in part from an unbalanced sectoral distribution of innovation over the last several decades. Because an industry's success in innovation depends on complementary innovations among its input suppliers, rapid productivity growth that is concentrated in a subset of sectors may create bottlenecks and consequently fail to translate into commensurate aggregate productivity gains. Using data on input-output linkages, citation linkages, industry productivity growth and patenting, we find evidence consistent with this hypothesis: the variance of suppliers' Total Factor Productivity growth or innovation adversely affects an industry's own TFP growth and innovation. Our estimates suggest that a substantial share of the productivity slowdown in the United States (and several other industrialized economies) can be accounted for by a sizable increase in cross-industry variance of TFP growth and innovation. For example, if TFP growth variance had remained at the 1977–1987 level, US manufacturing productivity would have grown twice as rapidly in 1997–2007 as it did—yielding a counterfactual growth rate that would have been close to that of 1977–1987 and 1987–1997.

Aggregate Lending and Modern Financial Intermediation: Why Bank Balance Sheet Models Are Miscalibrated

Greg Buchak, Gregor Matvos, Tomasz Piskorski, and Amit Seru

Existing macroeconomic models focused on bank balance sheet lending are deficient because they do not account for the modern industrial organization of financial intermediation. Utilizing publicly available micro-level lending data, we investigate two increasingly significant margins of adjustment in credit markets: *banks' ability to sell loans* and *shadow bank activity*. These adjustment margins are substantial and vary across time and regions with different incomes. We examine these margins in a parsimonious dynamic quantitative model featuring banks with balance sheet adjustment through loan sales and shadow banks. Using the calibrated model, we illustrate that these margins significantly dampen the immediate contraction following bank capital shock. Recovery is also faster, because profitable loan sales (e.g., securitization) allow banks to build capital faster and because shadow banks pick up lending slack. Failure to account for adjustment margins leads to significant errors when studying policies which rely on financial intermediation pass-through in the level of aggregate lending, its direction, and composition. Our model highlights the tension between bank balance sheet models and data. The model, which forces total lending to depend strongly on bank balance sheet health, must reconcile the weak correlation between bank capital and aggregate lending. These issues can be reconciled with now available data from bank balance sheets, overall bank lending, and aggregate lending, in conjunction with a model of modern financial intermediation.

Long-Term Expectations and Aggregate Fluctuations
Pedro Bordalo, Nicola Gennaioli, Rafael La Porta, Matthew OBrien, and Andrei Shleifer

In line with Keynes' intuition, volatility in the stock market and in real economic activity is linked by expectations of long term profits. We show that analysts' optimism about the long term earnings growth of S&P 500 firms is associated with a near term boom in major US financial markets, real investment, and other business cycle indicators. The same optimism however predicts disappointing earnings growth and a contraction in financial markets and real activity one to two years later. Overreaction of measured long term profit expectations emerges as a promising mechanism for reconciling Shiller's excess volatility puzzle with the business cycle.

1

An Anatomy of Monopsony: Search Frictions, Amenities, and Bargaining in Concentrated Markets

David Berger, *Duke University and NBER,* United States of America

Kyle Herkenhoff, *University of Minnesota, Federal Reserve Bank of Minneapolis, and NBER,* United States of America

Andreas R. Kostøl, *Arizona State University W. P. Carey School of Business,* United States of America, *Norges Bank,* Norway, and *NBER,* United States of America

Simon Mongey, *Federal Reserve Bank of Minneapolis and NBER,* United States of America

I. Introduction

There is a growing consensus that imperfect competition in the labor market is pervasive.[1] Many local labor markets are dominated by a few firms, which gives them the ability to set wages and pay workers less than their marginal product. In his 2022 AEA presidential address, David Card argued that developing a tractable framework combining preference heterogeneity (in the Daniel McFadden-industrial organization tradition) and search and matching frictions with job ladders (in the Postel-Vinay and Robin [2002] tradition) were key to understanding the importance of market power in the labor market. The goal of this paper is to take a first step toward answering this charge. We develop a theory of monopsony that incorporates the three paradigms of the modern monopsony literature: worker-firm-specific preference heterogeneity (Robinson 1933), search frictions (Burdett and Mortensen 1998), and firm granularity (Berger, Herkenhoff, and Mongey 2022a; Jarosch, Nimcsik, and Sorkin 2024). We then quantify our framework using Norwegian worker-firm data and use it to answer several pertinent questions: How do the three sources of monopsony interact to shape wages, job flows, and welfare? Which sources of monopsony account for the wedge between a worker's pay and marginal product (henceforth, the wage markdown)? How does monopsony power affect wage inequality?

NBER Macroeconomics Annual, volume 38, 2024.

We make three contributions. Empirically, we use Norwegian administrative data to document that, within an occupation, wage levels, wage inequality, and job flows correlate systematically with local labor market concentration. Theoretically, we develop a model of frictional labor markets with a finite number of firms, as well as on-the-job search, worker-firm-specific nonwage amenities, and vacancy posting. Although some recent papers include the first two, vacancy posting closes the model in equilibrium and provides the first theory of search in granular markets that admits counterfactuals. Quantitatively, we use the Norwegian data and the structure of our model to discipline and then quantify the wage, welfare, and job flow implications of each source of monopsony power. Our empirics motivate a number of assumptions in our theory and allow us to conduct overidentification tests on the role of concentration in the quantitative framework.

Our framework implies that granularity in the wage bargaining process, amenities, and search frictions account for one-half, one-third, and two-thirds of wage markdowns, respectively, with the nonadditivity arising from the nonlinearity of our model. Although amenities and search frictions are studied extensively in the literature, our results suggest that more exploration of granularity and strategic interactions in the bargaining process are an important next step for the monopsony literature.

A.   Empirics

We begin by using detailed data about workplace locations and workers' line of work to document the relationship between concentration levels, wages, wage inequality, and job flows. Using two separate fixed-effect specifications that isolate within occupation-year, across-region variation and within occupation-region, across-time variation, we document a set of covariances between market concentration and labor market characteristics. More concentrated markets are associated with lower wages, less wage dispersion, lower employer-to-employer job flow rates, and lower job-finding rates. It is well known that job-to-job transitions are a key source of wage growth (see, e.g., Postel-Vinay and Robin 2002). These strong links between job flows and concentration suggest that on-the-job search may be an important mechanism through which market structure affects the level and dispersion of wages.

B.   Theory

Motivated by these findings, we develop a theory that incorporates neoclassical sources of monopsony as well as frictional job flows and concentration. Our model features a finite number of firms, on-the-job search, worker-firm-specific nonwage amenities, and strategic wage setting. The first two are necessary to replicate our empirical finding that both employer-to-employer flows and wages are lower in more concentrated markets. Firm contact rates are determined in general equilibrium by optimal firm vacancy posting, given the endogenous distribution of workers across firms.

Our framework substantially extends Postel-Vinay and Robin (2002) to accommodate a finite number of firms in each labor market and worker-firm-specific nonwage amenities. The number of firms in each market is given by $M < \infty$, and firms differ in their idiosyncratic but fixed productivity levels. Unemployed workers randomly meet vacancies of the M firms within their labor market, whereas employed workers randomly meet vacancies of the remaining $M - 1$ firms, excluding their current employer. When an unemployed worker meets a firm, the worker draws a worker-firm-specific nonwage amenity, and the parties Nash bargain over surplus. When an employed worker meets a firm, the worker draws a new worker-firm-specific amenity, and the incumbent and poaching firms compete via alternating offers (e.g., Cahuc, Postel-Vinay, and Robin 2006), yielding equilibrium values in which outside options are determined by Bertrand competition and the remaining surplus is split by Nash bargaining. Last, we assume that firms optimally choose vacancies, taking match surplus and market contract rates as given. Modeling of a firm's vacancy-posting decisions explicitly generates endogenous contact rates, which both closes the model and delivers a meaningful firm size distribution.

The surplus-sharing protocol yields strategic complementarity between wage offers of incumbent and poaching firms. In the Cahuc et al. (2006) class of models, regardless of M, only two firms bargain. This "hardwired" duopsony is an important source of markdowns that operates through strategic wage setting. Allowing more firms at the bargaining table will reduce markdowns and increase efficiency. We contribute a stylized counterfactual that raises this point, and we leave more careful extensions of the theory to future research. Future researchers may try to (i) understand how changes in M affect the number of firms that are bargaining over any particular match and (ii) provide a theory for bargaining with more than two firms.

There are several caveats to our approach. Neoclassical models of monopsony focus on worker-firm-specific amenities as generating a mechanism by which firms must increase wages to attract more workers. We take those same worker-firm-specific amenities and study them in a search and matching model where we find they are necessary to match features of the data and provide market power for firms. However, we assume that they operate differently than in the neoclassical case. We allow firms to observe amenity draws and perfectly price discriminate. This differs with Robinson (1933), who treats amenities as unobserved and thus only allows for third-degree discrimination. An important implication of perfect price discrimination is that amenities themselves do not necessarily yield inefficient allocations.

C. Quantification

We use linked employer-employee data from Norway to discipline the quantitative model. The administrative data offer several advantages over other data sources. The Norwegian data include information about the type of work that each employee is hired to do (i.e., their occupation) and the workplace location of every employment contract from 2006 to 2016. These complete records allow us to accurately measure job flows and thus better classify local labor markets.

We contribute a simple clustering algorithm to define local labor markets, which we apply to these data. Rather than working with connected sets of firms (which is computationally demanding), our approach uses the much lower-dimensional occupation-to-occupation flow transition matrix. We first isolate single-occupation markets with high self-flow rates. Among the remaining occupations, we K-means cluster the rows of the occupation-to-occupation flow transition matrix. The resulting groups are occupations with similar job flow patterns. We determine the optimal number of clusters using an objective function that is increasing in the self-flow rate but decreasing in the concentration of occupations in each cluster. This rewards the lowering of self-flow rates but penalizes the classification of all occupations in one large cluster and thus "overfitting" the data.

We do not innovate on the dimension of geography; we simply define the boundary of a market to be the boundary of the commuting zone as computed in Bhuller (2009). This yields approximately 5,000 markets with a self-flow rate of 51% (among job transitioners, 51% transition back into the same market). Using three-digit occupation by commuting zone to define the market yields a similar number of markets but a lower self-flow rate of 45%. In an approach that intuitively groups connected sets of firms (stochastic blocks), Jarosch et al. (2024) find 376 markets with a self-flow rate of 40% in Austria. Worker occupation data allow us to define markets that both have high self-flow rates and are computationally easy to compute.

With market definitions in hand, we estimate the model to match key moments between 2006 and 2016 in Norway. First, we directly import market structures observed in the Norwegian data, including the number of firms in a market and the labor force in the market. Second, we discipline the role of amenities using the fraction of employer-to-employer (E-to-E) job moves down the ladder, where rungs are defined by the poaching index following Bagger and Lentz (2019). Third, we discipline the role of search frictions based on unemployment and E-to-E rates. Fourth, we discipline the bargaining power of workers using wage growth. We estimate the model on an overidentified set of moments to ensure that our model is consistent with observed covariances of market Herfindahl values and the level and standard deviation of wages. Despite its parsimony, the quantitative model fits nontargeted cross-market moments from our earlier empirics, generating lower E-to-E rates and unemployment-to-employment (U-to-E) rates in more concentrated markets.

D. Results

In our main results, we use the model to generate five counterfactuals that highlight the importance of labor market competition for markdowns, welfare, and wage inequality.

Concentration

We explore the role of concentration in depth because it is the newest element of our analysis. Our goal is to vary the number of firms (M) while holding the distribution of productivity (z) and bargaining protocol fixed. To implement this "idealized" heuristic experiment, we draw a vector of 10 productivities from the ergodic distribution and duplicate this productivity vector 10 times to construct 10 markets. We then organize the productivity vectors into three counterfactual economies (from most to least concentrated): 10 identical 10-firm markets, two identical 50-firm markets, and one 100-firm market. We hold the ratio of firms per worker fixed to remove mechanical effects from adding firms to a market. We find that workers' share of surplus monotonically increases as markets become less concentrated. A side effect of a higher surplus share is a reduction in compensating differentials; that is, the amenity wage penalty shrinks. With less concentration, wages w rise, markdowns narrow (i.e., w/z increases), and welfare increases. Inequality increases: across firms, more productive firms pay higher wages, and within firms, some workers are paid more due to better bargaining opportunities. Consolidating all 100 firms into a single market allows more workers to reach the highest-productivity firms, increasing output. Accordingly, unemployment falls, and E-to-E rates increase as more meetings result in job transitions.

We next explore the role of concentration in the actual Norwegian economy. We double the number of firms in the Norwegian economy by duplicating the existing productivity vector in every market (i.e., every firm's doppelgänger enters the market, leaving the job ladder rungs untouched) and double the number of workers in the market such that the number of firms per worker remains constant. Although this experiment yields results that are qualitatively consistent with our idealized heuristic experiment, the quantitative effects of concentration on wages and welfare are limited. Markdowns narrow by 1 percentage point, average wages rise by 0.68%, and the standard deviation of log wages increases by 0.81%. Why are the effects of changing M so small? There are two reasons: (1) approximately 70% of the labor force resides in markets with more than 150 firms, and hence, doubling the number of firms in these markets is irrelevant, and (2) the duopsony wage-setting assumption—that is, that only two firms at the bargaining table strategically set wages—remains unchanged regardless of M.

Exclusion

To explore the effect of firms removing themselves from future E-to-E contacts with the worker, we allow a worker at a given firm to meet that firm again, rebargain, and thus extract all the surplus. This mechanism is related to the approaches in Zhu (2012) and Jarosch et al. (2024).[2] We find that this leads to an economically small change in observed markdowns, narrowing them by approximately 1 percentage point compared with the 21-percentage-point markdown in the baseline economy. Again, the reason is that the bulk of the labor force resides in markets with many firms, limiting the impact of self-exclusion.

Preference Heterogeneity

To quantify the effects of preference heterogeneity (i.e., nonwage, worker-firm-specific amenities), we eliminate all variations in amenities and set them to a single value, resulting in a uniform level of amenities across the economy, while we maintain the same level of aggregate amenities as in our baseline economy. In this counterfactual, we find that the Herfindahl index more than triples. Workers now flow to the highest-productivity firm and stay there, unlike in our baseline economy, where differences in amenities can cause workers to leave the highest-productivity firms. High-productivity firms also post more vacancies, understanding that workers are less likely to leave due to idiosyncratic tastes. As a result, output, productivity, and welfare increase substantially. Without amenity dispersion, wage inequality falls, but wage levels rise as workers flow to—and stay at—more productive firms. Despite the level of amenities being the same, markdowns narrow by 7 percentage points.[3] This represents a 30% reduction in markdowns from the level in the baseline economy.

Search Frictions

To quantify the effects of search frictions, we increase worker contact rates to 100% per period, leading workers to always meet a firm in every period regardless of their employment status. Markdowns narrow by 14 percentage points, which represents a 60% reduction from the level in the baseline economy. Greater contact with lower-ranked firms allows workers at higher-productivity firms to bid up their share of surplus, and they are also more likely to meet the highest-ranked firms. The Herfindahl index rises to 0.75 (an eightfold increase), as workers rapidly climb the job ladder. Wage inequality falls dramatically, as a majority of workers work at the highest-productivity firm and quickly negotiate the highest-possible surplus share.

Bargaining

As in Cahuc et al. (2006), in our model, there are only ever two firms at the bargaining table. Duopsony is a feature of the economic environment regardless of the number of firms in a given market. We remove this "hardwired" role for duopsony by assuming that whenever a worker meets a firm whose surplus rank is K, the worker also meets the next-best firm (i.e., the rank $K - 1$ firm). Now three firms are always at the bargaining table. Holding vacancies fixed, this protocol does not alter allocations—the worker either stays put or goes to firm K—however, surplus is redistributed from firms to workers, increasing wages. In general equilibrium, however, vacancies adjust (because the firm's share of surplus is now lower), shifting the allocation of workers to firms. Our main result is that markdowns narrow to approximately half of the level in the baseline economy. This experiment suggests that future work on the precise structure of strategic wage setting is valuable, in particular how variation in M endogenously leads to differences in the number of firms at the bargaining table.[4]

Our counterfactuals have implications for policy makers who may seek to address inefficiencies arising from labor market power. Our wage decomposition results point to a significant role for policies that alleviate markdowns due to amenities and strategic wage setting. Merger policy—primarily focused on the number of firms in a market, M—may have more moderate effects on wage markdowns. However, we anticipate that in a model with multiparty bargaining, this conclusion may be different. The extent to which bargaining is between two, three, or more parties is an empirical question that deserves more attention in light of our findings.

Further research can use our framework to study the distributional consequences of policies in granular labor markets. It is tractable enough to incorporate realistic policies (e.g., minimum wages, taxation, and antitrust), richer theories of the household and firm (e.g., costly human capital accumulation), and alternative contractual environments (e.g., noncompetes, as in Gottfries and Jarosch 2023; Shi 2023).

We review the literature and then proceed as follows. Section II describes the Norwegian administrative data and offers motivating empirics. Section III describes the model and defines the equilibrium. Section IV provides details on model calibration and fit. Section V decomposes wages in the steady state to analyze the mechanisms through which concentration shapes wages. Section VI conducts the main counterfactual exercises and discusses potential policy implications of our findings.

E.   Related Literature

We contribute to a growing theoretical and quantitative literature by integrating the three existing monopsony paradigms into one framework: search frictions, nonwage amenities, and granularity. There are two main classes of monopsony models, each with two subgroups: (i) models in which frictional markets generate monopsony power with a continuum of firms (e.g., Burdett and Mortensen 1998; Manning 2003; Engbom and

Moser 2022; Hurst et al. 2022) and a finite number of firms (Burdett, Shi, and Wright 2001; Zhu 2012; Jarosch et al. 2024; Bagga 2023; Bloesch and Larsen 2023; Gottfries and Jarosch 2023) and (ii) models in which neoclassical markets in the presence of amenities generate monopsony power with a continuum of firms (e.g., Robinson 1933; Card et al. 2018; Kroft et al. 2020; Taber and Vejlin 2020; Lamadon, Mogstad, and Setzler 2022) and a finite number of firms (e.g., Bhaskar and To 1999; Bhaskar, Manning, and To 2002; Azkarate-Askasua and Zerecero 2024; Berger, Herkenhoff, and Mongey 2022a, 2022b). Unlike these existing frameworks, our model simultaneously features (1) search and matching frictions, (2) neoclassical nonwage amenities, (3) price discrimination within the firm, and (4) a finite number of firms. In addition, we model vacancy posting, and thus our general equilibrium model links employer concentration to both prices and quantities. This allows us to discuss welfare and conduct normative counterfactual exercises.

We contribute to a growing empirical literature that explores the relationship between worker and firm outcomes and market granularity. Recent work has documented cross-sectional relationships between standard measures of concentration (Herfindahl index values) and wages or employment (Benmelech, Bergman, and Kim 2022; Rinz 2022; Yeh, Macaluso, and Hershbein 2022) and vacancies (Azar et al. 2018; Azar, Berry, and Marinescu 2022; Azar, Marinescu, and Steinbaum 2022). To our knowledge, we are the first to (i) document reduced-form, cross-market relationships between Herfindahl values, job flows, and various measures of wage inequality, including within- and between-firm wage inequality, and (ii) combine occupational flow-data and clustering techniques to define markets.

II. Empirical Analysis

This section presents new evidence on market structure, job mobility, and wage-setting behavior in Norwegian labor markets.

A. Data and Measurement

Although the use of linked employer-employee data covering the universe of firms, establishments, and employees is now common among researchers, the Norwegian data have the key advantage that employers must record the type of work that each employee is hired to do and the workplace location of every employment contract from 2006 to 2018.

These bibliographic records allow us to define labor markets using geography and occupation rather than industry (as in Berger et al. 2022a).[5] We can then count the employers within each occupation-location market and track changes to individuals' wages when they move between employers.

Data. Data collection consists of two steps. In the first step, we use the information about the work contract that the employer submits to the employment agency (NAV). To comply with labor laws, the employer must enter a specific position from a list of more than 6,000 possible job titles and the workplace location, wage income, and work hours.[6] Job titles are then grouped into 354 four-digit occupations by Statistics Norway based on similarity of work.[7] We cluster these occupations using novel techniques to compute the occupational scope of labor markets. In the second step, we combine linked employer-employee data with socioeconomic variables from longitudinal population registers. These include demographic information (e.g., sex, age, residential municipality, education). We can therefore determine commuting distances between residence and workplace, which facilitates computation of the geographical scope of labor markets. We can therefore allow labor markets to cross administrative borders of municipalities and counties.[8]

Institutional detail. Norway has a population of 5 million, and Oslo, the capital, accounts for approximately one-fifth. The labor force aged 25–66 is some 2 million, and the labor share of income is approximately 70%.[9] In 2016, unemployment was approximately 4.5%. There were 176,019 firms and 234,941 establishments with workers on payroll.

Firms can hire employees on either fixed-term or permanent contracts and can dismiss workers if they underperform relative to their peers or if the firms are operating at a loss. Employment protection in Norway ranks near the median among Organization for Economic Cooperation and Development (OECD) countries and is comparable with that in France and Sweden.[10] Wages and typical working hours, in turn, tend to be set by collective bargaining at the industry level, after which wages are supplemented by local adjustments or wage drift, bargained over at the worker-firm and collective agreement level, which may vary by occupation within a firm (see, e.g., Bhuller et al. 2022). This two-tier framework gives rise to a relatively compressed wage structure. The Norwegian safety net covers lost income from unemployment. The primary insurance source is unemployment insurance (UI) benefits, which begin after a 3-day waiting period, replacing approximately two-thirds of workers' past earnings net of tax (see, e.g., Røed and Zhang 2003).[11]

B.   Defining Labor Markets

In our empirical analysis, we build markets from the ground up using individual data. To avoid issues of entry and exit from the labor force, we focus on residents aged 25–60. We define a local labor market as a group of four-digit occupations within a commuting zone region indexed by r, where the commuting zones are taken from Bhuller (2009). As shown later, the self-flow rate is the fraction of job-to-job transitions from one group of occupations back into the same group.[12] We then group occupations as follows:

1. First, we isolate single-occupation markets with high self-flow rates (e.g., those with rates of more than 50%, such as the market for dentists).

2. Among the remaining occupations, we K-means cluster the rows of the occupation-to-occupation flow transition matrix.

3. For each commuting zone region indexed by r, we compute the Herfindahl-Hirschman index of employment across clusters (HHI_r^K).[13] We then determine the optimal number of K clusters by maximizing an objective function that is (i) increasing in the self-flow rate but (ii) decreasing in HHI_r^K, such that we penalize the classification of all occupations in one large cluster:

$$\underbrace{\frac{\text{Average self- flow rate of all } K \text{ clusters}}{\text{Standard deviation self-flow rate of all } K \text{ clusters}}}_{\text{(i)Reward fit}} \times \underbrace{\left[1 - \mathrm{HHI}_r^K\right]}_{\text{(ii)Penalize overfitting}}.$$

Table 1 summarizes our market definitions. Our procedure yields a self-flow rate of 51%. We obtain approximately 103 clusters per commuting zone, and the average market has 404 workers. The unweighted number

Table 1
Market Definition Summary Statistics

Moment	Value
Fraction of E-to-E flows within market 2006–16 (%)	51.40
Number of markets per region	102.8
Average firm employment per market	6.20
Average labor force per market	404.7
Average markets per firm	2.30
Total number of markets	4,783

Note: E-to-E = employer-to-employer. Summary statistics are unweighted. All rows except top row are calculated from December 2016.

of employees per firm market is 6, and the average firm operates in 2.3 markets.

To ground our definition of markets, consider the fictitious example of a dental care firm in Oslo named ABC Dental. ABC Dental is an eight-person firm that hires workers in three occupations corresponding to its six dentists, one janitor, and one groundskeeper. The commuting zone region of ABC Dental is Oslo. Suppose dentists are in a single dentist cluster, and janitors and groundskeepers are both in a manual low-skill service cluster.[14] Markets are cluster–commuting zone pairs and indexed by j (e.g., "manual low-skill services-Oslo" is one market and "dentists-Oslo" is another). Firms are firm-market pairs (e.g., "manual low-skill services-ABC Dental-Oslo" is treated as a different firm than "dentists-ABC Dental-Oslo"). Occupations are the four-digit raw occupation (e.g., dentist, janitor, groundskeeper).

Figure 1 plots the distribution of firms and employment across markets, ordered by the number of firms in each market M_j. As we do in the calibration, we truncate the graph at $M_j = 150$ firms in a market. Only 10% of markets have more than 150 firms (panel A), but these markets employ more than 70% of the Norwegian labor force (panel B).

Table 2 provides summary statistics on key labor market outcomes for 2006–16. The economy-wide unemployment rate averaged 4%. The monthly job-to-job transition rate was 0.7%, the job-finding rate was 8% per month, and the layoff rate was 0.4%. Relative to those in US data, worker flows in the Norwegian labor market are noticeably lower. We note that all flow rates in the main body of the text are computed within

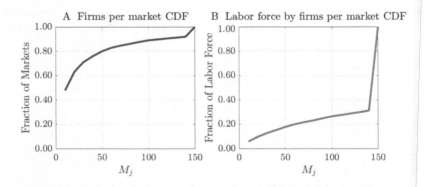

Fig. 1. Cumulative distribution functions (CDFs) of market size and labor force. Panel A is the CDF of the number of firms per market. We winsorize the data at 10 and 150 firms per market. Panel B is the CDF of the labor force by number of firms per market. A color version of this figure is available online.

Table 2
Summary Statistics: Worker Flows, Concentration, Wage Inequality

Moment	Value	Moment	Value
Unemployment rate (%)	4.01	Average firms per market	75.2
E-to-E rate (monthly %)	.65	HHI wage bill (wage bill weighted)	.09
U-to-E rate (monthly %)	8.08	HHI employment (employment weighted)	.08
E-to-U rate (monthly %)	.35	Standard deviation of log wages	.63
Fraction E-to-E moves down poach index	.15	Fraction of log wage variance within firms	.61

Note: E-to-E = employer-to-employer, E-to-U = employment-to-unemployment, U-to-E = unemployment-to-employment, and HHI = Herfindahl-Hirschman index. Flow rates are computed within markets (flows within markets divided by workers remaining within markets) to be consistent with the model definition of a market. Similar statistics are obtained when we include job flows outside of the market.

markets (flows within markets divided by workers remaining within markets) to be consistent with the model definition of a market. Including job flows outside of the market yields similar statistics and covariances (see app. D, http://www.nber.org/data-appendix/c14848/appendix .pdf). We then rank firms by the fraction of their hires coming from other firms—that is, the poach rank index (see Bagger and Lentz 2019)—and find that 15% of job-to-job transitions are down this ladder. We use this moment to discipline the role of nonwage amenities.

The average number of firms in a market is large: 75.2. However, markets are concentrated. The average wage bill Herfindahl index (weighted by the wage bill) is 0.09.[15] This is the same concentration as in a market with only 11 equally sized firms.[16] Similarly, the average employment Herfindahl index (employment weighted) is 0.08. The wage bill HHI is higher due to larger firms paying higher wages. The standard deviation of log wages is 63%, with the bulk of this (61%) accounted for by dispersion in wages within firms.

C. Regression Framework

Our goal is to study the relationship between employer concentration wage levels, the wage distribution, and job-to-job transitions. We provide a set of covariances between concentration and labor market outcomes that any theory of concentration and labor market dynamics should replicate. We do not attempt to attribute causality. We, along with the existing literature, lack credible instruments for measuring concentration. For example, take the change in local concentration due to a national firm exit used by Azkarate-Askasua and Zerecero (2024). Through the lens of our theory in Section III, this shock alters the rungs of the job ladder. Thus, it is not a pure "concentration" shock, ceteris paribus.[17] The same is true of instrumenting changes in local exposure with changes in national concentration (e.g., Azar, Marinescu, and Steinbaum 2022) because the second stage still implies changes in the number of rungs on the local job ladder.

Instead, we consider two different dimensions of variation in the Herfindahl values by using across-region variation within occupation-years and across-time variation within occupation-regions. Importantly, however, the unit of observation remains four-digit occupations in a commuting zone, allowing us to use occupation fixed effects. Each approach differs in its interpretation. Comparisons across regions may reflect sorting across space on unobservables. Comparisons across time may reflect changing demand patterns. We do not take a stance on what drives these covariances. However, both approaches provide similar negative correlations between Herfindahl values, wages, job flows, and wage inequality.

Let o denote the occupation, r the region (commuting zone), t the time (the data are monthly, and we denote the corresponding year as $\tau(t)$), and $m(o, r)$ the market to which the occupation-region was assigned by our algorithm.[18] Let γ_{FE} denote either (1) occupation-year fixed effects ($\gamma_{o\tau(t)}$), thus isolating across-region variation, or (2) occupation-region fixed effects γ_{or}, thus isolating across-time variation. Given our focus on market-level outcomes, we do not weight our regressions.[19] We estimate the following equation using ordinary least squares:

$$y_{ort} = \gamma_{FE} + \beta \text{HHI}_{m(or)t} + X_{ort} + \varepsilon_{ort}. \tag{1}$$

We include a vector of controls, X_{ort}, that vary at the occupation-region-time level. As we discuss in Section III, our model removes mechanical variation in the number of firms per worker. We therefore control for lagged quintiles of firms per worker measured at the market-time level. We also control for month of the year to hold seasonal fluctuations fixed, lagged labor force growth and age, gender, and education composition at the *ort* level.

D. Empirical Results

Across regions. Figure 2 provides a graphical representation of our regression evidence using across-region, within-occupation-year variation. The x-axis (Herfindahl index) and y-axis (labor market outcome) variables are residualized on occupation-year fixed effects and the controls X_{ort}. This leaves across-region variation (e.g., Oslo vs. Bergen, for dentists

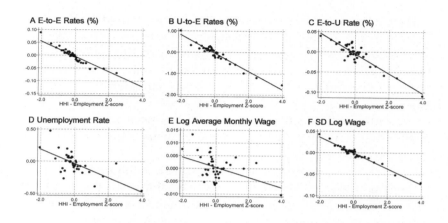

Fig. 2. The figures show scatter plots of employer-to-employer (E-to-E) rates, unemloyment-to-employment (U-to-E) rates, employment-to-unemployment (E-to-U) rates, unemployment rates, log average monthly wage and the standard deviation (SD) of the log wage against labor market concentration. Concentration and labor market outcomes residualized on occupation-year fixed effects (FEs), leaving across-region variation. For each market (where a market is defined, as in Sec. II, as a cluster of occupations within a commuting zone), we compute the employment Herfindahl-Hirschman index (HHI). For each four-digit occupation-commuting zone-year, we compute the average of the dependent variable within 40 centiles of the market HHI, unweighted. We then residualize all x and y variables on occupation-year FEs, age composition, gender composition, education composition, lagged firms-per-worker ventiles, lagged labor force growth, and month-of-year dummies. The average NOK/USD in 2021 was 9.

in 2008). We normalize the residualized Herfindahl value by its standard deviation and subtract its mean (i.e., convert it to a z-score) to ease interpretation. We also perform inference by clustering standard errors at the market level.

We find a statistically significant negative relationship between employment-to-employment transition rates and the market Herfindahl index (panel A). To interpret the relationships, we note that the unweighted employment Herfindahl index has a mean of 0.28 and a standard deviation of 0.27. The slope of the bin-scatter implies that a one-standard-deviation increase in the market employment Herfindahl index is associated with a 0.06-percentage-point reduction in the E-to-E rate ($= -0.00214 \times 0.27$), which corresponds to approximately 10% of the sample average E-to-E rate (see table 2). Panels B and C show similar negative relationships for U-to-E rates and E-to-U rates. On net, these yield a negative relationship with the unemployment rate (panel D). Later, we find that this negative unemployment-HHI relationship is not robust to the choice of fixed effects.

There is also a negative relationship between wages and the Herfindahl index (panel E). This relationship is significant with occupation-year fixed effects alone but insignificant with occupation-year fixed effects and controls. Nonetheless, with occupation-year fixed effects and controls, a one-standard-deviation increase in the market employment Herfindahl index is associated with a 0.27-percentage-point reduction in the wage ($= -0.0104 \times 0.27 \times 100$). Last, panel F illustrates a strong negative relationship between concentration and wage inequality (the standard deviation of log wages).

One concern is that these covariances reflect the sorting of better workers into less concentrated markets. We think that this is unlikely for two reasons. First, we control for education level and show that the main conclusions remain unaltered if we omit these controls in table 3. Second, high-skill workers are more likely to have high U-to-E rates but lower E-to-U rates. Nevertheless, we consider an alternative specification that isolates within-occupation-region across-time variation, thereby mitigating concerns regarding spatial sorting on unobservables.

Across time. Figure 3 repeats the exercise with both the Herfindahl index and labor market outcome residualized on occupation-region fixed effects and the controls X_{ort}. This leaves across-time variation (e.g., 2006 vs. 2007, for dentists in Oslo). Again we observe the negative correlation between concentration and labor market flows (panels A, B, and C), wages (panel E), and wage inequality (panel F). Here, however, the relationship with unemployment is flipped (panel D). However, with occupation-region fixed effects, the relationship between wages and concentration is robustly negative, regardless of controls. Panel E implies that a one-standard-deviation increase in the market employment Herfindahl index is associated with a 4.5-percentage-point reduction in the wage ($= -0.166 \times 0.27 \times 100$).

Regressions. The significant, negative relationship between concentration and all three worker flows and wage inequality is robust across all specifications (table 3, panels A, B, C, and F). Table 3 provides the regression tables corresponding to figures 2 and 3. We estimate equation (1) with and without controls and for both sets of fixed effects (occupation-year, denoted O-Y, and occupation-region, denoted O-R). The dependent variable in column 1 is the monthly E-to-E transition rate (not expressed as a percentage). The coefficient can be interpreted as follows: a one-standard-deviation increase in the HHI is associated with 0.05% ($= -0.00194 \times 0.27 \times 100$) reduction in the employment-to-employment transition rate. The relationship between concentration and unemployment rates is sometimes insignificant, negative, or positive depending on the fixed

Table 3

Regression Analysis: Concentration and Labor Market Outcomes

A. E-to-E rate

	(1)	(2)	(3)	(4)
HHI	-.00194***	-.00214***	-.00361***	-.00475***
	(7.58e-05)	(9.11e-05)	(.000232)	(.000312)
FE	O-Y	O-Y	O-R	O-R
Controls	N	Y	N	Y
Obs.	1,035,450	892,774	1,035,382	892,731
R^2	.066	.181	.047	.164

B. U-to-E rate

	(5)	(6)	(7)	(8)
HHI	-.0356***	-.0330***	-.0231***	-.0284***
	(.00208)	(.00234)	(.00443)	(.00520)
FE	O-Y	O-Y	O-R	O-R
Controls	N	Y	N	Y
Obs.	628,097	553,705	627,933	553,544
R^2	.065	.075	.094	.101

C. E-to-U rate

	(9)	(10)	(11)	(12)
HHI	-.00191***	-.00177***	-.000825**	-.00172***
	(.000154)	(.000177)	(.000325)	(.000415)
FE	O-Y	O-Y	O-R	O-R
Controls	N	Y	N	Y
Obs.	1,035,450	892,774	1,035,382	892,731
R^2	.069	.082	.095	.110

D. Unemployment rate

	(13)	(14)	(15)	(16)
HHI	.00251	-.00781***	.0631***	.0420***
	(.00302)	(.00298)	(.00650)	(.00668)
FE	O-Y	O-Y	O-R	O-R
Controls	N	Y	N	Y
Obs.	1,043,861	892,927	1,043,790	892,885
R^2	.408	.425	.509	.528

E. Log wage

	(17)	(18)	(19)	(20)
HHI	-.0328***	-.0104	-.167***	-.166***
	(.00956)	(.00970)	(.0197)	(.0211)
FE	O-Y	O-Y	O-R	O-R
Controls	N	Y	N	Y
Obs.	1,043,861	892,927	1,043,790	892,885
R^2	.793	.817	.784	.825

F. Standard deviation of log wage

	(21)	(22)	(23)	(24)
HHI	-.126***	-.134***	-.226***	-.216***
	(.00892)	(.00960)	(.0166)	(.0198)
FE	O-Y	O-Y	O-R	O-R
Controls	N	Y	N	Y
Obs.	1,042,160	892,176	1,042,089	892,134
R^2	.382	.402	.518	.537

Note: E-to-E = employer-to-employer, U-to-E = unemloyment-to-employment, E-to-U = employment-to-unemployment, HHI = Herfindahl-Hirschman index. Standard errors are clustered at the market level. For the fixed effects, (i) O-Y refers to occupation-year fixed effects, and (ii) O-R refers to occupation-region fixed effects. For the controls, Y indicates controls for quintiles of firms per worker measured at the market-month level, month of the year, lagged labor force growth, age, gender, and education composition at the ort level. In this table (unlike the figures), E-to-E, U-to-E, E-to-U, and unemployment rates take values between zero and one and are thus not expressed in percentage points.

**$p < .01.

***$p < .001.

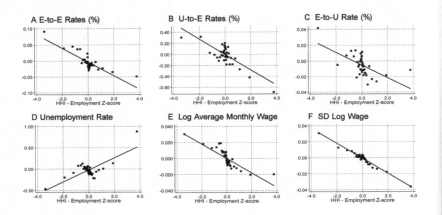

Fig. 3. The figures show scatter plots of employer-to-employer (E-to-E) rates, unemloyment-to-employment (U-to-E) rates, employment-to-unemployment (E-to-U) rates, unemployment rates, log average monthly wage and the standard deviation (SD) of the log wage against labor market concentration. Concentration and labor market outcomes residualized on occupation-region fixed effects (FEs), leaving across-time variation. For each market (where a market is defined, as in Sec. II, as a cluster of occupations within a commuting zone), we compute the employment Herfindahl-Hirschman index (HHI). For each four-digit occupation-commuting zone-year, we compute the average of the dependent variable within 40 centiles of the market HHI, unweighted. We then residualize all x and y variables on occupation-region FEs, age composition, gender composition, education composition, lagged firms-per-worker ventiles, lagged labor force growth, and month-of-year dummies. The average NOK/USD in 2021 was 9.

effects and inclusion of controls (panel D). Log wages are significantly negatively related to concentration in all specifications except for that with occupation-year fixed effects with controls (panel E).

Robustness to alternative labor market definitions. We explore the robustness of our empirical results to defining labor markets in alternative ways in appendix C, http://www.nber.org/data-appendix/c14848/appendix.pdf. Rather than clustering occupations by K-means using the occupational flow matrix within each commuting zone, we follow a recent literature (Lindenlaub and Postel-Vinay 2021) and extract the relevant clusters of occupations within a commuting zone using modularity maximization following the work of Schmutte (2014). Reassuringly, the patterns that we find are similar to those obtained when we use our baseline clustering algorithm. Last, an alternative approach to defining markets is to simply use raw three-digit occupations and commuting zones. We used this market definition in an earlier draft of this paper and found quantitatively similar results.

Summary. In the rest of the paper, we ask whether a benchmark theory of frictional labor markets with on-the-job search and bargaining (Cahuc et al. 2006) can quantitatively replicate these empirical relationships when extended to accommodate (i) concentrated markets, (ii) a vacancy-posting equilibrium, and (iii) worker-firm-specific tastes. We then use the model to decompose the role of different economic forces in determining wage markdowns, employment, and inequality.

III. Model

In our model, time is discrete and runs forever. We assume that there are J markets indexed by $j \in \{1, \dots, J\}$. Within each market, there are $\bar{N}_j$ workers and M_j firms. Firms are indexed by $i \in \{1, \dots, M_j\}$. The measure of firms is exogenous, and workers are assumed to be immobile across markets. For the remainder of the section, we suppress the market index j.

Workers. Workers have linear utility and maximize the net present value of discounted utility. Both workers and firms discount the future at a rate β. Workers are either employed or unemployed. Among the employed, a measure n_i is employed at firm i. Total employment in a labor market is therefore $n = \Sigma_{i=1}^{M} n_i$, and thus, the measure of unemployed individuals in a labor market is $u = \bar{N} - n$.

A worker's per period utility is the summation of income and a worker-firm-specific taste shock, ε. This taste shock is a stand-in for commuting times, how well a worker gets along with their boss and colleagues, and any other worker-firm-specific nonwage characteristics. We assume that the taste shock is independently drawn from the distribution $F(\varepsilon)$ when a worker contacts a firm, and we assume that ε is constant throughout a worker-firm match. Both the firm and worker observe and contract are on the amenity draw. Thus, we allow firms to first-degree price discriminate on amenities.[20]

Search is random. Each period, a random fraction ϕ of unemployed individuals searches for job openings. Unemployed individuals receive utility from home production, b. Employed workers search on the job with probability $\xi\phi$ and do not apply to jobs at their existing firm. We refer to this search protocol as partially directed search.

Firms. Firm i's productivity is fixed and is denoted z_i. Posting v_i vacancies costs $c(v_i, M, \bar{N})$, where c is convex in vacancies. Empirically, unemployment rates vary relatively little across markets that vary widely in terms of the number of firms per worker (see app. table 9, http://www.nber.org/data-appendix/c14848/appendix.pdf). For the model to scale and achieve this stylized fact, we remove variation in firms per worker by scaling the vacancy costs accordingly. Anticipating the calibration, we assume that vacancy costs are given by $c(v_i, M, \bar{N}) = (M/\bar{N})^\gamma 1/(1 + \gamma)v_i^{1+\gamma}$. The scaling factor achieves neutrality of the unemployment rate with respect to firms per worker $(M/\bar{N})$. For convenience, we suppress the market employment and firm arguments of $c(\cdot)$ and write $c(v_i)$ for vacancy costs.

We assume that firms post vacancies nonstrategically. In an earlier version of this paper, we solved the strategic vacancy-posting decision for markets with few firms and found that strategic vacancy-posting motives yield no discernible effects on aggregates while simultaneously making the model less tractable. Strategic vacancy posting, when combined with amenities, also gives rise to complex hiring rules.[21] We assume away this behavior and leave it to future researchers to find tractable solutions to this problem.

Meeting rates. When workers apply for jobs, only a fraction of those applications actually result in a meeting with a prospective employer via a vacancy. After meeting, the worker and prospective firm observe the nonwage amenity draw ε upon which they base their matching decision. A match occurs if the worker moves to the prospective employer. Matches end through on-the-job search as well as at an exogenous rate δ.

From the worker's perspective, let λ_{ik} denote the rate at which a firm i worker meets a firm k vacancy. From the firm's perspective, let λ_{ik}^f denote the rate at which firm i's workers meet a firm k vacancy. Our convention with subscripts is origin first (i), then destination (k).

To describe the meeting process, we must keep track of the origin and destination of job applicants. Let x_{ik} (x_{uk}) denote the measure of firm i workers (unemployed workers) who randomly apply for jobs at firm k. Then, $x_i = \Sigma_{k\neq i} x_{ki} + x_{ui}$ is the total measure of workers who randomly apply for jobs at i.

Throughout, we assume that meetings at each firm are governed by a constant-returns-to-scale meeting function $\bar{m}(v_i, x_i) \leq \min\{v_i, x_i\}$. In the absence of on-the-job search, firm-specific constant-returns-to-scale matching functions and the usual pooled random search model of Diamond-Mortensen-Pissarides are equivalent. Let A denote match efficiency. In practice, we use a Cobb-Douglas matching function:

$$\bar{m}(v, x) = \min\{Av^{\alpha-1}x^\alpha, 1\}.$$

We let $f(\theta_i)$ denote the job-finding rate at firm i, where the tightness at firm i is defined to be $\theta_i = v_i/x_i$. Constant returns to scale imply $\bar{m}(v_i, x_i) = x_i f(\theta_i)$.

From each firm i, there is a measure $\xi\phi n_i$ of workers who engage in partially directed on-the-job search. Because employed workers randomly apply only for vacancies posted by firms other than the one where they are currently employed, the measure of workers at firm i who apply to firm k is given by

$$x_{ik} = \frac{v_k}{\sum_{j\neq i}v_j}\xi\phi n_i.$$

A fraction ϕ of unemployed individuals apply to all M firms randomly. Therefore, the measure of workers who are unemployed and apply to firm k is given by

$$x_{uk} = \frac{v_k}{\sum_j v_j}\phi u.$$

We can now derive the probability that a worker at firm i meets firm k into three terms. The first term is the probability that a worker searches, $\xi\phi$. The second term is the conditional probability that the worker applies to a vacancy at firm k, $v_k/\sum_{j\neq i}v_j$. The third term is the conditional probability that a meeting occurs, $\bar{m}(v_k, x_k)/x_k$. These yield the worker meeting rate:

$$\lambda_{ik} = \xi\phi \times \left(\frac{v_k}{\sum_{j\neq i}v_j}\right) \times \left(\frac{\bar{m}(v_k, x_k)}{x_k}\right) = \xi\phi \times \left(\frac{v_k}{\sum_{j\neq i}v_j}\right) \times f(\theta_k). \quad (2)$$

The contact rate of unemployed workers is defined similarly, except that unemployed workers may meet any firm and, hence, $\lambda_{uk} = \phi(v_k/\sum_j v_j)f(\theta_k)$.

We similarly divide the probability of a meeting a firm k's vacancy with a worker at firm i into two terms: (i) the probability of a meeting between a worker and a vacancy, $\bar{m}(v_k, x_k)/v_k$, and (ii) the probability that the worker originated from firm i, x_{ik}/x_k. These yield the firm meeting rate:

$$\lambda_{ik}^f = \frac{\bar{m}(v_k, x_k)}{v_k} \times \left(\frac{x_{ik}}{x_k}\right). \quad (3)$$

The probability that firm k meets aunemployed worker is given by $\lambda_{uk}^f = \bar{m}(v_k, x_k)/v_k(x_{uk}/x_k)$.

Flow balance holds. Using the definitions of x_{ik} and x_k, one can check that $n_i\lambda_{ik} = v_k\lambda_{ik}^f$: firm i workers' rate of meeting firm k vacancies equals firm k's rate of meeting vacancies with firm i workers.

Bargaining over promised values. We follow Cahuc et al. (2006). When a worker meets a new firm, the incumbent and poaching firm propose sequential offers. We assume that firms offer workers promised values that they are committed to. There are three possible cases: the worker meets a firm that can deliver a maximum promised value that is (i) less than the value promised to the worker by their current employer, (ii) greater than the value promised to the worker by their current employer but less than the maximum promised value of the worker's current employer, or (iii) greater than the maximum promised value that the worker's current employer can offer.

In case (i), we assume no change to the worker's wage, and the worker remains with the incumbent firm. In case (ii), we assume that the incumbent firm offers a new promised value that delivers the full joint value of the match with the poaching firm. In case (iii), the worker moves to the poaching firm, and Nash bargaining determines the split of the remaining surplus between the poaching firm and worker, where the full joint value of the match with the incumbent firm constitutes the worker's outside option. Let $\theta \in [0, 1]$ denote the worker's Nash bargaining parameter. Let $\sigma \in [\theta, 1]$ denote the worker's share of the match surplus. Because of cases (ii) and (iii), σ may increase above the worker's Nash bargaining weight θ.

Wage determination. The bargaining protocol pins down the promised values, but the wage that delivers the promised values is indeterminate. We assume that firms deliver the promised values to workers as a constant wage unless the worker receives an credible outside option. This is a common assumption and delivers wage dynamics consistent with the empirical evidence in Cahuc et al. (2006), Jarosch (2023), and Lise and Robin (2017).

Let the continuation value of a worker at firm i with bargained surplus share σ and taste shock ε be given by $W_i(\sigma, \varepsilon)$. Likewise, let firm i's continuation value of a match with bargained surplus share σ and taste shock ε be given by $J_i(\sigma, \varepsilon)$. The continuation value of an unemployed individual is given by U. We will frequently work with both the joint value of a match, $P_i(\varepsilon) := W_i(\sigma, \varepsilon) + J_i(\sigma, \varepsilon)$, and the match surplus, $S_i(\varepsilon) := W_i(\sigma, \varepsilon) - U + J_i(\sigma, \varepsilon) \equiv P_i(\varepsilon) - U$. Because firms commit to the promised values and workers and firms have linear utility, it can be shown that the match surplus and joint value are independent of the division of surplus, σ.

We assume that once workers and firms separate, the job position is destroyed. To hire again, then, a firm needs to post new vacancies. Hence, implicit in these definitions is that the value of an unfilled vacancy is zero, similar to the setup in Lise and Robin (2017).

Before we exposit the continuation values of the worker, we note that appendix E (http://www.nber.org/data-appendix/c14848/appendix .pdf) provides a full derivation of the main equations in the text, including the joint value of a match, the surplus of a match, and the wage equation. In addition, appendix E shows how one may solve for surplus using a simple matrix inversion.

Unemployed workers. Unemployed workers enjoy home production b and meet with firm k with probability λ_{uk}. When they meet with firm k, they draw a taste $\varepsilon' \sim F$ for working at firm k. They receive a share θ of surplus. The continuation value of an unemployed worker is therefore

$$U = b + \beta \left[U + \theta \int \sum_k \lambda_{uk} \max\{S_k(\varepsilon'), 0\} dF(\varepsilon') \right].$$

Employed workers. The worker value is the value of unemployment plus some share σ of the match surplus (following Lise and Postel-Vinay 2020). In other words, σ is defined to be the number that satisfies the following equation:

$$W_i(\sigma, \varepsilon) = U + \sigma[P_i(\varepsilon) - U].$$

The Cahuc et al. (2006) bargaining protocol implies that when a worker at firm i with amenity ε meets a vacancy at firm k and draws amenity ε', there are three possible outcomes:

i) If $P_i(\varepsilon) > W_i(\sigma, \varepsilon) > P_k(\varepsilon')$, the worker stays at firm i with promised value $W_i(\sigma, \varepsilon)$.

ii) If $P_i(\varepsilon) > P_k(\varepsilon') > W_i(\sigma, \varepsilon)$, the worker stays at firm i but is now delivered a promised value $W_i(\sigma', \varepsilon) = P_k(\varepsilon')$, where $\sigma' = S_k(\varepsilon')/S_i(\varepsilon)$.

iii) If $P_k(\varepsilon') > P_i(\varepsilon)$, the worker moves to firm k and Nash bargains over the gains from trade $[P_k(\varepsilon') - P_i(\varepsilon)]$, with the full joint value at firm i, $P_i(\varepsilon)$, as their outside option.

Under this protocol, the worker policy function is to move to the firm with the greatest surplus. Note that workers may move down the productivity ladder if the amenity draw increases surplus above that associated with the incumbent firm.

In case (iii), the Nash bargaining solution delivers a worker continuation value that maximizes:

$$\max_{\hat{W}} \left(P_k(\varepsilon') - \hat{W}\right)^{1-\theta} \left(\hat{W} - P_i(\varepsilon)\right)^{\theta}.$$

The resulting promised value is equal to the entire joint value between the worker and firm i plus a fraction θ of the gains from trade:

$$\hat{W} = P_i(\varepsilon) + \theta[P_k(\varepsilon') - P_i(\varepsilon)],$$

which is convenient to express as a fraction of the match surplus:

$$W_k(\sigma', \varepsilon') = \hat{W} = U + \sigma'[P_k(\varepsilon') - U], \text{ where } \sigma' = \theta + (1-\theta)\frac{S_i(\varepsilon)}{S_k(\varepsilon')}.$$

Given the above, it can be verified that the worker's share of surplus evolves according to:

$$\sigma' = \begin{pmatrix} \left(\dfrac{\theta S_k(\varepsilon') + (1-\theta)S_i(\varepsilon)}{S_k(\varepsilon')}\right) & \text{if } S_k(\varepsilon') > S_i(\varepsilon) \\[2ex] \max\left\{\sigma, \dfrac{S_k(\varepsilon')}{S_i(\varepsilon)}\right\} & \text{if } S_k(\varepsilon') \leq S_i(\varepsilon) \end{pmatrix}.$$

As discussed earlier, we assume that the promised values are delivered as a constant wage $w_i(\sigma, \varepsilon)$ unless the worker has a meeting with an employer that triggers renegotiation. Employed workers at firm i meet with firm k with probability λ_{ik}. Under the bargaining protocol of Cahuc et al. (2006), the continuation value of the worker can be written as (see app. E):

$$\begin{aligned} W_i(\sigma, \varepsilon) = w_i(\sigma, \varepsilon) + \varepsilon + \beta \Bigg[& W_i(\sigma, \varepsilon) - \delta\sigma S_i(\varepsilon) \\ & + \int \sum_{k \neq i} \lambda_{ik} \max\{0, \min\{\theta[S_k(\varepsilon') - S_i(\varepsilon)], S_k(\varepsilon') - S_i(\varepsilon)\} \quad (4) \\ & + (1-\sigma)S_i(\varepsilon)\}dF(\varepsilon') \Bigg]. \end{aligned}$$

Joint value. Rather than exposit the value of a firm directly, we focus on the joint value of a match between worker and firm i with taste shock ε. They jointly produce z_i unless (i) the worker receives an outside offer at a firm that generates greater surplus or (ii) the match exogenously dissolves. Thus, the joint value takes into account the worker's future value of a new match or unemployment:

$$P_i(\varepsilon) = z_i + \varepsilon + \beta \left[P_i(\varepsilon) + \theta \int \sum_{k \neq i} \lambda_{ik} \max\{S_k(\varepsilon') - S_i(\varepsilon), 0\} dF(\varepsilon') - \delta S_i(\varepsilon) \right].$$

Surplus. The surplus of a match relative to unemployment can be expressed similarly. The costs include the flow value of unemployment, b, and the option value of unemployment forfeited by being employed at i: $\theta \int \sum_k \lambda_{uk} \max\{S_k(\varepsilon''), 0\} dF(\varepsilon'')$. The benefits are production, amenities, and potential gains from on-the-job search, $\theta \int \sum_{k \neq i} \lambda_{ik} \max\{S_k(\varepsilon') - S_i(\varepsilon), 0\} dF(\varepsilon')$:

$$S_i(\varepsilon) = (z_i + \varepsilon) - b + \beta \left[(1 - \delta)S_i(\varepsilon) + \theta \int \sum_{k \neq i} \lambda_{ik} \max\{S_k(\varepsilon') - S_i(\varepsilon), 0\} dF(\varepsilon') \right.$$
$$\left. - \theta \int \sum_k \lambda_{uk} \max\{S_k(\varepsilon''), 0\} dF(\varepsilon'') \right]. \tag{5}$$

Wage equation. Combining the worker's value (eq. [4]) and surplus (eq. [5]), we can compute the wage based on surplus values alone. The wage function $w_i(\sigma, \varepsilon)$ delivers a surplus share σ at firm i:

$$w_i(\sigma, \varepsilon) = \sigma z_i - (1 - \sigma)\varepsilon + (1 - \sigma) \left[b + \beta \theta \int \sum_k \lambda_{uk} \max\{S_k(\varepsilon'_u), 0\} dF(\varepsilon'_u) \right]$$
$$- \beta \int \sum_{k \neq i} \lambda_{ik} \max\{0, \min\{(1 - \sigma)\theta(S_k(\varepsilon') - S_i(\varepsilon)), (S_k(\varepsilon') - S_i(\varepsilon))\} + (1 - \sigma)S_i(\varepsilon)\} dF(\varepsilon'). \tag{6}$$

The wage equation includes four terms: (i) workers obtain σ of production, (ii) the firm can offer a lower wage to workers with higher taste shocks to deliver any given promised value, (iii) workers obtain $(1 - \sigma)$ of their outside option, and (iv) there is backloading because firms that offer greater future pay prospects can initially pay less.

Optimal vacancy posting. The firm vacancy-posting problem requires knowledge of the distribution of workers across amenity values and employers. The probability that a worker at firm k has amenity draw ε is given by the endogenous ratio $n_k(\varepsilon)/n_k$. As discussed earlier, we assume that the vacancy-posting decision is nonstrategic. Thus, the firm chooses v_i to maximize the following objective, taking all contact rates, worker stocks, and surplus values as given:[22]

$$\max_{v_i} -c(v_i) + \underbrace{(1 - \theta)v_i \int \lambda_{ui}^f \max\{S_i(\varepsilon'), 0\} dF(\varepsilon')}_{\text{Hire from unemployment}} \tag{7}$$

$$+ \underbrace{(1 - \theta)v_i \iint \sum_{k \neq i} \lambda_{ki}^f \left(\frac{n_k(\varepsilon)}{n_k} \right) \max\{S_i(\varepsilon') - S_k(\varepsilon), 0\} d\varepsilon \, dF(\varepsilon')}_{\text{Hire from employment}}.$$

This yields the following optimality condition for firms:

$$
v_i = c'^{-1} \left((1 - \theta) \int \lambda^f_{ui} \max\{S_i(\varepsilon'), 0\} dF(\varepsilon') \right.
$$
$$
\left. + (1 - \theta) \iint \sum_{k \neq i} \lambda^f_{ki} \left(\frac{n_k(\varepsilon)}{n_k} \right) \max\{S_i(\varepsilon') - S_k(\varepsilon), 0\} d\varepsilon dF(\varepsilon') \right).
$$

Laws of motion for employment. The laws of motion for employment and unemployment are given by the following equations, where primes denote next-period values:[23]

$$
n'_i(\varepsilon) = \left(1 - \delta - \sum_{k \neq i} \lambda_{ik} \int 1_{[S_k(\varepsilon') \geq S_i(\varepsilon)]} dF(\varepsilon') \right) n_i(\varepsilon) + \lambda_{ui} 1_{[S_i(\varepsilon) > U]} f(\varepsilon) u
$$
$$
+ \sum_{k \neq i} \lambda_{ki} \int 1_{[S_i(\varepsilon) \geq S_k(\varepsilon')]} f(\varepsilon) n_k(\varepsilon') d\varepsilon' \tag{8}
$$
$$
u' = \left(1 - \sum_i \lambda_{ui} \int 1_{[S_i(\varepsilon') \geq U]} dF(\varepsilon') \right) u + \delta(\bar{N} - u), n_i = \int n_i(\varepsilon) d\varepsilon, u = \bar{N} - \sum_i n_i.
$$

Equilibrium. Because markets do not interact, it suffices to define the equilibrium for a single market. We continue to suppress the market j index, and we note that, in the quantitative model, all J markets satisfy the following equilibrium definition.

In a given market with a mass of firms M and labor force $\bar{N}$, a *stationary equilibrium* is a stock of vacancies and employment $\{v_i, n_i(\varepsilon)\}^M_{i=1}$, an unemployed value U, surplus values $\{S_i(\varepsilon)\}^M_{i=1}$ (which implicitly define the worker's mobility policy function), meeting rates $\{\lambda^f_{ui}, \lambda_{ui}\}^M_{i=1}$ and $\{\{\lambda^f_{ki}, \lambda_{ik}\}_{k \neq i}\}^M_{i=1}$ such that

1. Worker optimality: Given surpluses and contact rates, worker mobility decisions are optimal—that is, mobility decisions are consistent with surpluses (eq. [5]) and deliver the worker value (eq. [4]).

2. Firm optimality: Given surpluses, contact rates, and worker stocks, v_i solves equation (7).

3. Market clearing: Worker mobility decisions (implicitly defined by $\{S_i(\varepsilon)\}^M_{i=1}$ and U) and optimal firm vacancy postings deliver a stationary distribution of workers given by equation (8) consistent with $\{n_i(\varepsilon)\}^M_{i=1}$.

IV.   Calibration and Model Fit

This section describes our calibration approach. We then explore the model fit relative to the data moments in Section II.

A. Calibration

Markets. We adopt the clustering method described in Section II to define markets. With these market definitions in hand, we can compute the labor force per market, $\bar{N}_j$, and the distribution of the number of firms per market, $G(M_j)$. Rather than parameterize the joint distribution of M_j and $\bar{N}_j$, we note that a linear relationship between labor force and firms per market fits the data quite well (see fig. 4 and the discussion in the following paragraph). Thus, we impose $\bar{N}_j = a\bar{M}_j$ so that once we draw the market size M_j, we know $\bar{N}_j$. We truncate the data at $M_j = 150$, above which we find very little difference with respect to equilibrium as we raise M_j. At the final truncated market size, for the labor force to add up to that of Norway, we deviate from the linear relationship and simply compute the necessary $\bar{N}_j$ to match the size of the Norwegian labor force (in particular, the characteristic that 70% of workers are in $M_j = 150$ markets).

Figure 4A illustrates the relationship between $\bar{N}_j$ and M_j, as well as our fitted values. We assume there are $J = 200$ markets (despite there being 3,700 in our data), and for each market, we draw the number of firms $M_j \sim G(M_j)$ where $G(\cdot)$ is the empirical cumulative distribution function (CDF) of firms per market. Figure 4B plots the distribution $G(M_j)$ in the data and in our $J = 200$ markets, illustrating the limited Monte Carlo simulation error in our quantitative experiments.

Preferences and technology. A period is 1 month. On an annual basis, the discount rate is 4% ($\beta = 0.96^{1/12}$). We assume that the matching function elasticity is given by $\alpha = 0.50$ and that unemployed workers

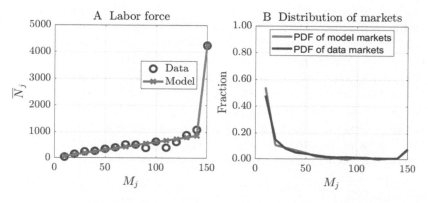

Fig. 4. Calibration of market size and labor force. Panel *A* plots the relationship between labor force size $\bar{N}_j$ and market size M_j. Panel *B* plots the probability density function of market sizes in the model versus the data. A color version of this figure is available online.

search every period, $\phi = 1$. Employed workers' intensity of on-the-job search $\xi = 0.32$ delivers the job-to-job transition rate shown in table 2. The match efficiency parameter $A = 0.18$ then delivers the unemployment rate. The home production parameter $b = 0.85$ is estimated to yield a 66% replacement rate as in Kostøl (2017).

We calibrate the amenity distribution to match the fraction of employment-to-employment moves that occur down the poaching index ladder. We assume that amenities are distributed uniformly $\varepsilon \sim U[0, \bar{\varepsilon}]$ and calibrate $\bar{\varepsilon} = 0.76$. As discussed in Section II, the poaching index is simply a firm's share of hires who are poached from competitors rather than hired from unemployment.[24] We construct the same index in our model to map this moment to the data. If $\bar{\varepsilon} = 0$, so that there were no amenities, then all job-to-job transitions would be to firms with a higher poaching index (we demonstrate this and provide deeper discussion of identification in app. F, http://www.nber.org/data-appendix/c14848/appendix.pdf). Through the lens of our model, the fact that only 85% of moves are up this ladder provides evidence for idiosyncratic tastes and disciplines $\bar{\varepsilon}$. The bargaining power $\theta = 0.18$ is calibrated to match the average wage growth rate in Norway.[25]

The remaining parameters control dispersion in productivity σ_z and vacancy cost convexity γ. We assume that firm productivity is log normal: $\log z \sim N(-\frac{1}{2}\sigma_z^2, \sigma_z)$. Conditional on other parameters, $\sigma_z = 0.14$ is determined by matching the standard deviation of log wages. Given the amount of productivity dispersion and number of firms in a market, γ determines the share of employment at large firms. A higher γ compresses vacancy posting at the most productive firms, impeding their growth. The vacancy cost convexity parameter $\gamma = 1.16$ is therefore pinned down by the employment Herfindahl index of 0.09.

To further discipline the parameters that govern concentration $(\gamma, \sigma_z, b, \theta)$ and its relationship with wages, we also target the regression coefficients of wages and the standard deviation of wages on the Herfindahl values in table 3 (cols. 18, 20, 22, and 24). Thus, our estimation is overidentified. We take a simple average of the regression coefficients based on occupation-year and occupation-region fixed effects. The results of the estimation are shown in table 4 along with the corresponding data moment that identifies each parameter.

B.   Model Fit

Table 5 compares the model's fit with the remaining reduced-form estimates from Section II. The first two rows are the wage moments that we explicitly target. These coefficients are negative, but this is not by

Table 4
Calibration

Parameter	Value		Moment	Model	Data
Match efficiency	A	.18	Unemployment rate	.03	.04
OJS intensity	ξ_e	.32	Aggregate E-to-E rate	.01	.01
Home production	b	.85	Replacement rate	.86	.66
Vacancy cost elasticity	γ	1.16	Employment HHI	.09	.08
Bargaining power	θ	.18	Average log wage growth	.01	.01
Upper-bound amenity	$\bar{\varepsilon}$	.76	Fraction of EE moves down poach index ladder	.21	.15
Standard deviation of productivity	σ_z	14	Standard deviation of log wages	.69	.63
			Regression β: Log market wage on HHI	−.09	−.09
			Regression β: Standard deviation of log wages on HHI	−.18	−.18

Note: E-to-E = employer-to-employer, HHI = Herfindahl-Hirschman index, OJS = on-the-job search (OJS).

construction. The model can generate a counterfactually positive relationship between concentration and wages. How? With a sufficiently high productivity dispersion, the most concentrated markets are the markets in which one firm has drawn an outlier draw of productivity, z_i. Workers bargain over a share of surplus that is proportional to z_i, and thus concentrated markets can offer higher wages.

In terms of nontargeted moments, the model naturally generates the negative relationship between employment-to-employment transition rates and concentration. In the extreme, a market with a solo monopsonist $N = 1$ has zero employer-to-employer job transitions. The model also generates the negative observed relationship between job-finding rates and concentration. Note that the model can generate a counterfactually positive relationship between concentration and the job-finding rate. If concentrated markets are also the most productive (i.e., a firm in such a market drew an extremely high z_i), then surplus and vacancy postings reflect the high surplus value, and hence, high job-finding rates and high concentration occur simultaneously. That the model correctly generates the right negative relationship between the UE rates and Herfindahl values is thus a positive contribution of the model.

In summary, we have a quantitative model that matches the cross-sectional empirical relationship between concentration and (i) wages, (ii) worker flows, and (iii) wage inequality.

V. Wage Decomposition and Mechanisms

Before we discuss our model counterfactuals, we first provide a decomposition of wages. Rewriting equation (6), we can express the wage as

Table 5
Model Fit Relative to Regression Estimates in Section II

| | | | Data | |
| | | Model | Occ-Year FE | Occ-Region FE |
Dependent Variable (Y_{ort})	Targeted in Estimation	(1)	(2)	(3)
Log wage	Yes—Target average of (2) and (3)	−.0915	−.0104	−.166***
Standard deviation of log wage	Yes—Target average of (2) and (3)	−.1799	−.125***	−.230***
E.-to-E rate	No		−.0027 −.00214***	−.00475***
U-to-E rate	No		−.0103 −.0330***	−.0284***

Note: E-to-E = employer-to-employer, U-to-E = unemployment-to-employment. Regression estimates are taken from table 3. Log wages correspond to columns 18 and 20. The standard deviation of wages corresponds to columns 22 and 24. E-to-E rate estimates correspond to columns 2 and 4. U-to-E rate estimates correspond to columns 6 and 8.
***$p < .001$.

the sum of four components: the output share, the opportunity cost, the amenity discount, and the quit/promotion discount. In our calibrated steady state, the sum of the output share components over the sum of total wages is 91.4%. The opportunity cost is approximately half as important, and the amenity discount and quit/promotion discounts lower wages by approximately 20%. We summarize these results as follows:

$$w_k(\sigma, \varepsilon) = \qquad\qquad\qquad\qquad\qquad (9)$$

1. Output share (91.4%) σz_k
2. Opportunity cost (42.0%) $+ (1-\sigma)(b + \beta\theta\Sigma_{k'}^M\lambda_{uk'} \int \max\{S_{k'}(\varepsilon'),0\}dF(\varepsilon'))$
3. Amenity discount (−18.8%) $-(1 - \sigma)\varepsilon$
4. Quit/promotion discount (−14.6%) $-(1 - \sigma)\beta \int \Sigma_{k'\neq k}^M\lambda_{kk'}\mathbf{1}_{[S'>S]}[S_k(\varepsilon) + \theta(S_{k'}(\varepsilon') - S_k(\varepsilon))]dF(\varepsilon') - \beta\int \sum_{k'\neq k}^M\lambda_{kk'}\mathbf{1}_{[\sigma S \leq S' < S]}[S_{k'}(\varepsilon') - \sigma S_k(\varepsilon)]dF(\varepsilon').$

The wage equation provides insight into how wage concentration, duopsonistic bargaining, and search frictions affect wages. First, concentration directly limits the surplus share σ. The finiteness of the number of firms implies that σ is bounded below one at the highest productivity-amenity match (i.e., the highest-ranked/highest-surplus firms). Consider the economy without amenities, and denote the highest attainable surplus share at the most productive firm $\bar{\sigma}_1$. In a single-firm market, workers coming out of unemployment can meet only the most productive firm, and thus, $\bar{\sigma}_1 = \theta < 1$. With two firms in a market where the $k = 1$ firm is the most productive, the highest-possible share of surplus is $\bar{\sigma}_1 = (\theta S_1 + (1 - \theta)S_2)/S_1$, which occurs when a worker at the lower-ranked firm meets the top-ranked firm via on-the-job search. A similar argument holds with amenities.

Concentration also manifests itself through future contact rates. Similar to Jarosch et al. (2024), we assume that workers cannot meet their current employer.[26] Hence, for a worker at firm k, the quit/promotion discount sums only over $k' \neq k$. Without nonwage amenities, this does not affect the surplus value but does affect the split of the surplus. With nonwage amenities, this affects the surplus value because the worker is restricted from drawing a new amenity value at their current employer (i.e., working for a new boss, changing departments), potentially creating surplus. Therefore, firms' ability to exclude themselves from future job-to-job transitions generates lower total surplus and thus lowers wages.

Neoclassical monopsony forces working through nonwage amenities contribute negatively to wages and thus drive a gap between a worker's wage and marginal product due to compensating differentials. Note that when $\sigma = 1$, workers are paid all the way up to their output z_i, and the amenity discount disappears. That is, a worker could obtain a high amenity value from working at firm i, but in a dynamic labor market with a high rate of outside offers, σ would quickly increase, and this idiosyncratic taste would no longer reduce pay. Hence, search frictions and amenities interact; furthermore, the mere finiteness of firms in the market bounds $\bar{\sigma}_1 < 1$, generating positive amenity discounts.

Given the wage-setting protocol in Cahuc et al. (2006), the worker's bargaining power θ limits wage payments. Perhaps more subtly, the duopsonistic bargaining protocol—that is, only two firms ever compete simultaneously for a worker's services—also lowers the share of worker surplus σ. We explain this more in detail later when we allow more than two firms to bargain for a worker's services.

VI. Counterfactuals

We now use the model to investigate a number of counterfactuals that isolate the roles of (1) concentration, (2) amenities, and (3) search frictions for wage markdowns, welfare, and inequality. As discussed, there are many facets of concentration. Concentration affects the set of possible meetings, attainable surplus shares, and outside options. In what follows, we attempt to thoroughly explore the various dimensions of concentration, as how we model the granularity of firms is arguably the most novel aspect of our framework. We then proceed to isolate the effects of amenity dispersion and search frictions on wages and welfare.

A. Isolating the Effect of the Number of Firms, **M**

An Ideal Experiment

Our first counterfactual exercise aims to isolate the role of firms per market, M. We first consider an idealized experiment in which we solve an economy with 10 identical 10-firm markets—that is, with the same vector of productivities in each market—and then combine these into two identical 50-firm markets and, finally, one 100-firm market. When we combine markets, we combine the labor force as well, ensuring that $M/\bar{N}$ is constant across exercises, thus removing any mechanical changes to firms per worker. The vector of productivities $\mathbf{z} = (z_1, ..., z_{10})$ that we consider is evenly spaced between the 10th and 90th percentiles of the ergodic distribution of z_i. When we combine five of the 10-firm markets to produce a single 50-firm market, our exercise keeps the rungs of the productivity ladder fixed but reduces concentration.

Figure 5A uses equation (9) to plot the effect of M on the average wage and its four components. We plot percentage changes relative to the 10-firm benchmark, reducing concentration as we move from left to right. We find that average wages increase by 2% (solid). As M increases from 10 to 100, the output share component increases by 4%, being responsible for more than all of the gains (x's). The output share component consists of $\sigma \times z$, and both increase. The share parameter σ increases by 3% alone due to a higher inflow of outside offers. The average productivity level z increases as workers flow to higher z firms.

When shares of surplus are higher, the opportunity cost of employment is lower, which reduces the wage (squares). Notably, this nearly offsets all gains due to reallocation to higher-productivity firms (x's). Once these offsetting effects are accounted for, the dominant force in increasing the wage is the change in the amenity discount. As the worker's surplus share increases due to more competitive outside offers in a denser labor market, the reduction in wages due to worker-firm-specific tastes is reduced.

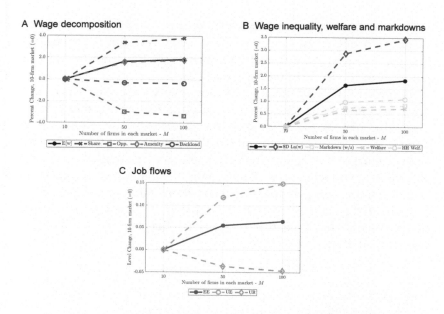

Fig. 5. Altering M in isolation: ideal experiment. EE = employer-to-employer, UE = unemployment-to-employment, EU = employment-to-unemployment. A color version of this figure is available online.

Wage discrimination on the basis of idiosyncratic factors is impossible when competition is tight, as workers receive more and better outside offers. The wage penalty due to amenities declines, pushing up wages by 2% (diamonds).

With more competition, workers are now more likely to meet with higher z firms in the future, which leads to more backloading of wages (circles). In the 50-firm and 100-firm markets, workers at z_{10} can meet with another z_{10} firm that they might like more due to personal preferences. As the worker will gain some surplus from that later transition, a lower wage is required today to deliver the promised values. Quantitatively, we find that this effect is small, contributing only a small negative effect on wages as we increase the number of firms per market by a factor of 10.

Figure 5B plots four other moments of interest, including wage inequality, welfare, and markdowns. First, wage inequality rises as we move from the 10-firm market to the 100-firm market. Workers at the top of the ladder now have many more possibilities in terms of competitive outside options, leading to higher wages to retain workers. Lucky workers receive many outside offers from good firms, fanning out the wage distribution and increasing wage inequality.

Total welfare—the sum of household utility and firm profits net of vacancy-posting costs—rises by 0.75%. As worker surplus shares rise, firm profits net of vacancy costs fall. As a result, household welfare, ignoring firm profits, rises by more than 1%.

A central focus of the literature on monopsony is the static wage markdown (e.g., Robinson [1933] and Berger et al. [2022a], among many others). In static economies, the definition of the markdown is universally agreed upon in the literature—it is the ratio of the spot wage to the marginal revenue product of the worker. In the dynamic context, markdowns can be defined in a number of ways. For example, the markdown could be logically defined as σ or perhaps via a comparison of the net present value of wages with the net present value of productivity. To stay as close as possible to the literature, we define markdowns following the static definition, here defined at the worker-firm level:

$$\text{Markdown definition: } \mu := w/z.$$

Thus, in our dynamic setting, μ reflects a variety of forces, including imperfect competition and its interaction with amenities, bargaining, and backloading. As a conceptual point, we are able to decompose what researchers would estimate in static models into its various components including backloading, which may not necessarily reflect noncompetitive behavior. We aggregate by taking the average across matches.

Figure 5B shows that markdowns narrow, with workers' spot wages relative to their marginal product increasing by 1% in the 100-firm market over the wages in the 10-firm markets. Importantly, the majority of the reductions in markdowns occur between the ten 10-firm markets and the two 50-firm markets. There is very little impact on markdowns between the two 50-firm markets and the single 100-firm market. This foreshadows our counterfactuals in Norway. The bulk of employment in Norway is in markets with 150 or more firms. Doubling the number of firms in an $M_j = 150$ firm market does little to markdowns, with the rungs of the productivity ladder held fixed. Conversely, markdowns are extremely sensitive to the number of firms in highly concentrated markets.

Last, figure 5C shows the increase in mobility that underpins the improvement in workers' shares of output. The effect of the ability to meet with a same-rank firm of higher personal preference is that job-to-job transition rates rise (open circles). A knock-on effect is that, in equilibrium, poaching workers becomes easier, incentivizing vacancy posting. Higher vacancies per worker support an increase in the U-to-E rate (filled circles) and hence a fall in the unemployment rate (diamonds). Importantly, with endogenous recruiting effort—here via vacancies—it is not only the split of surplus that is affected by the density of firms in the market but also quantities.

Application to Norway

We now extend the idealized experiment to the full Norwegian economy. Limited by computational resources, we conduct the following experiment: we duplicate the productivity vector in every simulated Norwegian market while simultaneously doubling the number of workers in each market. As in the ideal experiment, this preserves the rungs of the job ladder (i.e., the vector of z is duplicated but not altered otherwise), and the number of firms per worker remains the same. Table 6 column A contains statistics for our baseline economy, whereas column B considers the counterfactual economy. With the doubling of M in each market via duplication, the Herfindahl value is approximately halved from 0.09 to 0.05, which is mostly mechanical. As tighter competition leads workers to obtain a greater surplus share, the wage markdown narrows by 1 percentage point. The employer-to-employer job transition rate increases marginally, and labor productivity improves by 0.42% relative to that in

Table 6
Counterfactuals in Norway

Variable	A. Baseline $\{M_j, \bar{N}_j\}$	B. Duplicate z_j $2 \times \{M_j, \bar{N}_j\}$	C. Meet yourself	D. One ε $\frac{1}{N}\int \varepsilon_i di$ fixed	E. No search $\xi_e = 1$, $A = \infty$
I. Outcomes					
HHI$_n$	.09	.05	.12	.28	.75
Markdown (w/z), employment weighted	.79	.80	.80	.86	.93
E-to-E worker flow rate (%)	.55	.56	.62	.63	1.17
II. Comparison with baseline economy—percent difference					
Labor productivity	–	.42	.92	7.59	12.74
Welfare	–	.25	.57	6.60	14.75
Average wage	–	.68	1.43	16.82	30.88
Standard deviation of log wage	–	.81	2.05	−8.98	−91.66

Note: E-to-E = employer-to-employer, HHI = Herfindahl-Hirschman index.

our baseline economy. Similarly to the ideal experiment, welfare increases, the average wage increases, and wages become more dispersed. The welfare and labor productivity effects are nonnegligible: welfare increases by 0.25 percent. Throughout, the mechanisms are identical to those in the ideal experiment.

These results suggest a limited role of concentration in shaping Norwegian markdowns, but importantly, the exercise captures only one facet of concentration. There are two reasons that the doubling of M yields small effects on markdowns: (1) the duopsonistic wage setting remains unchanged: when we double M there are still only ever two firms at the bargaining table competing on wages, and (2) approximately 70% of the labor force resides in markets with more than 150 firms, and hence, doubling the number of firms in those markets is irrelevant (fig. 5B). To dig deeper, we next conduct two exercises designed to measure the effects of concentration and granularity operating through outside options and duopsonistic strategic wage setting.

B.   Additional Sources of Monopsony Power

Granularity and Outside Options

In our model, similar to the setups in Zhu (2012) and Jarosch et al. (2024), firms are able to partially exclude themselves from future meetings when bargaining with workers. Such an assumption makes sense in a granular market. In our model, this is operationalized by a restriction that workers cannot meet with their current employer through job-to-job transitions in the next period. Jarosch et al. (2024) go one step further and also exclude the current employer from the next period's possible U-to-E transitions during the bargaining process, which we do not consider.

Table 6, column C reports what happens when we remove this assumption. Now workers redraw their amenity value at the firm. One can interpret this as life events that change the utility of a firm. Even if they draw the same amenity value, the firm now bargains against itself. One can interpret this as a worker changing departments or bosses. We find that wage dispersion increases substantially. Because the firms may have to compete internally for workers, wage dispersion increases at the top of the ladder because surplus shares can now go all the way to one. Two offsetting forces limit the narrowing of markdowns, which narrow by only 1 percentage point. On the one hand, workers' ability to meet the same firm leads to higher surplus shares, especially at the top, which increases wages. On the other hand, their ability to redraw amenity values leads to large amenity wage penalties, which lower markdowns. The latter improves welfare, however, which increases by 0.57%.

Amenities

Similarly to Robinson (1933), we include a role for nonwage amenities in driving the employment and wage-setting decisions of firms. Unlike Robinson (1933), however, we allow firms to first-degree price discriminate over the amenity value. This puts greater downward pressure on wages but, in many settings, does not necessarily result in inefficient allocations.

We find that our removing amenity dispersion yields a large reduction in the wage markdown. In table 6, column D, we restrict the amenity distribution to one value, calibrated to deliver the same aggregate amenity per capita as in our baseline economy. In other words, we study a mean-preserving removal of amenity dispersion. Workers' spot wages as a ratio to their productivity are now 7 percentage points greater than in the baseline economy. This represents a 33% narrowing of markdowns compared with the initial 21-percentage-point markdown observed in our baseline economy. With no heterogeneity in the amenity penalty, wage dispersion declines by a tenth relative to its level in the baseline economy.

Workers' sorting due to the combination of firm productivity and idiosyncratic tastes reduces the level of output in the economy relative to that in an economy where only firm productivity determines mobility. Recall that heterogeneity in amenities was necessary to ensure consistency with the empirical frequency of down-the-ladder job moves in the Norwegian data. In the economy in column D, there are zero down-the-ladder job moves. Hence, when we remove amenities, workers are sorted across firms only on firm productivity. This causes aggregate productivity to increase substantially, by more than 7%.

Search Frictions

We next explore the role of search frictions by steeply increasing match efficiency A.[27] In practice, our counterfactual implies that all employed and unemployed workers meet with a firm every period with certainty. Because our model is in discrete time, it remains the case that workers can at most meet with one firm per period. Hence, search frictions still exist, but they are strongly mitigated.

In an economy with on-the-job search, mitigating search frictions leads to a large increase in productivity (12.74%), as workers rapidly ascend the job ladder (E-to-E rates triple). Table 6 column E shows that this is accompanied by a large increase in concentration as workers agglomerate at the most productive firms. The Herfindahl index increases by a factor of 8, from 0.09 to 0.75. When at the highest-ranked firm, workers now quickly bump into the next-highest-ranked firm, which bids up their surplus share. As a result, reducing search frictions leads to a substantial narrowing of the markdown, with wages now only 7% below marginal product. Markdowns remain positive for two reasons: (i) the recuperation of vacancy costs for firms that still operate and (ii) the fact that, with granular firms, some workers at the top of the productivity ladder are employed at an amenity discount and run out of potential outside offers to increase their wage. Both the sorting to higher z firms and greater surplus share contribute to a 30% increase in wages; meanwhile, inequality compresses dramatically, as workers end up in approximately the same boat relatively quickly.

Bargaining Protocol and Bargaining Power

Our final set of counterfactuals addresses a source of market power that is implicit in the assumptions of this framework: duopsony in the bargaining protocol. What if a worker could instead have three firms at the negotiating table? Or four? It is beyond the scope of this paper to solve a model with these features; however, we think that future progress in this area is important. The aim of our final set of counterfactuals is to show that work in this area may be of future interest.

As a first step, we consider a counterfactual bargaining protocol that involves three firms at the table. First, we abstract from amenities, which gives an unambiguous ranking of firms. Second, we assume that whenever a worker meets with a firm of rank K, it simultaneously meets with the firm at rank $K - 1$ (i.e., the next-best firm). We assume that the arrival of firm $K - 1$ at the table is frictionless and does not come at the cost of any vacancies. We refer to this as the next-highest-ranked bargaining protocol. Because firm K presents the highest surplus value, the protocol affects only how surplus is split. In partial equilibrium, with contact rates held fixed, there would be no change to allocations. In general equilibrium, making the bargaining table more competitive reduces firms' values of vacancy posting, which is taken into account.

Table 7
Bargaining Counterfactuals in Norway

Variable	A. Single ε $\frac{1}{N}\int \varepsilon_i di$ fixed	B. ... and meet next highest rank	C. ... and $\theta = .5$	D. ... and $\theta = .9$
I. Outcomes				
HHI_n	.28	.84	.54	.72
Markdown (w/z), employment weighted	.86	.97	.97	1.00
E-to-E worker flow rate (%)	.63	.48	.64	.67
II. Comparison with single ε economy—percent difference				
Labor productivity	–	4.90	3.75	5.08
Welfare	–	7.20	5.48	7.34
Average wage	–	18.3	15.4	20.3
Standard deviation of log wage	–	−95.2	−87.2	−93.8

Note: EE = employer-to-employer, HHI = Herfindahl-Hirschman index.

Table 7 reports the results, where the comparison case is the model with a single amenity value (col. A). The markdown narrows by 11 percentage points, which is around half of the baseline markdown. A lower surplus share due to more direct competition reduces the return to vacancy posting, and especially so for the least productive firms. The shift in the distribution of vacancies toward more productive firms increases labor productivity by an additional 5%. As workers tend toward more productive firms, concentration increases and the Herfindahl index rises from 0.28 to 0.84. Despite this, the reallocation of production and more competitive labor markets increases welfare by 7.2%. Wage inequality falls, driven by compression in wages within firms as all workers are hired against a highly competitive outside offer.

Expanding the bargaining table has implications similar to those of massive increases in the bargaining power of workers.[28] Counterfactual levels of θ provide context for the large effects of the next-highest-ranked protocol. A more straightforward way to understand the effect of bargaining power could be to study comparative statics with respect to the worker bargaining weight $\theta \in [0, 1]$. However, this is difficult to interpret by itself. Column C shows that the next-highest-ranked protocol reduces markdowns as much as an increase in θ from 0.18 (baseline) to 0.50. Column D shows that the next-highest-ranked protocol increases welfare as much as an increase in θ to 0.90. These are substantial increases in bargaining power, and similarly increase wages by 15%–20%.

C. Summary and Policy Implications

Our experiments have explored how the three paradigms of monopsony—concentration, amenities, and search frictions—interact. Concentration is multifaceted, and we find a significant role for the hardwired duopsonistic wage setting built into models descended from Cahuc et al. (2006). Giving a seat at the bargaining table to the next-highest-ranked firm lowers markdowns by 50%. On the other hand, we find little effect of firms excluding themselves from future contacts. We also find that leaving the bargaining protocol untouched and doubling the number of firms in Norway does very little to markdowns. These results do not necessarily imply futility of stricter antitrust enforcement. Welfare significantly increases when the number of firms in the market doubles (see table 6, row 5, col. B) and even more so when firms are prevented from removing themselves from future contracts.

Although outside the scope of the current formulation of our model, antitrust law may be an effective way to alter the bargaining protocol of firms. For instance, theoretical work by Shi (2023) argues that a near-ban on noncompetes is an efficient policy. Moreover, such a ban may be within the scope of the Federal Trade Commission's mandate. As this paper is written, the Federal Trade Commission has proposed a rule to ban noncompetes.[29] Our framework can be easily modified to include noncompete restrictions and thus be used to assess the effect of such policies in a setting with firm concentration.[30]

We find that amenity dispersion explains one-third of observed markdowns in Norway. Because our model features first-degree price discrimination, however, the presence of amenity-driven markdowns does not imply inefficiency per se. Nonetheless, any policy that tilts the bargaining protocol in favor of the worker (raising σ and θ) increases pay by an erosion of the compensating differential. Put simply, a firm obtains output from the worker, and when pushed—via outside offers—they will pay up to that level of output. This raises consumer surplus but may lower total surplus.

Finally, search frictions in our discrete-time setting account for two-thirds of observed markdowns. We view search frictions as immutable, with no practical policy to alleviate them (see also Naidu and Posner 2022). Despite search frictions alone accounting for the majority of observed markdowns, the nonlinear interaction of the sources of monopsony in our model implies that addressing concentration and neoclassical sources of monopsony can still yield sizable improvements in worker welfare and wages.

One direction that we hope that future work will explore further is the distributional consequences of monopsony and market power. As Schmitz (2016) and Herkenhoff and Raveendranathan (2019) emphasize, the deadweight costs of monopoly are sizable and borne primarily by low-income households. This might also be true for any deadweight costs due to monopsony. Our framework is well suited to addressing these questions, as it allows for wage dispersion both within and across firms.

Two additional factors that can be accommodated relatively well in the model are human capital and risk aversion. Adding human capital to the model would enable researchers to explore the impact of monopsony and market power on investment in education and skill development. This would help us understand how these market structures affect workers' long-term career prospects and their ability to adapt to changes in the labor market. Work by Jungerman (2023) makes progress along these lines by incorporating human capital accumulation into a framework with dynamic oligopsony. Incorporating risk aversion would allow a more comprehensive analysis of the welfare costs of market power. This would help researchers better understand the costs associated with job loss and the ways in which individuals' decisions and well-being are affected by market power dynamics. Last, similarly to Berger et al. (2022a), we observe that worker mobility across markets may be important for quantifying the aggregate consequences of policies. By exploring these additional factors, future research could provide a more complete picture of the distributional consequences of monopsony and market power and guide policy interventions aimed at mitigating their negative effects on workers and society at large.

VII. Conclusion

In this paper, we develop a general equilibrium theory of monopsony that features (1) search frictions, (2) amenities, and (3) firm granularity. We estimate the strength of each source of monopsony using administrative data from Norway. Our approach introduces a novel method for defining markets and offers an extensive empirical overview of the conditional covariances of concentration, job flows, wages, and wage dispersion. Our model successfully replicates these relationships.

We use our model as a testing ground to investigate the sources of labor market power, focusing on wage markdowns—a measure defined as the ratio of a worker's current wage to the worker's productivity at the firm. Our findings indicate that more than 50% of observed wage markdowns can be attributed to firm granularity and strategic wage setting during bargaining. Amenities account for 33% of observed markdowns, and eliminating search frictions (by setting contact rates to one in a discrete-time setting) reveals that they account for 66% of markdowns. Due to strong nonlinear interactions between the three monopsony channels, the sum of this decomposition does not equal 100%.

These results can inform policy discussions. Markdowns related to concentration could potentially be influenced by antitrust laws or restrictions on noncompete agreements, which may help reduce amenity wage penalties. In contrast, markdowns driven by search and matching processes are likely immutable and more influenced by technology than policy.

Our paper points to a number of fruitful avenues for future research. Allowing worker mobility across markets, incorporating human capital, and allowing for risk aversion are necessary to account for these first-order factors that may have an important bearing on policy recommendations. Likewise, structurally modeling natural experiments that affect the composition and productivity of firms within a market may yield novel insights into how labor markets respond to market structure and provide strong tests of our own and other existing theories of oligopsony.

Endnotes

Authors email addresses: David Berger (david.berger@duke.edu), Kyle Herkenhoff (kyle.herkenhoff@gmail.com), Andreas R. Kostøl (andreas.r.kostol@gmail.com), Simon Mongey (simonmongey@gmail.com). This paper is for the *NBER Macroeconomics Annual 2023*, and we thank the editors, Martin Eichenbaum, Erik Hurst, and Valerie Ramey. We also thank our discussants, Giuseppe Moscarini and Katarína Borovičková. Any opinions and conclusions expressed herein are those of the author(s) and do not necessarily represent the views of the Federal Reserve Bank of Minneapolis, the Federal Reserve System, or Norges Bank. Thanks to Alexander Weinberg for excellent research assistance. This work was supported by the Norwegian Research Council grant numbers 227115 and 315437 and National Science Foundation award #SES-2214431. For acknowledgments, sources of research support, and disclosure of the authors' material financial relationships, if any, please see https://www.nber.org/books-and-chapters/nber-macroeconomics-annual -2023-volume-38/anatomy-monopsony-search-frictions-amenities-and-bargaining-concentrated -markets.

1. See Manning (2003) for a summary of the literature and recent papers by Card et al. (2018), Dube et al. (2020), Azar, Marinescu, and Steinbaum (2022), Benmelech et al. (2022), Berger et al. (2022a), Lamadon et al. (2022), Schubert, Stansbury, and Taska (2022), and Yeh et al. (2022), as well as Brooks et al. (2019), Dodini et al. (2020), Dodini, Løken, and Willén (2022), Felix (2022), and Rubens (2023) outside of the United States, among others.

2. In our baseline model, firms do not exclude themselves from future U-to-E transitions, only contemporaneous E-to-E meetings. Thus, this particular experiment holds fixed the set of possible U-to-E transitions, differentiating what we do from the approach in Jarosch et al. (2024).

3. Roussille and Scuderi (2022) find a similarly large role for amenities in empirical analysis of online job-board wage postings.

4. Early progress on this question is being made by Flinn and Mullins (2021), among others.

5. For the United States, economists have used Burning Glass data for occupation and wage information (Schubert et al. 2022). These data pose serious issues for analyses such as the one here. First, the data do not contain information on the universe of employees, employers, and jobs or wages paid to employees. Second, data on advertisements lack information on the quantity of positions and hence cannot be used to compute market shares. Third, only 6% of the advertisements scraped and collated by Burning Glass have wage, employer, and occupation information. Table A4 of Hazell et al. (2022) shows that although the 2010–19 data contain 239 million ads, dropping those without wages or a range of wages posted and without firm, county, sector, or occupation data leaves only 15 million ads, which is 6.27% of the initial sample. Further screening reduces their analysis sample to less than 1.6% of all ads.

6. The four-digit occupational classification is based on the International Standard Classification of Occupations adapted to Norwegian labor markets by Statistics Norway and the employment agency. There are strong incentives for correct reporting. First, the Norwegian labor law stipulates that firms undergoing a mass layoff, defined as laying off more than 10 workers over 30 days, must follow the last-in, first-out principle. The ordering is typically defined within position and establishment. Second, the employment agency uses information about occupation and the workplace location for targeted job search assistance. In practice, employers report positions by a seven-digit system (see https://www.ssb.no/klass/klassifikasjoner/145/, in Norwegian), with new job titles added at regular intervals.

7. For example, the occupational code for "economics and business" includes consultants, controllers, junior and senior credit analysts, and research and chief economists, to name a few. The codes also cluster unskilled positions, such as maintenance workers and janitors, and different levels of management positions into distinct groups.

8. See data appendix A, http://www.nber.org/data-appendix/c14848/appendix.pdf, for a more detailed description of the sources and variables and Bhuller (2009) for commuting patterns.

9. The petroleum sector accounts for a large fraction of income but is excluded from the calculation of the labor share.

10. Union membership in Norway is high relative to that in other countries in the OECD and the United States but fell from 58% to 53% from 1992 to 2013 (OECD Statistics Trade Union Statistics, https://stats.oecd.org/Index.aspx?DataSetCode=TUD). Unions play an important role in ensuring that firms comply with labor law, stating, e.g., that downsizing requires a 1-month notification to employees, with the dismissal time varying from 1 to 6 months, depending on age and tenure. Wrongful discharge can end with a lawsuit, where firms must compensate the dismissed employees for lost income.

11. Payroll taxes finance the UI system, and there is no experience rating on the firm. The potential benefit period is 52 weeks for workers who have earned less than twice the National Insurance basic amount for the last 3 years. The "basic amount" of benefits is currently approximately USD 1,000 per month. UI benefits are capped at a maximum level of previous earnings, currently six times the basic amount, which creates a kink in the benefit formula. To remain eligible for the cash benefits, work hours must have fallen by at least 50%, and recipients must be actively looking for work and willing to take any employment.

12. In appendix A.3, http://www.nber.org/data-appendix/c14848/appendix.pdf, we describe the construction of self-flow rates and plot the employment distribution of occupations by their self-flow. Approximately 50% of the workforce has a rate above 50%.

13. $\mathrm{HHI}_r^K = \Sigma_{k=1}^K (s_r^k)^2$, where s_r^k is the employment share of occupation cluster $k \in \{1, \ldots, K\}$ in commuting zone region r.

14. Note the clustering algorithm does not produce labels. We only use the label "manual low-skill services" for heuristic purposes.

15. See Berger et al. (2022a) for why weighting by the wage bill is appropriate.

16. A market with M identically sized firms has an HHI of $\text{HHI}_M = \Sigma_i(1/M)^2 = 1/M$. Hence, an HHI of 0.09 is what one would obtain from a market with $1/0.09 \approx 11$ equally sized firms.

17. These natural experiments can only be interpreted through a structural model, as Azkarate-Askasua and Zerecero (2024) adeptly do.

18. Recall that our clustering approach has potentially clustered four-digit occupations into different groupings in different regions due to heterogeneity across regions in the occupation-to-occupation flow matrix. Hence, our unit of analysis is the occupation, but statistics such as concentration or wage inequality are measured at the level of the market (cluster-commuting zone) to which the occupation-commuting zone is assigned by our algorithm.

19. Small concentrated markets vs. large less concentrated markets are precisely the comparison that we want to study and thus should not be downweighted by labor force size.

20. Note that Robinson's (1933) class of models does not allow for wage discrimination based on amenity draws, thus yielding inefficient allocations. First-degree price discrimination, on the other hand, yields the efficient allocation, with zero consumer surplus and wages set below marginal products.

21. For example, a firm may turn down all hires with the lowest amenity draw so as to wait until it meets a worker with a better amenity draw, to whom it can pay lower wages via a compensating differential. In a market with 150 firms and 3 potential amenity draws, 3^{150}, such possible complex hiring rules exist.

22. Specifically, for example, firm i does not internalize that its vacancies affect the contact rates of workers at firm k and hence affect the surplus $S_k(\varepsilon')$, which then affects the cost of hiring a worker from firm k.

23. Note that search efficiency is accounted for by λ_{ik} and λ_{ui} and that the density of $F(\varepsilon)$ is denoted $f(\varepsilon)$.

24. See Bagger and Lentz (2019) table 2 for more detail.

25. In this class of models, low values of θ. can deliver negative wages, or near-zero wages, generating what look like fat-tailed wage growth distributions (e.g., in reasonable calibrations, workers can move from wages of 0.001 to a wage of 1, for instance, yielding 1,000% growth rates). Higher values of θ remove negative and near-zero wages, thus bringing the wage growth rates in line with the data.

26. Note that Jarosch et al. (2024) further exclude the unemployed from meeting their former employer.

27. Numerically, we implement this by setting A to 100, which is more than 500 times the level in our baseline (table 4). We also set ξ_e to 1, so that unemployed and employed workers have the same search efficiency. Because A is so large, this is almost irrelevant, but we do it nonetheless for completeness.

28. Anecdotally, this is well understood in the post-PhD economics job market and provides incentives for firms to make exploding offers, limiting workers' length of search and hence the number of competing firms at the negotiation stage.

29. See https://www.ftc.gov/legal-library/browse/federal-register-notices/non -compete-clause-rulemaking.

30. See Berger, Hasenzagl, et al. (2022) for an extensive discussion of the role antitrust authorities could play in addressing monopsony power.

References

Azar, José, Ioana Marinescu, and Marshall Steinbaum. 2022. "Labor Market Concentration." *Journal of Human Resources* 57 (S): S167–S199.

Azar, José A., Steven T. Berry, and Ioana Marinescu. 2022. "Estimating Labor Market Power." Discussion paper. https://www.nber.org/papers/w30365.

Azar, José A., Ioana Marinescu, Marshall I. Steinbaum, and Bledi Taska. 2018. "Concentration in US Labor Markets: Evidence from Online Vacancy Data." Working Paper no. 24395, NBER, Cambridge, MA.

Azkarate-Askasua, Miren, and Miguel Zerecero. 2024. "Union and Firm Labor Market Power." https://mzerecero.netlify.app/working_papers/labor_conc_occ.pdf.

Bagga, Sadhika. 2023. "Firm Market Power, Worker Mobility, and Wages in the US Labor Market." *Journal of Labor Economics* 41 (S1): S205–S256.

Bagger, Jesper, and Rasmus Lentz. 2019. "An Empirical Model of Wage Dispersion with Sorting." *Review of Economic Studies* 86 (1): 153–90.

Benmelech, Efraim, Nittai K. Bergman, and Hyunseob Kim. 2022. "Strong Employers and Weak Employees: How Does Employer Concentration Affect Wages?" *Journal of Human Resources* 57 (S): S200–S250.

Berger, David, Thomas Hasenzagl, Kyle Herkenhoff, Simon Mongey, and Eric Posner. 2022. "Merger Guidelines for Labor Markets." Working paper. https://www.nber.org/papers/w31147.

Berger, David, Kyle Herkenhoff, and Simon Mongey. 2022a. "Labor Market Power." *American Economic Review* 112 (4): 1147–93.

———. 2022b. "Minimum Wages, Efficiency and Welfare." Working Paper no. 29662, NBER, Cambridge, MA.

Bhaskar, V., A. Manning, and T. To. 2002. "Oligopsony and Monopsonistic Competition in Labor Markets." *Journal of Economic Perspectives* 16 (2): 155–74.

Bhaskar, V., and T. To. 1999. "Minimum Wages for Ronald McDonald Monopsonies: A Theory of Monopsonistic Competition." *Economic Journal* 109 (455): 190–203.

Bhuller, M. 2009. "Classification of Norwegian Labor Market Regions." *SSB Notater*, 24. https://www.ssb.no/a/publikasjoner/pdf/notat_200924/notat_200924.pdf.

Bhuller, M., K. O. Moene, M. Mogstad, and O. L. Vestad. 2022. "Fact and Fantasies about Wage Setting and Collective Bargaining." *Journal of Economic Perspectives* 36 (4): 29–52.

Bloesch, Justin, and Birthe Larsen. 2023. "When Do Firms Profit from Wage Setting Power? New vs. Classical Monopsony." Manuscript. https://drive.google.com/file/d/1KIO2elh7fbeKovtxqxS26prfkxOt_0OA/view.

Brooks, Wyatt J., Joseph P. Kaboski, Yao Amber Li, and Wei Qian. 2019. "Exploitation of Labor? Classical Monopsony Power and Labor's Share." Working Paper no. 25660, NBER, Cambridge, MA.

Burdett, K., and D. T. Mortensen. 1998. "Wage Differentials, Employer Size, and Unemployment." *International Economic Review* 39 (2): 257–73.

Burdett, Kenneth, Shouyong Shi, and Randall Wright. 2001. "Pricing and Matching with Frictions." *Journal of Political Economy* 109 (5): 1060–85.

Cahuc, Pierre, Fabien Postel-Vinay, and Jean-Marc Robin. 2006. "Wage Bargaining with On-the-Job Search: Theory and Evidence." *Econometrica* 74 (2): 323–64.

Card, David, Ana Rute Cardoso, Jörg Heining, and Patrick Kline. 2018. "Firms and Labor Market Inequality: Evidence and Some Theory." *Journal of Labor Economics* 36 (S1): S13–S70.

Dodini, Samuel, Katrine Vellesen Løken, and Alexander Willén. 2022. "The Effect of Labor Market Competition on Firms, Workers, and Communities." Discussion Paper no. 17, NHH Department of Economics, Oslo. https://openaccess.nhh.no/nhh-xmlui/handle/11250/3032278.

Dodini, Samuel, Michael Lovenheim, Kjell G. Salvanes, and Alexander Willén. 2020. "Monopsony, Skills, and Labor Market Concentration." https://ideas.repec.org/p/cpr/ceprdp/15412.html.

Dube, Arindrajit, J. Jacobs, Suresh Naidu, and Siddharth Suri. 2020. "Monopsony in Online Labor Markets." *American Economic Review: Insights* 2 (1): 33–46.

Engbom, N., and C. Moser. 2022. "Earning Inequality and the Minimum Wage: Evidence from Brazil." *American Economic Review* 112 (12): 3803–47.

Felix, Mayara. 2022. "Trade, Labor Market Concentration, and Wages." Job Market Paper. https://www.mayarafelix.com/papers/Felix_JMP.pdf.

Flinn, Christopher, and Joseph Mullins. 2021. "Firms' Choices of Wage-Setting Protocols." Discussion paper, New York University.

Gottfries, Axel, and Gregor Jarosch. 2023. "Dynamic Monopsony with Large Firms and an Application to Non-competes." Manuscript. https://www.nber.org/papers/w31965.

Hazell, Joe, Christina Patterson, Heather Sarsons, and Bledi Taska. 2022. "National Wage Setting." https://www.nber.org/system/files/working_papers/w30623/w30623.pdf.

Herkenhoff, Kyle F., and Gajendran Raveendranathan. 2019. "Who Bears the Welfare Costs of Monopoly? The Case of the Credit Card Industry." https://www.nber.org/papers/w26604.

Hurst, E., P. Kehoe, E. Pastorino, and T. Winberry. 2022. "The Distributional Impact of the Minimum Wage in the Short and Long Run." Discussion paper. https://www.nber.org/papers/w30294.

Jarosch, Gregor. 2023. "Searching for Job Security and the Consequences of Job Loss." *Econometrica* 91 (3): 903–42.

Jarosch, Gregor, Jan Sebastian Nimcsik, and Isaac Sorkin. 2024. "Granular Search, Market Structure, and Wages." *Review of Economic Studies*. https://doi.org/10.1093/restud/rdae004.

Jungerman, William. 2023. "Monopsony and Human Capital." Manuscript, University of Minnesota, Minneapolis.

Kostøl, Andreas R. 2017. "Mismatch and the Consequence of Job Loss." Discussion paper, Preliminary Working Paper, Arizona State University, Phoenix.

Kroft, K., Y. Luo, M. Mogstad, and B. Setzler. 2020. "Imperfect Competition and Rents in Labor and Product Markets: The Case of the Construction Industry." Working Paper no. 27325, NBER, Cambridge, MA.

Lamadon, Thibaut, Magne Mogstad, and Bradley Setzler. 2022. "Imperfect Competition, Compensating Differentials, and Rent Sharing in the US Labor Market." *American Economic Review* 112 (1): 169–212.

Lindenlaub, Ilse, and Fabien Postel-Vinay. 2021. "The Worker-Job Surplus." Working Paper no. 28402, NBER, Cambridge, MA.

Lise, Jeremy, and Fabien Postel-Vinay. 2020. "Multidimensional Skills, Sorting, and Human Capital Accumulation." *American Economic Review* 110 (8): 2328–76.

Lise, Jeremy, and Jean-Marc Robin. 2017. "The Macrodynamics of Sorting between Workers and Firms." *American Economic Review* 107 (4): 1104–35.

Manning, Alan. 2003. *Monopsony in Motion: Imperfect Competition in Labor Markets*. Princeton, NJ: Princeton University Press.

Naidu, S., and E. A. Posner. 2022. "Labor Monopsony and the Limits of the Law." *Journal of Human Resources* 57 (2): S284–S323.

Postel-Vinay, Fabien, and Jean-Marc Robin. 2002. "Equilibrium Wage Dispersion with Worker and Employer Heterogeneity." *Econometrica* 70 (6): 2295–350.

Rinz, Kevin. 2022. "Labor Market Concentration, Earnings, and Inequality." *Journal of Human Resources* 57 (S): S251–S283.

Robinson, Joan. 1933. *The Economics of Imperfect Competition*. London: Palgrave Macmillan.

Røed, K., and T. Zhang. 2003. "Does Unemployment Compensation Affect Unemployment Duration?" *Economic Journal* 113 (484): 190–206.

Roussille, Nina, and Benjamin Scuderi. 2022. "Bidding for Talent: Equilibrium Wage Dispersion on a High-Wage Online Job Board." Working paper, MIT, Cambridge, MA.

Rubens, Michael. 2023. "Market Structure, Oligopsony Power, and Productivity." *American Economic Review* 113 (9): 2382–410.

Schmitz, James A. 2016. "The Cost of Monopoly: A New View." Federal Reserve Bank of Minneapolis Region.

Schmutte, Ian. 2014. "Free to Move? A Network Analytic Approach for Learning the Limits to Job Mobility." *Labour Economics* 29 (C): 49–61.

Schubert, Gregory, Anna Stansbury, and Bledi Taska. 2022. "Employer Concentration and Outside Options." Mimeo. https://equitablegrowth.org/wp-content/uploads/2021/01/030822-WP-Employer-Concentration-and-Outside-Options-Schubert-Stansbury-and-Taska.pdf.

Shi, Liyan. 2023. "Optimal Regulation of Noncompete Contracts." *Econometrica* 91 (2): 425–63.

Taber, C., and R. Vejlin. 2020. "Estimation of a Roy/Search/Compensating Differential Model of the Labor Market." *Econometrica* 88 (3): 1031–69.

Yeh, Chen, Claudia Macaluso, and Brad Hershbein. 2022. "Monopsony in the US Labor Market." *American Economic Review* 112 (7): 2099–138.

Zhu, Haoxiang. 2012. "Finding a Good Price in Opaque Over-the-Counter Markets." *Review of Financial Studies* 25 (4): 1255–85.

Comment

Giuseppe Moscarini, Yale University and NBER, United States of America

In this ambitious chapter, Berger, Herkenhoff, Kostøl, and Mongey make a significant contribution to a recent lively debate on the origins of rising income inequality. A growing literature, which they exhaustively discuss in the introduction to the chapter and that includes important work by some of the same authors (Berger, Herkenhoff, and Mongey 2022), argues that profit rates and price markups, estimated to be rising in the United States over the last 4 decades, are better understood as wage markdowns, with market power manifesting itself more in labor than in product markets. The question is then: What gives firms labor market power? The answer is essential to understand what (if anything) policy makers can do about it.

A key step in this kind of analysis is how to delimit the confines of a labor market to determine measures of employer concentration and labor market power. The statistical definition of a labor market proposed and implemented in this chapter is novel and quite interesting. It fully leverages the exceptional scope of the Norwegian data, especially the availability of occupation information, rare in matched employer-employee data sets that originate from administrative sources. Both the scope of a labor market, based on job-to-job transitions that remain within its confines, and the ordering of employers in a labor market, based on net poaching ranks, exploit compelling revealed-preference arguments.

Building on this definition of a labor market, the authors offer new empirical evidence on the cross-market correlation between employment concentration and labor market flows, wage levels, and within-market wage

NBER Macroeconomics Annual, volume 38, 2024.

dispersion. Noteworthy is the addition of labor market flows, central to the macroeconomic analysis of unemployment and wage dispersion in the last half century and still largely absent from the monopsony literature. The authors then enrich a sequential auctions-cum-bargaining search model, à la Cahuc, Postel-Vinay, and Robin (2006), with vacancy posting and job creation, job amenities, and firm granularity. This flexible framework allows them to set up a horse race between neoclassical and frictional sources of wage compression and inequality. The estimated model addresses a classic question—What is the main source of residualized wage dispersion?—this time across labor markets defined by space and occupations rather than across individual workers.

The authors suggest that, of the three possible sources of market power, search frictions are the least tractable by policy, whereas amenities and firm granularity can be presumably addressed by fiscal and antitrust policy, respectively. But a natural mechanism to combat search and matching frictions is internal labor markets, certainly more developed within larger firms (e.g., Papageorgiou 2018). Paradoxically, the emergence in a local labor market of a large, dominating company may cause wage compression but also improve allocation via information-sharing and the resulting career progression opportunities within the firm. If we are concerned about the level of wages rather than just the labor share, the effects of employment concentration are a priori ambiguous.

More broadly, the general theme of my comment is that employer concentration is difficult to interpret in a world of search frictions. I will focus on a specific, possibly the most novel, aspect of the chapter, namely, the relationship between worker turnover rates and employment concentration. The empirical evidence on the association between employment concentration, job-to-job transitions, and unemployment (figs. 2 and 3 and table 3 in the paper) is new to the literature, and it is essential to identify frictional versus neoclassical sources of labor market power in the structural estimation of the model. Worker flows between employment states and employers can originate either from search frictions or from preference shocks. The authors do not consider the latter: job-specific preferences/amenities do not change during an employment relationship. Therefore, only frictions remain to explain dynamics. Accordingly, I formally investigate the relationship between labor market flows and the Herfindahl-Hirschman Index (HHI) concentration index in a class of frictional models. Specifically, I study the role of several latent and unobserved fundamentals of a labor market that can cause the heterogeneity in worker flows and in employer concentration observed across labor markets in Norway. These fundamental, market-specific factors include the efficiency of job search, job stability, and total factor productivity (TFP).

The basic insight I build upon is the role of outside offers as a counterweight to firms' market power. While searching for microfoundations to tatonnement to competitive equilibrium, Diamond (1971) came to a paradoxical conclusion. In a wage-posting game, where workers have no exogenous bargaining power but can only leverage their outside options, arbitrarily small frictions in finding jobs from unemployment, barring any outside offer during employment, generate maximum monopsony power and wage compression. Put more simply, even negligible frictions before matching are sufficient to enforce a unique equilibrium where workers are at the complete mercy of the firms. Burdett and Judd (1983) and Burdett and Mortensen (1998) are the seminal frameworks that bring outside offers, simultaneous or sequential, respectively, to break this Diamond paradox. The Postel-Vinay and Robin (2002) sequential auctions framework, on which this chapter ultimately builds, further developed this line of thinking by introducing ex post competition for employed workers. Importantly, on-the-job search is more effective against firms' bargaining power the more stable jobs are. If separations to unemployment are frequent, and the job ladder is slippery, workers can rarely climb it and are hired mostly from unemployment, at their reservation wages.

My main conclusions are as follows. A generic job ladder model generates an inverse relationship across markets between the pace of employer-to-employer (EE) transitions and employment concentration, as we observe in the data, under different parameter configurations that lead to opposite implications for market power. In this sense, the empirical evidence on this inverse relationship cannot reject the model, but it does not fully discipline it either. Intuitively, a labor market can be highly concentrated, and job-to-job transitions suppressed, when frictions are small, jobs are stable, outside offers are very frequent, the market is nearly perfectly competitive, so workers concentrate in the most productive firm, which nearly drives the other firms out of the market. There is no need for EE reallocation, as most workers are already on the top rung of the job ladder. Modest job instability thus reduces concentration and raises EE transitions. Conversely, close to the Diamond (1971) paradoxical limit of full monopsony, EE transitions are low, because they are infeasible. If job ladder rungs capture firm-specific productivity, the top rungs earn the highest profits and post the most vacancies and thus absorb most hires (from unemployment) and concentrate employment. In this case, modest on-the-job search opportunities raise EE transitions and might reduce concentration.

To draw more definite conclusions, we need to consider additional local labor market indicators. The patterns of unemployment rates and of transition rates from employment to unemployment (EU), observed across labor markets of different concentrations in Norway, support the view that high concentration is actually, and maybe counterintuively, a symptom of small frictions and intense competition. The observed patterns of transition rates from unemployment to employment (UE) are uninformative in the logic of job ladder models where only outside offers to employed workers matter. The observed patterns of wage levels and within-market wage dispersion support the view that concentration means monopsony but can be also rationalized by additional forces that the model abstracts from, most notably implicit insurance contracts, also consistent with the other patterns.

I. A Job Ladder with Rank-Preserving Equilibrium

Much of the notation follows the chapter's. There exists a measure of firms indexed by a fixed trait (including permanent amenities) $z \in [\underline{z}, \bar{z}] \sim P(z)$. Each firm of index z posts $v(z)$ vacancies; the total mass of vacancies is then $v = \int_{\underline{z}}^{\bar{z}} v(z) dP(z)$.

Employed workers lose jobs and become unemployed with probability $\delta \in (0, 1)$. The u unemployed workers search full-time; still-employed workers $(1 - \delta)(1 - u)$ can search with probability $\xi \in [0, 1]$ each period. Aggregate job market tightness is $\theta = v/[u + \xi(1 - \delta)(1 - u)]$. Searching worker contacts open vacancies with probability $\lambda = \Lambda(\theta) \in (0, 1)$, where $\Lambda(\cdot)$ derives from a homothetic random meeting function.

The "sampling weight" of firms of index z is $\gamma(z) = v(z)P'(z)/v = \Gamma'(z)$, so $\Gamma(z)$ is the probability that a worker, conditional on contacting a vacancy, draws a match with index less than z.

I assume that the allocation reflected in the data is the outcome of a decentralized equilibrium (or of an optimal social plan) that is "rank preserving": all workers have preferences for jobs monotonic in z, thus agree on a vertical ranking, and climb the same "job ladder." This is a strong restriction that unlocks some useful properties. In this allocation, more desirable firms typically post more vacancies, $v'(z) > 0$.

Let $L_t(z)$ denote the measure of workers employed at index less than z at time $t = 0, 1, 2, \ldots$ Rank-preserving dynamics on the job ladder imply that workers, when given the opportunity, move from lower to higher z index jobs:

$$L_t(z) = L_{t-1}(z)(1 - \delta)[1 - \xi\Lambda(\theta_t)(1 - \Gamma(z))] + u_{t-1}\Lambda(\theta_t)\Gamma(z),$$

where the unemployment rate is $u_t = 1 - L_t(\bar{z})$. The two terms multiplying past employment represent retention from, respectively, separations to unemployment and quits to preferred employers $z' > z$. The last term is the inflow from unemployment. Note that there is no inflow from other firms, because this is a cumulated distribution. Quits between firms of index either both lower or both higher than z do not change the mass; only quits that cross z (in the square brackets) affect this mass, and indeed reduce it.

In steady state, with $\lambda = \Lambda(\theta)$ for notational convenience:

$$L(z) = \frac{\lambda\Gamma(z)u}{\delta + (1 - \delta)\xi\lambda[1 - \Gamma(z)]},$$

where

$$u = 1 - L(\bar{z}) = \frac{\delta}{\delta + \lambda}.$$

II.   Worker Flows

The probability of observing a worker making an EE transition is the product of the meeting probability and of the "acceptance" probability (AC) that the new draw has a higher index:

$$EE = \underbrace{(1 - \delta)\xi\lambda}_{\text{Prob(offer)}} \cdot \underbrace{\int_{\underline{z}}^{\bar{z}}[1 - \Gamma(z)]\frac{dL(z)}{1 - u}}_{\text{Prob(accept|offer)"AC"}}.$$

We now state and prove that in a rank-preserving equilibrium the specific sampling distribution Γ is irrelevant for EE transitions: only quantiles matter, because workers always move up the ladder. This argument builds on Moscarini and Postel-Vinay (2023).

Let

$$\Delta = \frac{\delta}{(1 - \delta)\xi\lambda} \in [0, \infty).$$

This is a "frictional index" of search on the job, similar to the "κ_1" index in Burdett and Mortensen's (1998) continuous time model. Frictional index

Δ is higher the lower the on-the-job search meeting probability $\xi\lambda$ and the higher the job-losing probability δ, both contributing to misallocation on low z rungs. The case $\xi = 0$ yields the Diamond paradox of full monopsony. Frictional index Δ is equal to zero if nobody ever loses a job and falls off the job ladder ($\delta = 0$). In this case, assuming workers do receive outside offers ($\xi\lambda > 0$), they all end up employed at the top rung $\bar{z}$, the competitive equilibrium outcome.

Proposition 1. In steady state, the acceptance probability only depends on the model parameters through the frictional index Δ, and equals

$$AC = \Delta(1 + \Delta) \ln\left(\frac{1 + \Delta}{\Delta}\right) - \Delta.$$

In particular, AC does not depend on the distribution of job ranks P nor (directly) on the sampling distribution Γ, thus on vacancy postings per rank $v(z)$. AC is increasing and concave in frictions Δ, with

$$\lim_{\Delta \downarrow 0} AC = 0 \text{ and } \lim_{\Delta \to \infty} AC = \frac{1}{2}.$$

Proof.

$$
\begin{aligned}
AC &= \int_{\underline{z}}^{\bar{z}} [1 - \Gamma(z)] \frac{dL(z)}{1 - u} \\
&= \int_{\underline{z}}^{\bar{z}} \frac{L(z)}{1 - u} d\Gamma(z) \\
&= \int_{\underline{z}}^{\bar{z}} \frac{u\lambda\Gamma(z)}{\delta + (1 - \delta)\xi\lambda[1 - \Gamma(z)]} \frac{d\Gamma(z)}{1 - u} \\
&= \int_0^1 \frac{u}{\delta + (1 - \delta)\xi\lambda(1 - Y)} \lambda \frac{Y}{1 - u} dY \\
&= \int_0^1 \frac{\delta}{\delta + (1 - \delta)\xi\lambda(1 - Y)} Y dY \\
&= \Delta \int_0^1 \frac{Y}{\Delta + 1 - Y} dY \\
&= \Delta \int_0^1 \left(\frac{\Delta + 1}{\Delta + 1 - Y} - 1\right) dY \\
&= \Delta(1 + \Delta) \ln \frac{1 + \Delta}{\Delta} - \Delta,
\end{aligned}
$$

where in the second line we integrate by parts, in the third we replace for $L(z)$ from its expression, in the fourth we change the variable to $Y = \Gamma(z)$, in the fifth we replace for u from its expression, in the sixth for Δ, and the rest is standard. The other properties can be verified directly.

Now we return to the EE probability. The meeting probability of employed workers with competing firms decreases with the separation probability δ, because fewer workers can access outside offers if they are first separated into unemployment; it increases with the general contact probability per unit of search efficiency, λ, and with the (relative) efficiency of on-the-job search ξ. These parameters have exactly the opposite impact on the frictional index Δ and thus, from the proposition, on the acceptance probability AC. It is easy to verify that

$$\lim_{\delta\downarrow 0} \text{EE} = \xi\lambda \cdot 0 = 0$$

$$\lim_{\delta\uparrow 1} \text{EE} = 0 \cdot \frac{1}{2} = 0$$

$$\lim_{\xi,\lambda\downarrow 0} \text{EE} = 0 \cdot \frac{1}{2} = 0$$

$$\lim_{\xi,\lambda\uparrow 1} \text{EE} = (1 - \delta) \cdot \frac{\delta}{1 - \delta} = \delta.$$

In general, EE is nonmonotonic (hump-shaped) in δ, a fact that poses an identification challenge. When workers fall off the job ladder frequently, they have fewer chances to change jobs, so the fewer surviving employed are poorly distributed on the job ladder and thus accept more of the outside offers they receive, whereas firms have more labor market power. Therefore, a low observed EE probability is consistent with both very stable and very unstable jobs. The "competition" parameter $\xi\lambda$ too has two opposing effects: more frequent outside offers allow more job switches but also less misallocation and acceptance. But, in this case, the direct effect dominates.

III.   Employment Concentration

The same expression for the employment distribution $L(z)$ allows us to understand the impact of frictions on employment concentration. First, normalizing $L(z)$ by total employment $1 - u$ yields the employment cumulative distribution function (CDF)

$$\mathcal{L}(z) = \frac{L(z)}{1 - u} = \frac{\delta\Gamma(z)}{\delta + (1 - \delta)\xi\lambda[1 - \Gamma(z)]} = \frac{\Delta\Gamma(z)}{\Delta + 1 - \Gamma(z)}, \tag{1}$$

with $\mathcal{L}(\bar{z}) = 1$ independently of frictions Δ.

Let $\mathbb{I}$ denote the indicator function. In the frictionless limit

$$\lim_{\Delta \downarrow 0} \mathcal{L}(z) = \mathbb{I}\{z = \bar{z}\},$$

all employment concentrates on the top rung. If there is only one firm at the top, the HHI index, the sum of squared firms' employment shares, equals one, its maximum feasible value.

Conversely, as frictions grow unbounded:

$$\lim_{\Delta \to \infty} \mathcal{L}(z) = \Gamma(z),$$

no reallocation takes place up the job ladder, workers remain where they are hired from unemployment, until separation, and the employment distribution converges to sampling distribution Γ. This is the Diamond (1971) paradoxical equilibrium, with full monopsony power. As long as Γ is nondegenerate, as it is usually the case, the HHI index is unambiguously lower than one. If extreme frictions destroy any returns from vacancy postings, all firms post a vanishing measure of job openings, and the sampling distribution reduces to the population distribution $P(z)$. The same conclusion applies: the HHI index remains strictly below one.

Therefore, concentration is eventually decreasing in frictions and market power. Concentration is low when firms have maximum market power and extract all rents from helpless job applicants, whereas it is highest when competition not only pushes all workers to the top firms but also pushes wages up to productivity.

To understand what happens away from the limits, we can rewrite

$$\mathcal{L}(z) = \int_{\underline{z}}^{z} s(z) dP(z),$$

where $s(z)$ is the share of employment at each firm of type z. Therefore,

$$s(z) = \frac{\mathcal{L}'(z)}{P'(z)} = \frac{\Delta(1 + \Delta)}{[\Delta + 1 - \Gamma(z)]^2} \frac{\Gamma'(z)}{P'(z)} = \frac{\Delta(1 + \Delta)}{[\Delta + 1 - \Gamma(z)]^2} \frac{v(z)}{v},$$

where we used equation (1). In a rank-preserving equilibrium, this share is typically increasing in rank z. A sufficient condition is that firms higher on the ladder post more vacancies.

The HHI index is then

$$\mathrm{HHI} = \int_{\underline{z}}^{\bar{z}} s^2(z) dP(z).$$

How does it depend on our measure of labor market frictions Δ? Taking a derivative, because the firm population distribution $P(z)$ does not depend on the extent of labor market frictions:

$$\frac{\partial \text{HHI}}{\partial \Delta} = \int_{\underline{z}}^{\bar{z}} 2s(z)\frac{\partial s(z)}{\partial \Delta}P'(z)dz = \int_{\underline{z}}^{\bar{z}} 2s(z)\frac{\partial(s(z)P'(z))}{\partial \Delta}dz$$

$$= \int_{\underline{z}}^{\bar{z}} 2s(z)\frac{\partial \mathcal{L}'(z)}{\partial \Delta}dz,$$

where $\mathcal{L}$ is a proper CDF, so $\mathcal{L}'$ is a proper density. When $s(z)$ is increasing, the last integral is negative if an increase in frictions causes a downward shift in $\mathcal{L}$ in a first-order stochastic dominance sense, that is, if for every $z < \bar{z}$:

$$0 < \frac{\partial \mathcal{L}(z)}{\partial \Delta} = \frac{\Gamma(z)[1 - \Gamma(z)] + \Delta(1 + \Delta)\frac{\partial \Gamma(z)}{\partial \Delta}}{[\Delta + 1 - \Gamma(z)]^2},$$

where we again used equation (1) and rearranged terms. The first term in the numerator is unambiguously positive: more severe frictions amplify misallocation and reduce concentration. The second term can be negative. It is zero when firms do not post vacancies but stand ready to hire anybody who contacts them, as in Burdett and Mortensen (1998), so that $\Gamma = P$ is independent of frictions and employment concentration is globally, not just eventually, decreasing in frictions.

IV. The Relationship between EE Flows and Employment Concentration

We are now in a position to understand how the EE transition probability and the HHI index of labor market concentration comove across labor markets characterized by different unobservable fundamentals, summarized in the frictional index Δ. These fundamentals include not only job (in)stability δ and on-the-job search efficacy ξ but also any other, such as local TFP, that can determine vacancy creation; thus job market tightness θ and average meeting probability $\lambda = \Lambda(\theta)$. We distinguish between two cases and the resulting possible interpretations of the empirical evidence:

1. Job stability: Labor markets differ by δ. Figures 2C and 3C in the chapter show an inverse relationship between the separation probability EU and the HHI index of concentration. If δ is small, as is average EU in the data, then the EE probability declines and the HHI index rises as δ falls. That is, in figures 2 and 3 in the chapter, as we move from left to right,

less fluid and more concentrated labor markets are actually those that feature more stable jobs, a less slippery job ladder, and more opportunities for workers to climb it and to extract rents from firms. Thus, more fluid and less concentrated labor markets are actually, and maybe counterintuively, more monopsonistic.

2. On-the-job search frictions: Labor markets differ by $\xi\lambda$. For example, in some markets, on-the-job search is made very difficult by long work hours, or noncompetes are pervasive, or low market-specific TFP suppresses job creation. As $\xi\lambda$ decreases, and frictions Δ grow, markets become more monopsonistic, converging to the Diamond (1971) limit. As we showed, the EE probability declines. If concentration also declines, as in the example provided earlier, the resulting positive comovement between EE and concentration contradicts the evidence in figures 1A and 2A. To fit this evidence, concentration must be nonmonotonic in frictions. Because concentration is maximal near the frictionless benchmark $\Delta = 0$, where most employment joins the very top firms, it cannot increase in Δ near there. Therefore, Norwegian labor markets must be at the opposite, highly frictional end of the spectrum and feature very low, and heterogeneous, on-the-job contact rates $\xi\lambda$. In this scenario, more concentrated labor markets are indeed more monopsonistic.

These observations highlight the identification challenge faced by the authors. Job ladder models are a natural environment in which higher concentration does not imply nor signal market power.

V. Additional Labor Market Indicators

To further discriminate between the two scenarios, consider other local labor market outcomes, which may provide evidence of high or low frictions and monopsony power.

The job-finding rate from unemployment (UE rates) appears to be decreasing in concentration (figs. 2B and 3B). Although suggestive of higher monopsony power in more concentrated markets, this evidence is inconclusive. The logic of job ladder models with wage posting and on-the-job search indicates that UE flows are irrelevant to workers' bargaining power, which originates entirely from outside offers that they receive only once employed.

The unemployment rate (figs. 2D and 3D) is also inconclusive, as its relationship with concentration differs across markets and for a given market over time. The cross-market negative correlation supports the first interpretation, that markets differ by job stability and concentrated and less fluid markets are in fact more competitive. This is because unemployment declines despite falling job-finding UE rates from unemployment, so job-losing EU rates are the dominant force.

If job separations are endogenous, their heterogeneity across labor markets (figs. 2C and 3C) is naturally explained by local TFP: more productive labor markets feature more lenient retention standards and, as argued by Bilal (2023) for regions in France, lower EU separation probability. More productive labor markets are also more likely to generate, through firm entry, more vacancy openings and thus a higher meeting probability for job searchers. Whether separations to unemployment are exogenous or endogenous, the EU evidence supports the first interpretation.

What about wages? Those appear to provide direct evidence of markdowns and wage compression in more concentrated labor markets (figs. 2E and 3E). There are, however, alternative considerations that can reconcile lower wages with lower unemployment. One is an insurance component in employment contracts. Labor markets that offer more job stability—for example, because they are more productive and resilient to idiosyncratic productivity shocks—also offer more stable and compressed wages, as also indicated by the evidence on within-market wage inequality (figs. 2F and 3F). Workers accept lower wages to enjoy more job stability and be spared unemployment. Any empirical test of insurance in wage contracts must rely on dynamics, specifically on pass-through of firm revenues shocks to wages. A second possibility, inspired by the chapter itself, is that the job ladder rung z is dominated by amenities, and not by productivity; in this case, high poaching-index firms could be low-paying but extremely pleasant to work for.

The empirical evidence on wages calls for one final comment. Wages are not allocative in the model. If one takes a stand on wages, as the authors do, then the model predicts not only wage inequality across and within local labor markets but also individual wage career paths. Specifically, like any job ladder model, it generates a distribution of wage changes upon job switches, scarring effect of layoffs, and so forth. These dynamic properties are the litmus test of search models, which were built to explain the cross section of earnings, and can help to identify also the correct model of labor market power, thus to advance this exciting research agenda.

Endnote

Author email address: Moscarini (giuseppe.moscarini@yale.edu). For acknowledgments, sources of research support, and disclosure of the author's material financial relationships,

if any, please see https://www.nber.org/books-and-chapters/nber-macroeconomics-annual
-2023-volume-38/comment-anatomy-monopsony-search-frictions-amenities-and-bargaining
-concentrated-markets-moscarini.

References

Berger, D., K. Herkenhoff, and S. Mongey. 2022. "Labor Market Power." *American Economic Review* 112 (4): 1147–93.
Bilal, A. 2023. "The Geography of Unemployment." *Quarterly Journal of Economics* 138 (3): 1507–76.
Burdett, K., and K. L. Judd. 1983. "Equilibrium Price Dispersion." *Econometrica* 51 (4): 955–69.
Burdett, K., and D. Mortensen. 1998. "Wage Differentials, Employer Size and Unemployment." *International Economic Review* 39:257–73.
Cahuc, P., F. Postel-Vinay, and J.-M. Robin. 2006. "Wage Bargaining with On-the-Job Search: Theory and Evidence." *Econometrica* 74 (2): 323–64.
Diamond, P. A. 1971. "A Model of Price Adjustment." *Journal of Economic Theory* 3 (2): 156–68.
Moscarini, G., and F. Postel-Vinay. 2023. "The Job Ladder: Inflation vs Reallocation." Working Paper no. 31466, NBER, Cambridge, MA.
Papageorgiou, T. 2018. "Large Firms and within Firm Occupational Reallocation." *Journal of Economic Theory* 174:184–223.
Postel-Vinay, F., and J.-M. Robin. 2002. "Equilibrium Wage Dispersion with Worker and Employer Heterogeneity." *Econometrica* 70 (6): 2295–350.

Comment

Katarína Borovičková, *Federal Reserve Bank of Richmond,* United States of America

I.   Introduction

It is well understood that labor markets are not perfectly competitive. The goal of this paper is to evaluate how different aspects of monopsony power shape the gap between workers' marginal product and their wage.

The classical notion of a monopsony market is one where one dominant firm faces many workers who seek to sell their labor services to the firm. Labor supply is upward sloping as more workers are willing to work at higher wages. In this market, the dominant firm has power to choose its labor demand and wage, respecting the labor-supply curve, to maximize its profit. Compared with a competitive environment, the monopsony demands less labor and offers lower wages, exploiting the supply curve. Because of this inefficiency created by the monopsony, it is important to understand the degree of firms' market power and to potentially propose policies that limit it.

This paper features several deviations from a perfectly competitive labor market. First, search frictions prevent workers and vacancies from matching immediately. Second, workers differ in amenity values they attach to different jobs, allowing firms to offer a lower wage to workers with a high nonmonetary value of the given job. Third, bilateral monopoly in wage setting implies that workers and firms bargain over how to split the match surplus. Fourth, only a small number of firms operate in a given market. And finally, there is no worker and firm mobility across markets. The first four deviations are referred to as paradigms of monopsony. Hence, the notion of a monopsony is broader here, with some forces not creating inefficiency but all of them contributing to markdowns, the difference between workers' marginal product and wage. The no-mobility assumption is not treated as a paradigm of a monopsony; rather, it is used to set up the framework for evaluating the other paradigms.

II. Model and Its New Element

The model is based on Cahuc, Postel-Vinay, and Robin (2006) with several modifications. Workers in the model are assumed to be ex ante homogeneous and search for jobs in a local labor market with firms of varying levels of productivity. It is assumed that the number of workers and firms in the market is given and that there is no mobility across markets. Firms decide how many vacancies to post subject to convex vacancy-posting costs, after which workers meet them at an exogenous rate. After meeting, the worker draws an amenity value for the match, and the worker and firm decide whether to form a match. The worker and the firm bargain over a piece-rate contract following the bargaining protocol in Cahuc et al. (2006). The piece-rate contract is not updated until a worker meets another firm.

The novel element of the model is firm granularity, which affects three margins. First, it allows for partially directed search where employed workers cannot meet vacancies posted by their current employer, and firms cannot meet their current employees through the search process. Second, it enables the measurement of market concentration in the model to be based on the objects as in the data. Last, it introduces the concept of firms making their own vacancy-posting decisions, which is absent in the benchmark model where the distribution of vacancies is exogenous.

The authors take a shortcut when modeling the vacancy-posting decision. Firms understand that the per-vacancy meeting rate depends on the size of the firm; however, they are still acting as if they are atomistic when considering the impact of their actions. A dominant firm in the market does not factor in the effect that its own vacancy posting may have on the vacancy-filling probability of other firms, and therefore the outside option of workers and consequently the wages they receive. This shortcut eliminates the classical notion of a monopsony whereby a dominant firm can decrease employment to affect wages.

The most important margin of firm granularity is the partially directed search. Compared with an equilibrium with random search, workers receive fewer outside offers and, mechanically, fewer amenity draws, which translates into fewer opportunities to climb a ladder. Mobility declines. The bargaining protocol implies that the highest wage in the most productive firm is determined by the second-most productive firm a worker can meet. In a random search setup, this would be the most productive firm itself. In the partially directed search setup, workers cannot meet their employers, and hence this is the second-most productive firm. The highest achievable wage is lower, and so the wage distribution is compressed. This result depends on the important assumptions that there is no mobility across markets and workers are not able to meet a firm from a different market. However, this effect can be mitigated by introducing another high-productivity firm into the market. Past employers are not excluded from search, and hence workers would be able to move between multiple most productive firms, conditional on a good amenity draw, and through that increase their wage, prolonging the ladder again.

III.   Empirical Analysis and Its Connection to the Model

The strong assumption of no mobility across markets is a simplifying assumption that allows the model to be solved separately for each isolated market. However, when applying the proposed model to real-world data, a market must be clearly defined such that there are indeed no flows of workers or firms across its boundaries and other markets do not serve as outside options. This ensures that the model accurately accounts for the local nature of markets.

In the empirical analysis, a market is defined as a combination of groups of occupations and commuting zones. The geographic division into administrative units is assumed to be a given. However, occupation groups are determined endogenously using an algorithm that maximizes within-market worker flows while at the same time penalizes overfitting that would emerge from putting too many occupations into one group. This endogenous determination of occupation groups is done separately for each commuting zone, and hence occupation groups can vary across geographical locations.

Classifying occupations into groups is useful for several reasons. First, workers change occupations during their careers, and it would be too restrictive to study each of the occupations in isolation. Second, the classification of occupations varies across occupations in the sense that some occupations include a broad set of jobs, like teachers, and others are rather narrow, like dentists. This might be problematic from the perspective of a meaningful notion of the number of firms across markets, because having a market with five firms for a very narrow occupation is better for workers than five firms for a broad occupation. Creating groups of occupations mitigates this problem and helps maintain consistency across markets.

The resulting grouping of occupations is such that 50% of workers who switch an employer do so by moving outside their own labor market. Some of these market switches are due to workers changing their occupation group, and some of them are due to workers moving to a different commuting zone. Commuting zones are typically based on the administrative division of a country, which might be a relevant geographical boundary for some occupations but less so for others. Specifically, workers in low-skilled occupations, such as cashiers or plumbers, are less likely to move geographically for employment reasons. On the other hand, workers in high-skilled occupations, such as medical doctors or lawyers, are geographically mobile, and for many of these occupations the entire country is the relevant market. Hence, this definition of a market is more suitable for low-skilled occupations. However, the job-ladder model is a better description of the labor-market experience for workers in high-skilled occupations, because it is unlikely that firms compete for low-skilled workers by bidding up their wages. I view this as a discrepancy between the model and the data.

The goal of the empirical section is to document the relationship between labor-market concentration and several labor-market statistics, including average wages, unemployment rate, job-to-job transitions, and transitions between employment and unemployment. The authors use the standard market concentration measure, the Herfindahl-Hirschman index (HHI), and regress statistic of interest on HHI, exploring two different dimensions of variation. First, by including the occupation-year fixed effects into the regression, they explore across-region variation. By including occupation-region fixed effects, they explore time-variation in HHI.

The regression exploring across-region variation can be contaminated by spatial sorting. Bigger cities have less concentrated markets, but they also tend to have more productive firms and workers. Sorting between firms and workers has been well documented (e.g., Borovičková and Shimer 2017; Bonhomme, Lamadon, and Manresa 2019). Spatial sorting where more productive firms choose bigger cities is explored, for example, in Lindenlaub, Oh, and Peters (2022) or Bilal (2021). Therefore, the correlation between HHI and average wages and other labor-market statistics might not be representative of how firms' monopsony power shapes the labor market but rather the result of spatial sorting.

To address this concern, the authors explore variation over time in a given market by including occupation-region fixed effects. It remains a question what drives changes in HHI between different years in a given labor market. More concentrated markets are more likely to experience fluctuations in HHI because they consist of a small number of firms. Furthermore, given the definition of a market, an average firm in a market consists of only 6.2 employees. Thus, if only a few workers join or leave a single firm, it can significantly change the firm's employment share and have a noticeable impact on the HHI. In contrast, in a less concentrated market with many firms, a similar reallocation of workers will have a negligible effect on the HHI. Therefore, the observed variation in HHI is likely driven by the more concentrated markets and might not be informative about the less concentrated markets.

These regressions do not control for the distribution of firm productivities in the markets. Such controls would partially address the issue of spatial sorting, because now we would be able to see whether or not higher wages are driven by the presence of productive firms. This would also bring the regressions closer to measuring markdowns, the difference between workers' marginal product and wage, as is the ultimate objective of the analysis. This step requires bringing additional data sources containing value added of firms or sales per worker.

Finally, I want to discuss the question of to what extent HHI is a useful statistic in the context of a job-ladder model. Consider the following example. The average HHI in Norwegian data is 0.09. This value can be generated in several ways. For example, 11 equally sized firms or 15 firms with employment of 10, 20, . . . 150 workers. In the model, firm-size differences are generated through differences in firm productivities. Consider two markets, one with 11 equally productive firms and one with 15 firms with productivities $z_1 < z_2 < \ldots z_{15}$. These two markets have very different implications for workers' career wage profiles. In the first market, the wage profile is flat because all firms are identical. The second market yields wage profiles representative of a typical job ladder where workers move from worse to better firms over their careers. The average wage in these two markets will also differ. Therefore, HHI is not a sufficient statistic for average wage, let alone for the wage profiles, because these depend on the distribution of firm productivities.

IV.   Conclusion

This paper investigates the important question of how market structure affects workers' wages and their transitions between jobs and labor-market states. This question is studied through the lens of an extended job-ladder model that features firm granularity. The earlier comments explain that some of the empirical facts might be reflecting spatial sorting of better firms into larger cities, and assortative sorting between firms and workers, rather than the impact of market structure on wages. The model cannot address these concerns as it assumes all workers are ex ante homogeneous and all markets have the same distribution of firm productivities. To move forward with this research question, additional data sources are necessary to discipline differences in firm productivity across markets. The average productivity at the market level would not be sufficient; the entire distribution is needed, as the tails play an important role. For deeper understanding of the mechanism, it would be instructive to examine career profiles of workers. Does steepness of the career profile depend on market concentration? Workers might be better off in a market with a lower average wage if that market offers steeper wage growth early in the career.

The main finding of the paper is that the key determinants of the average wage in a market are search frictions and the bargaining protocol between firms and workers. This area of research does not have a data-driven bargaining protocol, making it a fruitful avenue for further exploration. Recent survey data have demonstrated that workers differ in their assessment of future labor-market conditions, which, in turn, directly affects their evaluation of outside options, a crucial element entering any bargaining situation. Several papers, such as Bhandari, Borovička, and Ho (forthcoming) and Menzio (2023), have shown that subjective expectations have a marked effect on firms' recruitment decisions and labor-market flows. Subjective expectations, disciplined by data, seem to be an important path toward improving our understanding of wage setting.

Endnote

Author email address: Borovičková (katarina.borovickova@rich.frb.org). The views expressed herein are those of the author and not necessarily those of the Federal Reserve Bank of Richmond or the Federal Reserve System. For acknowledgments, sources of research support, and disclosure of the author's material financial relationships, if any, please see https://www.nber.org/books-and-chapters/nber-macroeconomics-annual -2023-volume-38/comment-anatomy-monopsony-search-frictions-amenities-and-bar gaining-concentrated-markets-2.

References

Bhandari, Anmol, Jaroslav Borovička, and Paul Ho. Forthcoming. "Survey Data and Subjective Beliefs in Business Cycle Models." *Review of Economic Studies.*

Bilal, Adrien. 2021. "The Geography of Unemployment." Working Paper no. 29269, NBER, Cambridge, MA.

Bonhomme, Stéphane, Thibaut Lamadon, and Elena Manresa. 2019. "A Distributional Framework for Matched Employer Employee Data." *Econometrica* 87 (3): 699–738.

Borovičková, Katarína, and Robert Shimer. 2017. "High Wage Workers Work for High Wage Firms." Working Paper no. 24074, NBER, Cambridge, MA.

Cahuc, Pierre, Fabien Postel-Vinay, and Jean-Marc Robin. 2006. "Wage Bargaining with On-the-Job Search: Theory and Evidence." *Econometrica* 74 (2): 323–64.

Lindenlaub, Ilse, Ryungha Oh, and Michael Peters. 2022. "Firm Sorting and Spatial Inequality." Working Paper no. 30637, NBER, Cambridge, MA.

Menzio, Guido. 2023. "Stubborn Beliefs in Search Equilibrium." *NBER Macroeconomics Annual* 37 (1): 239–97.

Discussion

Daron Acemoglu opened the discussion by stating that this is a very exciting research agenda and that he liked the use of Norwegian data as well as the way the authors constructed labor markets. He agreed with the sentiment of the discussants that the model is too complicated. He explained that once you have the relevant frictions, you can think of the problem of a bilateral monopoly and consider where the wage is relative to the outside options of the two parties. He added that one could also explore how the level of employment varies as you reduce the friction. However, he noted that the predictions depend on the details of the model and that the authors had chosen very specific details. As such, it was hard to know which details matter for the prediction. Monopsony models are a very special type of model and imply certain comparative statics where amenities could play an important role. Switching to the empirical work, Acemoglu pointed out that even with the moments they estimated from the Norwegian data, it was not clear that those can really be identified. He pointed out that there is much more granularity in the data. For example, when you look at wage changes as workers move from one firm to another, that takes the bargaining-power differences between firms into account. He emphasized that this would be the direction to go for this exciting research agenda. He concluded that adding structural features to the model and trying to back those out in the data would make it difficult to generate credible conclusions.

Erik Hurst complemented Acemoglu's points. He agreed that this is an exciting research agenda but emphasized that it will be important to

NBER Macroeconomics Annual, volume 38, 2024.

think about which frictions relative to each other will matter for explaining labor-market dynamics. He also added that it would be helpful to understand what in the data allows authors to distinguish between different levels of a markdown. In relation to the decomposition, Erik Hurst asked what in the data is pinning down how much of the markdown is coming from search relative to other sources. Search appears to be doing a lot, and from his own work on minimum wages, which features a monopsony model with search, he noted that the importance of search depended significantly on preferences.

Building on the comments by the discussants, Gabriel Chodorow-Reich emphasized that the bargaining question is really central, and it is hard to get systematic data to discipline models. His intuition was that it is different for different types of workers and different parts of the labor market. He asked the authors about estimating these models. Specifically, whether heterogeneity by worker type or how specific a worker's skills are will affect how much they are subject to bargaining versus wage posting. He added that, at some point, we will have to move away from estimating one model for all workers to incorporating different types of bargaining protocols for different types of workers and different types of firms.

Giuseppe Moscarini highlighted a recent *Econometrica* paper by Faberman, Mueller, Şahin, and Topa. He pointed out that those who work on monopsony should read the search literature very carefully, because there is now so much relevant data. For example, we have data on the probability of accepting outside offers. Given all these data, we can now see the demand and supply sides, which gets to the points made earlier by Acemoglu and Hurst about where the identification is coming from. We have had demand on the vacancy side but not supply on the acceptance side. Therefore, using this additional data on the supply side, which the authors do not use yet, in conjunction with the demand side would be key.

Kyle Herkonhoff thanked Moscarini for his helpful response to the many comments and added that they can measure the delta (the ratio of the flows) and so can immediately reject atomistic firm models. Moreover, there is enough empirical work that simulates firm exits and wage and employment responses, so they can rule out a particular class of models.

David Autor noted that the assumption in the literature is that firms optimally mark down by some amount, which provides a labor-supply elasticity. However, in reality, most employers have no idea about the labor-supply elasticity. Moreover, recent experiments suggest firms do not even understand how much adjusting wages affects applications.

Recognizing that employers have wage-setting powers does not necessarily mean firms optimally mark down with a given formula. Simon Mongey responded that one of the nice things about their model is that you can essentially ask a firm in the model to run a reduced-form regression and they would get a number.

On the empirical side, Autor asked about the relationship between the Herfindahl-Hirschman Index (HHI) and wage level. Other papers have shown that most variation in concentration is driven by small and large places, which have different wage levels in general, so doing aggregated analysis is not necessarily informative about the effect of concentration and wages. However, if you are making within-market comparisons across occupations, then it is informative. He asked the authors which approach they were taking. Herkonhoff noted that this question was also touched on in Katarína Borovičková's discussion and responded that because of those concerns relating to HHI, their analysis focused on within region, within occupation, across year. For example, comparing a dentist in Oslo today to a dentist in Oslo tomorrow is informative, and it is highly unlikely to reflect sorting.

Mongey added that in terms of the regressions, when they do within occupation and across markets, they are controlling for size of the market (number of firms) and the density, so there is no mechanical effect in model; this is taken care of in the regression as well. He agreed with Chodorow-Reich that thinking about skill specificity is important. He also agreed with comments by Acemoglu and Hurst, and now that they have model laid out, they can turn off individual model elements as well as think about the identification of each of them. In relation to the comments made in Moscarini's discussion, Mongey agreed that the distribution of amenities matters. He added that if you turn off the amenities distribution and rank firms in terms of the fraction that hires those coming from other firms relative to unemployment, then 100% of job flows in the model are going up the "ladder," so the only way in the model to have flows going in both directions is to have the amenities distribution. So given the model, the identification argument for that parameter is clear, which Moscarini also alluded to in relation to search literature.

In relation to the job-flows data, Andreas Kostol added that people are about three times more likely to flow out of the market to different occupations. He explained that there is also a gradient in the flows. For example, people with children or higher education are less likely to flow out. He pointed out that they could add productivity using a classic value-added measure and agreed that they should add more data.

Ayşegül Şahin pointed out that the authors have endogenous vacancies, and there is a cost of posting vacancies. She asked how the cost of posting vacancies was disciplined. Mongey responded that Herkonhoff had put up the wage formula. Given there is heterogeneity in productivity in the market, wages are primarily driven by this heterogeneity, and the bargaining determines what shares workers are getting of that productivity. That maps one-to-one to dispersion in wages, and they match that. Given that dispersion in productivity and the number of firms in the market, then the convexity of the vacancy cost entirely pins down concentration in the market. If you increase this convexity, then large firms do not become too large. Therefore, the measure of concentration provides a key way to get at this, though not necessarily a sufficient statistic. He added that the way the markets are defined in the model allows them to do this analysis.

David Berger concluded the discussion by agreeing with Acemoglu. He emphasized that they wrote this paper because people do not know empirically where markdowns come from. These benchmark frameworks do not work well together. Specifically, bargaining frameworks do not work well with neoclassical frameworks, so more needs to be done here, and they are taking a small step in that direction.

2

Inflation Strikes Back: The Role of Import Competition and the Labor Market

Mary Amiti, *Federal Reserve Bank of New York,* United States of America

Sebastian Heise, *Federal Reserve Bank of New York,* United States of America

Fatih Karahan, *Central Bank of the Republic of Türkiye,* Turkey

Ayşegül Şahin, *University of Texas at Austin and NBER,* United States of America, and *IZA Institute of Labor Economics,* Germany

I. Introduction

"So we have now experienced an extraordinary series of shocks if you think about it. The pandemic, the response, the reopening, inflation, followed by the war in Ukraine, followed by shutdowns in China, the war in Ukraine potentially having effects for years here. ... You couldn't get this kind of inflation without a change on the supply side, which is there for anybody to see, which is these blockages and shortages and people dropping out of the labor force and things like that." (Federal Reserve Chair Jerome Powell, remarks at news conference on June 15, 2022)

US inflation has recently surged, with annual consumer-price index (CPI) inflation reaching 9% in June 2022, its highest reading since November 1981, as figure 1*A* shows. Many policy makers have attributed this high and persistent level of inflation to supply-chain pressures related to several unprecedented developments, such as the COVID-19 pandemic and the war in Ukraine, coupled with a very tight labor market as the unemployment rate retreated back to its prepandemic level in less than 3 years (see earlier quote). To illustrate how the post-COVID recovery differs from earlier expansions, figure 1*B* shows the increase in the core CPI for the past six expansions, starting at the quarter with the peak level of unemployment of the preceding recession. Price growth in the most recent expansion is markedly higher than in the expansions of the 1990s or '00s: 10 quarters after peak unemployment in 2020:Q2, prices have grown by more than 12%, following a trajectory similar to the 1980s expansion rather than the most recent past.

In this paper, we examine how supply-chain disruptions and labor-supply constraints have contributed to the recent rise of inflation and

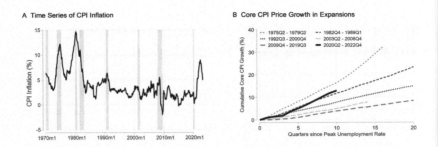

Fig. 1. CPI inflation. Bureau of Labor Statistics and authors' calculations. The left figure plots the annual rate of consumer-price index (CPI) inflation. The right figure plots the cumulative core CPI price growth (all items less food and energy, seasonally adjusted) against time, starting at the quarter of peak unemployment of a given recession, for the past six expansions. A color version of this figure is available online.

how they interacted with the shift of consumption from services to goods and expansionary monetary policy.[1] We consider three shocks to capture supply-chain and labor-market disruptions: first, supply-chain bottlenecks have led to an increase in the prices of imported intermediate inputs, driving up firms' marginal costs and contributing to price increases, in particular in the goods sector.[2] Second, supply-chain pressures affected US firms' foreign competitors as well, forcing them to raise their prices and allowing domestic firms to pass through price increases to customers without losing market share. Third, workers' willingness to work declined, and there was a rise in reservation wages, defined as the minimum wage that individuals require to work.[3] The decline in labor supply led to a rapid tightening of the labor market and worker shortages, contributing to high wage inflation and price pressures, particularly in services.

The supply-chain and labor-market disruptions coincided with a stark shift in consumption from services to goods in the recent period. The goods share in personal consumption expenditures (PCE) rose from 36% before the pandemic to a peak of 42% in 2020 and to about 38% by the end of 2022. In addition, monetary policy was highly accommodative in 2020 and 2021: the Federal Reserve cut its target for the federal funds rate by a total of 1.5 percentage points in 2020 and did not start tightening policy until March 2022.

A careful analysis of the role played by the different forces on goods and services inflation requires a framework with multiple factors of production, simultaneous cost shocks, and multiple sectors. In the first part of the paper, we therefore develop a two-sector New Keynesian model that allows for shocks to import prices, foreign competitors' prices, and workers' disutility of labor. Firms can substitute between domestic labor and intermediate inputs, which are in turn a combination of domestic and foreign inputs that are also substitutable. The substitution margins in our model reduce the effect of an individual cost shock on overall marginal costs, because firms can shift away from any factor experiencing an isolated cost increase (see, e.g., Feenstra et al. 2018). However, when multiple cost shocks hit at the same time, the scope for substitution is diminished, amplifying the cost pass-through into inflation. To capture the effect of foreign competition on firms' price setting, our model considers a finite number of domestic and foreign producers, which compete in a framework as in Atkeson and Burstein (2008). Markups are variable in this framework, and domestic firms have more pricing power at times when foreign competitors also experience cost pressures, because they can raise prices without losing market share. We assume that firms in only the "goods" sector are subject to foreign competition in their domestic output market, whereas firms in the "services" sector compete only domestically. The goods sector also exhibits a lower labor share than services (and hence a higher intermediates share), and it accounts for a smaller share in the final consumption basket. These sectoral differences generate heterogeneous responses of inflation across the two sectors. Finally, our model allows for a shift in the share of consumption expenditures toward goods. This shift can amplify the impact of supply-chain and labor-disutility shocks on inflation because it raises demand for production factors precisely when these are becoming more expensive.

In the second part of the paper, we calibrate the model to US data and use it to study the effects on inflation in 2021 of supply-chain disruptions, labor shortages, and shift of consumption to goods. We focus on 2021 because this is when the inflation surge happened and monetary policy remained highly expansionary. We characterize accommodative monetary policy by using a highly persistent Taylor rule and a negative monetary-policy shock, which keeps the nominal interest rate close to zero in 2021. We capture supply-chain disruptions by two shocks: first, a 20% shock to imported intermediate input prices, calibrated to approximately match the observed increase of these prices in the data. Second, a marginal cost shock to foreign competitors, which we set to match US firms' marginal cost increase. This shock delivers a roughly stable market share of foreign competitors, as US import penetration remained relatively unchanged in the recent period. To proxy labor-supply shocks, we use a labor-disutility shock that reduces potential hours by 0.5 percentage points, which mimics the negative effects of the pandemic on the participation rate and population growth rate estimated by Hobijn and Şahin (2022). Finally, we add a shift from services to goods by 2 percentage points to capture the rise in the goods share of consumption.

Our quantitative analysis shows that these shocks together increase aggregate consumer-price inflation by 4 percentage points, accounting for all of the rise in core inflation in 2021. Although these shocks generate substantial inflation, it is important to note that they could also be driven by demand factors. Recent work has emphasized the additional role of demand-side factors in contributing to the price increases (e.g., Di Giovanni et al. 2022, 2023; De Soyres, Santacreu, and Young 2023). These demand factors were partially driven by a large fiscal expansion in the United States due to stimulus payments.

Our model allows us to investigate the mechanisms by which supply-chain disruptions and labor-disutility shock contribute to the inflation surge. We obtain three key insights. First, the input-price shock prompts firms to substitute from imported inputs toward domestic suppliers. This shift generates demand for domestic labor and puts upward pressure on wages even without any separate shock to the labor market. This *substitution effect* due to supply-chain disruptions generates both wage and price inflation of about 0.5 percentage points. Second, the foreign-competitor shock shifts production from foreign producers to domestic ones, increasing domestic demand for inputs and labor. We refer to this mechanism as the *foreign-competition effect*. Last, the combination of supply-chain shocks and labor-disutility shock creates an amplified effect on inflation: the shocks increase wage inflation by 1 percentage point and price inflation by 0.7 percentage points more than they would have increased if the shocks had hit separately. This *amplification* arises because the joint shock to labor and imported input prices makes substituting between labor and intermediates less effective for domestic firms. Moreover, the simultaneous foreign-competition shock allows domestic producers to increase their pass-through into prices without losing market share.

We show that the simultaneous shift in consumption toward goods further amplified inflation. Although by itself the shift from services to goods would have caused a relatively muted inflationary effect of 0.5 percentage points, combined with the supply-side shocks the shift added in total nearly 1 percentage point to inflation. Intuitively, consumer demand for goods rose at precisely the time when there was already significant price pressure on the goods sector.

Given the persistence of high inflation, which remains well above target as of May 2023, the Fed has been criticized for being behind the curve, especially in the second half of 2021 and early 2022.[4] Our general-equilibrium framework allows us to analyze the effects that a more aggressive monetary policy would have had on the macro economy. In particular, what would have happened if the Fed had started tightening monetary policy earlier? To address this question, we compare our baseline monetary policy with two more aggressive scenarios. We find that although a less persistent Taylor rule calibrated with standard parameter values (e.g., Carvalho, Nechio, and Tristão 2021) would have lowered consumption and output significantly, it has little effect on price inflation in our model. Because supply disruptions still increase domestic labor demand due to the substitution from imported inputs toward labor and due to the substitution from foreign sellers toward domestic ones, price inflation is only partially tamed by more aggressive policy as the labor market remains strong. We show that controlling the surge in inflation earlier would have required an even more aggressive monetary policy, which would have led to a deep recession. These comparisons in our model suggest that even if the Fed had acted earlier, it was unlikely to bring inflation down substantially without scarring the labor-market recovery due to the unique factors that contributed to the surge in inflation. Our policy implications are somewhat similar to Harding, Lindé, and Trabandt (2023), who argue that the policy trade-off to stabilize inflation becomes larger as baseline inflation increases. In our case, the trade-off is larger because supply constraints are important for the ramp-up in inflation.

In the final part of the paper, we provide corroborating evidence for the key mechanisms in the model, using aggregate and industry-level data on prices and wages. First, we estimate pass-through regressions from wages and input prices to producer prices using the local projection method on aggregate data (Jordà 2005). We find a positive and significant interaction effect consistent with the model: when wages and input prices go up simultaneously, producer prices rise more strongly. We then turn to industry-level data. Although the aggregate analysis is informative, it is limited in scope to time-series variation. We therefore estimate reduced-form regressions derived from the model using prices at the six-digit North American Industry Classification System (NAICS) level from the producer-price index (PPI) and industry-level wages from the Quarterly Census of Employment and Wages (QCEW), covering about 500 industries over the period 2013–21. We find a pattern similar to what we see in the aggregate data: a given increase in wages translates into a larger increase in producer prices in industries that experienced a larger increase in input prices, and vice versa. In addition, prices have become more correlated with changes in foreign competitors' prices in 2021, consistent with both domestic and foreign firms experiencing similar shocks.

Related literature. Our paper is closely related to recent work on drivers of inflation dynamics in the post-COVID period and macroeconomic effects of supply-chain disruptions. Di Giovanni et al. (2022) build on the multisector model by Baqaee and Farhi (2022) to show that supply-chain pressures and labor shortages have contributed to higher inflation in both the Euro area and the United States in the recent period. They find that the demand shift from services to goods was amplified by global input-output linkages. Bunn et al. (2022) and Ball, Leigh, and Mishra (2022) find that energy prices and shortages of labor and materials were important drivers of the rise in inflation in both the United Kingdom and the United States, and Cavallo and Kryvtsov (2023) find that unanticipated shocks to stockout levels contributed to higher inflation, particularly for imported goods and import-intensive sectors.

Our findings are also related to recent work reexamining the slope of the Phillips curve. Crump et al. (2022) study the postpandemic Phillips curve and project underlying inflation to remain high due to strong wage growth. Cerrato and Gitti (2022) provide empirical evidence for an increasing slope of the Phillips curve in the recent period. Our findings are consistent with this literature in showing that the inflationary effects of labor-market shocks have been amplified in the recent period.

Several recent papers have studied the postpandemic inflation dynamics through the lens of dynamic stochastic general equilibrium (DSGE) models. Rubbo (2023) uses a multisector DSGE model with primary factors to study the aggregate inflation effect of shocks that are heterogeneous across industries and shows that supply shocks played the largest role in the early stage of the pandemic, whereas demand shocks became more important in 2021. Ferrante, Graves, and Iacoviello (2023) find an important role for the shift of consumption from services to goods in accounting for inflation. Comin, Johnson, and Jones (2023) use a multisector New Keynesian model to show that binding capacity constraints shift Phillips curves up. Our modeling strategy is similar to recent work incorporating a nonlinear Phillips curve into DSGE models. Harding et al. (2023) show in a DSGE model with Kimball demand that all shocks transmit more strongly to inflation when inflation is surging.

In particular, they find that cost-push shocks are amplified in booms and muted in recessions—a result that is supported by our industry-level empirical analysis. Benigno and Eggertsson (2023) propose a model with search and matching frictions and wage rigidity to generate a non-linear Phillips curve. They show that inflation can surge when the labor market is tight, consistent with our work.

Finally, we build on a recent literature that emphasizes the global nature of inflation dynamics. Several studies, such as Forbes (2019), Obstfeld (2019), and Heise, Karahan, and Şahin (2022), argue that foreign competition and firms' ability to outsource have weakened the link between wage pressures and prices in the United States over the past 2 decades. This substitution mechanism has also been highlighted by Elsby, Hobijn, and Şahin (2013) and Feenstra et al. (2018), and it has been used to explain the low inflation in the United States and the decline in the labor share. Relatedly, Heise et al. (2022) show that the lack of goods inflation in the United States in the past 2 decades can be linked to increased foreign competition that constrained firms' ability to pass through domestic wage shocks. We view pandemic-related disruptions as a partial reversal of these disinflationary factors in the economy and argue that large and simultaneous inflationary shocks to both labor and intermediate inputs contributed to the rise in inflation and overheating in the labor market in the recent period.

The rest of the paper is organized as follows. Section II documents some aggregate facts regarding behavior of inflation, import prices, and wages. Section III introduces our New Keynesian DSGE model, which we calibrate and analyze quantitatively in Section IV. Section V uses aggregate data to provide corroborating evidence for the model, and Section VI provides further support with industry-level data. Finally, Section VII concludes.

II.   Why Is This Time Different?

The pickup of inflation after nearly 3 decades of subdued price increases has surprised many. In this section, we document four key differences in the evolution of aggregates in the 2020–22 period compared with earlier expansions. First, goods inflation, which averaged around zero in the past 2 decades, accounted for roughly half of the rise in inflation in 2021. Second, there has been a notable shift toward goods from services in aggregate consumption. Third, workers' willingness to work has declined and reservation wages have increased, contributing to the unprecedented

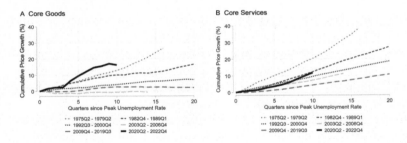

Fig. 2. Evolution of cumulative core goods and services CPI inflation. Bureau of Labor Statistics and authors' calculations. The left panel plots the cumulative core goods consume-price index (CPI) price growth (all items less food and energy, seasonally adjusted) against time, starting at the quarter of peak unemployment of a given expansion. The right panel plots the cumulative core services price growth (all items less energy services, seasonally adjusted) against time. A color version of this figure is available online.

tightness in the labor market. Finally, we show that there has been a sharp rise in both wages and input prices in the current period that far exceeds earlier expansions. These facts motivate our modeling choices later.

Reemergence of goods inflation. The left panel of figure 2 shows the cumulative-price growth of the core consumer-price index for goods (core goods CPI) in the United States, starting from the business cycle trough for each of the past six economic expansions. As the figure shows, the pickup in core goods prices in the current expansion is the strongest across all expansions, including even the 1970s and the 1980s expansions. After only 10 quarters since the unemployment peak, goods prices have risen by 16%. The right panel of figure 2 shows the analogous figure for core services. The pickup in services prices is significant but more modest initially. These inflation dynamics stand in sharp contrast to the typical pattern in the past 20 years, which consisted of procyclical services-price inflation and essentially no pickup in goods prices despite declining unemployment (see Heise et al. 2022). On the contrary, goods inflation picked up briskly in 2021 and far exceeded services inflation. Services inflation accelerated in 2022, as goods prices started to moderate.

Consumption share of goods increased relative to services. A defining feature of the pandemic period was the stark shift in the composition of consumption from services to goods. The lockdowns, which have been followed by an ongoing period of extended remote work, triggered a shift away from services such as restaurants, travel, and entertainment

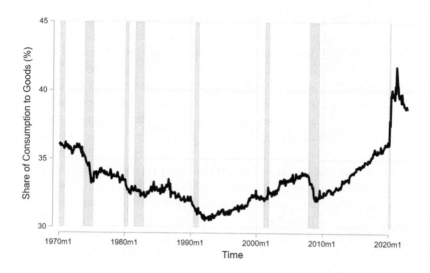

Fig. 3. Consumption share of goods. Bureau of Economic Analysis and authors' calculations. The figure plots the monthly share of real personal consumption expenditures attributed to goods.

to durable goods. Figure 3 shows the share of real PCE that is attributed to goods since 1970. This share was at around 36% before the pandemic and peaked at 42% in 2020. Since then, it has declined but was still 2 percentage points above its prepandemic level in 2021. Given the differences in goods and services production and the differential role of imports in these two categories of consumption, the shift toward goods is an important factor in understanding inflationary developments. Imported goods account for about one-third of manufactured-goods consumption, whereas services are mostly produced domestically.

Labor supply and willingness to work declined. The COVID-19 pandemic was a major disruption for the US labor market, with the unemployment rate rising from 3.5% in February 2020 to a peak of 14.7% in April 2020. Although the elevated unemployment rate was short lived compared with earlier recessions, labor-force participation has not returned to its prepandemic level. In addition to this persistent decline in labor-force participation, which is mostly due to demographic trends, the desired number of work hours also declined, according to Faberman, Mueller, and Şahin (2022). Another measure that captures changes in the work-leisure trade-off is the reservation wage, which is periodically reported by the Survey of Consumer Expectations Labor Market Survey. According to this survey, the *reservation wage*, defined as the average lowest wage a respondent would be willing to accept for a new job, was relatively stable at around $60,000 from March 2016 to March 2020 but has increased by roughly 20% to around $73,000 since then. We view the decline in the participation rate and desired work hours, and the increase in reservation wages, as indicative of a negative labor-supply shock that potentially contributed to the increase in wage growth we turn to next.

Wages and input prices have risen sharply. Two important factors that are often referred to as drivers of high inflation in the post-COVID period are strong wage growth and rising input prices, caused by supply-chain bottlenecks. Table 1 shows the average four-quarter change of different variables during the past four expansions. In row 1, we present wage growth from the employment cost index (ECI), a measure of labor costs that includes benefits and takes into account compositional shifts in industry and occupation. According to the ECI, average four-quarter wage growth in the most recent expansion was 4.5%, exceeding the previous three expansions by about 1–2 percentage points.

Row 2 shows the four-quarter growth in import prices from the Bureau of Labor Statistics (BLS). Import prices grew at a rate of around 6% after the onset of the pandemic in the 2020:Q2–2022:Q4 period. However, import prices combine both intermediate inputs and final goods. The third row therefore focuses on imported intermediate inputs, specifically

Table 1
Wage and Input-Price Growth and Prices

		Average 4-Quarter Change			
		1992:Q2– 2000:Q4 (%)	2003:Q2– 2006:Q4 (%)	2009:Q4– 2019:Q3 (%)	2020:Q2– 2022:Q4 (%)
(1)	Wage growth (ECI)	3.5	3.2	2.3	4.5
(2)	Import prices (excl. petroleum)	−.1	2.5	.2	5.7
(2i)	Industrial supplies excl. petroleum	1.5	9.5	.6	20.0
(4)	Intermediate PPI (excl. food and energy)	1.4	6.1	1.4	16.0
(5)	Core CPI	2.6	2.2	1.9	5.3

Source: Bureau of Labor Statistics and authors' calculations.
Note: The table shows the average four-quarter change in the listed variable for each of the past four economic expansions shown in the header. ECI = employment cost index, PPI = producer-price index, CPI = consumer-price index.

industrial supplies, such as metals, rubber, chemicals, and so on. These inputs are especially important because when the price of inputs increases, these costs are passed through into the prices of the goods that use them. The price of imported industrial supplies grew at a rate of about 20% in the current expansion, far higher than in the previous periods.

A rise in import prices affects domestic producers both by raising their marginal costs (due to higher imported intermediate prices) and due to a competition effect. Because foreign producers are increasing their prices, domestic firms can raise prices without losing market share. Consistent with these two forces, row 4 shows the average-price growth for domestically produced intermediate inputs from the PPI for intermediates, which excludes food and energy inputs. The average input-price growth in the most recent expansion was 16%, significantly higher than in the previous expansions.

Monetary policy. The Fed acted decisively at the onset of the pandemic and took a broad range of actions to minimize disruptions to the economy and support financial markets. It cut its target for the federal funds rate by a total of 1.5 percentage points, bringing it to a range of 0%–0.25%, and engaged in large purchases of US government and mortgage-backed securities.[5] The Fed did not start tightening until March 2022 despite high inflation readings because it attributed inflationary pressures to mostly transitory factors, as summarized in the transcript of Chair Powell's news conference on September 22, 2021:

Inflation is elevated and will likely remain so in coming months before moderating. As the economy continues to reopen and spending rebounds, we are seeing upward pressure on prices, particularly because supply bottlenecks in some sectors have limited how quickly production can respond in the near term. These bottleneck effects have been larger and longer lasting than anticipated, leading to upward revisions to participants' inflation projections for this year. While these supply effects are prominent for now, they will abate, and as they do, inflation is expected to drop back toward our longer-run goal. The median inflation projection from FOMC [Federal Open Market Committee] participants falls from 4.2% this year to 2.2% next year.

The Fed then reversed course in March 2022 as inflationary pressures continued and labor-market conditions have become tighter. It raised its target for the federal funds rate by a total of 5 percentage points, to a range of 5%–5.25%.

Taking stock. The behavior of inflation following the pandemic recession has been an exception to the subdued inflationary environment the

United States experienced since the 1990s. Moreover, the composition of inflation was different, with goods inflation leading the inflationary pressures. The pandemic also triggered a reversal in the declining trend of the goods share in consumption. These inflationary pressures were accompanied by stark increases in input prices, reflecting global disruptions in supply chains, and a rapid tightening of the labor market. Monetary policy remained accommodative amid these developments until the beginning of 2022. We next develop a model to evaluate how these developments have contributed to the drastic surge in inflation.

III.   A New Keynesian DSGE Model with Two Sectors and Import Competition

Our starting point is the standard New Keynesian DSGE model with two sectors: goods and services. The goods sector has a lower labor share than services and is subject to foreign competition, whereas all services are provided by domestic firms. We allow for strategic interactions between firms by assuming that there is only a finite number of firms as in Heise et al. (2022). On the production side, we assume that labor and intermediate inputs are combined via a constant elasticity of substitution (CES) production function. Intermediates are in turn a CES aggregate of domestic and foreign inputs. This structure allows for substitution between the different production factors.

The economy consists of four sets of agents. Households consume final consumption goods provided by a perfectly competitive final output firm. This firm aggregates differentiated products from two sectors: the goods-producing sector, which we also refer to as manufacturing, and services. The final output firm sources differentiated products from monopolistically competitive retailers subject to Rotemberg pricing frictions. Retailers aggregate inputs from a continuum of industries. Finally, the industries are populated by a finite number of producers, which combine labor and an intermediate input to produce a differentiated product. The intermediate input is produced using imported intermediates and domestic intermediates produced in a roundabout production structure. We next describe these building blocks of the model in more detail.

A.   The Household Sector

The household side follows closely Smets and Wouters (2003). There is a continuum of households, indexed by τ. Households supply differentiated labor at nominal wage $W_t^{s,\tau}$ to the goods and services sectors, indexed by $s \in \{M, S\}$. Each household τ maximizes the present discounted value of utility given by

$$E_0 \sum_{t=0}^{\infty} \mathcal{B}_0^t U_t^\tau,$$

where $\mathcal{B}_0^t$ indicates the discount factor, which is defined as $\mathcal{B}_0^t = \prod_{t'=0}^{t-1} \beta_{t'}$, with the convention $\mathcal{B}_0^0 = 1$. The discount factor follows the exogenous process:

$$\ln(\beta_{t+1}) = (1 - \omega_\beta) \ln(\beta) + \omega_\beta \ln(\beta_t) + \varepsilon_{t+1}^\beta,$$

where β is the discount factor in steady state and ε_t^β is a discount-factor shock.

Household τ's period utility is

$$U^\tau \left(C_t^\tau, \ell_t^{M,\tau}, \ell_t^{S,\tau}\right) = \frac{1}{1 - \sigma} \left(C_t^\tau - H_t\right)^{1-\sigma} - \frac{\kappa_t^M}{1 + \varphi} \left(\ell_t^{M,\tau}\right)^{1+\varphi}$$
$$- \frac{\kappa_t^S}{1 + \varphi} \left(\ell_t^{S,\tau}\right)^{1+\varphi}.$$

In this equation, C_t^τ is the household's consumption, $\sigma > 0$ is the coefficient of relative risk aversion, $\varphi > 0$ is the inverse of the Frisch elasticity of labor supply, and $H_t = hC_{t-1}$ is the habit stock of the household. The labor supply is additively separable across the two sectors and given by $\ell_t^{s,\tau}$ for sector s. The parameters κ_t^s govern the disutility of labor and follow an exogenous process:

$$\kappa_{t+1}^s = (1 - \omega_\kappa)\kappa^s + \omega_\kappa \kappa_t^s + \varepsilon_{t+1}^{\kappa,s}, \tag{1}$$

where κ^s is the disutility parameter in steady state and $\varepsilon_t^{\kappa,s}$ is a labor-disutility shock in sector s.

Households maximize their consumption subject to the intertemporal budget constraint

$$C_t^\tau P_{f,t} + b_t B_t^\tau + Q_{t+1} A_{t+1}^\tau \leq W_t^{M,\tau} \ell_t^{M,\tau} + W_t^{S,\tau} \ell_t^{S,\tau} + B_{t-1}^\tau + A_t^\tau + P_{f,t} \Pi_t^\tau,$$

where $P_{f,t}$ is the price index of the final good. Household τ invests B_t^τ into a one-period bond with price b_t at time t. Following Christiano, Eichenbaum, and Evans (2005), households also purchase A_{t+1}^τ of state-contingent securities with price Q_{t+1}. The state-contingent securities insure the households against fluctuations in household-specific labor income, and hence the labor income of household τ will be equal to aggregate labor income. Households own the firms and receive nominal dividends $P_{f,t}\Pi_t^r$.

We next discuss the household decisions in turn. We delegate all derivations of the model solutions to appendix A, http://www.nber.org/data-appendix/c14851/appendix.pdf.

Consumption and savings behavior. The solution to the household consumption-savings problem leads to the standard Euler equation

$$(C_t - hC_{t-1})^{-\sigma} = \beta_t E_t \left[\frac{1 + R_t}{1 + \pi_{t+1}} (C_{t+1} - hC_t)^{-\sigma} \right], \tag{2}$$

where R_t is the nominal interest rate on bonds and $\pi_t \equiv P_{f,t}/P_{f,t-1} - 1$ is the rate of consumer-price inflation.

Labor-supply decisions and wage setting. Households are wage setters in the labor market as in Smets and Wouters (2003). They face a labor-demand curve of

$$l_t^{s,\tau} = \left(\frac{W_t^{s,\tau}}{W_t^s} \right)^{-\eta^s} L_t^s, \tag{3}$$

where labor demand L_t^s and the nominal wage in sector s, W_t^s, are given by

$$L_t^s = \left(\int_0^1 (\ell_t^{s,\tau})^{\frac{\eta^s - 1}{\eta^s}} d\tau \right)^{\frac{\eta^s}{\eta^s - 1}}$$

and

$$W_t^s = \left(\int_0^1 (W_t^{s,\tau})^{1-\eta^s} d\tau \right)^{1-\eta^s}.$$

The parameter η^s governs the wage markup in sector s.

Households set wages subject to Rotemberg pricing frictions with a utility cost of changing price that is governed by a parameter ψ_w. The maximization problem leads to the following markup equation:

$$
\begin{aligned}
(\eta^s - 1)(C_t - hC_{t-1})^{-\sigma} w_t^s = {} & \kappa_t^s \eta^s (L_t^s)^\varphi - \psi_w \pi_t^{s,w} (1 + \pi_t^{s,w}) \\
& + E_t \beta_t \psi_w \pi_{t+1}^{s,w} (1 + \pi_{t+1}^{s,w}),
\end{aligned}
\tag{4}
$$

where $w_t^s \equiv W_t^s/P_{f,t}$ is the real wage and $\pi_t^{s,w} \equiv W_t^s/W_{t-1}^s - 1$ is the rate of wage inflation in sector s.

B. Final Output Firm

The final output good $Y_{f,t}$ consumed by the households is a Cobb-Douglas aggregate of two sectoral goods, manufacturing and services:

$$Y_{f,t} = (Y^M_{f,t})^{\gamma^M_t}(Y^S_{f,t})^{\gamma^S_t}, \tag{5}$$

where γ^M_t and γ^S_t is the share of expenditures in each sector. We assume that the share of expenditures in the goods sector follows

$$\ln(\gamma^M_{t+1}) = (1 - \omega_\gamma)\ln(\gamma^M) + \omega_\gamma \ln(\gamma^M_t) + \varepsilon^{\gamma,M}_{t+1},$$

where γ^M is the steady-state share of expenditures in the goods sector and $\varepsilon^{\gamma,M}_{t+1}$ is an expenditure-share shock. By definition, $\gamma^M_t + \gamma^S_t = 1$, and hence the evolution of γ^M_t also determines the value of γ^S_t. We will later analyze a shock that shifts the composition of expenditures toward goods, motivated by the empirical evidence earlier.

Both manufacturing and services are a CES aggregate of a continuum of products $j \in [0,1]$:

$$Y^s_{f,t} = \left(\int_0^1 y^s_{f,t}(j)^{\frac{\theta-1}{\theta}}dj\right)^{\frac{\theta}{\theta-1}}, \tag{6}$$

where θ is the elasticity of substitution across products j. Cost minimization implies that the final demand for product j is

$$y^s_{f,t}(j) = \gamma^s_t\left(\frac{P^s_{f,t}(j)}{P^s_{f,t}}\right)^{-\theta}\left(\frac{P_{f,t}}{P^s_{f,t}}\right)Y_{f,t}, \tag{7}$$

where $P^s_{f,t} = (\int_0^1 P^s_{f,t}(j)^{1-\theta}dj)^{1/(1-\theta)}$ is the sectoral-price index. The consumer-price index $P_{f,t}$ is a combination of the sectoral-price indices

$$P_{f,t} = \left(\frac{1}{\gamma^M_t}\right)^{\gamma^M_t}\left(\frac{1}{\gamma^S_t}\right)^{\gamma^S_t}(P^M_{f,t})^{\gamma^M_t}(P^S_{f,t})^{\gamma^S_t}. \tag{8}$$

Note that the aggregate price index may fluctuate as the shares γ^M_t and γ^S_t on each sector vary.

C. Retailers

Each product is sold by a retailer j. Retailers aggregate a continuum of industries $i \in [0,1]$ according to

$$y_{f,t}^s(j) = \left(\int_0^1 x_t^s(j,i)^{\frac{v-1}{v}} di\right)^{\frac{v}{v-1}}, \tag{9}$$

where v is the elasticity of substitution between industries and $x_t^s(j,i)$ is the quantity of industry i used by retailer j in sector s. The retailers are monopolistic competitors, taking price indices as given, and face a quadratic price-adjustment cost proportional to sectoral output with price-adjustment parameter ψ_p. We denote the cost of the input of industry i by $P_{x,t}(j,i)$. Given demand (eq. [7]) and solving for a symmetric equilibrium with $j = j'$ and $i = i'$, maximization of real profits results in the first-order condition

$$(\theta - 1) = \theta \frac{p_{x,t}^s}{p_{f,t}^s} - \psi_p(1 + \pi_t^s)\pi_t^s$$

$$+ \beta_t \psi_p E_t \left[\frac{\gamma_{t+1}^s}{\gamma_t^s} \frac{(C_{t+1} - hC_t)^{-\sigma}}{(C_t - hC_{t-1})^{-\sigma}} \frac{Y_{f,t+1}}{Y_{f,t}} (1 + \pi_{t+1}^s)\pi_{t+1}^s\right], \tag{10}$$

where $p_{x,t}^s \equiv P_{x,t}^s/P_{f,t}, p_{f,t}^s \equiv P_{f,t}^s/P_{f,t}$, sectoral inflation is $\pi_t^s = P_{f,t}^s/P_{f,t-1}^s - 1$, and we have omitted the i and j indices due to symmetry.

D.   Intermediate Goods Firms

Each industry i consists of a finite number of intermediate goods firms indexed by k that produce for retailer j in sector s. The finite number of firms allows for strategic interactions, which will generate potentially incomplete pass-through of shocks. We build on the canonical model by Atkeson and Burstein (2008) and its application in Heise et al. (2022). Firms can either be domestic, D, or foreign, F, and the total number of these firms in sector s is N_D^s and N_F^s, respectively. The number of domestic firms relative to foreign firms will govern the importance of foreign competition for the transmission of domestic shocks.

The production of intermediate goods firms is aggregated to the industry level according to

$$x_t^s(j,i) = (N^s)^{\frac{1}{1-\mu}} \left(\sum_{k=1}^{N_D^s} x_t^s(j,i,k)^{\frac{\mu-1}{\mu}} + \sum_{k=1}^{N_F^s} x_t^s(j,i,k)^{\frac{\mu-1}{\mu}}\right)^{\frac{\mu}{\mu-1}}, \tag{11}$$

where μ is the elasticity of substitution between firms and $N^s = N_D^s + N_F^s$. As in Jaimovich and Floetotto (2008), we include the scale term $(N^s)^{1/(1-\mu)}$ to ensure that there is no variety effect, which implies that, in an equilibrium in which all firms are symmetric, $N^s x_t^s(j,i,k) = x_t^s(j,i) = x_t^s(j)$. As in Atkeson and Burstein (2008), we assume that $\mu > \nu > 1$ so that it is easier to substitute across firms within industries than across industries.

Demand

Firms engage in Bertrand competition and set a producer price of $P^s_{x,t}(j, i, k)$. Demand for firm k's output is

$$x^s_t(j, i, k) = \left(\frac{P^s_{x,t}(j, i, k)}{P^s_{x,t}(j, i)}\right)^{-\mu} \frac{x^s_t(j, i)}{N^s}, \tag{12}$$

where $P^s_{x,t}(j, i, k) = P^s_{x,t}(j, i) = P^s_{x,t}(j) \equiv P^s_{x,t}$ in a completely symmetric equilibrium and

$$P^s_{x,t}(j, i) = (N^s)^{\frac{1}{\mu-1}} \left(\sum_{k=1}^{N^s_D} P^s_{x,t}(j, i, k)^{1-\mu} + \sum_{k=1}^{N^s_F} P^s_{x,t}(j, i, k)^{1-\mu}\right)^{\frac{1}{1-\mu}} \tag{13}$$

is the industry-price index. We will analyze the behavior of this producer-price index at the industry level in our empirical analysis later.

Production

We assume that firms combine two factors of production: intermediate inputs and labor. These factors of production are imperfectly substitutable via a CES production structure. Our setup will allow us to analyze the substitution patterns in response to a cost shock to one or both of the factors.

Domestic intermediate firm k supplying retailer j in sector s has a production function

$$x^s_t(j, i, k) = \left[(A_t L^s_t(j, i, k))^{\frac{\varrho_s-1}{\varrho_s}} + \Lambda_s^{\frac{1}{\varrho_s}} D^s_t(j, i, k)^{\frac{\varrho_s-1}{\varrho_s}}\right]^{\frac{\varrho_s}{\varrho_s-1}}, \tag{14}$$

where A_t is aggregate labor productivity, which is common across sectors, and $L^s_t(j, i, k)$ and $D^s_t(j, i, k)$ are labor and intermediate inputs used by the firm. The parameter ϱ_s is the sector-specific elasticity of substitution between the inputs. When one of the factors of production increases in cost, firms substitute toward the other factor, where the strength of the effect is governed by ϱ_s. The parameter Λ_s is a constant that we will use to match the share of intermediates in production in steady state.

The intermediate input $D^s_t(j, i, k)$ is a composite of domestic and foreign inputs, which are combined according to

$$D_t^s(j, i, k) = \left[M_t^s(j, i, k)^{\frac{\xi-1}{\xi}} + Z_t^s(j, i, k)^{\frac{\xi-1}{\xi}} \right]^{\frac{\xi}{\xi-1}}, \tag{15}$$

where $M_t^s(j, i, k)$ is an imported intermediate input and $Z_t^s(j, i, k)$ is an aggregate of domestic intermediate inputs. The equation highlights that firms can adjust to a change in imported input costs by substituting toward the domestic input with an elasticity of substitution that is governed by ξ.

The imported intermediate input $M_t^s(j, i, k)$ is supplied with a sector-specific price $P_{x,\text{imp},t}^s$. We assume that the relative import price $p_{x,\text{imp},t}^s \equiv P_{x,\text{imp},t}^s / P_{f,t}$ follows an exogenous process

$$\ln\left(p_{x,\text{imp},t+1}^s\right) = (1 - \omega_P) \ln\left(p_{x,\text{imp}}^s\right) + \omega_P \ln\left(p_{x,\text{imp},t}^s\right) + \varepsilon_{t+1}^{P,s}, \tag{16}$$

where $p_{x,\text{imp}}^s$ is the relative import price in sector s in steady state and $\varepsilon_t^{P,s}$ is an import-price shock. We will calibrate $p_{x,\text{imp}}^s$ to match the empirically observed imported input share in each sector.

The domestic input $Z_t^s(j, i, k)$ is assembled using all industries' output via a roundabout production technology that combines all industries as in equation (9) and combines sectors in the same way as the consumer good in equations (5) and (6). We assume that the domestic input is produced with the same weights γ_t^M, γ_t^S as the consumer good. This structure leads to a price index for domestic inputs of

$$P_{x,\text{dom},t} = \left(\frac{1}{\gamma_t^M} \right)^{\gamma_t^M} \left(\frac{1}{\gamma_t^S} \right)^{\gamma_t^S} (P_{x,t}^M)^{\gamma_t^M} (P_{x,t}^S)^{\gamma_t^S}, \tag{17}$$

analogous to equation (8) for the CPI, but using the sectoral producer prices $P_{x,t}^s$ defined previously. Because both sectors use the same input basket, the domestic input-price index is the same in both sectors. We assume that only domestic firms demand domestic intermediates, and thus our model does not include exports.

Domestic intermediate input producers optimally choose their input bundle of domestic and foreign intermediates and then optimize over intermediates and labor to minimize costs. Cost minimization implies that marginal costs of domestic firm k are

$$\text{MC}_{D,t}^s = \left[(W_t^s / A_t)^{1-\varrho_s} + \Lambda_s (P_{x,\text{input},t}^s)^{1-\varrho_s} \right]^{1/(1-\varrho_s)}, \tag{18}$$

where $P_{x,\text{input},t}^s$ is the intermediate input-price index. This price index aggregates the prices of domestic and foreign inputs according to

$$P^s_{x,\text{input},t} = \left[(P^s_{x,\text{dom},t})^{1-\xi} + (P^s_{x,\text{imp},t})^{1-\xi}\right]^{1/(1-\xi)}. \tag{19}$$

Real marginal costs are defined as $mc^s_{D,t} \equiv MC^s_{D,t}/P_{f,t}$.

We assume that foreign intermediate firms face an exogenous process for real marginal costs, $mc^s_{F,t} \equiv MC^s_{F,t}/P_{f,t}$, given by

$$\ln(mc^s_{F,t+1}) = (1 - \omega_F)\ln(mc^s_F) + \omega_F \ln(mc^s_{F,t}) + \varepsilon^F_{t+1}, \tag{20}$$

where mc^s_F is the foreign firm's real marginal cost in steady state and ε^F_t is a marginal cost shock. Foreign intermediates are produced abroad and do not use any domestic resources.

Profit maximization implies that producers set producer prices as

$$P_{x,t}(j,i,k) = \frac{\mathcal{E}^s_t(j,i,k)}{\mathcal{E}^s_t(j,i,k) - 1} MC^s_{D,t}, \tag{21}$$

where $\mathcal{E}^s_t(j,i,k) = \mu(1 - S^s_t(j,i,k)) + \nu S^s_t(j,i,k)$ is the effective elasticity of substitution faced by the firm, which depends on the market share

$$S^s_t(j,i,k) = \left(\frac{1}{N^s}\right)\frac{P^s_{x,t}(j,i,k)^{1-\mu}}{P^s_{x,t}(j,i)^{1-\mu}}. \tag{22}$$

Equation (21) highlights that firms set a variable markup $\mathcal{M}_t(j,i,k) \equiv \mathcal{E}^s_t(j,i,k)/(\mathcal{E}^s_t(j,i,k)-1)$ over marginal costs. Because $\mu > \nu$, firms with a higher market share face a lower effective elasticity of substitution and hence set higher markups.

E.   Monetary Authority

We close the model by assuming that a central bank sets monetary policy based on a Taylor rule. This rule is given by

$$R_t = \varrho R_{t-1} + (1 - \varrho)R + (1 - \varrho)\left[\Phi_\pi \pi_t + \Phi_y\left(\ln(Y_{f,t}) - \ln(Y_f)\right)\right] + \varepsilon^M_t, \tag{23}$$

where Φ_π and Φ_y are the central bank's weights on inflation and on final output, respectively, and Y_f is the steady-state value of final output. Monetary-policy shocks are represented by ε^M_t.

F.   Aggregation

We consider an equilibrium in which all domestic and foreign firms are symmetric but allow the two groups to differ in terms of their marginal costs. Thus, a domestic producer will set price $P^s_{D,x,t}$, and a foreign producer sets price $P_{F,x,t}^s$. Gross output by domestic producers in sector s, $Y_{g,t}^s$, is equal in equilibrium to the total demand for domestic output by consumers, from other firms, and for the price-adjustment cost:

$$Y_{g,t}^s = \frac{N_D^s}{N^s} \left(\frac{P_{D,x,t}}{P_{x,t}}\right)^{-\mu} \left[\gamma_t^s \left(\frac{P_{f,t}}{P_{f,t}^s}\right) C_t + \gamma_t^s \frac{\psi_p}{2} (\pi_t^s)^2 C_t \right.$$
$$\left. + \gamma_t^s \left(\frac{P_{x,dom,t}}{P_{x,t}^s}\right) Z_t^s + \gamma_t^s \left(\frac{P_{x,dom,t}}{P_{x,t}^s}\right) Z_t^{s'} \right].$$

The first term, $(N_D^s/N^s)(P_{D,x,t}/P_{x,t})$, represents the share of total demand that is satisfied by domestic producers. This share depends on the number of domestic producers in sector s, N_D^s, and their price relative to the industry price index, which also includes foreign firms. The terms in parentheses represent the output demand from four sources. The first term in parentheses is the demand from consumers, where in equilibrium $Y_{f,t} = C_t$. The second term is the output needed by retailers to cover the price adjustment. The third and fourth terms are the input demands by sector s and s' from sector s, which depend on the price of sector s relative to the domestic input-price index. The total demand for intermediates by sector s is given by

$$Z_t^s = \Lambda_s \left(\frac{P_{x,dom,t}}{P_{x,input,t}^s}\right)^{-\xi} \left(\frac{P_{x,input,t}^s}{MC_{D,t}^s}\right)^{-\varrho_s} Y_{g,t}^s.$$

Total gross output is

$$Y_{g,t} = Y_{g,t}^M + Y_{g,t}^S.$$

Aggregate labor demand in sector s is equal to

$$L_t^s = A_t^{\varrho_s - 1} \left(\frac{W_t^s}{MC_{D,t}^s}\right)^{-\varrho_s} Y_{g,t}^s,$$

which must equal the total supply of labor to that sector given by equation (4).

Going forward, we assume that foreign firms operate only in the goods sector, whereas the services sector contains only domestic firms. This assumption is consistent with the empirical analysis later, where a number of industries, mostly in services, do not record any imports and hence no competition by foreign firms. Figure 4 summarizes the components of the model. The light gray cells on the left show the household side. Households face a trade-off between consumption of final goods

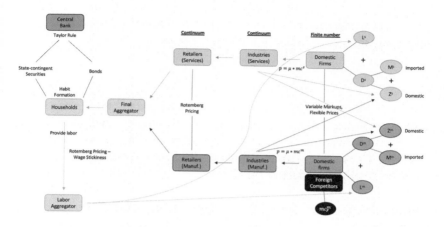

Fig. 4. Model diagram. The figure summarizes key components of the model. Households are represented by light gray cells, the central bank in darkest gray on the left. The medium-gray cells are for services and the medium-dark gray cells are for manufacturing. The black box highlights foreign competitors. A color version of this figure is available online.

and savings, and base their decision on the interest rate set by the monetary authority. The central bank sets monetary policy using a Taylor rule. The medium-gray cells are for services and the medium-dark gray cells are for manufacturing. Both sectors are populated by a continuum of retailers, which aggregate a continuum of industries that are populated by a finite number of producers. The producers assemble labor and intermediate inputs, where the latter are a combination of domestic inputs, produced using a roundabout production structure, and imported inputs in both sectors. Firms in the goods sector face competition from foreign firms, which set prices based on an exogenous marginal cost process. We list all equilibrium conditions of the final model in appendix A.6, http://www.nber.org/data-appendix/c14851/appendix.pdf#page=13.

IV.   Quantitative Analysis

In this section, we calibrate our two-sector model and analyze the effects of supply-chain disruptions and the labor-disutility shock. Our calibrated model implies that the supply-side shocks can account for about 2 percentage points of the rise in inflation in the pandemic period. We analyze the interactions of the shocks and show that they amplify each other. We then compare the inflationary effects of these supply shocks to the effects of a goods-biased demand shock. Finally, we examine the effect of monetary policy in response to the shocks and show that aggressive policy can reduce the risk of a recession in the case of a demand shock but is less advantageous in the case of the supply shocks.

A. Calibration

We calibrate our model using some standard parameters in the DSGE literature and a data set of disaggregated industry-level data, which we assemble at the six-digit NAICS level from publicly available data from the Census Bureau and from the BLS. We describe this data set in more detail in Subsection VI.B.

Standard parameters based on the DSGE literature. We set standard values for a number of parameters and summarize the parameter values in table 2. We choose the risk-aversion parameter, inverse of the Frisch elasticity of labor supply, steady-state discount factor, wage markup, and habit parameter as in Smets and Wouters (2003) and obtain $\sigma = 1.371$, $\varphi = 2.491$, $\beta = 0.99$, $\eta_M = \eta_S = 3$, and $h = 0.595$.

We calibrate the adjustment cost parameter for prices following Keen and Wang (2007). Assuming a steady-state markup of 20%, they find a value of $\psi_p = 72$. At that value, a simple model with Rotemberg adjustment costs corresponds to a Calvo model with a price-adjustment frequency of 12–15 months, consistent with empirical evidence. Given the rapid adjustment of wages in the recent period, we do not assume that wages are more sluggish than prices. Instead, we set $\psi_w = 72$. We specify the Taylor rule based on estimates by Carvalho et al. (2021), who follow a procedure similar to Clarida, Galí, and Gertler (2000). For the Greenspan-Bernanke era, they find a Taylor rule with a weight on inflation of $\Phi_\pi = 1.4$ and a weight on the output gap of $\Phi_y = 0.95$. Although Carvalho et al. (2021) find a persistence parameter of $\varrho = 0.8$, we choose a more persistent policy rule to capture the Fed's initially slow response to the higher inflation. Thus, we set $\varrho = 0.97$ in our baseline.

Labor share in goods and services sectors. Our model implies that the labor share in sector s in steady state is

$$\lambda_s \equiv \frac{(w^s/A)^{1-\varrho_s}}{(w^s/A)^{1-\varrho_s} + \Lambda_s(p^s_{i,\text{input}})^{1-\varrho_s}}, \tag{24}$$

where variables are without a time subscript to indicate a steady state. Given a calibrated λ_s, we can back out the parameter values Λ_s from this equation. We set the labor share in goods and services from the average

Table 2
Calibration Summary

Parameter	Description	Value	Source
σ	Risk aversion	1.371	Smets and Wouters (2003)
φ	Inverse elasticity of labor supply	2.491	Smets and Wouters (2003)
β	Steady-state discount factor	.99	Smets and Wouters (2003)
η_M, η_S	Wage markup	3	Smets and Wouters (2003)
h	Habit parameter	.595	Smets and Wouters (2003)
ψ_p	Adjustment costs prices	72	Keen and Wang (2007)
ψ_w	Adjustment costs wages	72	Assumed same as prices
ϱ	Taylor rule persistence	.97	Assumption based on early response
Φ_π	Taylor rule weight on inflation	1.4	Carvalho et al. (2021)
Φ_y	Taylor rule weight on output	.95	Carvalho et al. (2021)
λ_M, λ_S	Labor share goods (services)	.31 (.6)	Census Bureau, authors' calculations
γ_M, γ_S	Consumption share goods (services)	.35 (.65)	Bureau of Economic Analysis
κ_M, κ_S	Steady-state disutility of labor in goods (services)	122 (1)	Census Bureau, authors' calculations
N_D^M, N_D^S	Domestic firms goods (services)	13 (20)	Atkeson and Burstein (2008)
N_F^M	Foreign firms goods	7	Census Bureau, authors' calculations
α_M, α_S	Imported input share in goods (services)	.17 (.04)	Census Bureau, authors' calculations
θ	Elasticity final goods	6	Christiano et al. (2005)
μ	Elasticity across firms	3	Atkeson and Burstein (2008)
ν	Elasticity across industries	1	Atkeson and Burstein (2008)
ϱ_M, ϱ_S	Elasticity labor vs. intermediates	2 (1.5)	Chan (2021)
ξ	Elasticity domestic vs. foreign	2	Feenstra et al. (2018)

Note: The table summarizes key parameter values taken from the literature and authors' calculations.

share of labor costs relative to total costs in our disaggregated industry-level data. We obtain $\lambda_M = 0.31$ and $\lambda_S = 0.60$, and hence labor is significantly more important in services than in goods.

Consumption share in goods and services sectors. The steady-state consumption share of goods is obtained from the Bureau of Economic

Analysis (BEA) real PCE data. We average the goods share over time from 1970 to 2022 and obtain approximately $\gamma_M = 0.35$ and $\gamma_S = 0.65$.

Disutility of labor. We normalize the steady-state disutility of labor in the services sector to $\kappa_S = 1$. To set the disutility in the goods sector, we obtain the average monthly earnings of workers in goods and in services from the Quarterly Workforce Indicators (QWI) for 2013–21.[6] On average, wages in the goods sector are 17% higher than in services. We then set κ_M to match this wage gap in steady state, yielding $\kappa_M = 122$.

Number of firms—domestic and foreign. We calibrate the number of firms based on Atkeson and Burstein (2008). They set the number of firms to 20. To set the number of foreign competitors in the goods sector, we use the import share in total domestic sales from our disaggregated industry-level data. We find an import share in the goods sector of 0.3. We therefore set $N_D^M = 13$, $N_F^M = 7$, and $N_D^S = 20$.

Relative import price. To calibrate the steady-state relative import price, $p_{x,\text{imp}}^s$, we define the imported input share in sector s, α_s, in steady state as

$$\alpha_s \equiv \frac{\left(p_{x,\text{imp}}^s\right)^{1-\xi}}{\left(p_{x,\text{dom}}\right)^{1-\xi} + \left(p_{x,\text{imp}}^s\right)^{1-\xi}}, \tag{25}$$

where $p_{x,\text{dom}} \equiv P_{x,\text{dom}}/P_f$. We set the imported input share α_s to match the average share of imported input costs in intermediate costs in our disaggregated industry-level data. We obtain an imported input share in goods of $\alpha_M = 0.17$ and in services of $\alpha_S = 0.04$. Given these values, we can then back out $p_{x,\text{imp}}^s$ in steady state.

Key elasticities. Given the rich structure of our model, there are a number of elasticities that we need to calibrate.

First, for the elasticity of substitution across final goods, we follow Christiano et al. (2005) and set $\theta = 6$.

Second, because all domestic and all foreign firms are symmetric, the parameter μ essentially governs the elasticity of substitution between the domestic and foreign firm groups, rather than substitution between individual firms. We therefore set this elasticity toward the lower end of the range of 1–10 discussed by Atkeson and Burstein (2008) and follow estimates on the elasticity of substitution between foreign and domestic varieties from the trade literature. Feenstra et al. (2018) estimate this elasticity to be in the range of 1–4. We therefore set $\mu = 3$. We follow the conventional calibration from Atkeson and Burstein (2008) and Amiti, Itskhoki, and Konings (2019) and set the elasticity of substitution across industries to $\nu = 1$.

The third parameter is the elasticity of substitution between labor and intermediates, ϱ_s. This parameter is important because it governs to what extent firms can substitute between inputs when hit by a shock, and hence the importance of the substitution channel. We set this parameter based on Chan (2021), who estimates using disaggregated Danish data that labor and intermediates are gross substitutes. He estimates the elasticities by regressing the labor-to-intermediate ratio on the ratio of input prices and wages, instrumenting for wages to induce exogenous wage variation. Chan (2021) estimates elasticities of substitution in the range of 1.5–4, and we therefore choose an elasticity in the goods sector of $\varrho_M = 2$. We assume a lower elasticity between labor and intermediates in services and set $\varrho_S = 1.5$. We interpret these elasticities as medium-run elasticities. We analyze the robustness of our results later and study a short-run scenario where intermediates are perfect complements in a Leontief production function. We show that our overall conclusions are very similar to before.

Fourth is the elasticity of substitution between domestic and foreign intermediates, ξ. This parameter governs to what extent firms can switch to domestic intermediates in the event of a shock to foreign inputs. We again build on the estimated value of 1–4 in Feenstra et al. (2018). Because we prefer this elasticity to be at least as high as the elasticity of substitution between labor and intermediates, we set it to $\xi = 2$.

Our calibration implies that the model contains four key differences between the goods and the services sector. First, services account for a larger share of the consumption basket and of firms' inputs, $\gamma_S > \gamma_M$. Second, the labor share is lower in the goods sector, $\lambda_M < \lambda_S$, making intermediates more important. As a result, shocks to input prices will have a larger direct effect on goods. Third, it is easier to substitute between labor and intermediates in the goods sector, $\varrho_M > \varrho_S$. Finally, only the goods sector contains foreign competitors. The presence of foreign competition dampens the response of domestic producers to domestic shocks because these firms partially adjust their markups to preserve market share.

B. Shocks

We consider the effects of five different developments on macroeconomic aggregates and how they interacted with monetary policy. Our baseline experiment focuses on 2021, when the bulk of the inflation surge takes place. Although we refer to these developments as shocks, admittedly they are not identified as exogenous shocks. That is why we do not interpret our simulations as decomposition of inflation driven by exogenous factors. We rather use our model to evaluate the joint effects of these changes on the economy and their interaction with monetary policy. This choice allows us to evaluate the effect of alternative monetary-policy choices.

Import-price shock. We consider the effect of a positive imported input-price shock in both the goods and the services sectors on inflation by setting $\varepsilon_{t+1}^{P,s} = 0.18$ for both $s \in \{M, S\}$. This shock generates an increase in imported input prices of about 20% on impact, matching the rise of imported input prices during the current expansion from table 1. We set $\omega_P = 0.9$ to capture the persistence of the shock.

Labor-disutility shock. We interpret the disutility shock as representing workers' increased reservation wage and the tighter labor market conditions in the recent period. We calibrate this shock to match the part of the drop in participation that is due to the pandemic, which Hobijn and Şahin (2022) estimate to be in the range of 0.5 percentage points, taking into account the acceleration of a downward trend in participation and a slowdown in population growth. Because health concerns related to the pandemic have been more prominent in the services sector due to the social proximity of jobs in that sector, we feed in a disutility shock that increases labor disutility κ_t^s in goods and services by 6% and 10%, respectively. Given the different steady-state levels, these values translate into shocks of $\varepsilon_{t+1}^{\kappa,S} = 0.10$ in services and of $\varepsilon_{t+1}^{\kappa,M} = 8$ in goods. On their own, these shocks lead to a drop in labor demand of 0.6% in services and of 0.4% in goods at the peak, consistent with the empirical evidence. We set $\omega_\kappa = 0.9$.

Foreign-competition shock. The supply-chain disruptions also affected US firms' foreign competitors and increased their marginal costs of production. We feed into the model a shock that increases competitors' real marginal costs by 8.1% relative to the steady-state level, $\varepsilon_{t+1}^{F} = 0.081$. This shock generates an increase in real marginal costs similar to what domestic firms in the goods sector experience due to the combined domestic shocks, as we will show later. As a result, foreign competitors' market share remains roughly constant. This outcome is consistent with the fact that the US imports as a share of gross domestic product were virtually unchanged in 2021 relative to 2019. We set $\omega_F = 0.9$, in line with the persistence of the other shocks.

Rise in consumption share of goods. We consider a shift in composition of demand from services to goods by 2 percentage points. Specifically, we feed into the model an expenditure-share shock of $\varepsilon_{t+1}^{\gamma,M} = 0.06$. This shock increases the share of expenditures on goods from its steady-state level of 35% by approximately 6%–37.1%. As before, we set $\omega_\gamma = 0.9$, in line with the other shocks.

Monetary-policy shock. Our final shock is to monetary policy. As discussed, our calibration uses a standard Taylor rule, but with a persistence of the policy rule of 0.97, significantly higher than in the literature. To capture the accommodative stance of monetary policy in 2021, we add a monetary-policy shock of $\varepsilon_t^M = -0.003$ in period zero, which is calibrated so that the interest rate change in that period is zero. This response resembles the developments in 2021: CPI inflation averaged 4.7% in that year, and the effective federal funds rate remained close to zero until February 2022.

We hit the model with deterministic shocks of the magnitude described at time zero but assume that all shocks are drawn from mean-zero stochastic processes that the agents continue to face. Consequently, agents face uncertainty about the state of the economy, consistent with the highly uncertain environment of 2021. To reflect the unusual size of the shocks in 2021, we assume that the standard deviation of the stochastic processes is significantly smaller than the size of the shocks the agents faced in 2021. Specifically, we set the standard deviation of shocks to be 0.21 times the deterministic shock for all variables. We calibrate this factor using the standard deviation of the four-quarter growth in imported input prices excluding petroleum, which was 4.2% over the period 1982–2019 but rose to 20% in the recent expansion, as shown in table 1. We solve the model in Dynare using a combination of deterministic shocks and stochastic processes and use a second-order approximation to capture nonlinear effects.

C.   *Supply-Chain and Labor-Supply Disruptions, Shift to Goods,*
     and Monetary Policy

We first consider the joint effect of all developments on important macroeconomic aggregates as our baseline case. Our goal is to mimic the changes in 2021, especially the surge in inflation. Prices as measured by the core CPI increased by 5.5% in December 2021 relative to a year earlier, a big increase compared with the 12-month core CPI growth of 1.6% in December 2020. In our simulations, we seek to match this 3.9 percentage point rise in core prices. Although overall CPI inflation increased from 1.3% in December 2020 to 7.2% in December 2021, we do not aim to explain this almost 6 percentage point rise because we exclude petroleum from our import-price shock.[7]

In figure 5, we trace out the effects of these shocks over the next 20 quarters. We calibrate the deterministic shocks at time zero as described, to reflect all the developments we discussed for 2021. Thus, we feed into the model a labor-disutility shock, an imported input-price shock, and a competitor cost shock that matches the rise in domestic costs. Moreover, we include a shock that raises the share of consumption in goods by 2 percentage points and the monetary-policy shock discussed earlier.

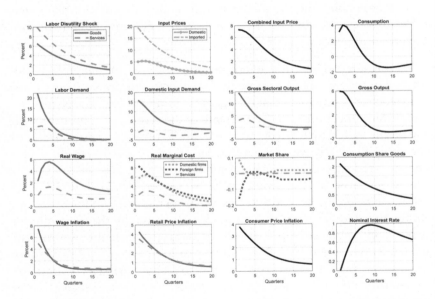

Fig. 5. Baseline: All shocks. The figure shows the effect of a joint disutility, imported input price, foreign-competitor cost shock, and shock to the share of goods consumption under the accommodative monetary policy with monetary-policy shock discussed in the main text. Each panel shows the percentage deviation of a variable from its steady-state value against the number of quarters passed since the initial shock. For wage and price inflation, the interest rate, the market share, and the consumption share of goods, we show percentage point changes from steady state. Consumer-price inflation is computed as the consumption share weighted average inflation rate across the two sectors. A color version of this figure is available online.

The first and second panels in the top row of figure 5 show the exogenous labor-disutility and imported input-price shocks. The disutility shock raises labor disutility κ_t^s in the goods and services sector by 6% and 10%, respectively. The imported input shock raises imported input prices in both sectors by about 20% on impact. Domestic input-prices rise as well due to a rise in equilibrium wages. The second row highlights that the shock leads to a substitution away from intermediates toward labor. This effect is much stronger in the goods sector, as consumer demand shifts to that sector. In services, labor demand rises only slightly as the substitution toward labor from intermediates is partially counteracted by the fall in consumer demand for services. The strong increase in labor demand we find is consistent with (though quantitatively larger than) the increase in payroll employment between December 2020 and December 2021, which was 5.1%. The second panel in the second row illustrates that firms also substitute away from imported intermediates toward domestic intermediates in the goods sector, as this sector is particularly exposed to foreign intermediates. Gross output rises in goods, as more intermediates are now produced domestically, and to a smaller extent in services. Consumption rises on impact but less than output because some of the additional output produced goes toward the replacement of inputs previously obtained from abroad. The big jump in output and consumption is also consistent with the data, where these variables rose by 5.7% and 7.2% in 2021, respectively.[8]

The third row of figure 5 illustrates that the substitution toward domestic labor increases real wages and therefore marginal costs. The real wage increase is significantly stronger for goods due to the significantly greater labor demand in that sector. Foreign firms' marginal costs increase exogenously and decline slowly back to steady state. Based on our calibration, their increase in marginal costs is somewhat in line with the real marginal cost of domestic firms in the goods sector, and thus foreign firms' market share changes little. The final row shows that wage inflation approaches 8% in the goods sector and 5% in services. Monetary policy is highly accommodative, keeping nominal interest rates at zero initially and raising them only slowly, which contributes to the consumption boom. Overall consumer-price inflation rises by 4% on impact, in line with the rise in core CPI inflation in 2021.[9] Moreover, retail-price inflation rises initially more in the goods sector than in services, as documented earlier.

The growth rate of wages we find is somewhat higher than in the data, in particular in goods: average hourly earnings of production and nonsupervisory employees in goods-producing industries increased by 5.4% in 2021 in the data and in private service-providing industries by 5.1%. However, nominal wages rose relative to core CPI inflation both in the data in 2021 and in our model. Although wage growth was below overall CPI inflation, we focus on nonenergy price increases in our simulations, and therefore we do not generate this decline in real wages. If we take into account the overall CPI inflation, real wage growth is negative in our simulation as well. Moreover, a recent study by Howard, Rich, and Tracy (2022) shows that workers have experienced real wage gains over the 2 years of the pandemic when composition effects are properly taken into account. Another recent study by Duran-Franch and Konczal (2021) has shown that the behavior of real wages has varied considerably by occupation. They find that relative to the same period in 2020, in September and October 2021 average real hourly wages were higher in most percentiles at the bottom of the wage distribution. The average wage growth for the bottom half of the occupational hourly wage distribution was 1.4% over 2021.[10] To capture these heterogeneous wage effects, we consider an extension of our model in appendix B.1, https://data.nber.org/data-appendix/c14851/appendix.pdf#page=16, with two types of worker skill levels. In this extension, real wages go up for low-skilled services workers, whereas they decline for high-skilled services workers due to differences in substitutability with intermediates.

D. Supply-Chain and Labor-Supply Disruptions

We now focus on the effects of the supply-side factors on their own and shut down the consumption shift toward goods. This exercise allows us to analyze how the supply-chain and labor-supply disruptions interact and contribute to inflation. The supply-side shocks consist of an interaction of three simultaneous developments: a rise in imported input prices, an increase in the disutility of work, and a rise in marginal cost of foreign competitors.[11] We keep the same accommodative monetary policy as in our baseline.

In figure 6, we trace out the effects of the three supply-side shocks. The first row illustrates that the labor-disutility shock and the imported input-price shock are the same as before, whereas in the third row we see that the shift in the consumption share is now omitted. Because we keep the foreign competitors' marginal cost shock as in the baseline, foreign competitors now experience a relatively larger cost increase than domestic firms and consequently lose market share. The three shocks together

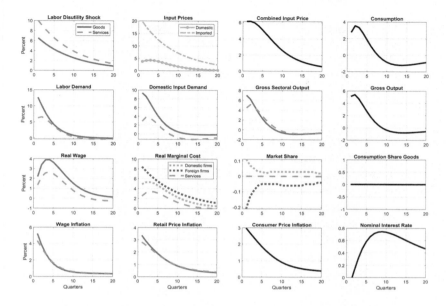

Fig. 6. Supply-chain and labor-supply disruptions. The figure shows the effect of a joint disutility, imported input price, and foreign-competitor cost shock under the accommodative monetary policy with monetary-policy shock discussed in the main text. Each panel shows the percentage deviation of a variable from its steady-state value against the number of quarters passed since the initial shock. For wage and price inflation, the interest rate, the market share, and the consumption share of goods, we show percentage point changes from steady state. Consumer-price inflation is computed as the consumption share weighted average inflation rate across the two sectors. A color version of this figure is available online.

generate a 3 percentage point rise in consumer-price inflation and a 5 percentage point increase in average wage inflation, accounting for a notable part of the pickup in wages and prices in 2021. These effects are combined effects of supply-side developments and a lax monetary policy that did not respond to inflation until March 2022.

To shed light on the role of the individual shocks and how they interact, we next analyze the effects of the imported input price shock and the shock to foreign competitors' marginal costs, respectively, in isolation, and then discuss the interaction of the shocks. We obtain three important insights. First, we demonstrate that an import-price shock on its own can lead to substantial wage and price inflation due to the substitution from imported inputs toward labor (*substitution effect*). Second, we show that a shock to foreign competitors' costs increases the demand for domestic inputs and allows domestic firms to increase their prices without losing market share (*foreign-competition effect*). Third, we show that a joint shock to import prices, marginal costs of foreign competitors, and labor disutility has an amplified effect on inflation by diminishing firms' ability to reduce costs by substituting across inputs or toward foreign competitors (*amplification*).

Substitution Effect

Figure 7 traces out the effect of the imported input-price shock in isolation. We adjust the monetary-policy shock so that the nominal interest rate is approximately zero on impact as before, setting $\varepsilon_t^M = -0.0004$. The first row shows again the imported input-price shock when there is no longer a labor-disutility shock. The second row shows that the import-price shock leads to a substitution away from intermediates toward labor, particularly in the goods sector due to its higher exposure to imported intermediates. Gross output falls due to a large decline in

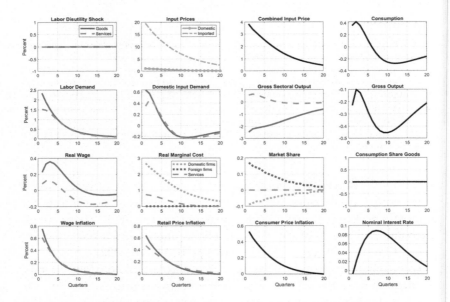

Fig. 7. Effect of imported input-price shock only. The figure shows the effect of an input-price shock under the accommodative monetary policy with monetary-policy shock discussed in the main text. Each panel shows the percentage deviation of a variable from its steady-state value against the number of quarters passed since the initial shock. For wage and price inflation, the interest rate, the market share, and the consumption share of goods, we show percentage point changes from steady state. Consumer-price inflation is computed as the consumption share weighted average inflation rate across the two sectors. A color version of this figure is available online.

goods output, which has become more expensive to produce. The third row illustrates that some of this production shifts to foreign firms, which have gained market share because in this experiment they are assumed not to be affected by supply-chain disruptions, and hence their real marginal cost stays flat. The substitution effect toward domestic labor increases real wages and therefore marginal costs in the goods sector. Real wages in the services sector fall slightly after several quarters, but real marginal costs in that sector still rise due to the higher cost of intermediate inputs. The real wage increase is larger in the goods sector than in the services sector due to the stronger substitution in goods. The final row highlights that there is significant wage inflation in both sectors of approximately 0.5% due to the substitution toward labor. The change in real marginal costs translates into consumer-price inflation of about 0.5%. Nominal interest rates are nearly unchanged due to the accommodative policy. As a result, real interest rates actually decline on impact, leading to a very short-lived consumption boom. This boom is supported by the additional sales of foreign firms.

This experiment highlights that an import-price shock on its own can generate substantial wage and price inflation due to the substitution effect. If supply-chain bottlenecks prompt firms to source more from domestic suppliers, the resulting additional labor demand can put upward pressure on wages. This substitution channel generates a 0.5 percentage point rise in wages—which is around 15% of the rise in the wages in our baseline experiment with three shocks.

Foreign-Competition Effect

Figure 8 shows the effect of the increase in foreign competitors' marginal costs by 8.1% in isolation. As for the imported input-price shock, we adjust the monetary-policy shock so that the nominal interest rate is zero on impact, by setting $\varepsilon_t^M = -0.0007$. The first row shows that there are no direct domestic shocks to the US producers. However, domestic input prices go up as production shifts from foreign producers toward domestic ones. The second row illustrates the source of this cost increase. When the marginal costs of foreign producers rise, domestic labor demand goes up, especially in the goods sector due to a shift from imports to domestic production. Foreign producers lose market share. As a result of the increase in labor demand, nominal wages rise. The shock generates price inflation of about 1 percentage point as the domestic firms' marginal costs rise and they pass these cost increases on to domestic consumers. We refer to this

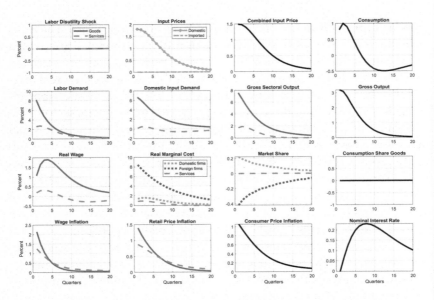

Fig. 8. Effect of foreign-competition shock only. The figure shows the effect of a shock to foreign competitors' real marginal cost under the accommodative monetary policy with monetary-policy shock discussed in the main text. Each panel shows the percentage deviation of a variable from its steady-state value against the number of quarters passed since the initial shock. For wage and price inflation, the interest rate, the market share, and the consumption share of goods, we show percentage point changes from steady state. Consumer-price inflation is computed as the consumption share weighted average inflation rate across the two sectors. A color version of this figure is available online.

effect as the *foreign-competition effect* because it highlights how shocks to relative marginal costs of domestic and foreign firms create inflation. The developments in the 2 decades before the pandemic were the opposite of this shock: low marginal costs of US firms' foreign competitors, in particular from China, held back price increases by domestic producers. Heise et al. (2022) find that increased import competition during this period reduced the pass-through of domestic wage increases to prices in the goods sector, as US firms were unable to raise prices without losing market share.

Amplification

The combination of imported input-price shock, foreign-competition-price shock, and labor-disutility shock creates an amplified effect on inflation. First, the combination of a labor-disutility and import-price shock makes substituting between labor and intermediates less effective for domestic firms. Feenstra et al. (2018) describe that US firms substitute away from labor and toward imported inputs to reduce costs. When the shocks hit jointly, substitution is impaired, which leads to higher inflation compared with when the shocks hit separately. Second, when the labor-disutility shock coincides with a price increase by foreign competitors, firms' ability to switch toward foreign products to mitigate the cost shock is weakened. This keeps demand for domestic output high and raises domestic wage pressures. Moreover, the concurrent price increase by foreign competitors allows domestic firms to pass through more of the wage and input-price shock into prices without loss of market share.

Figure 9 illustrates the amplification. The left panel shows the impulse response of the average wage inflation to a specific shock, where wage inflation is constructed by averaging across the two sectors' wage growth using each sector's share in consumption. The right panel shows the impulse response of price inflation. The three lines at the bottom trace out the impulse responses to the import price shock, labor-disutility shock, and competition shock separately. In each of these experiments, we adjust the monetary-policy shock in the first period so that the nominal interest rate in the first period does not change. We present the sum of these three separate impulse responses by the dashed line. The solid black line shows the effect of the joint shock, which corresponds to the experiment analyzed in figure 6 earlier. This line is clearly above the dashed line: when all three shocks hit together, wage inflation is about 1 percentage point higher and

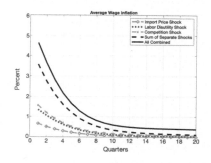 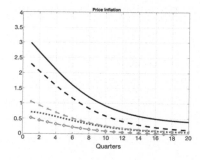

Fig. 9. Effect of joint shocks: Amplification. The figure shows the amplification effect of a joint shock compared with the three supply shocks separately. The left panel shows impulse responses of average wage inflation, constructed by averaging across the two sectors' wage growth using each sector's share in consumption. The right panel shows impulse responses of average consumer price inflation, constructed analogously. The dot-dashed, cross-dashed, and dotted lines trace out the impulse responses to a separate import-price shock, labor-disutility shock, and competition shock. The black dashed line sums over these impulse responses. The black solid line shows the joint effect of all three shocks simultaneously. A color version of this figure is available online.

price inflation is about 0.7 percentage points higher at the peak than when all shocks hit separately.[12]

Elasticity of Substitution

The degree of amplification in the model depends on the elasticity of substitution between labor and intermediates, ϱ_s, and on the elasticity of substitution between the domestic and foreign firm groups, μ. When the elasticity of substitution between inputs is higher, producers can substitute more between labor and intermediates when the shocks hit separately than when they hit jointly. Similarly, when the elasticity of substitution between the firm groups is higher, retailers can substitute more between foreign and domestic products. Figure 10 analyzes the difference between the impulse responses of inflation for the joint shock relative to the impulse response of the summed separate shocks on impact (the difference between the dashed and the black solid line from fig. 9 in quarter 1). Figure 10A shows the amplification on impact for different values of ϱ_s, here assumed to be the same in both sectors. Raising the elasticity of substitution between labor and intermediates from 1.5 to 5 increases amplification significantly from about 0.7 to 1.1 percentage points for price inflation and from 1.1 to 1.7 percentage points for wage inflation. Figure 10B shows the amplification as a function of μ. Reducing this elasticity from its baseline value of 3–1.5 would lower wage and price amplification to 0.6 and 0.4 percentage points, respectively.

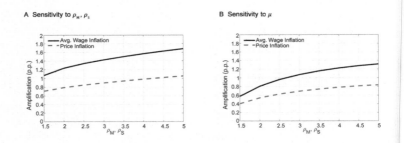

Fig. 10. Amplification on impact: Sensitivity to ϱ_s and μ. The figure plots the difference between the impulse responses of consumer price inflation and average wage inflation for the joint shock relative to the impulse response of the summed separate shocks on impact (the difference between the dashed line and the solid line from fig. 9 in quarter 1). Panel A shows this amplification as a function of the value of ϱ_M and ϱ_s. Panel B shows the amplification as a function of μ. A color version of this figure is available online.

For completeness, we show the impulse responses of an isolated labor-disutility shock in appendix B.2 (https://data.nber.org/data-appendix /c14851/appendix.pdf#page=20). We also analyze the sensitivity of amplification to changes in the elasticity of substitution between domestic and imported intermediates, ξ, and find that this variable also increases amplification.

E. Shift of Consumption from Services to Goods

A important development during the pandemic period was the stark shift in the composition of consumption from services to goods, which we take into account in our baseline simulation. We now analyze the role of this shift in driving up inflation and its interaction with the supply-side shocks.

Figure 11 considers the effect of a shift from services to goods in isolation. We do not add a separate monetary-policy shock in this experiment

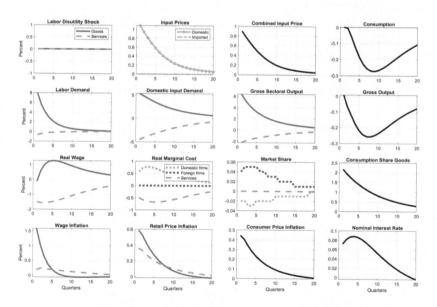

Fig. 11. Shift in consumption share of goods from services only. The figure shows the effect of a shock that shifts consumption from services to goods. Each panel shows the percentage deviation of a variable from its steady-state value against the number of quarters passed since the initial shock. For wage and price inflation, the interest rate, the market share, and the consumption share of goods, we show percentage point changes from steady state. Consumer price inflation is computed as the consumption share weighted average inflation rate across the two sectors. A color version of this figure is available online.

because the nominal interest rate on impact barely changes. As a result of the consumption shift, labor demand surges in goods at the expense of services. The percentage increase in goods is larger than the percentage decline in services because the steady-state level of labor is smaller in goods than in services. Domestic input demand also increases in goods, leading to a rise in sectoral output. However, overall gross domestic output shrinks slightly due to the shift toward goods, because some of the additional demand for goods is provided by foreign firms, which gain market share. The shift leads to an increase in the real wage in the goods sector and a decline in the real wage in services. Overall, the greater relative increase in labor demand in goods compared with the relative decline in services leads to about 0.4% consumer price inflation on impact. However, this effect cannot simply be added to the inflationary effect of the supply-side shocks. Because there are multiple shocks in the economy, they interact, and their joint effect can be amplified.

To quantify this interaction effect, figure 12 shows the average wage inflation and the average price inflation in response to the joint supply-side shocks, the consumption shift, and the sum of the two, similar to our analysis of the interaction of the individual supply-side shocks in Subsection IV.D. The dot-dashed and dotted lines trace out the separate impulse responses to the consumption shift to goods and to the supply-chain and labor-supply shocks (the import price shock, labor-disutility shock,

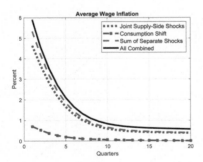 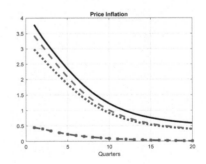

Fig. 12. Amplification of supply shocks due to consumption shift. The figure shows the amplification effect of a joint supply and consumption-shift shock compared with the two shocks separately. The left panel shows impulse responses of average wage inflation, constructed by averaging across the two sectors' wage growth using each sector's share in consumption. The right panel shows impulse responses of average consumer price inflation, constructed analogously. The dot-dashed and dotted lines trace out the impulse responses to a separate combined supply-side shock and to a consumption-shift shock. The dashed line sums over these impulse responses. The black solid line shows the joint effect of all shocks simultaneously. A color version of this figure is available online.

and competition shock), respectively. As before, we combine the supply-side shocks with a negative monetary-policy shock of $\varepsilon_t^M = -0.003$ and do not include a separate monetary-policy shock for the consumption shift, so that in both experiments nominal interest rates are approximately unchanged in the first period. The dashed line presents the sum of the two sets of shocks. If the only shock in the economy were a shift from services to goods, price inflation would have increased by 0.5 percentage points. If only supply-chain disruptions and the labor-disutility shock hit the economy, inflation would have increased by 3 percentage points. However, because this shift coincided with supply-chain disruptions and a decline in willingness to work, their impact on inflation has been higher. The solid black line shows the effect of the joint shocks. This line is above the dashed line: when all shocks hit together, wage inflation is about 0.6 percentage points higher and price inflation is about 0.4 percentage points higher than when the shocks hit separately. Intuitively, the increase in demand in the goods sector coincides with supply-chain disruptions and labor shortages in that sector, which make it harder to satisfy the demand. As a result, the consumption shift amplifies the impact of the supply-side shocks on inflation.

F. Complementarity between Labor and Intermediates

Our baseline calibration assumes that labor and intermediates are substitutes, allowing firms to respond to the shocks by shifting their production structure. In reality, adjusting production between labor and intermediates may take time. Hence, it is plausible that production looks more like a Leontief production function between labor and intermediates in the short run. To evaluate the effect of substitution between labor and intermediates, we replace the production function with a Leontief production function between labor and intermediates motivated by Boehm, Flaaen, and Pandalai-Nayar (2019). We replace equation (14) with

$$x_t^s(j, i, k) = \min\{A_t L_t^s(j, i, k), \Lambda_s D_t^s(j, i, k)\} \tag{26}$$

and recalibrate Λ_s to again match the labor share in steady state. We continue to assume that foreign and domestic intermediates are substitutes, motivated by Feenstra et al. (2018), who show an elasticity of substitution above one between foreign and domestic intermediates. These intermediates are plausibly more easily adjustable in the short term.[13]

Figure 13 shows our baseline case with the same shocks and the same monetary-policy rule as before under a Leontief production function

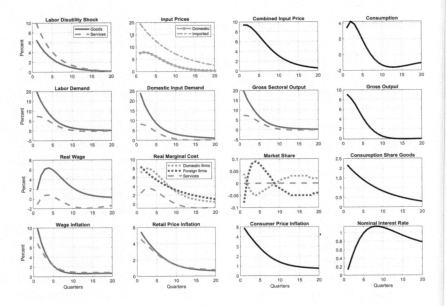

Fig. 13. Baseline with perfect labor-intermediate complementarity. The figure shows the effect of a joint disutility, imported input price, foreign-competitor cost shock, and shock to the share of goods consumption. Each panel shows the percentage deviation of a variable from its steady-state value against the number of quarters passed since the initial shock. For wage and price inflation, the market share, and the consumption share of goods, we show percentage point changes from steady state. A color version of this figure is available online.

between labor and intermediates. Compared with figure 5, labor demand in goods now increases slightly less strongly than before, by only about 20% on impact compared with 22% in the baseline, as firms cannot substitute from intermediates toward labor. The flip side is a stronger increase in domestic input demand under the Leontief production function. Domestic input demand rises because firms substitute away from imported intermediates toward domestic intermediates, which are still assumed to be substitutes. Because labor is a perfect complement of intermediates, the increase in intermediate demand is matched by an increase in labor demand. Thus, irrespective of whether labor and intermediates are complements or substitutes, labor demand in goods rises strongly. With a Leontief production function, real wages rise slightly more strongly in goods than the baseline case, leading to wage inflation of 10% on impact compared with 8% in the baseline. Real wages in services instead fall slightly, as substitution toward labor now does not

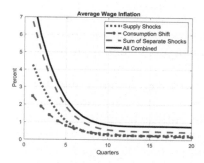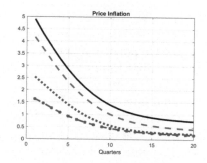

Fig. 14. Amplification of supply shocks due to consumption shift with perfect labor-intermediate complementarity. The figure shows the amplification effect of a joint supply and consumption-shift shock compared with the two shocks separately. The left panel shows impulse responses of average wage inflation, constructed by averaging across the two sectors' wage growth using each sector's share in consumption. The right panel shows impulse responses of consumer price inflation. The dot-dashed and dotted lines trace out the impulse responses to a separate combined supply-side shock and to a consumption-shift shock, respectively. The dashed line sums over these responses. The black solid line shows the joint effect of all shocks simultaneously. A color version of this figure is available online.

prop up demand in that sector. Overall, these shifts lead to consumer price inflation of 4.8% in the Leontief case.

We repeat the analysis of the interaction between the supply-side shocks and the demand shift under the Leontief production function (i.e., when labor and intermediates are not substitutable). Figure 14 shows that in this case amplification is even higher, raising inflation by about 0.8 percentage points. Intuitively, in this case firms cannot adjust their relative mix of labor and intermediates in response to the shocks, and hence the combination of demand shift and supply-side shocks has a bigger effect on prices.

G.   Role of Monetary Policy

Given the persistence of high inflation, which remains well above target as of May 2023, the Fed has been criticized for being behind the curve, especially in the second half of 2021 and early 2022.[14] Our general-equilibrium framework allows us to analyze the effects of a more aggressive monetary policy on the macro economy. In particular, what would have happened if the Fed had started tightening monetary policy earlier? To address this question, we compare our economy with all shocks under the baseline monetary policy with two more aggressive scenarios. First, we consider a standard Taylor rule calibrated as in, for example, Carvalho et al.

(2021), with a persistence of $\varrho = 0.8$ and without the accommodative monetary-policy shock in period zero. Second, we consider an even more aggressive policy that increases the weight on inflation from $\Phi_\pi = 1.4\text{–}4$ and has even less persistence, with $\varrho = 0.2$.

Figure 15 shows the behavior of main aggregates under different nominal interest rates. Interestingly, although the baseline Taylor rule lowers consumption and output significantly, it has little effect on price inflation. The reason for this result is that the joint shock still leads to a strong increase in labor demand of about 10%. The lack of an employment decline is due to firms' substitution from intermediate goods to labor, which supports aggregate employment. Consequently, price inflation is only partially tamed by the standard Taylor rule, as the labor market remains strong. The large rise in labor demand and inflation are consistent with an overheating labor market.

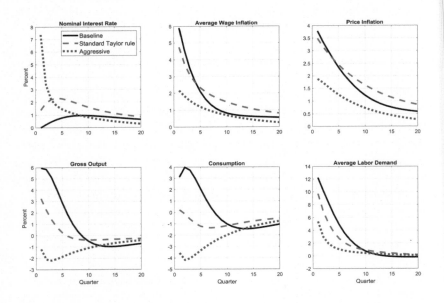

Fig. 15. Monetary policy. The figure shows the effect of three monetary-policy rules on outcomes. The solid black lines show our baseline policy with high persistence, $\varrho = 0.97$, and an accommodative monetary-policy shock in period zero of $\varepsilon_t^M = -0.003$. The dashed lines show a standard Taylor rule with persistence $\varrho = 0.8$ and no accommodative shock. The dotted lines show an aggressive policy with a higher weight on inflation, $\Phi_\pi = 4$, and lower persistence, $\varrho = 0.2$. Labor demand and wage inflation are averaged across the two sectors with each period's consumption weights on each sector. A color version of this figure is available online.

Controlling the surge in inflation earlier would have required an even more aggressive monetary policy. As figure 15 shows, this strong policy comes at the expense of a sharp contraction in consumption and output. Moreover, the increase in labor demand would have been substantially lower. These comparisons suggest that even if the Fed had acted earlier, it was unlikely to bring inflation down substantially without scarring the labor market recovery due to the unique factors that contributed to the surge in inflation.[15]

V. Empirical Evidence: Aggregate Analysis

Our quantitative model suggests that supply-chain disruptions and labor-supply constraints contributed significantly to the rise in inflation in the postpandemic period. Moreover, the effects of these supply-side shocks were amplified because they hit the economy at the same time. This section examines whether aggregate data corroborate these findings with respect to the supply-side shocks.

A curious feature of inflation has been the disappearance of goods inflation in the late 1990s and its reemergence during the pandemic. As Heise et al. (2022) showed, the disinflationary effect of goods inflation can be traced back to lack of pass-through from wages to prices. According to their analysis, there has been a notable decline in the pass-through from wages to producer prices; specifically, firms did not pass through wage increases to prices due to rising import competition. Our analysis implies that this trend should have reversed after the pandemic due to the rise in import prices and the decline in foreign competition.

We investigate this implication of the model by estimating pass-through regressions using aggregate data and the local projection method following Jordà (2005). In particular, we estimate the impulse response of price inflation to changes in wage and input-price inflation for each quarter $h = 0, \ldots, 20$ by running a series of regressions of the form

$$\pi_{t+h}^{\text{price}} = \alpha + \beta_h \pi_t^{\text{wage}} + \gamma_h \pi_t^{\text{input}} + \sum_{j=1}^{8} \delta_j \pi_{t-j}^{\text{price}} + \sum_{j=1}^{8} \zeta_j \pi_{t-j}^{\text{wage}} + \sum_{j=1}^{8} \xi_j \pi_{t-j}^{\text{input}} + \varepsilon_t, \ (27)$$

where π_{t+h}^{price} is the inflation rate of prices in quarter $t + h$, π_t^{wage} is wage inflation in quarter t, and π_t^{input} is input-price inflation in quarter t. We also include eight lags of the price inflation rate π_{t-j}^{price}, wage inflation rate π_{t-j}^{wage}, and input-price inflation π_{t-j}^{input}.

We measure price inflation using the core PPI capturing the inflation of finished goods less food and energy.[16] We measure wage inflation as average hourly earnings of production and supervisory workers. We measure intermediate input-price inflation using the core intermediate PPI, capturing intermediates less food and energy inputs. All inflation measures have been annualized to facilitate the interpretation of the results. Our sample starts in 1988.

Figures 16*A* and 16*B* present the impulse response of core finished PPI to an innovation in wages and core intermediate PPI, respectively. We find a strong positive pass-through from both wages and intermediate input prices to producer prices. Pass-through rises for about nine quarters and peaks around 2 for wages. Pass-through rises faster for intermediate prices, and peaks after five quarters at around 0.5.

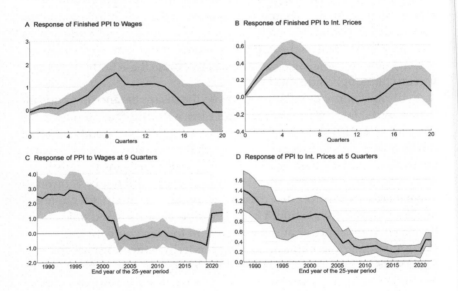

Fig. 16. Response of producer price inflation to wages and intermediate input prices. Bureau of Labor Statistics and authors' calculations. The top two panels present the estimated coefficients β_h and γ_h and their 90% confidence intervals from specification (27) run at quarterly frequency, for horizons $h = 0, \dots, 20$ quarters. In the top left panel, we present the coefficients β_h showing pass-through from wage inflation and producer price inflation. Wages are average hourly earnings of production and nonsupervisory employees. Producer prices are the PPI of finished goods less food and energy. All variables are transformed into a quarterly series by taking a simple average across the months in each quarter. In the top right panel, we show the coefficients γ_h of the pass-through from intermediate prices into producer prices. Intermediate prices are the PPI of intermediate goods less food and energy inputs. The bottom two panels estimate specification (27) over 25-year rolling windows for $h = 9$ for wages and $h = 5$ for intermediate prices, where the ending year of the 25-year period is indicated on the x-axis. A color version of this figure is available online.

To examine whether pass-through has increased after the pandemic, we estimate equation (27) over 25-year rolling windows and plot the estimate at the peak lag length ($h = 9$ for wages and $h = 5$ for intermediate prices) over time. As shown in Heise et al. (2022), wage-to-price pass-through has significantly declined over time until the beginning of the pandemic. However, it has picked up again following the onset of the pandemic and became significantly positive (see fig. 16C). We find a qualitatively similar, though less strong, pattern for intermediates (fig. 16D). Pass-through declined until the 2010s and slightly increased in the recent period.

The recent emergence of pass-through could be an outcome of the simultaneous increase in wages and input prices as suggested by our model. We investigate this possible interaction by adding an interaction term between wage inflation and input-price inflation to equation (27), both contemporaneously and with eight lags as for the other variables. Figure 17 shows the estimated impulse response to the contemporaneous interaction term. We find a positive and significant interaction effect on producer price inflation. When wages and input prices go up simultaneously, producer prices rise more strongly, consistent with our model's implications. We analyze this interaction in more detail using disaggregated industry-level data in the next section.

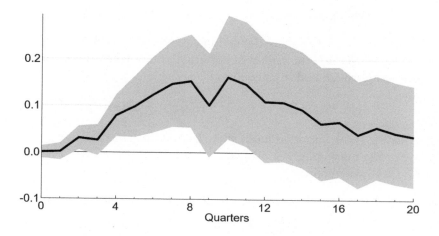

Fig. 17. Interaction effect of wage inflation and input price inflation. The figure shows the estimated coefficient on the interaction term $\pi_t^{\text{wage}} \pi_t^{\text{input}}$ and its 90% confidence interval from an augmented version of specification (27) that includes interactions run at quarterly frequency, for horizons $h = 0, \ldots, 20$ quarters. A color version of this figure is available online.

VI. Empirical Evidence: Industry-Level Analysis

Although the aggregate analysis is informative, it is limited in scope to time-series variation. In the remainder of this section, we exploit rich industry-level panel data on wages, import prices, and producer prices to run within-industry panel regressions. These regressions have the advantage that they can control for any aggregate trends, such as changes in inflation expectations. We derive an estimating equation from the model and use industry-level data to provide empirical evidence for the key implications of the model.

A. Linking the Theory to Data

The firms' price-setting equation (21) implies that domestic producers set prices equal to marginal cost times a variable markup $\mathcal{M}_t(j, i, k) \equiv \mathcal{E}_t(j, i, k)/(\mathcal{E}_t(j, i, k) - 1)$. Taking logs and differentiating this equation for a domestic firm, we obtain

$$d\ln(P_{x,t}(j, i, k)) = d\ln(MC^s_{D,t}) + d\ln(\mathcal{M}_t(j, i, k)), \qquad (28)$$

which is a log-linear approximation of a price change. Using the expression for marginal costs, equation (18), a log-linear approximation yields

$$d\ln(MC^s_{D,t}) = \lambda_s[d\ln W^s_t - d\ln A_t] + (1 - \lambda_s)d\ln P^s_{x,\text{input},t},$$

where λ_s is the labor share defined in equation (24), and the input price $P^s_{x,\text{input},t}$ is itself a combination of imported and domestic input prices. It can be approximated from equation (19) as

$$d\ln\left(P^s_{x,\text{input},t}\right) = (1 - \alpha_s)d\ln(P_{x,\text{dom},t}) + \alpha_s d\ln\left(P^s_{x,\text{imp},t}\right), \qquad (29)$$

where α_s is the imported input share from equation (25).

For the markup, given our functional form of the demand elasticity $\mathcal{E}^s_t(j, i, k)$, we obtain

$$d\ln(\mathcal{M}_t(j, i, k)) = -\Gamma_t(j, i, k)[d\ln P_{x,t}(j, i, k) - d\ln P_{x,t}(j, i)],$$

where $\Gamma_t(j, i, k) = -(\partial\log\mathcal{M}_t(i, j, k)/\partial\log P_{x,t}(j, i, k)) \geq 0$ is the elasticity of the markup with respect to a firm's own price.[17] Plugging the expression for marginal costs and the markup into equation (28) and rearranging, we obtain a firm's price change as a function of changes in the components of marginal costs and of changes in competitors' prices

$$d \ln(P_{x,t}(j,i,k)) = \frac{\lambda_s}{1 + \Gamma_t(j,i,k)} [d \ln W_t^s - d \ln A_t] + \frac{(1 - \lambda_s)}{1 + \Gamma_t(j,i,k)} d \ln P_{x,\text{input},t}^s$$

$$+ \frac{\Gamma_t(j,i,k)}{1 + \Gamma_t(j,i,k)} d \ln P_{x,t}(j,i). \tag{30}$$

Equation (30) illustrates how producers' prices are related to wages and input prices. The first and second terms in the equation reflect the direct effect of input costs on prices (i.e., the effect of marginal costs). An increase in wages W_t^s that exceeds productivity growth passes through into prices with an elasticity that is proportional to the labor share in marginal costs, λ_s. Wage increases only raise prices to the extent that they exceed productivity growth. Changes in input costs pass through to prices with an elasticity that is proportional to $(1 - \lambda_s)$, where the pass-through of imported input prices in turn depends on the imported input share α_s. The third term in equation (30) captures the indirect effect on pass-through that operates via firms' markup adjustment. An increase in a firm's competitors' prices $P_{x,t}(j,i)$ allows the firm to raise its prices itself by increasing its markup. The relative strength of this channel relative to the marginal cost channel is modulated by the markup elasticity $\Gamma_t(j,i,k)$. Firms with a higher markup elasticity put a higher weight on the aggregate price index. As shown in appendix A.7, https://data.nber.org/data-appendix/c14851/appendix .pdf#page=16, the markup elasticity is increasing in a firm's market share holding everything else fixed, $d\Gamma_t(j,i,k)/dS_t(j,i,k) > 0$, and satisfies $\Gamma_t(j,i,k) = 0$, if $S_t(j,i,k) = 0$.

Equation (30) is a version of a standard pass-through equation (see, e.g., Amiti et al. 2019). One shortcoming of this specification is that due to the log-linearization, it does not account for the nonlinearity of the response arising from the substitution between labor and intermediates. In particular, in our model the labor share adjusts in response to a shock: when import prices rise, firms substitute toward labor, raising the labor share. We therefore also perform a second-order approximation to the marginal cost term to derive the alternative nonlinear estimating equation

$$d \ln(P_{x,t}(j,i,k)) = \frac{\lambda_s}{1 + \Gamma_t(j,i,k)} [d \ln W_t^s - d \ln A_t] + \frac{(1 - \lambda_s)}{1 + \Gamma_t(j,i,k)} d \ln P_{x,\text{input},t}^s$$

$$+ \frac{(\varrho_s - 1)\lambda_{s,t}(1 - \lambda_s)}{1 + \Gamma_t(j,i,k)} \{(d \ln W_t^s - d \ln A_t) d \ln P_{x,\text{input},t}^s \tag{31}$$

$$- \frac{(d \ln W_t^s - d \ln A_t)^2}{2} - \frac{(d \ln P_{x,\text{input},t}^s)^2}{2}\} + \frac{\Gamma_t(j,i,k)}{1 + \Gamma_t(j,i,k)} d \ln P_{x,t}(j,i).$$

This equation contains in the second row the interaction between the wage change and the input-price change and in the third row quadratic terms of the wage change and the input-price change. The negative sign of the quadratic terms highlights that, absent the interaction effect, the response of producer prices to a shock is smaller than that implied by the linear effect, due to the possibility to substitute. The importance of the substitution rises with the elasticity of substitution ϱ_s and with the product of the steady-state shares of the two inputs, $\lambda_s(1 - \lambda_s)$. We will estimate both the standard linear equation and this specification with nonlinear terms.

B. Data

Estimating equations (30) and (31) requires industry-level data on input prices, wages, and productivity and detailed controls for worker characteristics. We use various publicly available data sources to construct our data set.

Prices. We construct the industry-level producer prices P_{it} from the PPI, which we have at the six-digit NAICS level. The PPI measures the price received by domestic producers for their goods and services, consisting of both final goods and intermediate goods. It is constructed by the BLS from a monthly survey of establishments representing nearly the entire goods sector and 70% of services. We aggregate the monthly PPI data to the quarterly level. We drop the bottom 5% of industries in terms of 2012 shipment value from all regressions to eliminate very small and noisy industries.[18] Our sample consists of 497 industries for the period 2013:Q1–2021:Q3.[19]

Wages. We obtain quarterly industry wages, W_{it}, as the average weekly earnings per quarter from the QCEW from the BLS. In principle, hourly earnings would be preferable, to account for changes in hours worked. In practice, however, using the QCEW has several advantages over other data sets, such as greater coverage of establishments and industries (see Heise et al. 2022).

Input prices. We construct an industry's input-cost index, $P_{it,\text{input}}$, as a weighted average of the domestic input-price index and the imported input-price index, consistent with equation (29). Specifically, the four-quarter change in industry input prices is

$$\Delta \ln\left(P_{it,\text{input}}\right) = \alpha_{i,2012}\sum_{n}w_{n,i,2012}\Delta \ln\left(P_{nt,\text{imp}}\right) + (1 - \alpha_{i,2012})\sum_{n}w_{n,i,2012}\Delta \ln(P_{nt}), \quad (32)$$

where $\alpha_{i,2012}$ is the industry's share of intermediate imported inputs in total material costs in 2012. The four-quarter change in the domestic input price ΔP_{nt} is constructed as the change in the log PPI across all industries n that provide inputs to industry i, where the weights $w_{n,i,2012}$ are the time-invariant cost shares from the 2012 input-output table from the BEA.[20] We omit the domestic input industry n that is the same as industry i because we cannot disentangle the own industry's input prices from its output prices using our industry-level data.[21] We construct the imported input-price index of industry i analogously as a weighted average over the import-price indices $P_{nt,\text{imp}}$ of all industries n that provide inputs to industry i. Because the import-price indices provided by the BLS are too aggregated for our purposes, we construct our own measures using disaggregated import data from the Census Bureau. Our six-digit NAICS industry-level import-price index is a weighted average of the log change in import unit values (equal to import values divided by quantities) across all 10-digit Harmonized Tariff Schedule (HTS10) country observations, h, c, within each NAICS industry i, where the weights are lagged annual import value weights

$$\Delta \ln \left(P_{it,\text{imp}} \right) = \sum_{h,c} w_{h,c,\text{year}-1} \Delta \ln \left(\text{import unit values}_{h,c,t} \right). \qquad (33)$$

We construct a mapping between HTS10 codes and six-digit NAICS industries throughout our sample period using the concordance by Pierce and Schott (2012).

Productivity. We construct industry-level labor productivity, A_{it}, using industries' real value added from the BEA. Although the BLS provides disaggregated industry-level productivity measures, these are only available on an annual basis and with significant delay. We obtain quarterly real value added for 50 two-digit and three-digit industries from the BEA and divide by each industry's number of workers from the QCEW to obtain real value added per worker. For each six-digit NAICS industry in our sample, we assign the real value added per worker of the corresponding two-digit or three-digit industry.

C. Price Dynamics in the Industry Data

It is useful to examine the changes in input prices and wages at the industry level to see whether the facts we have reported in table 1 also apply to industry-level data. Table 3 provides summary statistics on the average

Table 3
Changes in Input Prices and Wages in Goods and Services

	Goods		Services	
	$\Delta\ln(P_{it,\text{input}})$	$\Delta\ln(\text{Wage}_{it})$	$\Delta\ln(P_{it,\text{input}})$	$\Delta\ln(\text{Wage}_{it})$
2013:Q1–2019:Q4:				
Mean	.001	.022	−.005	.028
P50	.005	.024	.005	.029
Mean of fourth quartile	.062	.078	.077	.072
Correlation		.045		.077
Correlation (ind. FE)		.046		.076
2020:				
Mean	−.023	.035	−.064	.051
P50	−.014	.028	−.024	.044
Mean of fourth quartile	.028	.116	.004	.128
Correlation		.296		.205
Correlation (ind. FE)		.312		.205
2021:				
Mean	.148	.049	.170	.061
P50	.124	.051	.124	.056
Mean of fourth quartile	.296	.130	.390	.149
Correlation		.226		.165
Correlation (ind. FE)		.229		.192

Note: The table shows summary statistics on the average four-quarter change in wages and input prices for goods (first two columns) and services (last two columns). Each panel focuses on changes in a specific time period. The first row shows the mean of the four-quarter change. The second row presents the median and the third row the average over industries in the fourth quartile. The fourth row shows the correlation between wage and industry price changes. The fifth row presents the correlation between wage and input price changes after they have been residualized by industry fixed effects.

four-quarter change in wages and input prices in our sample of industries. The first two columns present statistics for industries in the goods sector.[22] The last two columns present statistics for the services sector, consisting of all industries that are nontraded, mostly services.[23]

The first panel presents statistics for the pre-COVID period. We find that the average industry's change in input prices is virtually zero in this period, with average nominal wage growth between 2% and 3%. The raw correlation between wage growth and input-price changes is also negligible prior to COVID-19 (row 4). In the fifth row, we residualize the four-quarter wage and input-price changes with industry fixed effects and find similar results.[24]

The second panel shows the same statistics for 2020. Input prices declined in that year, and wages grew slightly faster growth than in the earlier period. What stands out most, however, is the significantly higher correlation between wage and input-price changes in 2020 compared with the pre-COVID period. The last panel shows the statistics for 2021, when both wages and input prices had risen significantly. Moreover, these changes were highly correlated across industries. This observation reinforces the interaction effect we have seen in the aggregate analysis. It also suggests that there is scope for amplification: our model predicts that simultaneous wage and input-price increases would lead to bigger increases in prices.

We exploit a reduced-form version of equation (30) to examine the relationship between labor costs, input prices, and producer prices and whether the predictions of our model have empirical support in the cross-industry data. Specifically, we estimate

$$\Delta\ln(P_{it}) = \beta_1\Delta\ln W_{it} + \beta_2\Delta\ln A_{it} + \beta_3\Delta\ln P_{it,\text{input}} + \beta_4\Delta\ln P_{it,\text{imp}}$$
$$+ \alpha X_{it} + \delta_i + \psi_t + \varepsilon_{it}, \tag{34}$$

where P_{it} denotes the PPI and Δ indicates four-quarter changes. W_{it} and $P_{it,\text{input}}$ are wages and the input-price index, respectively, and capture components of marginal costs. The term $\Delta\ln(P_{it,\text{imp}})$ picks up the effect of competition on US firms' price setting.[25] The controls X_{it} include the shares of prime-age and 55+ workers, the share of women, and the shares of workers with a high school degree, associate's degree, and bachelor's degree or higher.[26] Finally, δ_i is an industry fixed effect and ψ_t is a time fixed effect that captures any aggregate variation that affects all industries, such as changes in aggregate inflation expectations or general business-cycle trends. We estimate our regression specification (34) separately for goods and for services. Our regressions use Driscoll-Kraay standard errors with bandwidth two quarters to account for cross-sectional and time-series correlation. We also estimate the regression interacted with a dummy for 2021 to examine whether the predictions of our model are consistent with the data.

Note that in this regression, β_1 to β_4 cannot be interpreted as structural coefficients because we do not generate plausibly exogenous variation in input costs and wages. Instead, we interpret our estimation results as conditional correlations that are informative about the model's predictions. We also note that we cannot compare the coefficients with the model's implications because the model includes general-equilibrium effects and the regression exploits within-time, within-industry variation. Nevertheless, we find our results useful to detect changes in wage and price dynamics after the pandemic.

Price Dynamics in the Goods Sector

We first estimate our baseline regression for the goods sector (i.e., traded industries) and report the results in table 4. Column 1 presents the coefficients from specification (34) for the entire sample period 2013:Q1–2021:Q3. Because different industries have different degrees of import penetration, we multiply the foreign competitors' price index, $P_{it,imp}$, by the industry's import share, s_i, in 2013. Focusing first on the coefficient on the import-price index in the first row, we find that for an industry with the average import share of 31%, a 10% increase in import prices leads to an increase in producer prices of 0.7%. The following coefficients show a positive and significant correlation between producer prices and input costs. A 10% increase in input prices is associated with a 3.5% rise in producer prices. We also find a positive pass-through from wages to producer prices, although the effect is small. A 10% increase in wages is associated with a 0.4% rise in producer prices. This small pass-through from wages to prices in the goods sector is consistent with earlier work (Heise et al. 2022). Finally, productivity improvements have a negative impact on producer prices, as expected.

Our model implies that correlated shocks should have bigger effects on price inflation. Because wage and input prices increased drastically in 2021, it is informative to consider 2021 separately. In particular, the foreign-competition effect implies that US producer prices should have become more strongly correlated with foreign competitors' prices in the recent period because all firms are experiencing similar shocks due to global supply-chain disruptions. Therefore, US firms can raise their prices by more without losing market share. Similarly, the amplification result in the model implies that the effects of wages and input prices on producer prices should have increased in 2021. Because the cost of both input factors rose at the same time in that year, the inflation impact should be larger. Column 2 reestimates the regression by interacting the variables with a dummy for the year 2021.

First, we find that US and foreign firms' price changes have become more synchronized. The correlation between foreign competitors' prices and US producer prices was around 5% in an industry with the average import share in the pre-2021 period, but it rose to around 21% in 2021. Second, simultaneous wage and input-price changes have a higher correlation with producer price inflation. In particular, a 10% rise in input prices was associated with a 2.8% rise in producer prices in the pre-2021 period but led to a 4.4% increase in 2021. Even more strikingly, we find that the entire positive correlation between wage changes and producer prices is accounted for by 2021. Although in earlier years the pass-through from wages to producer prices was insignificant, it rose to 13.8% in 2021.

In column 3, we run the specification with additional nonlinear marginal cost terms using equation (31). This specification includes an interaction term between wage changes and input-price changes, an interaction between productivity and input-price changes, and squared wage and input-price terms. We interact all terms with dummies for 2021 to examine changes in the coefficients.[27] We find a positive and highly significant effect of the product of wage and input-price changes on producer prices in 2021. Moreover, once this term is included in the regression, the 2021 interaction terms on wages and input prices become insignificant. This result suggests that the interaction between wages and input prices can completely explain the pickup in the pass-through of costs in 2021.

The nonlinear regression results indicate a positive and significant interaction effect in 2021 but not in earlier years. As shown in table 3, changes in wages and input prices were small until 2021, and the changes were virtually uncorrelated until 2020. This could explain the lack of an effect in prior years if smaller changes have a lower pass-through. As a robustness check, we next exploit the high correlation between wage and input-price shocks in 2020 and construct dummies for whether an industry was above the median of the wage-change distribution and above the median of the input-price-change distribution in our sample period. For industries that exhibited large changes in wages and input prices, we should pick up an interaction effect. Column 4 reruns our nonlinear specification with additional interactions for 2020, where the interaction between wages, input-price changes, and the 2020 dummy is also interacted with a dummy for whether an industry was in the top half of both the wage-change and the input-price-change distributions. We call this dummy "HH." The positive and significant coefficient on the quadruple interaction with the "HH" dummy indicates that there was a positive and significant interaction between wage changes and input-price changes for this group of industries. This finding is consistent with our hypothesis that both large and positively correlated shocks are needed.

As we have stated earlier, we do not interpret our estimates of β_1 to β_4 as structural pass-through coefficients. In appendix C, https://data.nber .org/data-appendix/c14851/appendix.pdf#page=23, we consider pass-through regressions using an instrumental variable local projection (IV-LP)

Table 4
Pass-Through for Goods, 2013:Q1–2021:Q3

	$\Delta\ln(p_{it})$	$\Delta\ln(p_{it})$	$\Delta\ln(p_{it})$	$\Delta\ln(p_{it})$
	(1)	(2)	(3)	(4)
$s_i \times \Delta\ln(p_{it,\text{imp}})$	.238***	.189***	.190***	.172***
	(.045)	(.026)	(.026)	(.026)
$s_i \times \Delta\ln(p_{it,\text{imp}}) \times \text{Year} = 20$				.097**
				(.044)
$s_i \times \Delta\ln(p_{it,\text{imp}}) \times \text{Year} = 21$		.488***	.502***	.518***
		(.137)	(.136)	(.136)
$\Delta\ln(p_{it,\text{input}})$	.353***	.280***	.316***	.334***
	(.030)	(.026)	(.027)	(.032)
$\Delta\ln(p_{it,\text{input}}) \times \text{Year} = 20$				−.101**
				(.038)
$\Delta\ln(p_{it,\text{input}}) \times \text{Year} = 21$		.156***	−.115	−.119
		(.029)	(.094)	(.099)
$\Delta\ln(\text{Wage}_{it})$	.036**	.017	.011	.003
	(.015)	(.013)	(.011)	(.012)
$\Delta\ln(\text{Wage}_{it}) \times \text{Year} = 20$				.033
				(.028)
$\Delta\ln(\text{Wage}_{it}) \times \text{Year} = 21$		.121***	−.038	−.031
		(.020)	(.044)	(.044)
$\Delta\ln(\text{Wage}_{it}) \times \Delta\ln(p_{it,\text{input}})$			−.464*	−.511
			(.241)	(.316)
$\Delta\ln(\text{Wage}_{it}) \times \Delta\ln(p_{it,\text{input}}) \times$ Year = 20				−.294
				(.497)
$\Delta\ln(\text{Wage}_{it}) \times \Delta\ln(p_{it,\text{input}}) \times$ Year = 21			1.887***	1.939***
			(.297)	(.338)
$\Delta\ln(\text{Wage}_{it}) \times \Delta\ln(p_{it,\text{input}}) \times$ HH × Year = 20				1.216*
				(.714)
$\Delta\ln(A_{it})$	−.160***	−.157***	−.145***	−.145***
	(.024)	(.023)	(.022)	(.029)
Time fixed effects	Yes	Yes	Yes	Yes
Industry fixed effects	Yes	Yes	Yes	Yes
Worker composition	Yes	Yes	Yes	Yes
Nonlinear effects	No	No	Yes	Yes
R^2	.153	.169	.173	.175
Observations	9,549	9,549	9,549	9,549

Note: The table shows the results from running the baseline regression (34) for goods. The first column shows the results for the baseline regression. The second column includes interactions for 2021. The third column includes an interaction between wage changes and intermediate input-price changes. The fourth column includes additional interactions for 2020. All regressions include time and industry fixed effects and controls for the log share of workers 25–54, log share of workers 55+, log share of women, and log shares of workers with a high school degree, associate's degree, and bachelor's degree or higher. The last two columns also include nonlinear terms from equation (31), that is, an interaction term between approach following Ramey (2016) and find strong pass-through from wages and import prices to producer prices. Although this approach measures the pass-through in a way that properly accounts for dynamics and endogeneity, it is not easily applicable to the specification we consider in equation (30). Instead, to alleviate concerns that our results only hold at one specific time horizon, we reestimate our regressions where, instead of four-quarter changes, we use eight-quarter changes or 12-quarter changes for all variables. The results in appendix D show that our findings are robust over longer time periods.[28]

Price Dynamics in the Services Sector

The evolution of goods and services inflation has been different since the onset of the pandemic, as we discussed earlier. Services industries are not directly affected by foreign competitors' prices. However, these industries can still be indirectly affected by imported input prices. We next turn to services and show analogous results in table 5. Column 1 shows that there is a significant and positive correlation of both input prices and wages with producer prices. A 10% increase in input prices is associated with a 1% rise in producer prices, on average. Similarly, a 10% rise in wages is associated with a 1.1% increase in producer prices. Column 2 shows that, in contrast to the goods sector, there was no increase in input-price pass-through in 2021 for the services sector. However, the correlation between wages and prices rose significantly. A 10% rise in wages is associated with price growth of 0.7% in the earlier years, but with a 2.4% rise in prices in 2021. This rise in correlation between wages and producer prices is consistent with our model, because the substitution toward labor and domestically produced intermediates, especially in the goods sector, drives up wages at the same time prices rise. The last column shows that the coefficient on the interaction between wages and input prices is actually negative in services in 2021. This absence of an amplification effect in services is consistent again with the model because the substitutability

wage changes and input-price changes, an interaction between productivity and input-price changes, and squared wage and input-price terms. We interact all terms with dummies for 2021. The last column also contains interactions of competitors' prices, input prices, wages, and productivity with a dummy for 2020, as well as interactions between wages, input-price changes, a dummy for 2020, and dummies for whether both wage and input-price changes were above median (HH), the wage change was below median and the input-price change above median (LH), and the wage change was above median and the input-price change below median (HL). We only report in the table the main coefficients of interest.
Significance: * = 10%, ** = 5%, *** = 1%.

Table 5
Pass-Through for Services, 2013:Q1–2021:Q3

	$\Delta\ln(p_{it})$	$\Delta\ln(p_{it})$	$\Delta\ln(p_{it})$
	(1)	(2)	(3)
$\Delta\ln(p_{it,input})$	.097***	.097***	.079***
	(.011)	(.016)	(.027)
$\Delta\ln(p_{it,input}) \times$ Year $= 21$		.001	.129**
		(.027)	(.061)
$\Delta\ln(Wage_{it})$	.112***	.073**	.072**
	(.035)	(.033)	(.030)
$\Delta\ln(Wage_{it}) \times$ Year $= 21$		.165***	.352***
		(.047)	(.102)
$\Delta\ln(Wage_{it}) \times \Delta\ln(p_{it,input})$			.086
			(.183)
$\Delta\ln(Wage_{it}) \times \Delta\ln(p_{it,input}) \times$ Year $= 21$			−1.092***
			(.294)
$\Delta\ln(A_{it})$	−.030	−.029	−.012
	(.020)	(.019)	(.012)
Time fixed effects	Yes	Yes	Yes
Industry fixed effects	Yes	Yes	Yes
Worker composition	Yes	Yes	Yes
Nonlinear effects	No	No	Yes
R^2	.047	.050	.059
Observations	5,012	5,012	5,012

Note: The table shows the results from running the baseline regression (34) for services. The first column shows the results for the baseline regression. The second column includes interactions for 2021. The third column includes an interaction between wage changes and intermediate input-price changes. All regressions include time and industry fixed effects and controls for the log share of workers 25–54, log share of workers 55+, log share of women, and log shares of workers with a high school degree, associate's degree, and bachelor's degree or higher. The last column also includes nonlinear terms from (31); that is, an interaction term between wage changes and input-price changes, an interaction between productivity and input-price changes, and squared wage and input-price terms. We interact all terms with dummies for 2021. We only report in the table the main coefficients of interest. Significance: * = 10%, ** = 5%, *** = 1%.

between labor and intermediates in services is low, and hence there is no change in substitution patterns when both labor and intermediates' costs rise.

VII. Conclusion

In this paper, we have developed and calibrated a DSGE model to quantify the effects of supply-chain and labor-market disruptions, shift from services to goods in consumption, and accommodative monetary policy on inflation. Our analysis delivers three key insights: First, supply-chain disruptions on their own can generate significant wage and price inflation due to the substitution from imported intermediates to domestic labor (substitution effect). Second, the marginal cost shock to foreign competitors shifts production from foreign producers to domestic ones, increasing demand for domestic inputs and labor, which raises price and wage inflation (foreign-competition effect). Third, a joint supply-chain and labor-disutility shock has an amplified effect on inflation because the joint shock to labor and imported input prices makes substituting between labor and intermediates less effective for domestic firms. Moreover, the simultaneous foreign-competition shock allows domestic producers to increase their pass-through into prices without losing market share. Because firms cannot shift toward foreign producers to mitigate the increase in costs, demand for domestic inputs and labor remains high, which may lead to an overheating of the labor market. In addition, we show that, although by itself the shift from services to consumption would have caused a relatively muted inflationary effect, its effects have been amplified because of supply-chain and labor-market disruptions. Using aggregate data and disaggregated industry-level data, we provide empirical support for our predictions.

Our general-equilibrium framework allows us to analyze the potential effects of a counterfactual, more aggressive monetary policy in 2021. We find that although a baseline Taylor rule would have lowered consumption and output significantly, it would have had little effect on price inflation. Controlling the surge in inflation in 2021 would have required a more aggressive monetary-policy response than a standard Taylor rule and would have stalled the labor-market recovery.

Our analysis helps shed light on the changing dynamics of inflation. We interpret the supply-chain disruptions during the COVID-19 pandemic as a partial reversal of disinflationary effects of globalization on US inflation. Better and more interconnected supply chains and improvements in trade allowed firms to substitute between labor and imported labor-intensive intermediate inputs in the past decades, thus cushioning any cost shock due to one of the two input factors. Moreover, foreign competition in output markets affected firms' pricing decisions significantly. The pandemic-related disruptions weakened firms' ability to optimize across domestic and imported input factors, raised demand for domestic inputs and labor, and increased firms' pricing power. These effects contributed significantly to the rise in inflation and the overheating of the labor market.

Endnotes

Author email addresses: Amiti (amiti@gmail.com), Heise (sebastian.heise@ny.frb.org), Karahan (yfkarahan@gmail.com), Şahin (aysegul.sahin@austin.utexas.edu). We are grateful to Stefano Eusepi, Sebnem Kalemli-Özcan, Valerie Ramey, and Mathias Trabandt for detailed comments and suggestions. We thank David Dam, Will Schirmer, Aidan Toner-Rodgers, Aidan Wang, and Julia Wu for excellent research assistance. The views expressed in this paper are those of the authors and do not necessarily reflect the position of the Federal Reserve Bank of New York or the Federal Reserve System. For acknowledgments, sources of research support, and disclosure of the author's or authors' material financial relationships, if any, please see https://www.nber.org/books-and-chapters/nber-macroeco nomics-annual-2023-volume-38/inflation-strikes-back-role-import-competition-and -labor-market.

1. For anecdotal evidence on supply-chain disruptions and labor-supply constraints, see "Daily Business Briefing: Supply Chain Snags Continued to Drive Up Prices" (*New York Times*, January 12, 2022) and "Could Wages and Prices Spiral Upward in America?" (*New York Times*, February 17, 2022).

2. For example, LaBelle and Santacreu (2022) document that higher import prices were associated with higher producer prices for US output in the recent period.

3. See, for example, Crump et al. (2022) and Faberman et al. (2022). Reservation-wage increases are documented in the Survey of Consumer Expectations of the NYFed: https://www.newyorkfed.org/microeconomics/sce/labor#/expectations-job-search16.

4. See, for example, http://larrysummers.com/2021/11/16/on-inflation-its-past -time-for-team-transitory-to-stand-down.

5. See https://www.brookings.edu/research/fed-response-to-covid19 for a discussion of the Fed's actions in 2020 and 2021.

6. We define the manufacturing and mining sectors as the goods sector and set utilities, construction, wholesale and retail trade, transportation, and all other services as services.

7. Prices as measured by the core PCE increased by 5.0% in December 2021 relative to 1 year earlier. This increase compares with a 12-month core PCE growth of 1.5% in December 2020.

8. We calculate annual growth rates in the fourth quarter of 2021.

9. For expositional purposes, we plot here the average consumer-price inflation rate across the two sectors, using each sector's time-varying consumption share γ_t^s as weight. We do not plot the change of $P_{f,t}$ itself because that depends on the levels of $P_{f,t}^M$ and $P_{f,t}^S$, due to the changing consumption weights. In our calibration, the price level in goods tends to be higher than in services, and therefore the shift to goods in the first period mechanically leads to a significant increase in $P_{f,t}$ even without any within-sector inflation. We prefer to omit this inflationary effect.

10. Out of the 349 occupations for which there is information available, 196 (56%) have seen real mean wage gains over this period. These occupations represented 64% of all nonfarm employment in September and October 2021.

11. Note that although we refer to these shocks as supply-side shocks, they might be capturing the effects of various developments such as domestic and foreign fiscal stimulus, health concerns, or changing preferences.

12. Although policy is set to be the same in the first period under all experiments, it is more restrictive under the joint shock than under the sum of the shocks in later periods. Hence, the amplification we find is a conservative estimate.

13. As shown by Ruzic (2023), the capital-labor ratio responds 30%–80% more strongly to the price of labor than to the price of capital; hence there may be asymmetries in substitution patterns dependent on the direction of the substitution.

14. See, for example, http://larrysummers.com/2021/11/16/on-inflation-its-past -time-for-team-transitory-to-stand-down.

15. Instead, it would have been better to be ahead of the curve to reduce inflation if inflation was purely demand driven, as we show in an earlier version of our paper.

16. Because the BLS started collecting services prices only in 2004, we do not have a comprehensive series covering both goods and services.

17. See appendix A.7, https://data.nber.org/data-appendix/c14851/appendix.pdf #page=16, for the derivations in this section.

18. Our regression results are similar if we include these industries.

19. We do not include earlier years due to revisions in the Census trade codes and NAICS codes, which make a consistent mapping from import prices to six-digit PPI codes over longer time horizons more difficult.

20. The latest input-output table with sufficiently disaggregated industries available is 2012. It consists of 405 BEA industries, which are mapped to six-digit NAICS codes.

21. As an example, if the auto industry uses 70% rubber and 30% steel, its domestic input-price index will be constructed as 0.7 times the change in the log rubber price plus 0.3 times the change of the log steel price.

22. We define that sector to comprise all industries with positive imports in at least 1 year; that is, there is some import competition. These industries are predominantly in manufacturing, with a few industries in agriculture and mining. Manufacturing accounted for about 63% of employment in goods-producing industries in the past decade.

23. Import prices can still affect nontraded industries through imported intermediate inputs. For example, a dentist may use a computer that was manufactured abroad.

24. In appendix D.1, https://data.nber.org/data-appendix/c14851/appendix.pdf #page=26, we repeat the same table using wage and input-price changes residualized by industry fixed effects for all statistics.

25. Because we use industry-level data, we do not have domestic competitors' prices within the same industry. We therefore estimate the effect of competition on US producer prices using only an industry's foreign competitors' prices. These are given by the import-price index $P_{it,imp}$ constructed earlier. In contrast to the imported input-price index, which is a weighted average of import prices across all industries that provide inputs to i, the competitors' price index is simply the import-price index of industry i; for example, the price of imported cars for the car industry.

26. We obtain these variables from the Census Bureau's QWI.

27. We show only a subset of the regression coefficients in table 4.

28. In appendix D, https://data.nber.org/data-appendix/c14851/appendix.pdf #page=26, we perform several additional robustness checks of our findings. First, our structural equation (30) indicates that the effect of wages and productivity on prices should be of equal and opposite sign. We therefore run a constrained regression that imposes this requirement. Second, we introduce a proxy for domestic competitors, using the prices of the more aggregated four-digit NAICS industry, to attempt to capture the competition that is missing from our baseline analysis. Third, we attempt to control for demand shocks by rerunning our regression with three-digit NAICS industry by quarter fixed effects. This specification absorbs all factors that are common to the same three-digit industry and quarter and identifies our coefficients of interest from variation within broad industries. If demand shocks are common within three-digit industries, then the remaining variation can be attributed to the shocks we focus on. The results in appendix D indicate that our results continue to hold with these alternative specifications.

References

Amiti, M., O. Itskhoki, and J. Konings. 2019. "International Shocks, Variable Markups, and Domestic Prices." *Review of Economic Studies* 86:2356–402.

Atkeson, A., and A. Burstein. 2008. "Pricing-to-Market, Trade Costs, and International Relative Prices." *American Economic Review* 98:1998–2031.

Ball, L. M., D. Leigh, and P. Mishra. 2022. "Understanding U.S. Inflation during the COVID Era." Working Paper no. 30613, NBER, Cambridge, MA.

Baqaee, D., and E. Farhi. 2022. "Supply and Demand in Disaggregated Keynesian Economies with an Application to the COVID-19 Crisis." *American Economic Review* 112:1397–436.

Benigno, P., and G. B. Eggertsson. 2023. "It's Baaack: The Surge in Inflation in the 2020s and the Return of the Non-Linear Phillips Curve." Working Paper no. 31197, NBER, Cambridge, MA.

Boehm, C. E., A. Flaaen, and N. Pandalai-Nayar. 2019. "Input Linkages and the Transmission of Shocks: Firm-Level Evidence from the 2011 Tohoku Earthquake." *Review of Economics and Statistics* 101:60–75.

Bunn, P., L. S. Anayi, N. Bloom, P. Mizen, G. Thwaites, and I. Yotzov. 2022. "Firming Up Price Inflation." Working Paper no. 30505, NBER, Cambridge, MA.

Carvalho, C., F. Nechio, and T. Tristão. 2021. "Taylor Rule Estimation by OLS." *Journal of Monetary Economics* 124:140–54.

Cavallo, A., and O. Kryvtsov. 2023. "What Can Stockouts Tell Us about Inflation? Evidence from Online Micro Data." *Journal of International Economics* 146:103769.

Cerrato, A., and G. Gitti. 2022. "Inflation since COVID: Demand or Supply." Working Paper no. 4193594, SSRN.

Chan, M. 2021. "How Substitutable Are Labor and Intermediates?" https://www.monschan.com/wp-content/uploads/2022/01/Mons-Chan-2021-Working-Paper-How-Substitutable-Are-Labor-and-Intermediates.pdf.

Christiano, L. J., M. Eichenbaum, and C. L. Evans. 2005. "Nominal Rigidities and the Dynamic Effects of a Shock to Monetary Policy." *Journal of Political Economy* 113:1–45.

Clarida, R., J. Galí, and M. Gertler. 2000. "Monetary Policy Rules and Macroeconomic Stability: Evidence and Some Theory." *Quarterly Journal of Economics* 115:147–80.

Comin, D. A., R. C. Johnson, and C. J. Jones. 2023. "Supply Chain Constraints and Inflation." Working Paper no. 31179, NBER, Cambridge, MA.

Crump, R. K., S. Eusepi, M. Giannoni, and A. Şahin. 2022. "The Unemployment-Inflation Trade-Off Revisited: The Phillips Curve in COVID Times." Working Paper no. 29785, NBER, Cambridge, MA.

De Soyres, F., A. M. Santacreu, and H. L. Young. 2023. "Demand-Supply Imbalance during the COVID-19 Pandemic: The Role of Fiscal Policy." International Finance Discussion Papers 1353, Board of Governors of the Federal Reserve System, Washington, DC.

Di Giovanni, J., C. Kalemli-Özcan, A. Silva, and M. A. Yildirim. 2022. "Global Supply Chain Pressures, International Trade, and Inflation." https://www.ecb.europa.eu/pub/pdf/sintra/ecb.forumcentbank202206~a6bc0541ca.en.pdf.

———. 2023. "Quantifying the Inflationary Impact of Fiscal Stimulus under Supply Constraints." *American Economic Review Papers and Proceedings* 113:76–80.

Duran-Franch, J., and M. Konczal. 2021. "Real Wages Are Increasing for Those in the Bottom Half of the Income Distribution." *Roosevelt Institute Blog*, November 17.

Elsby, M. W., B. Hobijn, and A. Şahin. 2013. "The Decline of the US Labor Share." *Brookings Papers on Economic Activity* 2013:1–63.

Faberman, R. J., A. Mueller, and A. Şahin. 2022. "Has the Willingness to Work Fallen during the COVID Pandemic?" *Labour Economics* 79:102275.

Feenstra, R. C., P. Luck, M. Obstfeld, and K. N. Russ. 2018. "In Search of the Armington Elasticity." *Review of Economics and Statistics* 100:135–50.

Ferrante, F., S. Graves, and M. Iacoviello. 2023. "The Inflationary Effects of Sectoral Reallocation." *Journal of Monetary Economics* 140:S64–S81.

Forbes, K. J. 2019. "Inflation Dynamics: Dead, Dormant or Determined Abroad?" *Brookings Papers on Economic Activity* 2019:257–338.

Harding, M., J. Lindé, and M. Trabandt. 2023. "Understanding Post-COVID Inflation Dynamics." *Journal of Monetary Economics* 140:S101–S118.

Heise, S., F. Karahan, and A. Şahin. 2022. "The Missing Inflation Puzzle: The Role of the Wage-Price Pass-Through." *Journal of Money, Credit and Banking* 54:7–51.

Hobijn, B., and A. Şahin. 2022. "Missing Workers and Missing Jobs since the Pandemic." Working Paper no. 30717, NBER, Cambridge, MA.

Howard, S., R. Rich, and J. Tracy. 2022. "Real Wages Grew during Two Years of COVID-19 after Controlling for Workforce Composition." Federal Reserve Bank of Dallas, February 15.

Jaimovich, N., and M. Floetotto. 2008. "Firm Dynamics, Markup Variation and the Business Cycle." *Journal of Monetary Economics* 55:1238–52.

Jordà, Ò. 2005. "Estimation and Inference of Impulse Responses by Local Projections." *American Economic Review* 95:161–82.

Keen, B., and Y. Wang. 2007. "What Is a Realistic Value for Price Adjustment Costs in New Keynesian Models?" *Applied Economics Letters* 14:789–93.

LaBelle, J., and A. M. Santacreu. 2022. "Global Supply Chain Disruptions and Inflation during the COVID-19 Pandemic." *Federal Reserve Bank of St. Louis Review* 104 (2): 78–91. https://doi.org/10.20955/r.104.78-91.

Obstfeld, M. 2019. "Global Dimensions of U.S. Monetary Policy." *International Journal of Central Banking* 16:73–132.

Pierce, J. R., and P. K. Schott. 2012. "A Concordance between Ten-Digit U.S. Harmonized System Codes and SIC/NAICS Product Classes and Industries." *Journal of Economic and Social Measurement* 37:61–96.

Ramey, V. A. 2016. "Macroeconomic Shocks and Their Propagation." *Handbook of Macroeconomics* 2:71–162.

Rubbo, E. 2023. "What Drives Inflation? Lessons from Disaggregated Price Data." https://sites.google.com/view/elisarubbo/research?authuser=0.

Ruzic, D. 2023. "Factor-Biased Outsourcing: Implications for Capital-Labor Substitution." https://www.druzic.com/research.

Smets, F., and R. Wouters. 2003. "An Estimated Dynamic Stochastic General Equilibrium Model of the Euro Area." *Journal of the European Economic Association* 1:1123–75.

Comment

Şebnem Kalemli-Özcan, *University of Maryland and NBER,* United States of America

The paper by Amiti, Heise, Karahan, and Sahin quantifies drivers of the US inflation during 2021. They write down a model to explain the almost 4 percentage point increase in core consumer price index (CPI) inflation, from 1.6% in December 2020 to 5.5% in December 2021. To allow for the peculiarities of the COVID-19 era inflation, they enrich an otherwise standard two-sector dynamic stochastic general equilibrium model with exogenous supply shocks coming from higher import prices, lower foreign competition, and higher disutility of labor. They further add a reallocation shock where consumption shifts from services to goods. On top of all these exogenous shocks, they also factor in the "no-response" monetary policy of 2021, keeping monetary policy accommodative. This effectively introduces a negative monetary-policy shock. All the shocks (supply and reallocation of consumption) fully account for the 3.9 percentage point rise in core CPI inflation. The accommodative monetary policy helped the surge in inflation, and all the shocks together overexplain the observed rise in inflation. Put differently, the model shows that tight monetary policy in 2021 would have crushed the overrecovery in the labor market.

The key intuition comes from the weak adjustment in relative prices due to a multitude of shocks, where each shock interacts with each other and amplifies each other's effect. For example, consumption of traded goods increased exactly at the time their shipping costs went up. Such amplification can be quantified given the nonlinear solution. They feed deterministic shocks into a stochastic model and use second-order approximation to capture the nonlinear effects.

NBER Macroeconomics Annual, volume 38, 2024.
© 2024 National Bureau of Economic Research. All rights reserved. Published by The University of Chicago Press for the National Bureau of Economic Research. https://doi.org/10.1086/729201

This is a general-interest paper on an important topic that has been widely debated since 2021. The following two facts indicate that the debate will continue for some time: (1) not only the United States but also all other advanced countries are going through the highest inflationary episode of the past 4 decades, and (2) none of these countries have brought the inflation back to their targets.

The paper is part of a growing literature that links inflation to factor prices and labor market in global networks/multisectors and in nonlinear closed/open economy models.[1] Similar to di Giovanni et al. (2022), they abstract from energy/oil shocks and focus on core inflation in 2021 to focus on the "sectoral" supply shocks that were the dominant drivers of inflation early in 2021. This also allows them to quantify, exactly as in di Giovanni et al. (2022), the amplification effect of supply disruptions due to consumption shift between sectors. Different from di Giovanni et al. (2022) and the existing literature on this topic that works with multisectors and networks, all the foreign shocks including price shocks are exogenous to the United States even though the United States is not a small open economy and shocks are global. When labor does not want to work and imported inputs are expensive, substitution from imported inputs to labor cannot smooth the inflationary impact of the foreign-price shock. This happens because domestic firms increase markups without losing market share to foreign competition, as foreigners also got hit by the same shocks.

I will organize my comments into three groups. First, I discuss the suitability of the modeling features to the facts of the past 3 years. Second, I discuss the pros and cons of the paper's methodology, running impulse responses by feeding shocks to the model, instead of estimating the model, and doing a full variance decomposition on inflation drivers. Finally, I evaluate the key role of certain parameters, such as the elasticities governing substitution between labor and domestic inputs and between domestic and foreign inputs, on the quantitative implications of the model.

The model has many shocks. This might be needed to match the real-life COVID-19 era, characterized by a multitude of shocks. However, assuming all these shocks to be exogenous sets the deck against monetary policy being helpful. Higher disutility of labor (lower labor supply) and higher foreign prices are partly endogenous responses to generous fiscal stimulus programs of advanced countries, which itself was a response to the original negative aggregate demand shock due to the pandemic (e.g., Gourinchas et al. 2021). The paper's focus is on import prices for the United States as a small open economy. This is not appropriate, as any demand shock in the United States will affect both export and import prices and the amount of net exports, not only imports. This is important because import and export price endogeneity to the consumption reallocation shock (shift from domestic services to traded goods during 2021 and shift back to services in 2022) is a first-order issue to get the timing and persistence of inflation right. As shown by di Giovanni et al. (2022), goods inflation started earlier than services inflation in 2021, and in 2022 when goods inflation was coming down, services inflation started picking up and drives inflation in 2023, as shown in di Giovanni et al. (2023).

The exogeneity of the labor-supply shock, being a disutility shock, raises a similar issue. The decline in labor-force participation in the data is due to a combination of demand and supply shocks. There are various reasons for the declining labor supply, such as the pandemic affecting desire to work in contact-intensive sectors, lockdowns, higher reservation wage given government support, and numerous lifestyle changes. Modeling the labor-supply shock as a preference parameter of not wanting to work creates difficulties in terms of calibrating this parameter, because it is hard to make it consistent with the health shock, fiscal impulse, and hand-to-mouth agents share all at once. Most importantly, as an exogenous preference shock, disutility of labor will not allow people to go back to work in the model, as happened in reality, and hence the model will assign the inflationary impact of the reduced unemployment and tight labor markets to somewhere else, underestimating the interaction between demand and labor-supply shock on labor-market tightness and the related sticky inflation.

My second set of comments is on the methodology of estimating impulse-response functions to different shocks in the calibrated model. An alternative strategy would be to estimate the model and let the data speak to which shocks are important in driving inflation in a formal variance decomposition. An exercise of this latter sort is done in di Giovanni et al. (2022, 2023). These papers can account for the timing in inflation—goods sector first, services sectors later—and also can account for the simultaneous occurrence of slack and inflation in the aggregate economy in 2021, the focus year of the current paper. The above papers quantify that two-thirds of inflation is due to demand shocks and one-third from supply shocks in the United States. The current paper does not do this but shows that their model is consistent with the behavior of inflation and also with consumption, output, and wages. However, this requires one to assume several exogenous shocks and flexible adjustment of factors of production across two sectors; a counterfactual, because factor markets including labor remain segmented during this period, where jobs lost/

gained in the tradable sector were not smoothed out by jobs gained/lost in the nontradable sector, keeping labor markets tight in the nontradable sector for more than 2 years.

My final comments are on the quantitative importance of the parameters governing the elasticity of substitution. CPI inflation in this model comes from higher markups and higher marginal costs. Each good (i) price is given by $\log P_i = \log \mu_i + \log MC_i$. How important are markups and cost pass-through quantitatively? The answer will depend on the elasticity of substitution parameter. And the effect of this parameter can be different on first- and second-order terms, as typical in nonlinear models. To see this, take equation (1):

$$
d\log MC_i = \underbrace{\alpha_{iL}\, d\log W + \alpha_{iM} d\log P_M + \alpha_{iD} d\log P_D}_{\text{First-Order Term}}
$$

$$
+ \frac{1}{2}(1-\rho)\underbrace{\left[\alpha_{iL}(1-\alpha_{iL})(d\log W)^2 + \alpha_{iM}(1-\alpha_{iM})(d\log P_M)^2 + \alpha_{iD}(1-\alpha_{iD})(d\log P_D)^2\right]}_{\text{Isolated Effects}}
$$

$$
+ (\rho-1)\underbrace{\left[\alpha_{iM}\alpha_{iL} d\log W d\log P_M + \alpha_{iM}\alpha_{iD} d\log P_D d\log P_M + \alpha_{iL}\alpha_{iD} d\log P_D d\log W\right]}_{\text{Cross-Term Effects}}.
$$

$$(1)$$

The paper's benchmark assumption is $\rho > 1$; that is, inputs into production are substitutable. This assumption drives all the results in the paper, because when foreign inputs become expensive, there will be substitution toward domestic inputs, leading to a cost-push shock and inflation. If only the price of a single input changes, this affects marginal costs less, as firms can substitute away toward other inputs. So in this case, substitution dampens the single shock via "isolated effects" as seen in equation (1). However, if all input prices change with multiple shocks, their benchmark case, then substitution ($\rho > 1$) amplifies the effect on the marginal cost via "cross-term effects" as seen in the equation. This is the key insight coming from multiple shocks, showing up in the second-order term, affecting all inputs so the standard smoothing effect of substitution from one input to other input is muted. This is an important insight, because the original view that inflation led by supply-chain disruption should be transitory relies on this substitution from one input to another and relative prices adjusting, totally ignoring the global nature of the shock where all sorts of inputs used through vertical supply chains get shocked. If substitution is muted, relative price adjustment will not happen and foreign-input shocks will have a larger inflationary effect.

What happens if $\rho < 1$? These effects are exactly reversed; now isolated effects get amplified and cross-effects are muted. However, ρ is estimated in the US data to be less than 1 (e.g., Atalay 2017; Raval 2019; Carvalho et al. 2021; Oberfield and Raval 2021) and internationally (e.g., Boehm, Flaaen, and Pandalai-Nayar 2019; Boehm, Levchenko, and Pandalai-Nayar 2023). This literature estimates the elasticity of substitution between value-added and intermediate inputs as 0.6, the elasticity between labor and capital as 0.5, and the elasticity between domestic and foreign inputs as 0.2. The authors estimate that one-third of the inflation comes from supply shocks, assuming high elasticity of substitution between domestic and foreign inputs; under their robustness exercise of the Leontief production function, where domestic and foreign inputs remain to be substitutes based on evidence in Feenstra et al. (2018), which contradicts the recent *American Economic Review* paper by Boehm et al. (2023). This is because Feenstra et al. (2018) estimate long-run elasticities, whereas the recent work estimates short-run elasticities that should be the relevant elasticity for the current paper focusing only on a single year, 2021. Different models assuming the exact reverse, a high degree of complementarity, also find a similar effect: one-third of inflation coming from supply shocks. How is this possible? The exercise below explains.

With complementarity between domestic and foreign inputs, amplification of marginal costs comes from isolated wage changes, whereas under substitution it comes from cross effects. To reconcile these two seemingly contradictory outcomes, we need to take sectoral heterogeneity seriously: having 66 sectors of the US economy instead of just two sectors matters. Same for factors of production: having 66 labor markets instead of just two matters and can better describe the real-life inflation.

To show this, let me run a simple simulation. Elasticity in these experiments can be either $\rho = 0.6$ or $\rho = 1.5$, to consider cases of both complementarity and substitution. I draw price changes from a uniform distribution with mean 0.16, to coincide with the import-price changes they fed in. This means that all prices in my exercise go up, but some go up more than others, to highlight the story they have in mind and to be as clear as possible. I conduct 100 simulations per each case. For example, I simulate the case when the number of inputs is $N = 2$ 100 times, and then I take the mean of the isolated effect, the cross-terms, and their sum across these 100 cases. Then I do the same for $N = 3, 4, \ldots, 150$. All results I show below are averaged across these 100 simulations.

Whenever I add an input, it is not obvious how input shares should be set. To address this, I consider three possible distributions for the input shares and their correlation with the price changes:

• Symmetric: I assume all inputs have the same share equal to $1/N$. An additional input thus decreases the shares of all other inputs in the same proportion. Hence, here input shares are symmetric. This is shown in the solid line in each case in figure 1.

• Positive: I draw the input share distribution from a Pareto distribution with a tail parameter equal to 1.16 and position parameter equal to 1. I ordered shares so that they are positively correlated with the price changes: inputs in which a firm spends more are the ones that experience the larger price increases. This is shown in the dotted line in figure 1.

• Negative: I draw the input share distribution from a Pareto distribution with a parameter equal to 1.16. I ordered shares so that they are negatively correlated with the price changes: inputs in which a firm spends more are the ones that experience the lower price increases. This is shown in the dashed line in figure 1.

Regardless of how input shares are drawn, the sum of the isolated effects and cross-effects—that is, the overall effect—is positive only when $\rho = 0.6$ and not when $\rho = 1.5$. This suggests that second-order terms in this model cannot generate inflation but rather decrease the overall impact of input-price changes on inflation (relative to a log-linear world). Increasing the level of disaggregation (number of sectors on the x-axis) increases the effect on inflation of the second-order term when $\rho = 0.6$ and decreases it when $\rho = 1.5$. This is true with any configuration of

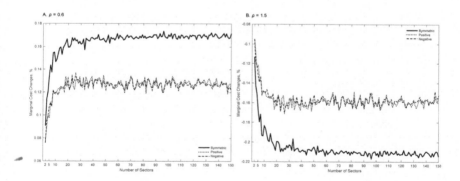

Fig. 1. Channels' strength as number of inputs increases. Panel A shows the second-order terms with an elasticity of substitution among inputs equal to $\rho = 0.6$. Panel B repeats the exercise with an elasticity of $\rho = 1.5$. Each point in the figure is the average across 100 simulations. The solid line assumes expenditure share in all inputs is the same and equals $1/N$. The dotted (positive) line means shares are drawn from a Pareto distribution with shape parameter 1.16 and are ordered such that inputs with larger expenditure shares receive larger shocks. The dashed (negative) line uses the same distribution but ordered shares in increasing order, meaning that inputs with larger expenditure shares experienced lower price increases. A color version of this figure is available online.

the input shares. Hence, disaggregation coupled with a low elasticity of substitution raises inflation in a nonlinear world relative to a log-linear world, and the opposite happens with values of the elasticity of substitution higher than 1. As a result, working with substitution between domestic and foreign inputs, as the authors do, decreases the quantitative importance of nonlinearity in the calibrated model.

Endnotes

Author email address: Kalemli-Özcan (kalemli@econ.umd.edu). For acknowledgments, sources of research support, and disclosure of the author's material financial relationships, if any, please see https://www.nber.org/books-and-chapters/nber-macroeconomics-annual-2023-volume-38/comment-inflation-strikes-back-role-import-competition-and-labor-market-kalemli-ozcan.
1. See Pasten, Schoenle, and Weber (2020), Baqaee and Farhi (2022), di Giovanni et al. (2022, 2023), Guerrieri et al. (2022), La'O and Tahbaz-Salehi (2022), Woodford (2022), Afrouzi and Bhattarai (2023), and Ferrante, Graves, and Iacoviello (2023).

References

Afrouzi, Hassan, and Saroj Bhattarai. 2023. "Inflation and GDP Dynamics in Production Networks: A Sufficient Statistics Approach." Working Paper no. 31218, NBER, Cambridge, MA.

Atalay, Enghin. 2017. "How Important Are Sectoral Shocks?" *American Economic Journal: Macroeconomics* 9 (4): 254–80.

Baqaee, David, and Emmanuel Farhi. 2022. "Supply and Demand in Disaggregated Keynesian Economies with an Application to the COVID-19 Crisis." *American Economic Review* 112 (5): 1397–436.

Boehm, Christoph E., Aaron Flaaen, and Nitya Pandalai-Nayar. 2019. "Input Linkages and the Transmission of Shocks: Firm-Level Evidence from the 2011 Tōhoku Earthquake." *Review of Economics and Statistics* 101 (1): 60–75.

Boehm, Christoph E., Andrei A. Levchenko, and Nitya Pandalai-Nayar. 2023. "The Long and Short (Run) of Trade Elasticities." *American Economic Review* 113 (4): 861–905.

Carvalho, Vasco M., Makoto Nirei, Yukiko U. Saito, and Alireza Tahbaz-Salehi. 2021. "Supply Chain Disruptions: Evidence from the Great East Japan Earthquake." *Quarterly Journal of Economics* 136 (2): 1255–321.

Feenstra, Robert C., Philip Luck, Maurice Obstfeld, Katheryn N. Russ. 2018. "In Search of the Armington Elasticity." *Review of Economics and Statistics* 100 (1): 135–50.

Ferrante, Francesco, Sebastian Graves, and Matteo Iacoviello. 2023. "The Inflationary Effects of Sectoral Reallocation." *Journal of Monetary Economics* 140 (Supplement): S64–S81.

di Giovanni, Julian, Şebnem Kalemli-Özcan, Alvaro Silva, and Muhammed A. Yıldırım. 2022. "Global Supply Chain Pressures, International Trade, and Inflation." Working Paper no. 30240, NBER, Cambridge, MA.

———. 2023. "Quantifying the Inflationary Impact of Fiscal Stimulus under Supply Constraints." *AEA Papers and Proceedings* 113:76–80.

Gourinchas, Pierre-Olivier, Şebnem Kalemli-Özcan, Veronika Penciakova, and Nick Sander. 2021. "Fiscal Policy in the Age of COVID: Does It 'Get in All of the Cracks'?" Technical report presented at the Jackson Hole Economic Policy Symposium, Jackson Hole, WY, August.

Guerrieri, Veronica, Guido Lorenzoni, Ludwig Straub, and Iván Werning. 2022. "Macroeconomic Implications of COVID-19: Can Negative Supply Shocks Cause Demand Shortages?" *American Economic Review* 112 (5): 1437–74.

La'O, Jennifer, and Alireza Tahbaz-Salehi. 2022. "Optimal Monetary Policy in Production Networks." *Econometrica* 90 (3): 1295–336.

Oberfield, Ezra, and Devesh Raval. 2021. "Micro Data and Macro Technology." *Econometrica* 89 (2): 703–32.

Pasten, Ernesto, Raphael Schoenle, and Michael Weber. 2020. "The Propagation of Monetary Policy Shocks in a Heterogeneous Production Economy." *Journal of Monetary Economics* 116:1–22.

Raval, Devesh R. 2019. "The Micro Elasticity of Substitution and Non-neutral Technology." *RAND Journal of Economics* 50 (1): 147–67.

Woodford, Michael. 2022. "Effective Demand Failures and the Limits of Monetary Stabilization Policy." *American Economic Review* 112 (5): 1475–521.

Comment

Mathias Trabandt, *Goethe University Frankfurt and Halle Institute for Economic Research,* Germany

I. Introduction

Amiti et al. (2024) seek to answer a very topical and important research question: How much did supply-side disruptions and the tight labor market contribute to the recent surge in inflation? The answer provided by the authors is: about 2 percentage points. To arrive at their answer, the authors use a calibrated two-sector New Keynesian model in which they use three correlated shocks in a perfect-storm type setting. The paper also has an interesting empirical part that provides evidence that the channels emphasized in the theoretical model are at work in the data.

Amiti et al. have written a fine paper with interesting and intriguing analysis and results. There is a lot to like about the paper, and it provides lots of food for thought for possible extensions of the model and the analysis in future work.

My discussion consists of two parts. The first part summarizes the model, intuition, and key results of the paper. The second part offers remarks and comments. My comments are based on the April 1, 2023, version of the paper, which I discussed at the 38th Annual Conference on Macroeconomics on April 21, 2023. The slides of my discussion are available on my website. Amiti et al. have subsequently revised their paper, taking on board parts of my comments.

NBER Macroeconomics Annual, volume 38, 2024.

II.   The Amiti et al. (2023) Paper

A.   The Model

The model, which I will refer to as the AHKS model, is a calibrated two-sector model. There is a goods sector and a services sector. There is multistage production with multiple input factors such as labor, domestic, and foreign intermediate inputs. There is roundabout production and foreign competitors that compete in the domestic market. The model also features endogenous markups. Finally, the model contains sticky prices and sticky wages as well as a central bank that follows a Taylor rule.

The authors feed three correlated shocks into the model. The first shock is a run-up in imported intermediate inputs prices. The second shock is a decline in foreign competition in the domestic market. The third shock is a decline in the willingness to work in the labor market. After feeding these three shocks into the model simultaneously, the authors measure the effect on the rate of inflation in the United States.

B.   Key Results

The three correlated shocks result in a rise in inflation of about 2 percentage points. Importantly, there is an amplification effect when the three shocks are fed into the model jointly and occur at the same time. When the authors feed the shocks into the model separately—that is, one shock a time—each of these shocks itself generates about 0.5 percentage points of inflation. Thus, mechanically adding up the effect of each shock results in a rise of inflation of about 1.5 percentage points, whereas when all shocks hit jointly at the same time, the total effect on inflation is amplified and raises inflation by about 2 percentage points.

What is the reason for the amplification effect? In the model, firms can substitute various inputs. For example, firms can substitute between labor and intermediate inputs. In turn, intermediate inputs can be substituted between domestic inputs and foreign inputs. So when shocks hit separately, the effect on firms' marginal cost is relatively small because firms can use multiple margins to substitute across different input goods. By contrast, in a perfect-storm setting—that is, when all three shocks hit at the same time—the three input margins in the model are hit at the same time, and thus the ability to substitute inputs is diminished, which results in the amplification effect.

The authors also use their model to study the effects of monetary policy. Specifically, the authors show that the effects of more aggressive monetary policy depend on whether inflation is supply-side driven or demand-side driven. When inflation surges are driven by supply disruptions, it is difficult for the central bank to combat inflation, because a steep rise in interest rates implies sizable costs in terms of economic activity. By contrast, when inflation surges are demand-driven, the central bank can combat inflation without triggering a recession.

Finally, the authors also provide empirical results based on aggregate and industry-level data. The authors show that when wages and input prices rise together, the pass-through of wages and input prices into product prices tends to accelerate. In other words, there is empirical support for the amplification effect suggested by the model.

III. Comments

A. Variable Capital Utilization

In their model, the authors have abstracted from capital services; that is, physical capital coupled with variable capital utilization. How much does this matter for the resulting post-COVID inflation dynamics? Capital services are a standard feature in estimated medium-sized New Keynesian models such as, for example, Christiano, Eichenbaum, and Evans (2005), Smets and Wouters (2007), and many more. Christiano et al. (2005) have shown that variable capital utilization is a crucial model feature that is necessary so that the estimated model can account well for the observed dynamics of inflation.

In response to the adverse supply shocks considered by Amiti et al., variable capital utilization would constitute a further margin of adjustment that would allow firms to substitute toward in the wake of adverse supply shocks in other input markets. In this sense, one might consider the quantitative results of Amiti et al. (2023) as providing an upper bound for the effects on inflation. With variable capital utilization, the effects of adverse supply shocks could at least in principle be attenuated if firms had the opportunity to adjust their utilization of physical capital.

B. Implications for Wage Inflation

The model implications for wage inflation appear at odds with the data. In the model, wage inflation jumps by 4 percentage points while price inflation jumps by 2 percentage points in response to the supply shocks. In other words, wage inflation increases by more than price inflation after supply shocks. Likewise, when looking at the model implications for demand shocks, the same result obtains: wage inflation goes up by more than price inflation. So the model predicts wage inflation to jump more than price inflation during the post-COVID episode. In US data, however, the opposite is true: wage inflation increased by less than price inflation during the past 2 years. It would be useful to shed light on the reason(s) why the model struggles to come to terms with the data on the relative response of wage versus price inflation. Is this due to the missing capital services/variable capital utilization channel? That is, is labor demand driven up too much due to firms' inability to substitute away from domestic labor toward capital services? Or are wages just too flexible relative to prices in the calibration of the model?

C.   Model versus Data Comparison

The paper would benefit from a more rigorous model-data comparison so that the reader can assess the quantitative match between the model and the data. The authors state that US Consumer Price Index (CPI) inflation stood at 1.8% in 2019, 4.7% in 2021, and 8% in 2022. So the change in inflation between 2019 and 2021 is 2.9 percentage points, and the change in inflation between 2019 and 2022 is 6.2 percentage points. Unfortunately, the authors do not take a stand on whether they view 2.9 or 6.2 percentage points as a target to assess the model performance against. The authors write, "Our calculations suggest that supply-chain disruptions and labor supply constraints can account for one-third [of 6.2 pp] to two-thirds [of 2.9 pp] of the rise in inflation depending on the time period we consider" (square brackets added).

Importantly, the shocks are calibrated using 2021–22 data. With this in mind, 6.2 percentage points seems to be the right target number for the inflation surge to be explained by the model.

In addition, the paper focuses entirely on explaining the surge in inflation during the post-COVID episode. What about quantities? How well does the model match gross domestic product, consumption, labor, etc. in the data? Ideally, the model should account not only for the surge in inflation but also for the dynamics of quantities in the post-COVID data. Christiano, Eichenbaum, and Trabandt (2015) compare Great Recession data with the predictions of a New Keynesian model and show that their model can account well for inflation and quantities. It would be very interesting to see a similar comparison based on the AHKS model for the post-COVID episode.

Finally, it would be useful to provide a quantitative comparison between the empirical analysis based on aggregate and industry-level data and the theoretical model. So far, the comparison between the regression analysis and the theoretical model is qualitative. Does the model imply the same quantitative regression results as in the data? Ideally, one would like to simulate data from the theoretical model and rerun the regression analysis on the simulated model data. Are the regression coefficients similar to those when using actual data?

D.   Monetary Policy

In US data, inflation went up by 6 percentage points in the past 2 years. According to the authors' analysis, adverse supply shocks account for 2 percentage points, and demand shocks account for another 2 percentage points. What accounts for the missing 2 percentage points? There is a possibility that monetary policy has played a crucial role to account for the missing 2 percentage points. Let me expand. In the model, supply and demand shocks together drive up the nominal interest rate by about 4.5 percentage points. In the data, the Federal Funds rate also increased by about 4.5 percentage points in the past 2 years. That said, the timing of monetary tightening is of essence. Most of the tightening in the model occurs very front loaded during the first 4 quarters after the shocks occur. By contrast, in the data, the Federal Funds rate was kept unchanged for about 2 years before tightening started. Put differently, the model suggests much more up-front tightening than had occurred in the data. A natural question to ask is how much monetary policy contributed to the run-up in US inflation by keeping the interest rate unchanged for about 2 years. To shed light on this question, I suggest conducting a counterfactual simulation with the model in which the nominal interest rate is kept unchanged for 1 or 2 years in the wake of the adverse supply and expansionary demand shocks. Does this explain the missing 2 percentage points run-up in inflation?

E.   Relation to Literature on Optimal Monetary Policy

The authors emphasize that the nature of the shock matters for the benefits and costs of aggressive monetary policy. If inflation is demand-driven, aggressive monetary policy can contain inflation without inducing a recession. By contrast, if inflation is driven by cost-push type shocks (e.g., supply-chain disruptions), then aggressive monetary policy toward inflation leads to negative effects on the labor market and the economy. It would be useful if the authors would relate their results to the literature on optimal monetary policy in the New Keynesian model. For example, Clarida, Galí, and Gertler (1999) report that in the standard New Keynesian model, the central bank faces no trade-off between inflation and output when the economy is hit by demand shocks. By contrast, after adverse cost-push shocks, the central bank does face a trade-off, and inflation and output outcomes depend on the preferences of the central bank. It would be useful if the authors could relate their findings to this literature.

F.   Labor-Market Model

The labor market is at center stage in the analysis. The authors have chosen a labor-market setup developed in Erceg, Henderson, and Levin (2000) and used in, for example, Christiano et al. (2005), Smets and Wouters (2007), and many others. One fruitful avenue for further research would be to consider an alternative labor-market setup. Specifically, a labor-market search and matching framework along the lines of Diamond (1982), Mortensen (1982), and Pissarides (1985), which has been used in medium-sized New Keynesian models (see, e.g., Christiano, Eichenbaum, and Trabandt 2016). That labor-market framework has been shown to work well in New Keynesian models. In addition, that labor-market framework would allow the authors to make contact with a rich set of labor-market data such as, for example, unemployment, employment, job-finding rates, labor-market tightness, and so on. Finally, a search and matching labor-market framework would allow the authors to make contact with an ongoing debate about the tightness of the labor market and the effects thereof on inflation. It would be particularly interesting to revisit and contribute to the recent debate about the Beveridge curve between Waller (2022), Figura and Waller (2022), and Blanchard, Domash, and Summers (2022a, 2022b) by using a quantitative medium-sized New Keynesian model with search and matching labor-market frictions that is subject to adverse supply shocks and expansionary demand shocks.

G.   Autocorrelation of Shocks

The authors calibrate their model, including the size of the exogenous shocks, carefully. That said, the authors assume an AR(1) coefficient of

0.9 for all three shocks. It would be useful to elaborate about this common choice for the persistence of the three exogenous shocks that drive all model results.

H.   Model Estimation and Filtering of Shocks

Is the AHKS model useful to study the 2021–22 episode only, or does it also fit pre-2021 (postwar) data? It would be very interesting to estimate the model on pre-2021 (postwar) data like, for example, Christiano et al. (2005) or Smets and Wouters (2007). Does the AHKS model offer new insights about postwar data?

   Given an estimated version of the model, one could then measure the shocks by Kalman-filtering the data with the model. This would allow the authors to study historical decompositions of the post-COVID period, examining the contributions of shocks to the run-up in inflation through the lens of the estimated model.

   Relatedly, when using a standard Christiano et al. (2005) or Smets and Wouters (2007) model that abstracts from the various features in AHKS, what would these models tell us about the post-COVID inflation drivers? Would these models provide radically different answers/insights than the AHKS model?

I.   Solution Method

The authors use a third-order Taylor series approximation to solve their model. How much does the solution method matter for the results? How would the results look like if the authors had used a first- or second-order approximation? What about solving the fully nonlinear model using the two-point boundary value solution method proposed by Fair and Taylor (1983), which is available in standard computational software such as Dynare? And finally, what are the implications when solving the model with global methods for the resulting conclusions of the paper?

J.   Concluding Remarks

All told, this is a very nice paper with interesting and intriguing analysis and results. There is much to like about the paper, and it provides considerable food for thought for possible extensions of the model and the analysis in future work.

Endnote

Author email address: Trabandt (mathias.trabandt@gmail.com). For acknowledgments, sources of research support, and disclosure of the author's material financial relationships, if any, please see https://www.nber.org/books-and-chapters/nber-macroeconomics-annual -2023-volume-38/comment-inflation-strikes-back-role-import-competition-and-labor-market -trabandt.

References

Amiti, Mary, Sebastian Heise, Fatih Karahan, and Ayşegül Şahin. 2024. "Inflation Strikes Back: The Role of Import Competition and the Labor Market." *NBER Macroeconomics Annual* 38 (1): 71–131.
Blanchard, Olivier, Alex Domash, and Lawrence H. Summers. 2022a. "Bad News for the Fed from the Beveridge Space." Policy Brief 22-7, Peterson Institute for International Economics, Washington, DC.
———. 2022b. "The Fed Is Wrong: Lower Inflation Is Unlikely without Raising Unemployment. Why We Disagree with Governor Chris Waller and Andrew Figura." Realtime Economics, Peterson Institute for International Economics, Washington, DC. http://www.piie.com/blogs/realtime-economic-issues -watch/fed-wrong-lower-inflation-unlikely-without-raising.
Christiano, Lawrence J., Martin Eichenbaum, and Charles Evans. 2005. "Nominal Rigidities and the Dynamic Effects of a Shock to Monetary Policy." *Journal of Political Economy* 113 (1): 1–45.
Christiano, Lawrence J., Martin Eichenbaum, and Mathias Trabandt. 2015. "Understanding the Great Recession." *American Economic Journal: Macroeconomics* 7 (1): 110–67.
———. 2016. "Unemployment and Business Cycles." *Econometrica* 84 (4): 1523–69.
Clarida, Richard, Jordi Galí, and Mark Gertler. 1999. "The Science of Monetary Policy: A New Keynesian Perspective." *Journal of Economic Literature* 37: 1661–707.
Diamond, Peter A. 1982. "Aggregate Demand Management in Search Equilibrium." *Journal of Political Economy* 90 (5): 881–94.
Erceg, Christopher J., Dale W. Henderson, and Andrew T. Levin. 2000. "Optimal Monetary Policy with Staggered Wage and Price Contracts." *Journal of Monetary Economics* 46:281–313.
Fair, Ray C., and John B. Taylor. 1983. "Solution and Maximum Likelihood Estimation of Dynamic Rational Expectations Models." *Econometrica* 51 (4): 1169–85.
Figura, Andrew, and Chris Waller. 2022. "What Does the Beveridge Curve Tell Us about the Likelihood of a Soft Landing?" FEDS Notes, July 29, Board of Governors of the Federal Reserve System, Washington, DC. https://doi.org /10.17016/2380-7172.3190.
Mortensen, Dale T. 1982. "Property Rights and Efficiency in Mating, Racing, and Related Games." *American Economic Review* 72 (5): 968–79.
Pissarides, Christopher A. 1985. "Short-Run Equilibrium Dynamics of Unemployment, Vacancies, and Real Wages." *American Economic Review* 75 (4): 676–90.

Smets, Frank, and Raf Wouters. 2007. "Shocks and Frictions in US Business Cycles: A Bayesian DSGE Approach." *American Economic Review* 97 (3): 586–606.

Waller, Christopher J. 2022. "Responding to High Inflation, with Some Thoughts on a Soft Landing." http://www.federalreserve.gov/newsevents/speech /waller20220530a.htm.

Discussion

Jennifer La'O opened the discussion by asking whether, in the model, import-price shocks are isomorphic to productivity or markup shocks. Understanding the nature of the shock matters for policy implications. For example, if the import-price shock is a negative productivity shock, the Federal Reserve should aggressively fight inflation, which generates a recession. Hence, to make a statement on whether the Federal Reserve reacts too aggressively or not to the import-price shocks, it is necessary to understand the nature of the import-price shocks. The authors thanked La'O for the comment and explained that the import-price shocks are isomorphic to productivity shocks in the model.

Gianluca Violante commented that the model is very rich on the production side but has a representative household, which implies that the aggregate marginal propensity to consume is low. Indeed, in the model presented, the aggregate marginal risk to consume is around 3% or 4%, which is about three or four times smaller than what it is in the data. The aggregate marginal risk to consume is important for the dynamics and the amplification mechanism of the shocks. Hence, Violante suggested a two-agent model. Furthermore, a two-agent model opens the door to other interesting questions that are important for amplification dynamics. For example, in the model, how is a fiscal stimulus shock distributed? The authors agreed with Violante saying that they are not taking a clear stance on the importance of demand in the model. However, a fiscal stimulus would augment the amplification effect discussed in the paper.

Ricardo Reis followed up on a point made by discussant Mathias Trabandt: the Taylor rule is the less accurately calibrated parameter in the model. The benchmark calibrated Taylor rule generates a response by the monetary authority that is much more aggressive than what happened in the past year. Therefore, Ricardo Reis suggested the authors do a counterfactual where the monetary authority is less aggressive and more in line with the data. With looser monetary policy, it is possible that the shocks studied in the model can explain more of the inflation than they do now. The authors thanked Reis and Trabandt for the comment on the Taylor rule. They added that they will follow the suggestion and show what happens when a less-aggressive Taylor rule is used.

Jason Furman then asked why the authors interpret the import-price shocks as a supply shock and not as a demand shock. Imports went up, and it seemed to be a movement along the supply curve and not a shift of it. Furthermore, at the beginning of 2021, in some cases people were getting more money if they were not working rather than working. Therefore, modeling the labor supply during this period is challenging, and the model is not facing this issue. Finally, Furman added that globalization affects relative prices but not inflation directly. The authors replied that the import-price shock can be seen as a reduction in productivity and thus can be seen as a supply shock. Furthermore, modeling the labor market à la Diamond-Mortesen-Pissarides increases the complexity of the model, so it is harder to link wages with inflation.

Gabriel Chodorow-Reich suggested being careful in distinguishing between supply and demand forces and shocks, especially when the focus is on understanding the role of policy. Labor supply is an example. It could be that there has been a drop in the labor force due to COVID-19 because people were worried about getting sick. Another possibility could be the wealth effect, given that stock prices and housing prices went up and the relative price of working and not working had changed. Therefore, it is important to make a distinction between incentives and shocks. Furthermore, the motivation behind the movements in wages in the '00s and the 2020s could be very different. Indeed, in the '00s, labor demand was moving wages, whereas in the 2020s, it is labor supply moving wages. Labor supply comoves with prices, and this could be an alternative story to the empirical finding of the paper that the correlation between prices and wages went up in recent periods.

Erik Hurst wanted to know whether the participants agreed on what happened to real wages in the past 2 years. His assessment, looking at the data, is that real wages are falling. Nominal wages have grown on average around 5%, and inflation has been slightly above 5%, so real wages have been decreasing. This fact is important to understand for the calibration of the model and to answer some of the earlier questions. The authors pointed out that it is hard to measure real wages. For example, in other work, the authors find that the wage for the same job for a low-skilled worker posted by the same firm after 1 year increased by 20%. For this reason, the authors have an extension of the model presented with low- and high-skilled workers. Low-skilled workers have a larger elasticity of substitution between intermediate inputs. This extension delivers similar results to the benchmark model.

The last comment was made by Valerie Ramey. She agreed with the discussants and Furman that movements along the supply curve were more important than supply shocks, particularly in light of the huge aggregate demand shocks in the United States and other parts of the world.

3

Bottlenecks: Sectoral Imbalances and the US Productivity Slowdown

Daron Acemoglu, *Massachusetts Institute of Technology and NBER,* United States of America

David Autor, *Massachusetts Institute of Technology and NBER,* United States of America

Christina Patterson, *University of Chicago Booth School of Business and NBER,* United States of America

I. Introduction

One of the most enduring macroeconomic puzzles of the past several decades is the pervasive slowdown in productivity growth across industrialized nations, despite breakneck advances in information and communication technologies (ICT) and electronics. Figure 1 provides a glimpse of recent breakthroughs in ICT and electronics by plotting the distribution of patents granted over the past several decades.[1] Two patterns are evident from the figure: first, a rapid takeoff in the total number of patents in the 1980s; and second, a surge in the share of ICT and electronics patents during the same time interval. Between 1990 and 2010, the total number of patents granted rose from 99,000 to 208,000, and the combined number of ICT and electronics patents granted increased by approximately 87,000, accounting for the bulk of the increase. Figure 2 depicts the growth rate of total factor productivity (TFP) in the US economy and in the leading Organisation for Economic Co-operation and Development (OECD) economies in recent decades. Productivity growth in the United States has been minimal since the mid-'00s, and it has been slower still in many OECD countries, with the possible exception of Germany.

How can these facts be reconciled? The exponential advance of innovations in ICT and electronics has led some commentators to conclude that we are on the verge of a new age of abundance, or even "technological singularity," driven by "superintelligent" machines (e.g., Kurzweil 2005; Diamandis and Kotler 2012; Bostrom 2014). Others looking at the

NBER Macroeconomics Annual, volume 38, 2024.

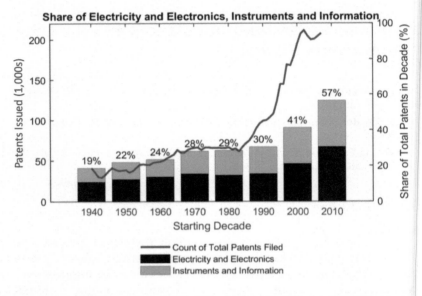

Fig. 1. Counts of US patents issued 1940–2010 and shares in (i) Electricity and Electronics and (ii) Instruments and Information. This figure plots the evolution of the counts and share (among all US utility patents) of Electricity and Electronics as well as Instruments and Information patents. Specifically, the left-hand y-axis gives the count of US utility patents issued in each year (black line), and the right-hand y-axis corresponds to the share of patents granted in each decade that are in Electricity and Electronics (black) and Instruments and Information (gray). Instruments and Information is synonymous with information and communications technologies (ICT). A color version of this figure is available online.

TFP data conclude that we have entered an age of slower growth because the most impactful technologies have already been developed and exploited (e.g., Cowen 2011; Gordon 2017).[2]

This paper offers a potential reconciliation of these trends based on the idea that technological advances over the past several decades have been unbalanced across sectors and have thus created endogenous bottlenecks, holding back aggregate productivity. We propose a simple framework in which the development of new technologies or products in a given sector requires simultaneous improvements in the quality of several inputs. For example, breakthroughs in automotive technology cannot be achieved solely with improvements in engine-management software and safety sensors but will also require complementary improvements in energy storage, drivetrains, and tire adhesion. Consequently, when some of those innovations, say batteries, do not keep pace with the rest, we may simultaneously observe rapid technological

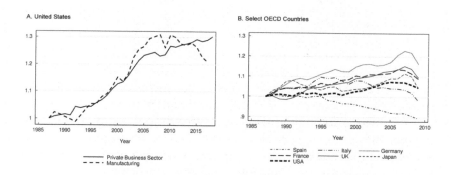

Fig. 2.   Time series for aggregate total factor productivity (TFP). This figure plots the time series for aggregate TFP for the US private business sector and manufacturing (left panel) and for selected Organisation for Economic Co-operation and Development (OECD) countries (right panel). The US TFP in the left panel is normalized to 1 in 1987 and spans 1987–2017 (data from the Bureau of Labor Statistics Major Sector and Major Industry TFP database). All TFP series are normalized to 1 in 1987 in the right panel as well and span 1987–2009 (data from the 2012 release of the EU KLEMS Growth and Productivity Accounts). A color version of this figure is available online.

progress in a subset of inputs and yet slow productivity growth in the aggregate. The bottleneck created by slow progress in battery technology, in this example, is endogenous in the sense that it is the advances of nonbattery inputs that have caused batteries to become a bottleneck.

Our perspective also emphasizes how a more balanced distribution of technological progress (and research and development) can improve aggregate productivity performance. In fact, current bottlenecks may offer the potential for significantly faster aggregate productivity growth: rapid progress in these technologies could enable broader gains that are held back at present.

Several transformative technologies of the past 3 decades illustrate how bottlenecks emerge and how their alleviation can accelerate innovation and growth. High-energy-density rechargeable batteries, which power the mobile electronics and electric vehicle industries (figuratively and literally), provide a key example. Batteries were a bottleneck even prior to the 1970s, when the best available technology for rechargeable batteries (lead-acid electrochemistry) had low energy density, a slow charging rate, a short lifecycle, and an unwelcome property of releasing explosive hydrogen gas during recharging. Lead-acid batteries were succeeded in the 1970s by nickel-cadmium and nickel metal hydride (NiMH) cells, which enabled the first commercially successful gasoline-electric "hybrid" car, the Toyota Prius, introduced in 1997. However, the primary drive unit in the Prius remained a conventional gas engine;

its NiMH battery provided only supplemental electric propulsion and regenerative braking capacity. The battery bottleneck was substantially overcome by lithium-ion batteries, invented in 1973 and refined in the 1980s. The lithium-ion battery's high energy density not only enabled fully electric vehicles for mass production but also catalyzed a host of unforeseen innovations: a surge in onboard automotive processing power, enabling vehicle autonomy; battery-powered drone aircraft, now used in weather forecasting, emergency response, construction planning, filmmaking, and building inspection; and the emerging electric passenger-airplane industry. In awarding the Nobel Prize in Chemistry 2019 to John B. Goodenough, M. Stanley Whittingham, and Akira Yoshino for their invention of the lithium-ion battery, the Nobel committee observed that their work had enabled the "wireless revolution."[3]

Even more foundational to the current era is the transistor, an electronic switch that is capable of amplifying, switching, and rectifying electrical signals (Park, Steigerwald, and Walker 1976). Through the 1950s, electromechanical switches and vacuum tubes were a clear bottleneck. Though used in all kinds of electronic devices, telephone lines, radios, transmitters, audio amplifiers, and early computers, they were bulky, fragile, and slow (Sosa 2013). The transistor supplied a tiny, fast, and (ultimately) very cheap, mass-produced alternative to vacuum tubes, thus breaking the bottleneck that had impeded progress in technologies as disparate as computers, long-distance telephones, and audio amplifiers. Due to its extraordinary switching speed, the transistor also ushered in the age of digital communications. Many of the central technologies of the present—the internet, artificial intelligence (AI), mobile computing, digital imaging, autonomous vehicles—are transistor-dependent innovations that were largely unforeseen prior to digital switching. The transistor is estimated to be the most-manufactured device in history, at 13 sextillion (10^{21}) units to date, with billions more produced each day (Laws 2018; Iancu 2019). The transistor's immense footprint is also visible in figure 1, where the patenting surge in electronics and ICT would not have been feasible without this breakthrough technology.

The Global Positioning System (GPS) constitutes a third innovation that broke a technological bottleneck and enabled a suite of technologies that have become foundational to modern life. Historically, navigating an offshore or airborne vessel required either sight lines to charted objects or a combination of optical instruments, precise clocks, and detailed tables to track progress. Traditional navigation was supplemented with radio positioning systems in the 1970s, but these tools suffered from either poor accuracy or limited geographic coverage and hence did not penetrate beyond military and commercial shipping applications. GPS overcame these shortcomings and added a second crucial feature: time-keeping with atomic-level accuracy. First launched in 1978, GPS satellites now provide geolocation and date and time information to any GPS receiver on or near the earth. Although GPS was built by and for the US military, it was opened to worldwide public use in 1983, after a Korean commercial airliner inadvertently navigated over Soviet airspace and was shot down. In addition to breaking the geopositioning logjam, GPS enabled a set of highly consequential innovations that were surely not envisioned by the military planners who commissioned the system. These include precision agriculture, mining, and oil exploration; atomic-precision time information for synchronization of power transmission systems; remote surveying for geology and weather prediction; and innumerable consumer-facing services such as ride hailing, targeted advertising, and object trackers.

We first outline a simple conceptual framework that helps formalize the ideas embodied in the earlier examples. In our model, technological advances (modeled as quality improvements) in a given sector depend upon simultaneous improvements in the sector's supplier industries. Although advances in each upstream sector are potentially beneficial, these advances are complements, so that an imbalance among them is detrimental to further innovation. Our conceptual framework thus emphasizes that a balanced distribution of technological advances across sectors is important for the viability of further innovations. This mechanism is distinct from a standard Neoclassical channel where changes in input prices cause a sector to move along a fixed production possibility frontier. Our framework yields a simple estimating equation that links growth in sectoral TFP to both the average TFP and the dispersion (variance) of TFP among that sector's inputs. We estimate this equation using 462 manufacturing industries between 1977 and 2007 and also for the entire US economy between 1987 and 2007 by combining our manufacturing data with 42 nonmanufacturing industries.

Our estimates indicate that greater dispersion of TFP growth among an industry's suppliers exerts a powerful negative influence on its own growth opportunities. Our preferred specification suggests that doubling the variance of input-supplier TFP growth for a sector is associated with about 0.9 percentage points slower TFP growth for that sector.

We further document that, as conjectured, the dispersion of TFP growth among key industries has increased significantly over the past several decades. Our estimates suggest that this higher dispersion can, in an accounting sense, explain essentially all of the aggregate productivity slowdown in manufacturing between the 1970s and 2007. For example, our results imply that if the cross-industry dispersion of TFP growth in manufacturing had remained at the 1977–87 level, then aggregate TFP growth in manufacturing would have been slightly faster (rather than considerably slower) in 1997–2007 than in either of the previous 2 decades.

Our methodology also clarifies which sectors are major bottlenecks and singles out a number of industries—including pharmaceutical preparation, basic inorganic chemicals, electronic connectors, and surface active agents—as the leading bottlenecks. According to our results, a 20% decrease in the TFP growth of the 10 fastest-growing industries and a simultaneous increase in the TFP growth of each of the bottom 50% of industries—so as to keep average upstream TFP growth the same—would have led to 0.6 percentage points higher aggregate TFP growth in manufacturing. In addition, our estimates reveal that surgical and medical instruments, gas engines, and industrial valves are among the most consequentially bottlenecked sectors—meaning that they are large contributors to gross domestic product (GDP) but are inhibited by high TFP growth dispersion among their suppliers.

We confirm that these empirical patterns are broadly robust. They hold for the entire economy, and within the manufacturing sector (where TFP is better measured), they are present in weighted and unweighted specifications, in different subperiods, with varying additional controls, and with alternative measures of productivity dispersion. We also verify that these patterns are not driven by outliers, nor are they exclusively due to the rapid advances in computers and electronics sectors (though these sectors do play a central role in our results).

There is an obvious endogeneity concern in the results we present: technological trends or productivity shocks may affect supplier and customer sectors simultaneously, which could cause us to conflate the impact of sectoral linkages with correlated shocks. As a partial remedy to this threat, we exploit international (non-US) technological opportunities as an external source of identification for the variance of supplier TFP growth and obtain very similar results. We also document that it is the contemporaneous dispersion of TFP among suppliers, not the future dispersion, that predicts an industry's own TFP growth.

Another important concern relates to whether these results could be driven by relative price effects that change input intensity (e.g., less innovative inputs become more expensive and are used less intensively).[4] We show that this is unlikely to be the case. For one, we document that our results are driven by TFP, not by quantities and prices. More important, we document a similar relationship in patents: sectors with greater patenting variance across "idea suppliers" are less likely to patent themselves.[5] We also establish the same relationship at the firm level: firms facing greater variance of patenting activity across the patent classes that they cite are less likely to patent themselves.

Finally, we document analogous patterns using international data and establish that dispersion in productivity among key domestic and international supplier industries has also been a major impediment to productivity growth for several leading OECD economies.

We view our results as suggestive of a potentially important linkage between (endogenous) productivity bottlenecks and productivity growth. Although further work is needed to test whether unbalanced sectoral innovation is indeed constraining aggregate productivity growth, our evidence raises the possibility of a more nuanced explanation for the productivity slowdown experienced by industrialized nations than is available in current literature. Our analysis further suggests that, following major breakthroughs in sectors acting as bottlenecks, there should be an acceleration of both industry and aggregate productivity growth.

A conceptual issue raised by our paper is whether the dispersion of productivity growth across sectors is inefficiently unbalanced. High dispersion may result either from evolving technological opportunities or from inefficient allocation of research effort across industries. Our strategy is not geared toward identifying which allocation would be most efficient. Nevertheless, our evidence indicates that a more balanced trajectory of technological change would generate substantial aggregate gains.

Our paper is related to a small but growing literature on the causes of the productivity slowdown. Alongside the views that productivity growth is high but mismeasured or, alternatively, that good ideas are becoming increasingly scarce, several other perspectives may help to explain the productivity slowdown.[6] First, and most closely related to our work, several authors have argued that productivity growth from new technologies, especially from new general-purpose technologies, tends to lag the underlying breakthroughs substantially because the relevant sectors only slowly discover how to harness new technological capabilities. This idea was first proposed in the economics literature by David

(1990) in the context of the effects of the electrification of American industry, which David argued took place after considerable delays. It was further elaborated by Bresnahan and Trajtenberg (1995) and Helpman and Trajtenberg (1996), who proposed mechanisms for the slow emergence of productivity gains from general-purpose technologies. Closer still to our hypothesis, Brynjolfsson, Rock, and Syverson (2021) argue that productivity gains from AI and other digital technologies will trace a J-shaped curve because complementary investments and capabilities will take time to develop. Our approach, emphasizing that imbalanced innovation across sectors will act as a bottleneck, provides a specific mechanism for extensive delays in the realization of productivity gains from new technologies and platforms. Differently from these works, our paper emphasizes how the extent and duration of the productivity slowdown depend on the sectoral imbalance of innovation and the speed with which breakthroughs can take place in lagging sectors—rather than just slow adjustment in general-purpose technologies.

Second, Andrews, Criscuolo, and Gal (2016) provide evidence suggesting that, although leading firms have continued to experience steadily growing productivity, much of the aggregate productivity slowdown is related to the poor productivity performance of nonleader firms across various sectors and countries. Several other works have emphasized specific market imperfections or failures as contributing to the productivity slowdown. These include barriers to innovation and entrepreneurship (Decker et al. 2017; Aghion et al. 2019; Akcigit and Ates 2019); overinvestment in automation (Acemoglu and Restrepo 2019); insufficient government investment in research and development (Gruber and Johnson 2019); and patent rent-seeking by so-called nonpracticing entities ("trolls"), which discourages further innovation (Cohen, Gurun, and Kominers 2016). Our explanation is complementary to these ideas but distinct in its focus on productivity interactions across sectors rather than on sector-specific or aggregate factors.

Conceptually, our framework builds on models of input-output (IO) and idea linkages. Acemoglu and Azar (2020) provide a framework where innovation depends on the endogenous combinations of inputs a sector uses. Our approach here is related but emphasizes that innovation depends on the advancement of (and the balance across) the set of exogenously specified inputs. Our framework also relates to the motivating model in Acemoglu, Akcigit, and Kerr (2016), where patenting activity in a sector depends on the number of patents in "upstream" sectors that the given sector typically cites, and to the more detailed investigation of differential knowledge flows over the ideas/citation network in the recent work by Liu and Ma (2021). The key distinction between our approach and prior work is our focus on the drag that dispersion across sectors imposes on aggregate innovation and productivity growth.

The rest of the paper is organized as follows. Section II presents a motivating conceptual framework that will guide our empirical exploration. Section III overviews our data sources. Section IV presents our main results, focusing on the variance of supplier TFP growth as the measure of sectoral imbalance of innovation. This section also draws out the quantitative implications of our estimates and establishes their robustness. Section V provides several pieces of evidence that support our claim that the variance of supplier TFP growth captures the effects of imbalanced innovation across sectors. Section VI presents analogous results for a cross-country panel, and Section VII concludes. Additional information on our data, industry correspondences, and robustness checks are presented in the online appendix, http://www.nber.org/data-appendix/c14854/appendix.pdf.

II. Model

In this section, we provide a motivating conceptual framework, which will then be used to derive our estimating equations.

A. Basic Setup

Our starting point is the idea that new product or quality innovations in a sector depend on improvements in the quality of the inputs that they use—a point emphasized by our case studies of technological bottlenecks in the introduction. To develop this idea with minimal complexity, we consider a framework that borrows elements from existing models of IO linkages (e.g., Long and Plosser 1983; Acemoglu et al. 2012; and especially Acemoglu and Azar 2020) and also from canonical quality-ladder models (e.g., Grossman and Helpman 1991; Aghion and Howitt 1992).

Suppose that there are N sectors, denoted by $i = 1, 2, \ldots, N$. Assume also that the production function of sector i at time t is

$$Y_{it} = B_i A_{it} L_{it}^{1-\sum_{j \in S_i} \alpha_{ij}} \prod_{j \in S_i} X_{ijt}^{\alpha_{ij}}. \tag{1}$$

Here, Y_{it} denotes the output of sector i at time t, A_{it} is the productivity of this sector at time t, and B_i is a normalizing constant.[7] In addition, each sector uses labor, L_{it}, and inputs that are necessary for production, X_{ijt}, which are those in the time-invariant set S_i.[8] For simplicity, these inputs are assumed to be combined with a constant returns to scale Cobb-Douglas technology, where α_{ij} are input shares and $1 - \Sigma_{j\in S_i}\alpha_{ij}$ is the share of labor in production.

We model technological improvements by using a quality-ladder structure. In particular, we assume that $A_{jt} = \lambda^{n_{jt}}$, where $\lambda > 1$ and n_{jt} are the number of innovations this sector has experienced in the past. Each innovation, therefore, increases productivity by a factor of λ.

Our critical assumption is that the arrival rate of innovations depends on the distribution of input technologies that the sector uses:

$$\phi_{it} = H\left(\sum_{j\in S_i}\alpha_{ij}h(A_{jt})\right), \tag{2}$$

where ϕ_{it} denotes the arrival rate of innovations at time t, h and H are monotone continuous functions, and we normalize $H(0) = 0$.[9] Different choices for these functions give different relationships between the distribution of a sector's input quality and its innovation propensity. For example, we could take $h(x) = x^\rho$ and $H(x) = x^{1/\rho}$ to obtain a constant elasticity of substitution (CES) aggregator. Particularly important in this context is whether the function h in equation (2) is convex or concave. The former indicates that innovation in each sector is determined by its most advanced inputs, which means that innovations across input sectors are substitutes, implying that greater (mean-preserving) dispersion of technological know-how across inputs helps innovation. Alternatively, the concave case arises when innovations across different input sectors are complements, so that greater (mean-preserving) dispersion hinders innovation. We consider the concave case to be empirically relevant because it captures the intuitive idea, highlighted by the case studies in the introduction, that new product and quality improvements require simultaneous improvements in a range of inputs, and that if some of the relevant inputs fall behind, they will act as a bottleneck, slowing technological progress.[10] In both the convex and the concave cases, because h and H are monotone, a higher level of technology for any input always helps innovation in the sector in question.

A second-order Taylor expansion of the right-hand side of equation (2) around its mean gives

$$\phi_{it} \approx H\left[\alpha_{ij}h(\bar{A}_{it}) + h''(\bar{A}_{it})\text{var}(\{\alpha_{ij}A_{jt}\}_{j\in S_i})\right],$$

where $\bar{A}_{it} \equiv \Sigma_{j\in S_i}\alpha_{ij}A_{jt}$ is the (cost-share weighted) mean of the productivities of the inputs to sector i, and $\text{var}(\{\alpha_{ij}A_{jt}\}_{j\in S_i})$ is the (weighted) variance of those productivities. Next, taking a first-order expansion of H around 0 and also approximating $h(\bar{A}_{it})$ by $h'(\bar{A}_{it})\bar{A}_{it}$ gives

$$\phi_{it} \approx \eta^i_{\text{mean}}\bar{A}_{it} + \eta^i_{\text{variance}}\text{var}(\{\alpha_{ij}A_{jt}\}_{j\in S_i}), \tag{3}$$

where $\eta^i_{\text{mean}} \equiv H'(0)h'(\bar{A}_{it})$ represents the effect of the mean productivity of the technological advances across inputs, which we always control for in our empirical work, while $\eta^i_{\text{variance}} \equiv H'(0)h''(\bar{A}_{it})$ captures the effect of dispersion across inputs (holding the mean constant). Equation (3) will be the basis of our empirical work. The estimates of the parameter η_{variance} will show whether, in terms of our framework, the function h is convex or concave. This coefficient will also indicate the extent to which the imbalance of innovations across key input sectors in the economy may hold down aggregate productivity growth.[11]

To illustrate this point succinctly, suppose that $S_i = S$ for all i and some $S \subset \{1, \dots, N\}$ and that $\alpha_{ij} = \alpha_j$ for all i and $j \in S$. Suppose also that h is concave, so that $\eta_{\text{variance}} \equiv H'(0)h''(\bar{A}_t) < 0$, and we start with $A_{jt} = \bar{A}_t$ for all $j \in S$. Then, consider a mean-preserving spread of the A_{jt}'s so that the weighted variance, $\text{var}(\{\alpha_{ij}A_{jt}\}_{j\in S_i})$, is given by σ^2. Equation (3) implies that the aggregate productivity of the economy will be reduced by $\eta_{\text{variance}}\sigma^2$. So, if σ^2 and η_{variance} are both large, there will be a sizable negative impact on aggregate productivity.[12]

B. Endogenous Innovation Effort

It is straightforward to endogenize innovation and characterize the general equilibrium.[13] Although endogenous innovation does not play an important role in our empirical work, it is nevertheless useful to consider it to motivate our later discussion of potential inefficiencies from unbalanced innovative efforts. We add this channel to the model by modifying equation (2) to

$$\phi_{it} = \frac{1}{\gamma} H\left(\sum_{j\in S_i}\alpha_{ij}h(A_{jt})\right)^{1-\gamma} z_{it}^\gamma, \tag{4}$$

where $\gamma \in (0, 1)$ and z_{it} is research effort devoted to innovation in industry i at time t (e.g., overall research spending or research-related resource use, such as scientific effort). This specification implies that there are intratemporal diminishing returns to research effort in a given field, which could arise from crowding out when multiple researchers simultaneously pursue similar ideas. We include $1/\gamma$ as a constant in front of the H function, for simplicity. Note also that the H function here represents a pure knowledge externality, and thus the fact that sector i builds on the industries in the set S_i does not generate additional profits for these industries.

Suppose also that the per unit cost of research in industry i is κ_i, and the reward to an innovation in the sector at time t is π_{it}. The cost κ_i depends on the opportunity cost of research-related resources in nonresearch activities and may also include sector-specific distortions, as well as misperceptions or fads among researchers (i.e., motivations of researchers to pursue a particular field beyond its social value). We interpret the reward π_{it} as a market outcome determined by prices, market sizes, and markups (though here also, fads and misperceptions may affect rewards as well).

Given this setup, privately optimal research effort devoted to sector i at time t will be

$$z_{it}^* = \left(\frac{\pi_{it}}{\kappa_i}\right)^{\frac{1}{1-\gamma}} H\left(\sum_{j\in S_i} \alpha_{ij} h(A_{jt})\right),$$

and thus

$$\phi_{it}^* = \frac{1}{\gamma}\left(\frac{\pi_{it}}{\kappa_i}\right)^{\frac{\gamma}{1-\gamma}} H\left(\sum_{j\in S_i} \alpha_{ij} h(A_{jt})\right), \tag{5}$$

which is proportional to the exogenously specified success probability in equation (2). This ensures that equation (3) applies as before and highlights that whether the probability of successful innovation is endogenous or exogenous is not central for our empirical work.

Equation (5) emphasizes that, if the cost of research, κ_i, varies across sectors for reasons unrelated to the social cost of innovation in sector i, the unequal (unbalanced) rates of technological progress across sectors could be inefficient. In such a scenario, policies that reduce the dispersion of technological progress rates across sectors would improve the allocation of resources. For example, if the marginal cost of innovation were the same across sectors, a social planner could reduce dispersion without affecting the mean productivity of new innovations, thereby improving aggregate productivity (and welfare). Conversely, if differences in κ_i across sectors reflect differences in the social costs of innovation, then it may be infeasible to reduce the sectoral dispersion of technological progress without lowering mean productivity in the economy. Because we do not know where differences in the rate of innovation across sectors come from, these observations caution against drawing strong normative conclusions from the results that follow.

III.   Data Sources

The data sources that form the backbone of our paper combine time series for industry TFP growth with IO linkage data. For manufacturing industries, we use data from the National Bureau for Economic Research and Center for Economic Studies (NBER-CES) Manufacturing Industry Database.[14] These data are sourced from the Annual Survey of Manufacturers and include annual industry-level data for 1958–2011 on output, employment, input costs, investment, capital stocks, TFP, and industry-specific prices. We include 462 manufacturing industries, corresponding to six-digit North American Industry Classification System (NAICS) codes. In accordance with the literature, TFP is defined as the residual change in real output after subtracting the (cost-share weighted) change in each of five factors: capital, production labor, nonproduction labor, energy, and nonenergy materials. We supplement the manufacturing data with annual TFP estimates for 42 nonmanufacturing industries, corresponding to three-digit NAICS codes, from the Bureau of Labor Statistics (BLS) Major Sector and Major Industry TFP database 1987–2011. As with the manufacturing data, TFP outside of manufacturing is defined as the difference between real output growth and a shares-weighted combination of growth in five inputs: capital, labor, energy, materials, and purchased services.[15]

We construct IO tables using the detailed Make and Use tables provided by the US Bureau of Economic Analysis for 1977–2007, which are available every 5 years, corresponding to the years of the Economic Census. These tables provide information on the amount that each industry produces of various commodities and the amount that they spend on each commodity, respectively. From these two tables, we construct our basic IO network, $\{\alpha_{ijt}\}$, whose entries are the dollar value of inputs that industry i uses from industry j at time t relative to the dollar value of its total intermediate costs. Because each year's release of these tables uses industry coding particular to that year's classification, we convert each table to a set of time-consistent NAICS-based industry codes, the details of which are documented in the appendix, http://www.nber.org/data-appendix /c14854/appendix.pdf. Table A1 presents summary statistics across upstream (supplying) and downstream (customer) industries. Panel A shows results for only manufacturing industries 1977–2007, and panel B depicts averages for all industries 1987–2007. In the former, we see that the average 5-year TFP growth across manufacturing sectors was 1.8 percentage points. The average TFP growth of upstream manufacturing industries is substantially higher, at 3.3 percentage points, reflecting the fact that more-productive industries are used more intensely as intermediate inputs.

To explore innovation outcomes directly, we look at patent data, starting from the Fung Institute Patent Data Project at the University of California, Berkeley, which spans the years 1976–2016. These data include every patent application and patent granted by the US Patent and Trademark Office (USPTO) during this time period. Although the data do not include patents granted outside the United States, they contain patents filed at the USPTO by non-US firms. The data include classification codes, application dates, and (importantly) cross-citations to other patents. Firm names and locations are cleaned using machine learning and natural language processing (see Balsmeier et al. 2018 for additional details on the disambiguation algorithm). The patent classification codes refer to 633 unique Cooperative Patent Classification (CPC) classes. We construct a time series that tracks the total number of patents in each CPC class by application date, as well as a similar time series for the patenting activity of each firm.[16]

We also use these data to construct the CPC-level citation network (what Acemoglu et al. 2016 refer to as the "innovation network"), which represents the knowledge flows between CPC classes. Specifically, following Acemoglu et al. (2016), we calculate a citation network, γ_{cj}, whose entries are the fraction of citations to patents in CPC class j among total citations of patents in CPC class c. To achieve greater precision and remove the time-dependent measurement error problem introduced by the increasing number of patents over time, we use the average number of citations for each class over the entire sample. We exclude all within-CPC citations, meaning citations by patents in CPC c to other patents within-CPC c.

Likewise, we construct firm-level citation networks. In this case, we calculate a citation network, ω_{kc}, whose entries are the share of citations by firm-k patents (i.e., patents that belong to firm k) to the patents of other firms within the CPC class, c. We exclude all within-firm citations (i.e., citations by firm-k patents to other firm-k patents).

Last, we supplement the domestic, US data with data for select European countries. We use data on value-added and TFP from the 2012 EU KLEMS Growth and Productivity Accounts. In this exercise, we use data from 1987 to 2007 for 30 industries in Austria, Finland, France, Germany, Italy, the Netherlands, Spain, and the United Kingdom. We combine these data with country-specific IO tables from the Groningen Growth and Development Centre (GGDC) World Input-Output Database for 2000. The relevant entry in the world IO table, $\alpha_{ik,jl}$, is the share of inputs for industry i in country k that came from industry j in country l.[17] Panel C of table A1 (http://www.nber.org/data-appendix/c14854/appendix.pdf) presents the TFP growth for this sample. Overall, the average 5-year TFP growth within this sample was 4.6 percentage points. For patenting outside of the United States, we use Google Patents global patent data from Liu and Ma (2021), which contains patents from more than 40 major patent authorities around the world. Each patent is assigned to a geographical unit using the country of residence of the inventor, the country of residence of the assignee(s), and country of the patent authority, in that order. We construct the number of patents in each country in each CPC code in each year, using the date of application for each patent. We further restrict our attention to the 20 countries with the most patenting over the sample period.

IV.   Sectoral Imbalances and Productivity Growth

This section presents our main results, linking the TFP growth of an industry to the dispersion of productivity growth among its suppliers—with this dispersion representing an imbalance under our hypothesis. Concretely, we estimate a version of equation (3), derived earlier, using data on 462 six-digit NAICS-based manufacturing industries between 1977 and 2007, and 42 three-digit nonmanufacturing industries during 1987–2007. We also report the quantitative implications of these estimates and document their robustness to additional controls, different sample periods, and sources of variation in productivity growth.

A.   Main Results

Our main estimating equation is the empirical analogue of (3):

$$\Delta \text{TFP}_{it} = \beta_{\text{mean}} \sum_j \alpha_{ijt-1} \Delta \text{TFP}_{jt} + \beta_{\text{variance}} \text{VAR}(\Delta \text{TFP}_{jt})$$
$$+ \mathbf{X}'_{it-1} \beta_{\text{other}} + \delta_t + \varepsilon_{it} \tag{6}$$

where t refers to 5-year time periods, ΔTFP_{it} is the TFP growth of industry i during the 5-year time interval denoted by t,

$$\text{VAR}(\Delta\text{TFP}_{jt}) \equiv \sum_j \alpha_{ijt-1}\left(\Delta\text{TFP}_{jt} - \sum_j \alpha_{ijt-1}\Delta\text{TFP}_{jt}\right)^2,$$

and $\sum_j \alpha_{ijt-1}\Delta\text{TFP}_{jt}$ is the average TFP growth among the suppliers of industry i during the 5-year time period, calculated using the α_{ijt-1}'s as weights. Recall that α_{ijt} represents the ratio of industry i's spending on inputs from industry j relative to its total intermediate spending time t. The variance of TFP growth among the suppliers of industry i is also computed using these cost shares as weights. In addition, X'_{it-1} denotes a vector of other (predetermined) covariates, which in some specifications includes sector fixed effects, introducing sector-specific linear trends; δ_t denotes a full set of time dummies; and ε_{it} is a heteroscedastic and (potentially) serially correlated error term, capturing all omitted factors.

This equation is comparable to our model-derived equation (3), with several operational refinements. First, we use TFP growth as our primary measure of innovation because we do not have direct measures (though we will look at patenting as well). Second, instead of relating innovation to the level of technology across inputs, as in equation (3), we link TFP growth in each sector to the TFP growth rate across inputs, because the level of TFP is not well defined. Third, we have included an error term and additional covariates. Fourth, instead of the sector-specific coefficients in front of the mean and the variance in equation (3), η^i_{mean} and η^i_{variance}, we have imposed constant coefficients, which should be interpreted as local average treatment effects.

Throughout, we always control for the mean effect of supplier TFP growth, but the main coefficient of interest for our study is β_{variance}, which captures the effect of supplier TFP growth dispersion (or innovation dispersion, in the case of our patent analyses) on a sector's productivity (innovation), holding constant the mean of supplier TFP growth (innovation). We expect this coefficient to be significantly negative if, as we hypothesize, imbalances in the rates of technological progress across an industry's suppliers impose a productivity penalty on the industry.

Table 1 reports estimates of equation (6) for 462 six-digit manufacturing and 42 three-digit nonmanufacturing industries. Panel A is for manufacturing industries, where TFP estimates are more reliable and available for a longer time period. Panel B combines the manufacturing and the nonmanufacturing industries to include the full set of sectors. All models

Table 1

Relationship between Industry TFP Growth and Supplier TFP Growth

	(1)	(2)	(3)	(4)	(5)	(6)	(7)	(8)
				A. Manufacturing Only				
Input average	.425	.810	.653	.676	.255	1.096	.530	.187
	(.139)	(.130)	(.074)	(.170)	(.122)	(.372)	(.132)	(.156)
Input variance		−.744	−.912			−.617	−.624	
		(.121)	(.118)			(.255)	(.198)	
Input bottom decile				.059	.378			.367
				(.113)	(.091)			(.129)
Input top decile				−.110	−.081			−.068
				(.033)	(.032)			(.039)
Ind. fixed effects	no	no	yes	no	yes	no	yes	yes
Industry weighting	None	None	None	None	None	Nom. Sales	Nom. Sales	Nom. Sales
Observations	2,772	2,772	2,772	2,772	2,772	2,772	2,772	2,772
R^2	.108	.133	.371	.118	.361	.159	.598	.598
				B. All Industries				
Input average	.343	.915	.780	.636	.387	.708	.365	.248
	(.178)	(.161)	(.119)	(.183)	(.170)	(.399)	(.230)	(.268)
Input variance		−.905	−1.087			−.303	−.712	
		(.158)	(.191)			(.280)	(.280)	
Input bottom decile				.164	.422			.295
				(.099)	(.115)			(.190)
Input top decile				−.117	−.139			−.154
				(.034)	(.035)			(.058)
Ind. fixed effects	No	No	Yes	No	Yes	No	Yes	Yes
Industry weighting	None	None	None	None	None	Nom. Sales	Nom. Sales	Nom. Sales
Observations	2,016	2,016	2,016	2,016	2,016	2,016	2,016	2,016
R^2	.079	.102	.399	.090	.395	.033	.522	.531

Note: This table reports estimates of equation (6). The dependent variable is an industry's total factor productivity (TFP) growth in a 5-year period, and the two key right-hand-side variables are mean and variance of TFP growth among that industry's suppliers. Time dummies are included in all regressions, and industry dummies (corresponding to linear industry trends) are included in columns 3, 5, 7, and 8. Columns 1–5 report unweighted ordinary least squares regressions, and columns 6–8 use the industry's 1987 share of shipments as weights. Panel A is for manufacturing industries only 1977–2007, and panel B is for all industries 1987–2007. Industries are defined using 1997 North American Industry Classification System codes. Standard errors are clustered at the industry level.

include time fixed effects, and each specification includes an alternative with industry fixed effects, allowing each industry to have its own linear time trend in TFP. Odd-numbered columns include no covariates other than time dummies, whereas even-numbered columns also include industry fixed effects, thus allowing each industry to have its own linear time trend in TFP. The standard errors account for arbitrary heteroscedasticity and serial correlation at the industry level throughout. Our baseline regressions, shown in columns 1–5, are unweighted. We weight industries by their share of 1987 nominal sales in columns 6–8.

Column 1 shows the relationship between industry TFP growth and mean supplier (upstream) TFP growth, focusing only on the first term in equation (6). We detect a positive relationship between mean supplier TFP growth and downstream industry TFP growth. Adding the variance term in columns 2 and 3 strengthens the effect of mean supplier TFP growth and, more importantly, shows a precisely estimated and quantitatively large negative relationship between the variance of supplier TFP growth and industry TFP growth. For example, in our baseline specification, column 2 of panel A, the coefficient estimate of the variance term is -0.744 (standard error $= 0.121$). Adding linear industry trends in column 3 modestly increases this coefficient to -0.912 (standard error $= 0.118$). When we include nonmanufacturing industries in panel B, the point estimates are similar and only slightly larger. Figure 3 depicts the industry-level variation that produces these estimates. Specifically, we report binscatters for the regression model in column 2 of panel A. The left panel depicts the strong positive relationship between average supplier TFP growth and downstream industry TFP growth, and the right panel showcases the strong negative relationship between the variance of supplier TFP growth and downstream industry TFP growth.

The specification in equation (6) is a natural one, using the variance term to capture the effects from supplier TFP growth dispersion, as in our second-order approximation earlier. Nevertheless, it is useful to see whether well-performing and poorly performing supplier sectors both affect TFP growth. To investigate this question, columns 4 and 5 replace the variance term with TFP growth in the 10th and 90th percentiles of the (weighted) TFP distribution of suppliers (as we continue to control for mean supplier TFP growth). Consistent with our hypothesis, holding mean supplier TFP fixed, higher bottom-decile supplier TFP growth predicts faster own-industry TFP growth, whereas the top-decile supplier TFP growth predicts slower own-industry TFP growth

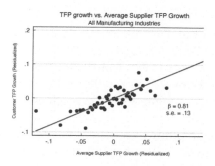 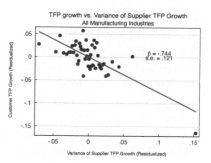

Fig. 3. Bottleneck patterns: distribution of upstream TFP growth. This figure reports binscatters (50 bins) for the regression model in table 1 from panel A, column 2 for the (conditional) relationship between manufacturing TFP growth and either the mean (left panel) or the variance (right panel) of supplier TFP growth. Specifically, the left panel plots the residuals from independent regressions of the x- and y-axis variables on the supplier variance of TFP growth, with time fixed effects. The right panel plots the residuals from independent regressions of the x- and y-axis variables on the supplier average of TFP growth, with time fixed effects. A color version of this figure is available online.

(with these relationships typically exhibiting statistical significance at the 5% level or below).

Last, columns 6 through 8 replicate our main specifications, but now using nominal industry sales in 1987 as weights. These weighted estimates are very similar to the unweighted specifications. For example, in column 6, the coefficient on the variance term is −0.617 (standard error = 0.255), which is only a little smaller than the estimate in the corresponding unweighted specification in column 2, −0.744.

Overall, the estimates in table 1 uniformly show a negative estimated impact of TFP growth dispersion across a sector's suppliers on own-industry TFP growth. In terms of our motivating conceptual framework, this suggests that productivity growth in a sector is held back when advances among its suppliers are unbalanced. In the rest of the paper, we demonstrate the robustness of these results and document a similar relationship in innovation activity. Before moving on to innovation, we draw out the quantitative implications of the productivity growth estimates in the next subsection.

B. Quantitative Implications

The results in table 1 imply that an imbalance in productivity growth across sectors could be a drag on aggregate growth. Temporarily deferring robustness checks, we explore whether such sectoral imbalances could be a quantitatively meaningful contributor to the productivity slowdown in the United States. For this to be the case, two conditions must be satisfied. First, the coefficient estimates in table 1 must be economically large. Second, the dispersion of sectoral TFP growth must have increased over the decades during which we witnessed the productivity slowdown.

Figure 4 confronts the latter issue by plotting the evolution of the variance of TFP across manufacturing industries. Panel A of figure 4 depicts the simple variance of TFP growth across all manufacturing industries, and panels B and C show the average variance of industry supplier TFP growth: for manufacturing only and for the economy overall, respectively. Both within upstream manufacturing and across all manufacturing industries, there was a striking rise in the dispersion of sectoral productivity growth in the US economy over the past several decades. This is true both overall and when weighting industries by their input share. Quantitatively, the TFP variance in manufacturing was about 0.002 before the mid-1970s and now is three times as large, around 0.006. As suggested by the patenting time series in figure 1, the electronics and computer sector accounts for a large portion of the increase in TFP variance through the 1990s. The right-hand-side plots of figure 4 document that when this sector is taken out, the rise in the variance of TFP growth is noticeably smaller—though still present—in recent decades. When we zoom out to include nonmanufacturing supplier industries, there is a similarly large increase in the variance of TFP growth from the 1980s to the present, but the pattern is not monotone, perhaps reflecting the fact that TFP is measured less reliably outside of manufacturing.

How much of the productivity slowdown can be explained by the rising variance of TFP growth? Figure 5 addresses this question by applying our (nominal sales-) weighted estimates reported in column 7 of panels A and B in table 1. We find a sizable productivity penalty from TFP growth dispersion. The estimates imply that TFP dispersion reduced manufacturing TFP growth significantly in both the 1987–97 and the 1997–2007 periods, as shown by the gray bars in the figure. If, counterfactually, input TFP variance remained at its 1977–87 value throughout the sample, then during 1987–97, instead of a 0.8 percentage point slowdown in aggregate TFP growth, we would have seen a 1.5 percentage point faster growth (as shown by the counterfactual patterned bar). Similarly, during 1997–2007, instead of the much slower 3.3% average TFP growth, the US manufacturing sector is predicted to have had only a mild TFP slowdown, to 6.5%. In

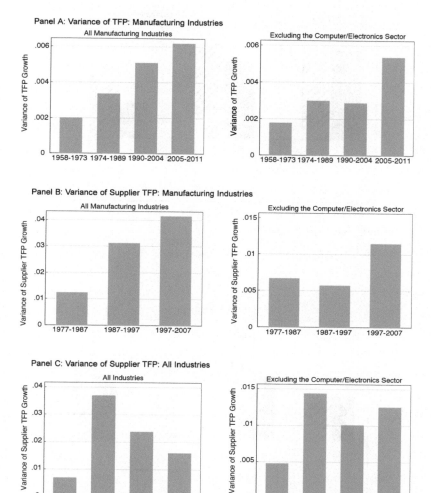

Fig. 4. Variance of total factor productivity (TFP) growth. This figure plots the variance of TFP across manufacturing industries, variance of supplier TFP across manufacturing industries, and variance of supplier TFP across all industries. Each industry observation is weighted by its share of total nominal sales. Panel *A* is for the variance of TFP growth across manufacturing industries for each 5-year period, spanning 1958–2011 (averaged into 15-year bars). Panel *B* reports the variance of supplier TFP growth across 462 six-digit North American Industry Classification System (NAICS)-based manufacturing industries, again for 1977–2007 (averaged into 10-year bars). Panel *C* reports the variance of supplier TFP growth across all industries (adding 42 three-digit nonmanufacturing industries). Figures on the right exclude the computer and electronics sector (NAICS 334). In panels *B* and *C*, the input-output network is defined at the beginning of each 5-year period. A color version of this figure is available online.

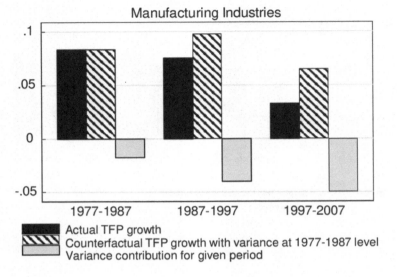

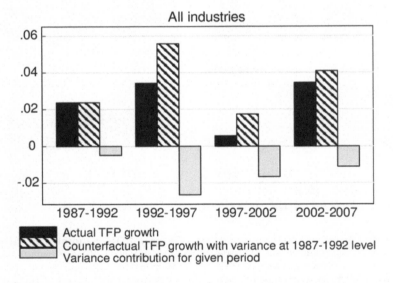

Fig. 5. Magnitude of bottleneck estimates. This figure reports actual and counterfactual total factor productivity (TFP) growth, and the contribution from supplier variance, for manufacturing and all industries for the periods 1977–87, 1987–97, and 1997–2007. The counterfactuals are based on regression estimates from the column 7 specification of table 1. Counterfactual TFP (patterned bars) is computed from the regression coefficients as the TFP growth that would have been observed in the given period if the variance of TFP growth had remained at the same level as during the initial period (1987–92). Specifically, we calculate counterfactual TFP growth by subtracting the contribution of the increase in supplier variance relative to 1977–87; the 1977–87 supplier variance is shown with the black bar, and by construction, counterfactual TFP growth in 1977–87 is equal to actual growth in this period. A color version of this figure is available online.

the lower panel of this figure, we see similar patterns for all industries. Thus, the quantitatively sizable estimates in table 1 can potentially account for the bulk of the US productivity slowdown in recent decades. We emphasize that these magnitudes are suggestive but far from definitive, given the limitations of our measurement and identification.

To provide more detailed insight into these aggregate relationships, we explored the identities of the sectors that have contributed to this quantitative effect. The variance of supplier TFP in manufacturing increased over this period both because lagging industries failed to grow and because leading industries pulled away from the rest. Panel A of table 2 lists illustrative examples of the fastest-growing industries, which are defined as those that have had the largest impact on supplier TFP variance between 1997 and 2007. These industries include electronic

Table 2
Examples of Limiting and Limited Industries

Panel A: List of Select Fastest-Growing Industries That Drive Rising TFP Variance
Semiconductor and related devices
Electronic computers
Iron and steel mills
Computer storage devices
Motor vehicle electrical and electronic equipment

Panel B: List of Select Bottleneck Industries
Petroleum refineries
Pharmaceutical preparation
Turbine and turbine generator set units
Printed circuit assembly
Basic organic chemicals

Panel C: List of Select Limited (Bottlenecked) Industries
Surgical and medical instruments
Relay and industrial controls
Gasoline engine and engine parts
Guided missile and space vehicles
Industrial valves

Note: Bottleneck industries (panel B) are defined as those for which a 10% increase in total factor productivity (TFP) would result in the largest aggregate reduction in the variance of TFP growth across all supplying industries (i.e., $VAR(\Delta TFP_{jt})$ from eq. [6]). Fastest-growing industries (panel A) are conversely defined as those for which a 10% increase in TFP would result in the smallest aggregate reduction in the variance of TFP growth across supplying industries. Limited ("bottlenecked") industries (panel C) are defined as the 50 manufacturing industries with the highest variance of TFP among suppliers, after limiting to the 100 industries with the highest value-added. Sample is restricted to 462 manufacturing industries 1997–2007. See table A2, http://www.nber.org/data-appendix/c14854/appendix.pdf, for an ordered list of the top 10 industries in each category 1997–2002 and 2002–07.

computers, computer storage devices, and semiconductors. To gauge the economic leverage of these outlier industries, consider a hypothetical mean-preserving contraction of TFP growth dispersion: reduce the TFP growth of the 10 fastest-growing industries between 1997 and 2007 by 0.2 percentage points and increase the TFP growth of each of the bottom 50% of industries just enough to keep the average TFP growth constant.[18] In this scenario, the variance of supplier TFP growth between 1997 and 2007 would have been 23% lower, and aggregate TFP growth in manufacturing would have been 0.6 percentage points higher.

The remaining panels of table 2 round out the evidence on bottleneck industries. Panel *B* reports illustrative examples of slow-growing industries that became the biggest bottlenecks over the same time period. These include pharmaceutical preparation, basic organic chemicals, printed circuit assembly, and turbine generators. Panel *C* reports example industries that are most *bottlenecked*—that is, held back by the uneven innovation across their suppliers. These include surgical and medical instruments, gas engines, and industrial valves.

C.   Endogeneity Concerns

Because the estimates in table 1 are obtained from regressions of an industry's TFP growth on the contemporaneous TFP growth of its suppliers, productivity shocks that are common across several industries might generate mechanical correlations between our right-hand-side and left-hand-side variables. In this subsection, we explore two strategies that, in net, lend support to the case that these results are informative about the effects of productivity bottlenecks.

Our first strategy is to isolate industry productivity changes that emanate from common technological developments across several advanced economies. We do this in table 3 by exploiting changes in industry TFP in major OECD countries, as reported by the 2012 EU KLEMS Growth and Productivity Accounts. For this exercise, we focus on all 504 industries (both manufacturing and nonmanufacturing), mapped to 29 EU KLEMS industries.[19] In panel *A*, we use the mean and variance of supplier TFP in France, Germany, and the United Kingdom as instruments for the corresponding variables in the United States. To purge measurement error in these instruments, panel *B* uses the rank of TFP growth by industry within-country. In both panels, columns 1 and 2 present the baseline ordinary least squares (OLS) results, and columns 3 and 4 depict two-stage least squares (2SLS) estimates.

Table 3
Country-Specific Instruments

	OLS Estimates		IV Estimates			
	(1)	(2)	(3)	(4)	(5)	(6)
	A. Average TFP Growth					
Upstream average	.951	.780	1.369	1.416	1.387	1.509
	(.232)	(.119)	(.363)	(.655)	(.378)	(.758)
Upstream variance	−.876	−1.066	−.902	−.887	−.897	−.795
	(.155)	(.135)	(.385)	(.527)	(.391)	(.588)
Estimate	OLS	OLS	2SLS	2SLS	LIML	LIML
Ind. fixed effects	No	Yes	No	Yes	No	Yes
Observations	2,478	2,478	2,478	2,478	2,478	2,478
R^2	0	0	0	0	0	0
First-stage F-stat			1.38	.63	1.38	.63
	B. Rank of TFP Growth					
Upstream average	.951	.780	.928	1.093	.928	1.094
	(.232)	(.119)	(.338)	(.348)	(.342)	(.349)
Upstream variance	−.876	−1.066	−.667	−1.480	−.664	−1.482
	(.155)	(.135)	(.445)	(.661)	(.449)	(.665)
Estimate	OLS	OLS	2SLS	2SLS	LIML	LIML
Ind. fixed effects	No	Yes	No	Yes	No	Yes
Observations	2,478	2,478	2,478	2,478	2,478	2,478
R^2	0	0	0	0	0	0
First-stage F-stat			.8	2.1	.8	2.1

Notes: This table reports instrumental-variables (IV) estimates of equation (6) for all industries 1982–2007. The dependent variable is an industry's total factor productivity (TFP)
growth in a 5-year period, and the two key right-hand-side variables are mean and variance
of TFP growth among that industry's suppliers. Excluded instruments are mean and variance of supplier TFP growth in France, Germany, and the United Kingdom. All columns
report unweighted regressions. Time dummies are included in all columns, and industry
dummies (corresponding to linear industry trends) are included in even-numbered columns. Columns 3 and 4 report two-stage least squares (2SLS) estimates, and columns 5
and 6 report limited information maximum likelihood (LIML) estimates. Panel A defines
the upstream moments, taking the average and variance of TFP growth across industries.
In panel B, we rank industries in each country according to their TFP growth and calculate
the input-share weighted average and variance of TFP ranks. Standard errors are clustered
at the aggregated KLEMS industry level. OLS = ordinary least squares.

The first-stage F-statistics are given at the bottom of panels A and B in
table 3; these are somewhat low in both panels (the full first stages are
reported in table A8, http://www.nber.org/data-appendix/c14854
/appendix.pdf). This motivates the limited information maximum likelihood (LIML) estimates presented in columns 5 and 6, which are consistent even in the presence of weak instruments. These estimates confirm
that our findings are not driven by weak instruments.

The instrumental-variables (IV) estimates of the relationship between industry TFP growth and supplier TFP mean and variance correspond closely to our earlier OLS estimates. In both panels, the OLS and IV estimates are very similar across columns 1–2 and 3–4. For example, in columns 1 and 3 of panel *A*, which do not include industry fixed effects, the OLS coefficient on the variance term is -0.876 (standard error $= 0.155$), and the IV estimate for the same variable in the same specification is -0.902 (standard error $= 0.385$). The variance term estimates are also quite close in columns 2 and 4, where we add industry fixed effects. We see a similar pattern in panel *B* when we exploit the variation in the rank of TFP growth: -0.667 (standard error $= 0.445$) for the IV estimate without industry fixed effects in column 3 and -1.480 (standard error $= 0.661$) for the IV estimate with industry fixed effects in column 4. The LIML estimates in columns 5 and 6 are also comparable. For example, in panel *B*, the variance term's coefficient estimate is -1.482 (standard error $= 0.665$) with industry fixed effects—similar to the 2SLS estimates in column 4 and the OLS estimates in column 2.

The congruence between the baseline OLS estimates and the IV estimates that exploit TFP changes in other leading economies bolsters our confidence that these results are not driven by shocks that are common across US industries and their suppliers. We also note that because the IV coefficient estimates are similar to the OLS estimates from table 1, the implied quantitative magnitudes are comparable as well.

Panel *A* of table 4 explores whether there is a correlation between future average and variance of TFP across suppliers and an industry's current TFP growth. Such a relationship would be concerning for the interpretation of productivity bottlenecks as a constraint on TFP growth. Across the eight columns (the first four for manufacturing industries and the last four for all industries), we do not see any evidence that future variance of TFP growth of suppliers has a negative relationship with current TFP growth of an industry. When we focus on all industries and look at the relationship between future variance and current TFP growth, the correlation is positive, but it disappears when we include our main regressors, contemporaneous average and variance of TFP across suppliers. It is also zero across all specifications for manufacturing industries. This pattern is reassuring for our overall interpretation.

Panel *B* of the same table explores whether a similar relationship exists between the variance of TFP growth among an industry's customers and its own TFP growth. Such a correlation is a distinct possibility, because many industries have customers and suppliers that are overlapping.

The general pattern is that customer variance is also negatively correlated with an industry's TFP growth, but typically only when it is entered by itself (without the variance of TFP among input suppliers). When both sets of variables are included, the coefficient on customer variance becomes less significant and smaller, whereas the variance of TFP across input suppliers remains negative and significant. This pattern is broadly supportive of our overall interpretation, even if it raises the possibility that in some specifications, there is a high enough correlation between downstream and upstream variances that we cannot rule out additional effects working from customers' TFP growth.

Panel C of table 4 investigates whether mean-reversion dynamics may be confounding our estimates. In particular, if TFP growth is serially correlated, then failing to account for this could lead to a spurious

Table 4
Relationship between Industry TFP Growth and the Distribution of TFP Growth

	Manufacturing Industries				All Industries			
	(1)	(2)	(3)	(4)	(5)	(6)	(7)	(8)
	A. Future Supplier TFP Growth							
Future input average	.166	.154	−.006	.083	−.003	.016	−.171	−.063
	(.145)	(.123)	(.079)	(.077)	(.178)	(.168)	(.110)	(.104)
Future input variance	.065	.011	−.010	−.066	.244	.239	.343	.149
	(.098)	(.120)	(.101)	(.103)	(.133)	(.156)	(.158)	(.146)
Input average		.787		.670		.867		.752
		(.121)		(.076)		(.158)		(.116)
Input variance		−.810		−.919		−.982		−1.061
		(.124)		(.122)		(.163)		(.186)
Ind. fixed effects	No	No	Yes	Yes	No	No	Yes	Yes
Industry weighting	None	None	None	None	None	None	None	None
Observations	2,772	2,772	2,772	2,772	2,016	2,016	2,016	2,016
R^2	.085	.137	.334	.371	.073	.106	.375	.399
	B. Customer TFP Growth							
Customer average	.626	.499	.499	.367	.460	.344	.383	.280
	(.066)	(.066)	(.074)	(.078)	(.077)	(.078)	(.102)	(.099)
Customer variance	−.503	−.302	−.796	−.529	−.443	−.264	−.907	−.662
	(.200)	(.236)	(.161)	(.151)	(.257)	(.314)	(.265)	(.254)
Input average		.466		.454		.765		.687
		(.123)		(.083)		(.173)		(.122)
Input variance		−.566		−.634		−.778		−.784
		(.127)		(.125)		(.178)		(.201)
Ind. fixed effects	No	No	Yes	Yes	No	No	Yes	Yes
Industry weighting	None	None	None	None	None	None	None	None
Observations	2,769	2,769	2,769	2,769	2,015	2,015	2,015	2,015
R^2	.157	.173	.373	.387	.093	.115	.393	.408

Table 4
(Continued)

	Manufacturing Industries				All Industries			
	(1)	(2)	(3)	(4)	(5)	(6)	(7)	(8)
	C. Lagged TFP Growth: Dependent Variable and Supplier Metrics							
Input average	.641	.637	.509	.530	.915	.921	.724	.744
	(.101)	(.097)	(.077)	(.081)	(.151)	(.153)	(.117)	(.121)
Input variance	−.678	−.715	−.753	−.776	−.923	−.939	−.889	−1.014
	(.111)	(.112)	(.121)	(.126)	(.152)	(.163)	(.173)	(.183)
Lagged input average		.056		.208		.069		.330
		(.110)		(.085)		(.137)		(.112)
Lagged input variance		.015		−.471		−.049		−.793
		(.146)		(.130)		(.195)		(.177)
Lagged dep. var.	.089	.086	−.255	−.280	.070	.066	−.362	−.391
	(.099)	(.103)	(.042)	(.045)	(.115)	(.122)	(.045)	(.050)
Ind. fixed effects	No	No	Yes	Yes	No	No	Yes	Yes
Industry weighting	None	None	None	None	None	None	None	None
Observations	2,310	2,310	2,310	2,310	1,974	1,974	1,974	1,974
R^2	.129	.130	.418	.425	.107	.108	.464	.476

Note: This table reports estimates of equation (6). The dependent variable is an industry's total factor productivity (TFP) growth in a 5-year period, and the right-hand-side variables are mean and variance of TFP growth among that industry's suppliers, plus lead terms, mean, and variance of TFP growth among the industry's customers, and lagged dependent variables. Time dummies are included in all regressions, and industry dummies (corresponding to linear industry trends) are included in columns 3, 4, 7, and 8. Columns 1–4 are for manufacturing industries 1977–2007 and columns 5–8 for all industries 1987–2007. All columns report unweighted ordinary least squares regressions. In addition to the mean and variance of TFP growth among an industry's suppliers, panel A includes the 5-year lead of the same variables. Panel B includes the mean and variance of TFP growth among the industry's customers. Panel C includes the 5-year lagged mean and variance of TFP growth among the industry's suppliers and the lag of the dependent variable (the industry's TFP growth rate). Standard errors are clustered at the industry level.

relationship between supplier TFP variance and own TFP growth. Panel C addresses this issue by including the lag of own TFP growth, as well as lagged input average and variance terms (in some specifications). Overall the results prove quite robust, and the statistical significance and quantitative impact of the input variance term are hardly affected. For example, in specifications that include only the lagged dependent variable, the input variance has a coefficient of −0.747 (standard error = 0.115) for manufacturing industries and −0.923 (standard error = 0.152) for all industries, similar to our baseline findings in table 1 in both cases. The estimates are again similar when we include lagged input average and variance terms.

D.   Robustness

Table 5 further investigates the robustness of our results to a battery of controls and specifications. For brevity, we focus on the manufacturing sample and report analogous results for all industries in the appendix (see table A7, http://www.nber.org/data-appendix/c14854/appendix .pdf). Panel A documents robustness for the specification without industry fixed effects, and panel B includes industry fixed effects that allow for linear trends in industry TFP.

For ease of reference, columns 1 and 2 report our unweighted and (nominal sales-) weighted specifications from table 1, which include only the mean and the variance of TFP as well as time dummies. The rest of the table focuses on our unweighted specification. Column 3 estimates the same models but now using 10-year periods rather than the 5-year intervals in table 1. This specification purges higher-frequency variation in TFP and focuses on longer-term variation. The results from these models are similar to the baseline estimates.

Our estimating equation (3) defines sectors that are falling behind as those that have relatively slow TFP growth in the contemporaneous 5-year period. However, if high variance in the current period reflects mean reversion following rapid growth in the recent past, this would not correspond to an imbalance but rather to a potential rebalancing. Column 4 checks this possibility by adding the covariance between the supplier TFP growth in the current and the prior periods to our specification.[20] Intuitively, this covariance term accounts for potential persistence and reversal patterns in industry-level TFP changes. We find that the covariance of TFP across periods does not meaningfully affect the relationship of primary interest. The coefficient on the variance term in panel A is only slightly larger, -0.640 (standard error $= 0.127$), and the covariance term is relatively small and imprecisely estimated. The estimate on the covariance term is larger and statistically significant in panel B, but the coefficient on the variance of upstream TFP growth remains unaffected by the inclusion of this covariance term. We infer from these results that the first and second moments of the upstream TFP distribution provide informative measures of sectoral imbalances.

The subsequent columns of table 5 provide additional robustness checks. Another factor that could affect measured industry TFP is changing import penetration. Column 5 controls for average imports from China by other countries in the industry and in the input-weighted average of the supplying industries (from Autor, Dorn, and Hanson

Table 5
Robustness for Downstream TFP and Upstream TFP: Manufacturing Industries

	Baseline	Weighted	10-Year	Cov.	China Shock	No Comp.	Outlier Robust	Fixed IO	All Inputs	3-Digit Leaveout
	(1)	(2)	(3)	(4)	(5)	(6)	(7)	(8)	(9)	(10)
					A. Without Industry Trends					
Input average	.810	1.096	.931	.660	.565	.560	.592	.878	1.154	.076
	(.130)	(.372)	(.182)	(.116)	(.123)	(.066)	(.043)	(.115)	(.163)	(.106)
Input variance	-.744	-.617	-.477	-.640	-.724	-1.231	-.774	-.711	-.903	-.360
	(.121)	(.255)	(.094)	(.127)	(.113)	(.587)	(.059)	(.161)	(.171)	(.120)
Input covariance				-.069						
				(.170)						
Observations	2,772	2,772	1,386	2,310	1,386	2,604	2,772	2,772	2,772	2,772
R^2	.133	.159	.100	.123	.126	.122	.208	.153	.147	.080

					B. With Industry Trends					
Input average	.653	.530	.704	.482	.502	.652	.597	.716	.968	.231
	(.074)	(.132)	(.122)	(.074)	(.100)	(.072)	(.048)	(.071)	(.097)	(.099)
Input variance	−.912	−.624	−.641	−.647	−.820	−1.197	−.757	−.961	−1.149	−.449
	(.118)	(.198)	(.107)	(.131)	(.146)	(.624)	(.068)	(.139)	(.163)	(.155)
Input covariance				−.399						
				(.143)						
Observations	2,772	2,772	1,386	2,310	1,386	2,604	2,772	2,772	2,772	2,772
R^2	.371	.598	.549	.385	.472	.252	.487	.379	.378	.338

Note: This table reports estimates of equation (6) for manufacturing industries 1977–2007. The dependent variable is an industry's total factor productivity (TFP) growth in a 5-year period, and the right-hand-side variables are mean and variance of TFP growth among that industry's suppliers plus additional controls. Time dummies are included in all regressions. Panel B also includes industry dummies (corresponding to linear industry trends). Column 1 repeats our baseline regression from column 2 of table 1. Column 2 weights observations by the industry's share of 1987 shipments. Column 3 uses 10-year observations. Column 4 controls for the covariance between the supplier TFP growth in the current and the prior 5-year periods. Column 5 controls for the China shock, following Autor et al. (2013). Column 6 excludes the computers and electronics manufacturing sector (NAICS 334) from the regression sample and from the construction of the average and variance of TFP growth among suppliers. Column 7 runs an outlier-robust regression (rreg). Column 8 fixes the input-output (IO) table at 1987. Column 9 defines the IO network to use the share among all inputs instead of among intermediaries. Column 10 excludes the industry's own three-digit North American Industry Classification System (NAICS) code when constructing the IO network.

183

2013), addressing the concern that Chinese import penetration may itself affect productivity growth (e.g., Autor et al. 2020). Accounting for imports does not appreciably change the coefficient on supplier TFP variance.[21]

We noted the importance of the electronics and computer sectors earlier. Column 6 confirms that the negative relationship between industry TFP growth and supplier TFP dispersion holds even when computers and electronics manufacturing (NAICS 334) is excluded from the estimation sample as well as from the calculation of upstream metrics. With these key sectors excluded, the variance term is less precisely estimated, as expected. Nevertheless, it remains statistically significant at the 5% level or below in all of our specifications: -1.231 (standard error $=$ 0.587) in panel A and -1.197 (standard error $= 0.624$) in panel B. These estimates reveal that our hypothesized mechanism is present even when the ICT and electronics sectors are excluded, but also that the ICT and electronics sectors showcase our mechanism and contribute substantially to its identification and quantitative implications (as corroborated by the examples in table 2).

Column 7 shows a similar relationship to our baseline results when we estimate a robust regression that downweights outliers that have a major effect on the slope of the relationship between upstream TFP variance and downstream TFP growth. Notice that in this case, the standard error of the input variance term is much smaller, highlighting that outliers were, indeed, reducing the precision of our estimates, though not affecting their magnitudes much.

Column 8 confirms that the results are again similar when we use a fixed IO matrix, rather than the time-varying IO matrix from our baseline specification. Column 9 probes robustness to our definition of input shares. Here, we define upstream shares, α_{ijt-1}, as total-cost shares rather than as intermediate-cost shares (as in our baseline specification). These two share measures will differ to the extent that the intermediate share of total costs varies across sectors. The results are once again very similar. Finally, column 10 excludes own three-digit industry when constructing the IO network. This does change the magnitude of the coefficient estimates but not their signs or statistical significance. Table A7 (http://www.nber.org/data-appendix/c14854/appendix.pdf) shows analogous estimates for the entire economy, rather than just the manufacturing sector. These results are again similar to our baseline estimates.

Because our empirical analysis is confined to the 462 manufacturing (or the 504 total) industries, our estimates will not capture any imbalances in innovation or productivity growth that happens at more-disaggregated levels. To explore whether these more-micro imbalances may also matter, and to further probe the robustness of our results, in the appendix we use estimates of within-industry, across-establishment TFP growth from the US Census Bureau's Dispersion Statistics on Productivity. These measures of dispersion have also increased during our sample period, but table A3 documents that the average upstream TFP growth dispersion among input suppliers, when added to our regression, is not statistically significant and does not change the relationship between our measure of supplier TFP growth dispersion and own TFP growth.

A final concern is that TFP growth estimates from the NBER-CES manufacturing data do not allow for fully subtracting the contribution of intermediate inputs, and this might be one reason why they are lower than estimates at more-aggregated levels that incorporate such corrections. To verify that this aspect of the data is not responsible for our results, in tables A4–A6 we repeat our main analysis (in particular, the regression models and tables 1–4) using an adjusted TFP series. This series is computed using factor shares for each disaggregated industry that are adjusted by a factor calculated to equate the factor shares at the three-digit industry level in the NBER-CES data with those in the National Income and Product Accounts data. We apply the same factor to all disaggregated industries in our data that belong to the same three-digit industry.[22] These results show very similar patterns to our main estimates.

In summary, these results confirm that the negative relationship between industry TFP growth and supplier TFP variance is statistically significant, pervasive, and largely unaffected by the inclusion of a variety of potential confounders.

E.   Prices, Quantities, and Productivity

Could these patterns be explained by mismeasurement of TFP? In a standard Neoclassical setting, industries benefit when the productivity of their suppliers increases because this reduces input costs (e.g., Acemoglu et al. 2012). If TFP is measured correctly, it will be unaffected by fluctuations in employment, demand factors, and input costs that induce industries to move along (rather than changing) their production possibility frontiers. If TFP is mismeasured, however, these Neoclassical effects could erroneously spill over to TFP estimates. If, in addition, elasticities of substitution between inputs are nonunitary, as explored in Atalay (2017) and Baqaee and Farhi (2019), changes in sectoral production may affect our TFP estimates and confound our results.

We investigate the role of these Neoclassical channels in table 6. Because these Neoclassical effects work through sectoral prices or through output changes that affect sectoral outputs and prices, we do this by adding the mean and variance of supplier prices and employment levels to our baseline regressions.[23] For comparison, columns 1 and 2 restate our baseline estimates. The alternative specifications in columns 3–8 indicate that controlling for these Neoclassical channels does not qualitatively change the relationship between supplier TFP variance and industry TFP growth (and that the coefficients on these channel variables are typically insignificant). For example, when we include the mean and variance of supplier prices in column 3 (without industry fixed effects), the TFP variance term has a coefficient of -0.686 (standard error $= 0.232$), which is 90% of the baseline estimate, though less precisely estimated. When we include the mean and variance of supplier employment levels

Table 6
Exploring Neoclassical Effects

	Baseline		Prices		Employment		Combined	
	(1)	(2)	(3)	(4)	(5)	(6)	(7)	(8)
Input TFP average	.810	.653	.815	.692	.720	.497	.602	.436
	(.130)	(.074)	(.113)	(.083)	(.134)	(.075)	(.107)	(.089)
Input TFP variance	−.744	−.912	−.686	−.527	−.703	−.786	−.655	−.424
	(.121)	(.118)	(.232)	(.243)	(.118)	(.115)	(.233)	(.245)
Input price average			.006	.077			−.141	−.069
			(.085)	(.061)			(.091)	(.065)
Input price variance			−.051	−.329			−.123	−.381
			(.204)	(.198)			(.201)	(.201)
Input employment average					.224	.244	.264	.262
					(.045)	(.056)	(.051)	(.062)
Input employment variance					.166	−.106	.117	−.213
					(.219)	(.235)	(.218)	(.246)
Ind. fixed effects	No	Yes	No	Yes	No	Yes	No	Yes
Observations	2,772	2,772	2,772	2,772	2,772	2,772	2,772	2,772
R^2	.133	.371	.133	.373	.149	.384	.152	.387

Note: This table reports estimates of equation (6) for manufacturing industries 1977–2007. The dependent variable is an industry's total factor productivity (TFP) growth in a 5-year period, and the right-hand-side variables are mean and variance of TFP growth among that industry's suppliers plus the mean and variance of supplier prices and employment. Time dummies are included in all regressions, and industry dummies (corresponding to linear industry trends) are included in even-numbered columns. All columns report unweighted ordinary least squares regressions. Industries are defined using 1997 North American Industry Classification System codes. Standard errors are clustered at the industry level.

in column 5 (also without industry fixed effects), the coefficient estimate on TFP variance is -0.703 (standard error $= 0.118$), which is nearly identical to the baseline estimates in column 1. The results remain similar when we include both sets of variables (prices and employment) together. When we include industry fixed effects, the estimates are once again similar to our baseline results.

The evidence in table 6 suggests that the relationship between supplier TFP and industry TFP is not a reflection of (potentially mismeasured) Neoclassical effects. Instead, the evidence suggests that it captures economic effects that work through the innovation or product-quality mechanism identified by our model. We next offer more direct evidence on this mechanism.

V.   Innovation

This section investigates whether innovation, as encoded in patents, is one of the underlying mechanisms that could explain our results. For this exercise, we replace the IO network (comprised of α_{ijt} entries) with the patent citation network (corresponding to the γ_{cj}'s capturing citation patterns across CPCs). Our sectoral analysis starts at the CPC level, but we also consider firm-level results later in this section. The main question explored in this section is whether a greater imbalance of innovation across upstream sectors or firms ("idea suppliers") reduces the innovation of a downstream sector or firm. We will see that the answer to this question is a strong yes.[24]

A.   CPC-Level Results

We begin the analysis at the patent-class level and estimate the following variant of equation (6):

$$\Delta \text{Patent}_{ct} = \beta_{\text{mean}} \sum_j \gamma_{cj} \Delta \text{Patent}_{jt} + \beta_{\text{variance}} \text{VAR}\left(\Delta \text{Patent}_{jt}\right) + \delta_t + \varepsilon_{ct}, \quad (7)$$

where t refers to 5-year time periods, $\Delta \text{Patent}_{ct}$ is a measure of patenting growth within-CPC c during the 5-year time interval denoted by t,

$$\text{VAR}\left(\Delta \text{Patent}_{jt}\right) \equiv \sum_j \gamma_{cj} \left(\Delta \text{Patent}_{jt} - \sum_j \gamma_{cj} \Delta \text{Patent}_{jt} \right)^2 ,$$

and $\sum_j \gamma_{cj} \Delta \text{Patent}_{jt}$ is the average patent growth during the 5-year time period among the CPCs that are upstream to c (i.e., among the CPC codes that c, the focal CPC, cites). As indicated earlier, its entries, the γ_{cj}'s, are the share of total citations over the entire sample period from patents in CPC c that go to patents in CPC j. The upstream variance of patenting growth is also computed analogously to the upstream variance of supplier TFP, though now using the γ_{cj}'s as weights.

Table 7 presents our main estimates of the patent-based version of equation (6). The first three columns measure innovation activity by log patents, which implies that sectors with zero patenting activity are dropped (this produces a sample of around 4,326 observations for our main specifications). Columns 4–6 instead focus on the Davis-Haltiwanger-Schuh (DHS) transformation (Davis, Haltiwanger, and Schuh 1998), which allows us to define growth rates when there are zero patents in a CPC in either the beginning or the end period.[25] This expands our sample slightly to 4,379 CPC observations. Throughout, we focus on unweighted specifications.

Columns 1 and 4 show a strong positive association between average patenting activity in a sector's upstream CPCs and the sector's own patenting activity. Columns 2–3 and 5–6 add the variance of patenting activity in the upstream CPCs to proxy for the imbalance of innovation activity across sectors. The latter two columns also include CPC fixed effects, which allow for linear trends at the CPC level. The estimates show

Table 7
Bottleneck Regressions Using Patenting by CPC Code

	Log Patent			DHS Specification		
	(1)	(2)	(3)	(4)	(5)	(6)
Citation average	1.291	1.335	1.473	1.284	1.307	1.402
	(.064)	(.064)	(.093)	(.065)	(.064)	(.098)
Citation variance		−.959	−.876		−1.040	−.911
		(.266)	(.314)		(.381)	(.532)
CPC fixed effects	No	No	Yes	No	No	Yes
Observations	4,326	4,326	4,323	4,379	4,379	4,376
R^2	.245	.250	.372	.202	.207	.307

Note: Standard errors are clustered at the Cooperative Patent Classification (CPC) level. All columns report unweighted ordinary least squares estimates. Year fixed effects are included in all regressions, and CPC fixed effects are included for columns 3 and 6. All regressions consider changes across 5-year averages 1975–2014. Columns 1–3 specify patent growth using the change in the log number of patents. Columns 4–6 specify patent growth as the change in patenting activity, normalized using the Davis-Haltiwanger-Schuh (DHS) transformation: $(P_{it} - P_{t-1}/\frac{1}{2}(P_{it} + P_{t-1}))$. In both cases, these specifications apply to both the dependent variable and the citation-weighted moments (i.e., the independent variables).

a powerful negative effect of upstream variance. In column 2, for example, the coefficient estimate for the variance is −0.959 (standard error = 0.266). The variance estimate remains essentially unchanged in column 3 when CPC fixed effects are included. The coefficient estimates are very similar in columns 5 and 6 with the DHS transformation, though standard errors are somewhat larger.

Table 8 is the patenting analogue of table 3 from our IV analysis for TFP, but now focusing on patents and exploiting variation in upstream patenting among foreign patents contained within the Google Patents global database. The estimates in table 8 are broadly supportive of the negative relationship between upstream variance and a sector's own patenting. Panel *A* depicts specifications using the change in log patenting (as in cols. 1–3 of table 7), and panel *B* shows results with the DHS transformation (as in cols. 4–6 of table 7). In each panel, columns 1 and 2 show the OLS relationship in this sample, columns 3 and 4 report 2SLS estimates, and columns 5 and 6 present the LIML estimates (which are again motivated by the weak first stages in cols. 3 and 4). Across essentially all columns, we see negative and statistically significant estimates of the impact of upstream variance.

Following the design of table 4, table 9 explores whether downstream patenting variance also matters, the possible relationship between future upstream variance and current patenting, and whether mean-reversion dynamics may be confounding our results. Reassuringly, the results in this table confirm the robustness of the estimates in table 7 to these checks. In particular, in panel *A* future citations have a smaller and often insignificant coefficient when entered at the same time as our main citation variables, and the coefficient on our citation variance measure remains similar to the baseline estimates.

In panel *B*, downstream variance—that is, variance among citing, rather than cited, patents—is negative and significant when entered by itself, which reflects the fact that, just as in the IO network, upstream and downstream measures are correlated. Nevertheless, when we also include our upstream citation variables, the downstream variance is no longer statistically significant and is in fact positive in most specifications, whereas our upstream citation variance has a similar coefficient to our baseline estimates and is statistically significant with log patents in columns 2 and 4, though it becomes less precise with DHS in columns 6 and 8.

Finally, in panel *C* we find that the inclusion of lagged patenting (the dependent variable) and the lagged citation average and variance terms

Table 8

Bottleneck Regressions Using Cross-Country Variation in Patenting as Instruments for US-Firm Patenting

	(1)	(2)	(3)	(4)	(5)	(6)
	Panel A: Log Patents					
Citation average	1.335	1.473	1.495	1.788	1.497	1.802
	(.064)	(.093)	(.075)	(.144)	(.076)	(.148)
Citation variance	−.959	−.876	−1.289	−2.289	−1.300	−2.477
	(.266)	(.314)	(.452)	(1.067)	(.469)	(1.201)
Year-by-CPC FEs	No	Yes	No	Yes	No	Yes
Estimator	OLS	OLS	2SLS	2SLS	LIML	LIML
Observations	4,326	4,323	4,285	4,283	4,285	4,283
R^2	.250	.372	.162	.095	.162	.092
First-stage F-stat	0	0	14.53	8.51	14.53	8.51
	Panel B: DHS Specification					
Citation average	1.307	1.402	1.446	1.679	1.447	1.687
	(.064)	(.098)	(.076)	(.150)	(.076)	(.153)
Citation variance	−1.040	−.911	−1.206	−2.176	−1.208	−2.288
	(.381)	(.532)	(.475)	(1.097)	(.483)	(1.179)
Year-by-CPC FEs	No	Yes	No	Yes	No	Yes
Estimator	OLS	OLS	2SLS	2SLS	LIML	LIML
Observations	4,379	4,376	4,325	4,324	4,325	4,324
R^2	.207	.307	.138	.078	.138	.077
First-stage F-stat	0	0	30.8	13.73	30.8	13.73

Note: Standard errors are clustered at the Cooperative Patent Classification (CPC) level. Year fixed effects (FE) are included in all regressions, and year-by-CPC fixed effects are included where indicated. All regressions consider changes across 5-year averages 1975–2014. All observations are unweighted. We use patenting growth in the 10 countries with the most patents over the sample period as instruments (Canada, China, Germany, France, the United Kingdom, Italy, Japan, Korea, Russia, Taiwan, and the United States). Specifically, we calculate the average and variance of patenting growth for each cited-CPC code in each of the five countries. Then, we use these 20 variables—the average and variance for each of the 10 countries—to instrument the average and variance of patenting growth in each cited-CPC code across US firms. Columns 3 and 4 report two-stage least squares (2SLS) estimates; columns 5 and 6 report limited information maximum likelihood (LIML) estimates. Panel A specifies patent growth using the change in the log number of patents; panel B specifies patent growth as the change in patenting activity, normalized using the Davis-Haltiwanger-Schuh (DHS) transformation: $(P_{it} - P_{t-1} / \frac{1}{2}(P_{it} + P_{t-1}))$. In both cases, these specifications apply to the dependent variable and the citation-weighted moments (i.e., the independent variables). OLS = ordinary least squares.

has very little effect on our results when focusing on the log patents measure. This is also the parent we find with the DHS transformation without fixed effects (col. 6), though with DHS and CPC fixed effects, the coefficient on the citation variance falls and becomes statistically insignificant (col. 8).

Table 10 confirms the robustness of our main CPC-level estimates to the same battery of tests we conducted in table 7 for TFP. (For brevity, we focus on log patents as the dependent variable.) We see broadly similar patterns across specifications that include or exclude CPC trends, are weighted by their share of total patenting, are at the 10-year frequency, include the covariance term, exclude the ICT and electronics sectors, leave out all citations to patents in the focal sector's three-digit CPC, limit the sample to years before 2005 to make the sample more similar to the data used for the TFP growth analyses, or focus on patents filed by US residents. The only two specifications in which the variance term is significantly weakened are columns 5 and 8. The former of these excludes the ICT and electronics sectors, and the weaker results likely reflect the factors discussed for the analogous specification in table 5—computers and electronics are emblematic of the imbalances that are our focus, so excluding these industries weakens the relevant economic forces and the precision of the estimates. The latter, column 8, excludes 54% of total patents filed by non-US residents at the USPTO, which likely accounts for the reduced precision of these estimates.

Quantitatively, these estimates suggest that upstream innovation imbalances have a major impact on overall innovation. For example, the weighted coefficient estimate in column 2 of panel A in table 10 suggests that a one standard deviation higher upstream variance (which is 0.03) is associated with a decline in the growth rate of patenting in a CPC code of 0.042 log points. This is a 47% reduction relative to the weighted mean of patenting across sectors, which is equal to 0.09 (weighting by the total number of patents in the CPC code in the initial 5-year period). These numbers are in the same ballpark as those implied by our TFP models.[26]

In sum, although the results in this subsection show a few specifications where the estimates are less stable than our main results reported in the prior section, they are overall supportive of a robust negative association between upstream variance of innovation activity and downstream patenting at the CPC level.

B.   Firm-Level Evidence

We next turn to the firm-level relationship between upstream imbalances and patenting. For this exercise, we disaggregate the patents data to the firm level and allow for variation across firms: specifically, the extent to which they rely on different CPCs for their patenting. This produces our firm-level citation network, summarized by $\{\omega_{kc}\}$,

Table 9

Bottleneck Regressions Using Patenting by CPC Code: Robustness to Lags, Leads, and Citing CPCs

	Log Patent				DHS Specification			
	(1)	(2)	(3)	(4)	(5)	(6)	(7)	(8)
A. Future Patenting Growth among Cited CPCs								
Citation average	.927	1.284		1.458		1.317		1.442
	(.067)	(.079)		(.098)		(.087)		(.104)
Citation variance	−.756	−.733		−.697		−1.100		−1.303
	(.246)	(.242)		(.299)		(.418)		(.532)
Future citation average		.064	.414	.180	.907	.024	.349	.129
		(.077)	(.089)	(.086)	(.073)	(.088)	(.113)	(.108)
Future citation variance		−.530	−.629	−.351	−.981	−.643	−.923	−.647
		(.233)	(.290)	(.278)	(.421)	(.505)	(.589)	(.568)
CPC fixed effects	No	No	Yes	Yes	No	No	Yes	Yes
Observations	3,712	3,712	3,709	3,709	3,753	3,753	3,753	3,753
R^2	.193	.275	.362	.424	.167	.243	.315	.370
B. Patenting Growth among Citing Patents								
Citation average		.919		.395		.726		.252
		(.237)		(.328)		(.296)		(.368)
Citation variance		−1.003		−1.374		−1.437		−1.628
		(.442)		(.524)		(.883)		(1.169)
Citing patent average	1.276	.429	1.516	1.152	1.262	.600	1.482	1.252
	(.066)	(.234)	(.089)	(.326)	(.067)	(.292)	(.084)	(.356)
Citing patent variance	−1.204	−.111	−.897	.240	−1.159	.296	−.848	.546
	(.245)	(.425)	(.306)	(.512)	(.299)	(.808)	(.365)	(1.011)
CPC fixed effects	No	No	Yes	Yes	No	No	Yes	Yes
Observations	4,326	4,326	4,323	4,323	4,378	4,378	4,376	4,376
R^2	.243	.252	.375	.379	.204	.211	.312	.314

	C. Lagged Patenting Growth: Dependent Variable and Citation Metrics							
Citation average	1.278	1.260	1.460	1.394	1.365	1.225	1.526	1.428
	(.061)	(.081)	(.101)	(.102)	(.068)	(.092)	(.103)	(.105)
Citation variance	-.985	-.965	-1.092	-1.017	-.793	-.797	-.581	-.488
	(.271)	(.269)	(.340)	(.341)	(.369)	(.399)	(.493)	(.491)
Lagged citation average		.032		.509		.226		.704
		(.103)		(.115)		(.121)		(.138)
Lagged citation variance		-.061		-.332		-.073		-.165
		(.257)		(.316)		(.398)		(.449)
Lagged dep. var.	.055	.052	-.097	-.132	-.068	-.084	-.197	-.238
	(.034)	(.038)	(.033)	(.036)	(.042)	(.046)	(.040)	(.041)
CPC fixed effects	No	No	Yes	Yes	No	No	Yes	Yes
Observations	3,695	3,695	3,693	3,693	3,743	3,743	3,742	3,742
R^2	.256	.256	.399	.406	.224	.226	.377	.388

Note: Standard errors are clustered at the Cooperative Patent Classification (CPC) level. All columns report unweighted ordinary least squares estimates. Year fixed effects are included in all regressions, and CPC fixed effects are included where indicated. All regressions consider changes across 5-year averages 1975–2014. Cols. 1–4 specify patent growth using the change in the log number of patents. Cols. 5–8 specify patent growth as the change in patenting activity, normalized using the Davis-Haltiwanger-Schuh (DHS) transformation: $(P_{it} - P_{i,t-1})/1/2(P_{it} + P_{i,t-1}))$. Panel A includes the leading average and variance of patent growth from the 5-year period. Panel B includes the average and variance of citation growth. Panel C includes the lagged average and variance of patent growth among idea suppliers, as well as the lagged dependent variable (downstream-CPC patenting growth), from the previous 5-year period.

193

Table 10
Robustness for Bottleneck Regressions Using Patenting by CPC Code

	Baseline	Weighted	10-Year	Cov.	No Comp.	3-Digit Leaveout	Excluding Post-2005	US Firms Only
	(1)	(2)	(3)	(4)	(5)	(6)	(7)	(8)
			A. Without CPC Trends					
Citation average	1.335	1.305	1.378	1.330	1.377	1.175	1.292	1.299
	(.064)	(.084)	(.073)	(.065)	(.074)	(.078)	(.072)	(.060)
Citation variance	−.959	−1.414	−.840	−.730	−.102	−.624	−.945	−.323
	(.266)	(.393)	(.197)	(.298)	(.260)	(.219)	(.271)	(.218)
Citation covariance				−.337				
				(.454)				
CPC fixed effects	No	No	No	No	No	No	No	No
Observations	4,326	4,305	1,853	3,094	3,783	4,326	3,098	4,224
R^2	.250	.442	.347	.279	.265	.195	.230	.207
			B. With CPC Trends					
Citation average	1.473	1.433	1.555	1.466	1.474	1.211	1.326	1.363
	(.093)	(.129)	(.112)	(.107)	(.087)	(.109)	(.113)	(.091)
Citation variance	−.876	−1.215	−.594	−.765	−.310	−.574	−.724	−.209
	(.314)	(.400)	(.247)	(.356)	(.318)	(.295)	(.370)	(.284)
Citation covariance				.179				
				(.471)				
CPC fixed effects	yes	yes	yes	yes	yes	yes	yes	yes
Observations	4,323	4,304	1,846	3,090	3,781	4,323	3,096	4,221
R^2	.372	.580	.601	.453	.369	.333	.414	.303

Note: Standard errors are clustered at the Cooperative Patent Classification (CPC) level. All columns report unweighted ordinary least squares estimates. All regressions consider stacked, sequential 5-year changes 1975–2014, except for column 3, where we consider stacked, sequential 10-year changes. In all columns, we specify patent growth using the change in the log number of patents. Time fixed effects are included in all specifications, and CPC fixed effects are included in panel B. Column 2 weights observations by the CPC code's share of total patenting in the sample period. Column 4 controls for covariance between the idea-supplier patenting growth in the current and the prior 5-year periods. Column 5 removes patents that belong to CPC class G, which includes computers. Column 6 excludes the CPC's own three-digit CPC code when constructing the citation network. Column 7 limits the sample to years before 2005. Column 8 limits to the patents of US-based firms.

representing citations by firm k to CPC class c. We estimate the following equation:

$$\Delta\text{Patent}_{kt} = \beta_{\text{mean}}\sum_c \omega_{kc}\Delta\text{Patent}_{ct} + \beta_{\text{variance}}\text{VAR}(\Delta\text{Patent}_{ct}) + \delta_t + \varepsilon_{kt}, \quad (8)$$

where t refers to 5-year time periods, ΔPatent_{kt} is a measure of patenting growth of firm k during the 5-year time interval denoted by t,

$$\text{VAR}(\Delta\text{Patent}_{ct}) \equiv \sum_c \omega_{kc}\left(\Delta\text{Patent}_{ct} - \sum_c \omega_{kc}\Delta\text{Patent}_{ct}\right)^2,$$

and $\sum_c \omega_{kc}\Delta\text{Patent}_{ct}$ is the average patent growth in the 5-year time period among the CPCs upstream to firm k (meaning those cited-to by firm k). As indicated earlier, these are calculated using the share of total citations over the entire sample period by firm k's patents to patents in CPC c. The variance of patent growth among the cited CPCs is computed using the ω_{kc}'s as weights.

This disaggregation produces a much larger sample, consisting of almost 2 million observations at the firm level. For many firm-period combinations, however, there are no patents. Thus, in this table, we use the DHS transformation. In particular, in columns 1–3 we use the standard DHS transformation, where observations are dropped when there are two consecutive zeros. In columns 4–6, we use a modified DHS transformation, where in such cases, the transformation imputes a value of zero.[27]

Table 11 presents the main results from this exercise. The firm-level structure of the data in this table enables us to control for firm fixed effects or for CPC-times-year fixed effects, thus purging a large fraction of the variation in patenting between firms. The general pattern is a negative relationship between upstream variance at the CPC level and a firm's own propensity to patent. For example, in column 1, the coefficient estimate of the citation variance is -0.264 (standard error $= 0.042$). In column 3, when we include CPC-times-year fixed effects, the coefficient increases slightly, to -0.292 (standard error $= 0.045$). The exception to this pattern is in column 2, where we see a positive and significant coefficient when firm fixed effects are included with the standard DHS transformation. We suspect that this is driven by firms that have many zeros and thus many missing observations. Indeed, in columns 4–6, when we use the modified DHS so that all zeros are kept, the coefficients on the variances are more stable and always negative (and strongly statistically significant except in col. 5).

Table 11
Bottleneck Patterns Using Firm-Level Patenting

	DHS Specification			DHS Specification with Zeros		
	(1)	(2)	(3)	(4)	(5)	(6)
Citation average	1.089	1.048	1.039	.234	.282	.233
	(.010)	(.024)	(.015)	(.003)	(.006)	(.004)
Citation variance	−.264	.337	−.292	−.065	−.025	−.051
	(.042)	(.083)	(.045)	(.011)	(.017)	(.012)
Firm FEs	No	Yes	No	No	Yes	No
CPC × Year FEs	No	No	Yes	No	No	Yes
Observations	654,583	617,894	640,397	1,888,705	1,888,705	1,828,778
R^2	.037	.414	.044	.009	.038	.013

Note: Standard errors are clustered at the firm level. Year fixed effects (FE) are included in all regressions and firm fixed effects or year-by-CPC (Cooperative Patent Classification) fixed effects are included where indicated. All regressions consider changes across 5-year averages 1975–2014. Observations are unweighted. In all columns, we specify patent growth as the change in patenting activity, normalized using the Davis-Haltiwanger-Schuh (DHS) transformation: $(P_{it} - P_{t-1} / \frac{1}{2}(P_{it} + P_{t-1}))$. In columns 1–3, we replace missing values with 0 for these specifications. In columns 4–6, we leave missing values as is.

Table 12 provides a number of robustness checks for these firm-level results, considering analogous specifications to those we presented for the TFP and CPC-level patenting models and focusing on the standard DHS measure. Panel *A* of this table corresponds to column 1 of table 11, and panel *B* adds CPC-times-year fixed effects, as in column 3 of that table. The results are robust across specifications that are weighted by the firm's share of total patenting, control for the lagged dependent variable, change the sample period, or focus only on domestic patents. As a further robustness test, column 6 adds the mean and variance of future citations in a firm's patenting network. Future citations as well as our main measures are now statistically significant. Given the high degree of serial correlation in patenting within classes, these patterns are not surprising. They highlight, however, that future tests of our proposed mechanism should attempt to exploit shocks that affect patenting during certain discrete periods.

Quantitatively, these estimates imply that upstream firm-level imbalances have similarly sized innovation effects as we measure at the CPC level. For example, the coefficient estimate in column 2 of panel *A* of table 12, which shows the weighted regression specification, suggests that a one standard deviation higher upstream variance (which is again 0.03, as in the CPC case in the previous section) is associated with a decline in firm-level patenting of 0.13 log points. This is a sizable (73%) decline relative to a baseline of 0.18. These numbers are similar when we include

Table 12
Robustness for Bottleneck Regressions Using Firm-Level Patenting

	Baseline	Weighted	Lagged	Excluding Post-2005	US Only	Lead Horserace
	(1)	(2)	(3)	(4)	(5)	(6)
	A. Without CPC-by-Year Fixed Effects					
Citation average	1.089	2.029	0.593	1.242	1.074	1.014
	(.010)	(.143)	(.011)	(.012)	(.012)	(.016)
Citation variance	−.264	−2.567	−.290	−.446	−.055	−.187
	(.042)	(.407)	(.038)	(.057)	(.045)	(.059)
Lagged 5-year growth			−.261			
Future citation average			(.002)			.176
						(.018)
Future citation variance						−.341
						(.059)
CPC × Year FEs	No	No	No	No	No	No
Observations	654,583	654,583	378,905	384,258	363,911	528,162
R^2	.037	.206	.076	.020	.035	.029
	B. With CPC-by-Year Fixed Effects					
Citation average	1.039	2.391	.591	1.209	1.018	1.064
	(.015)	(.133)	(.016)	(.019)	(.019)	(.022)
Citation variance	−.292	−2.687	−.104	−.462	−.088	−.286
	(.045)	(.414)	(.041)	(.060)	(.049)	(.063)
Lagged 5-year growth			−.253			
Future citation average			(.002)			.096
						(.024)
Future citation variance						−.225
						(.063)
CPC × Year FEs	Yes	yes	yes	yes	yes	yes
Observations	640,397	640,397	373,321	380,680	356,228	520,627
R^2	.044	.233	.083	.025	.043	.035

Note: Standard errors are clustered at the firm level. Year fixed effects (FE) are included in all regressions, and Cooperative Patent Classification (CPC) by year fixed effects are included in panel B. In all regressions, we specify patent growth as the change in patenting activity, normalized using the Davis-Haltiwanger-Schuh transformation: $(P_{it} - P_{t-1}/\frac{1}{2}(P_{it} + P_{t-1}))$. Observations are unweighted except for column 2, where we weight observations by the firm's share of total patenting in the sample period. All regressions consider changes across 5-year averages 1975–2014. Column 3 controls for the lagged dependent variable (downstream-firm patenting growth) from the previous 5-year period. Column 4 only limits the sample to years before 2005. Column 5 only includes US-firm patents, which applies to both the dependent variable and the citation-weighted moments (i.e., the independent variables). Columns 6 and 7 include the leading average and variance of patent growth from the 5-year period.

CPC-by-year fixed effects in the same column of panel *B*. Overall, these numbers are broadly comparable to those from the CPC-level analysis in Subsection V.A.

VI. International Evidence

Our primary analysis focuses on TFP growth and innovation in the United States (except when instrumenting domestic TFP growth and innovation with contemporaneous foreign development in tables 3 and 8). We supplement this evidence here by estimating a variant of equation (6) for TFP growth across European countries. As outlined in Section III, we use the GGDC World Input-Output Database to construct consistent IO linkages for 30 industries in Austria, Finland, France, Germany, Italy, the Netherlands, Spain, the United Kingdom, and the United States. We fix the global IO table at the year 2000 and focus on industry TFP growth in this cross-country sample between 1987 and 2007. These data enable us to include international IO linkages, which we exploit in our calculations of the mean and variance of supplier TFP growth.[28]

We report these cross-country estimates in table 13. We report the baseline specifications in the first four columns. These specifications are unweighted and include combinations of country effects, year effects, year-by-country effects, and year-by-industry effects, as noted at the bottom of each column. In column 1, we focus on a specification containing country and year effects. This estimate verifies that an industry's TFP growth is predicted by the average TFP growth of its suppliers. Column 2 includes the variance of supplier TFP growth. The coefficient on this measure is negative, highly significant and broadly similar to the US-based estimate, at -0.820 (standard error $= 0.211$).

Subsequent columns probe the robustness of this finding. Column 3 includes industry-by-year effects, so that the identifying variation is within-industry rather than cross-industry, as in the main specifications of the paper. The relationship is similar to column 2, although somewhat smaller. In particular, the coefficient on the variance term is -0.528 (standard error $= 0.142$). Column 4 includes both industry-by-year and country-by-year interactions, restricting to variation within-industry and within-country. In this demanding specification, the coefficient on the variance term remains negative and statistically significant, at -0.441 (standard error $= 0.158$).

The negative effect of supplier TFP variance is also present when we include the lagged dependent variable to control for mean-reversion

Table 13

Evidence on Bottlenecks from Cross-Country Regressions Using TFP

	Baseline				Lagged Dep. Var.	VA Weight	VA Weight	10-Year Changes	Within-Country IO
	(1)	(2)	(3)	(4)	(5)	(6)	(7)	(8)	(9)
Upstream average	.258	.270	.107	−.225	.264	.278	.266	.276	.280
	(.074)	(.078)	(.079)	(.112)	(.085)	(.103)	(.084)	(.115)	(.081)
Upstream variance		−.820	−.528	−.442	−.815	−.560	−.758	−.722	−.713
		(.211)	(.142)	(.158)	(.180)	(.579)	(.420)	(.362)	(.215)
Year FEs	Yes	Yes	No	No	Yes	Yes	Yes	Yes	Yes
Country FEs	Yes	Yes	Yes	No	Yes	Yes	Yes	Yes	Yes
Year × Country FEs	No	No	No	Yes	No	No	No	No	No
Year × Industry FEs	No	No	Yes	Yes	No	No	No	No	No
Lagged dep. var.	No	No	No	No	Yes	No	Yes	No	No
Observations	982	982	982	982	896	982	896	462	982
R^2	.065	.076	.364	.401	.120	.062	.192	.119	.075

Note: This table reports estimates of equation (6) for 1987–2007 using cross-country observations. The dependent variable is total factor productivity (TFP) growth of an industry in a given country in a 5-year period, and the two key right-hand-side variables are mean and variance of TFP growth among that country-industry pair's suppliers. All regressions are unweighted unless otherwise indicated. Time and country dummies are included in all regressions. The sample includes 30 industries in nine countries: Austria, Finland, France, Germany, Italy, the Netherlands, Spain, the United Kingdom, and the United States. Columns 1 and 2 are cross-country analogues of columns 1 and 2 in table 1. Column 3 includes industry-by-year fixed effects (FE), and column 4 adds country-by-year fixed effects. Column 5 includes the lagged dependent variable, and columns 6 and 7 weight each industry observation by its share of within-country value-added (VA; countries themselves are not weighted). Column 8 uses 10-year periods. Although columns 1–8 exploit variation in input shares across both countries and industries, column 9 focuses on within-country, cross-industry input-output (IO) linkages. See text for details. Standard errors are clustered at the industry level.

dynamics (col. 5). It is weaker but still present when we use 1992 within-country (nominal) value-added weights instead of our baseline unweighted specification (cols. 6 and 7, with and without controlling for the lagged dependent variable).[29] It is equally large, and (in this case) statistically significant, when we focus on a 10-year panel rather than stacked 5-year changes in column 8. In column 9, we show that the estimates are similar when we only use each country's domestic IO network, rather than the full international IO table (which incorporates inputs from each country-industry pair).[30] Finally, in table A9 (http://www.nber.org/data-appendix /c14854/appendix.pdf), we report cross-country regressions that include both own-country (domestic) values and foreign-country average values of the mean and variance of upstream (supplier) TFP growth as explanatory variables for sectoral productivity growth. These models show that own-country supplier TFP values are a far more robust predictor of sectoral productivity growth than the corresponding other-country values. This is especially the case for the variance term, where the own-country coefficient is negative and significant in all columns, whereas the other-country measure is neither significant nor consistently signed. This pattern is reassuring against the concern that our upstream TFP variance

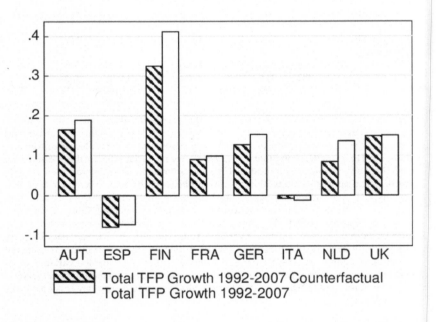

Fig. 6. Magnitude of bottleneck estimates in international data. This figure reports actual and counterfactual total factor productivity (TFP) growth between 1992 and 2007 across the countries in our international panel data (Austria, Spain, Finland, France, Germany, Italy, the Netherlands, and the United Kingdom). The counterfactuals are based on regression estimates from the column 2 specification of table 13. Specifically, counterfactual TFP (white bars) is computed from the regression coefficients as the TFP growth that would have been observed in the given country and year if the variance of supplier TFP growth had remained at the same level as during the initial period (1992–97). This is calculated by subtracting the contribution of supplier TFP variance from the actual TFP growth (patterned). A color version of this figure is available online.

Table 14

Evidence on Bottlenecks from Cross-Country Regressions Using Patenting

	Log Patent				DHS Specification			
	(1)	(2)	(3)	(4)	(5)	(6)	(7)	(8)
Citation average	1.231	1.240	1.229	1.404	1.103	1.096	1.077	1.200
	(.021)	(.022)	(.022)	(.054)	(.013)	(.013)	(.013)	(.033)
Citation variance		−.031	−.030	−.025		−.048	−.034	−.056
		(.010)	(.011)	(.018)		(.020)	(.020)	(.031)
Year-by-CPC Fes	no	no	yes	yes	no	no	yes	yes
Year-by-country FEs	no	no	no	yes	no	no	no	yes
Observations	84,870	84,870	84,862	84,862	85,698	85,698	85,694	85,694
R^2	.223	.223	.278	.281	.241	.241	.306	.309

Note: Standard errors are clustered at the Cooperative Patent Classification (CPC) level. We consider the 20 countries with the greatest number of patents in the sample period (Austria, Australia, Belgium, Canada, Switzerland, China, Germany, Denmark, Spain, Finland, France, the United Kingdom, Italy, Japan, Korea, the Netherlands, Russia, Sweden, Taiwan, and the United States). Fixed effects (FE) for year and country are included in all regressions, and year-by-CPC or year-by-country fixed effects are included where indicated. Observations are unweighted. All regressions include changes across 5-year averages 1975–2014. Cols. 1–4 specify patent growth using the change in the log number of patents. Columns 5–8 specify patent growth as the change in patenting activity, normalized using the Davis-Haltiwanger-Schuh (DHS) transformation: $(P_{it} - P_{t-1}/\frac{1}{2}(P_{it} + P_{t-1}))$.

terms may be misspecified because they do not include productivity growth among important intermediates (see endnote 21).

These cross-country models also enable us to investigate whether our mechanism can account for the international slowdown in productivity growth. Figure 6, which is analogous to figure 5 for the United States, reports the results of this exercise. Across the European countries in our sample, we estimate that the rising variance of supplier TFP reduced aggregate productivity growth in eight of nine countries—all except Italy. This bottleneck effect is largest in Finland and the Netherlands, where we estimate that it reduced aggregate TFP growth 1992–2007 by 30% and 60%, respectively.

We also implement a similar specification where the outcome is patenting among firms located in different countries. We use the same CPC-citation linkages for each country (calculated using all patents within the USPTO database), but we apply a variant of equation (6) for patenting growth of firms located in the 20 largest countries within Google global patent data. Table 14 reports these cross-country estimates (which are again unweighted). Columns 1 through 4 use log patents, and columns 5 through 8 use the DHS transformation. Exploiting the cross-country variation, we see in columns 2 and 6 that, with either specification, there is a negative effect of upstream imbalances on patenting. This remains true in columns 3 and 7, where we include year-by-CPC fixed effects, thus identifying the relationship exclusively from cross-country variation in the upstream variance. The relationship is also broadly robust, though a little less precisely estimated, in columns 4 and 8, where we further include year-by-country fixed effects, thus focusing entirely on within-country variation.

VII. Conclusion

Despite the exponential pace of innovation in the ICT and electronics sectors, aggregate productivity growth in the United States and many other industrialized nations has been disappointing since the 1970s—and only more so since the early 2000s. Some have interpreted this pattern, variously, as reflecting a severe underestimation of quality and actual productivity growth, a temporary lull that proceeds a major surge in productivity, or an exhaustion of the potential supply of truly transformative innovations—leading to a long-term deceleration of productivity growth.

We proposed an alternative hypothesis that implies neither a permanent slowdown in productivity growth nor an incipient surge. We then investigated this new hypothesis empirically. The foundational idea of our approach is that innovation in any one industry relies on complementary innovations in—and subsequent productivity gains from—its input and idea suppliers. When innovation is unbalanced across industries, this holds back aggregate productivity growth by creating innovation "bottlenecks" along the IO or patent citation (idea) networks.

After presenting a simple version of this productivity bottleneck hypothesis, we explored it using data on IO linkages, citation linkages, patenting, and TFP growth. Across a variety of measurement approaches, productivity outcomes, and countries, we verify the primary prediction of this hypothesis: an industry's productivity growth is augmented by the mean productivity growth of its suppliers (measured by TFP or innovation) and, crucially, it is hampered by the variance of their productivity growth.

Our primary evidence exploits IO linkages and TFP growth to document the sensitivity of industry productivity growth to the mean and variance of supplier productivity growth. We supplemented this evidence by looking at patenting as a direct measure of innovation. This analysis suggests that there is a similarly powerful linkage between the innovativeness of a sector or firm and the imbalances it faces across its upstream (idea-supplier) sectors. For these results, we measured the upstream sectors based on industry- or firm-level citation networks.

At face value, our evidence implies that the bulk of the productivity slowdown in the United States (and several other industrialized economies) can be explained by the sizable increase in the cross-industry variance of TFP growth and innovation. For example, if TFP growth variance had remained at its 1977–87 level for the subsequent 2 decades, US manufacturing productivity would have grown twice as rapidly in 1997–2007 as it did—yielding a counterfactual growth rate that would have been close to its observed level in either of the 2 prior decades. These estimates illustrate the potential importance of our mechanism, but given the limitations of our measurement and sources of variation, they do not constitute a definitive assessment of its quantitative contribution.

We view our paper as a first step in the theoretical and empirical investigation of the interlinked nature of innovation across sectors. Based on the earlier findings, many areas of research appear fruitful. First, our hypothesis raises a critical theoretical question: Will the endogenous direction of technological progress tend to clear productivity bottlenecks, or might the market mechanism exacerbate imbalances? Second, this initial evidence highlights the need for additional empirical strategies to explore dependencies among innovating sectors and the innovations generated by their suppliers. These same relationships could be tested, for example, using firm-level IO data, where we suspect that the importance of supplier-customer linkages would be even larger. Third, another interesting context to explore is the role of global supply chains in productivity bottlenecks. On the one hand, imported intermediates and technologies can relax domestic bottlenecks. On the other hand, global supply chains may introduce more extensive technological dependencies, which could intensify bottlenecks if those trade channels become constrained. Fourth, it would be valuable to investigate the bottleneck hypothesis using historical data—focusing, for example, on major technological breakthroughs in the first half of the twentieth century. Finally, our framework makes a strong—perhaps even rash—prediction, whose verification awaits the passage of time: if and when lagging industries ultimately increase their innovation and productivity growth rates, a rapid takeoff in aggregate productivity should ensue.

Endnotes

Author email addresses: Acemoglu (daron@mit.edu), Autor (dautor@mit.edu), Patterson (christina.patterson@chicagobooth.edu). We thank Nick Bloom, Steve Davis, John

Fernald, Hugo Hopenhayn, Bill Kerr, Jennifer La'O, Valerie Ramey, and John van Reenen for their helpful comments; Rebecca Jackson, Zhe Fredric Kong, and Austin Lentsch for expert research assistance; and Ernest Liu and Song Ma for sharing international patenting data. Acemoglu and Autor acknowledge support from the Hewlett Foundation, Google, and the Smith Richardson Foundation. Acemoglu also acknowledges support from the National Science Foundation, the Sloan Foundation, and the Toulouse Network on Information Technology. Autor also acknowledges support from the Washington Center for Equitable Growth. For acknowledgments, sources of research support, and disclosure of the authors' material financial relationships, if any, please see https://www.nber.org/books-and-chapters/nber-macroeconomics-annual-2023-volume-38/bottlenecks-sectoral-imbalances-and-us-productivity-slowdown.

1. The black bars correspond to the share of US Patent and Trademark Office (USPTO) patents granted in Electricity and Electronics (i.e., "electronics"), and the gray bars plot the share of patents granted in Instruments and Information (i.e., "ICT"). The black line shows the total number of patents granted.

2. Those who subscribe to the first view often highlight that growth is mismeasured, which is undoubtedly true. Nevertheless, mismeasurement does not seem to account for the broad outlines of the productivity slowdown since the 1970s. First, growth was almost surely mismeasured in the decades that followed World War II, when many new consumer goods and technologies were introduced. Second, many implications of the growth mismeasurement thesis, such as faster productivity growth in sectors with less potential for mismeasurement, do not receive support from the data (Byrne, Fernald, and Reinsdorf 2016; Syverson 2017). Third, there is no evidence for even the most basic predictions of fast, ICT-driven productivity growth; for example, industries with more-intensive use of ICT (outside of the ICT-producing industries themselves) have exhibited, if anything, slower growth of nominal and real value-added (Acemoglu et al. 2014).

3. See https://www.nobelprize.org/prizes/chemistry/2019/popular-information.

4. See Atalay (2017) and Baqaee and Farhi (2019) for such Neoclassical effects, which arise once we depart from unitary elasticities in production.

5. Specifically, using the Cooperative Patent Classification (CPC) scheme, we look at the mean and variance of patenting at the "upstream" patent classes. Upstream classes are constructed according to the citation network, which follows the approach in Acemoglu et al. (2016). We do not mix the patenting and TFP analyses, both because the idea network based on citations and the IO network are different and because the link between patents and productivity in our sample is modest, which may be due to the imperfect correspondence between industry classifications and patent technology classes.

6. The most sophisticated version of the "running out of ideas" hypothesis is developed in Bloom et al. (2020), who argue that innovations have become difficult in many fields but the rate of innovation has not declined commensurately because the amount of effort devoted to invention and innovation has increased.

7. $B_i = \left((1 - \Sigma_{j \in S_i} \alpha_{ij})^{1 - \Sigma_{j \in S_i} \alpha_{ij}} \prod_{j \in S_i} \alpha_{ij}^{\alpha_{ij}}\right)^{-1}$. See Acemoglu and Azar (2020) for more details on this functional form.

8. It is straightforward to allow these sets to be time-varying, but we do not do so, to reduce notation. In our empirical work, we explore models both with and without time-varying input sets.

9. We have equated the importance of an input to its share in production, α_{ij}. This is not necessary for any of our main arguments, but it is the benchmark functional form assumption that we use in our empirical work. We also consider an alternative where the importance of an input innovation is measured by the number of citations to the innovation by patents from other industries.

10. The inputs that need to make technological advances before sector i can successfully innovate may be a subset of the inputs in S_i. Because we do not have a way to empirically determine which subset of inputs is important for innovation, we assume that all inputs in S_i are relevant, then verify robustness using other measures of industry linkages.

11. Even when $\eta_{\text{variance}}^i < 0$, an increase in the productivity of an input-supplier industry is always beneficial (and thus, the negative effect through the variance is weaker than the positive impact through the mean, η_{mean}^i) because the functions h and H are monotone.

12. As we discuss in the next subsection, it may not be possible to reduce the dispersion of technological progress across sectors without affecting the mean. In particular, such a mean-preserving dispersion reduction would require that the cost of improving technology in every sector is the same.

13. Finding the general equilibrium will also require us to solve for the wage rate (and the allocation of labor across sectors) and the interest rate (as a function of the aggregate growth rate of the economy). We do not derive these (standard) aspects of the general equilibrium.

14. See https://www.nber.org/research/data/nber-ces-manufacturing-industry-database.

15. The BLS also produces similar statistics for aggregated three-digit NAICS manufacturing industries. Although we do not use these BLS measures in our analysis, these statistics are highly correlated with the multifactor productivity measures for manufacturing in the Census data.

16. If there is more than one CPC code provided for a patent, we use the first-reported (i.e., primary) code.

17. In our baseline specification, this share includes inputs from all other countries. We explore alternative definitions and, in table A9 (http://www.nber.org/data-appendix /c14854/appendix.pdf), show that our results are mostly driven by TFP growth patterns among a country's domestically sourced inputs, with a more limited role for imported intermediates.

18. Like the fastest-growing industries, the bottom 50% industries are defined in terms of their contribution to supplier TFP variance between 1997 and 2007. Table A2 (http:// www.nber.org/data-appendix/c14854/appendix.pdf) reports the full set of industries corresponding to each panel of table 2.

19. More specifically, we calculate these instruments using the US-based IO table, but taking the TFP growth across industries from each of three European countries (France, Germany, and the United Kingdom). Because the international industry data are more aggregated than our underlying NAICS data, six-digit NAICS codes are mapped to the most similar international industry code available, and the TFP growth value observed in the European instrument panel is assigned to US industries based on these mappings. To reflect this, we cluster the standard errors at the level of the 29 KLEMS industries in table 3. Throughout this exercise, we focus on our main, unweighted specifications, corresponding to cols. 2 and 3 of table 1.

20. Specifically, we calculate the covariance between the TFP growth of suppliers in the previous 5-year period ($t - 10$ to $t - 5$) and the current period ($t - 5$ to t), weighting each supplying industry by their input share in $t - 10$.

21. An additional concern is whether our variance term is misspecified, because it does not account for the productivity of offshored and imported inputs. Here we note that this concern would create attenuation toward zero and hence is unlikely to account for our findings. It also does not apply when we turn to patenting, because our analysis there will include foreign patents as well. We further discuss this issue in Sec. VI.

22. We are grateful to our discussant John Fernald for pointing out this problem and proposing the adjustment we implement here.

23. We use employment rather than output, because output numbers would be directly correlated with TFP estimates. We also focus on unweighted specifications, as in our other robustness explorations.

24. Because the mappings between CPCs and Standard Industrial Classification/ NAICS classifications are imperfect, we do not explore the relationship between upstream patenting and downstream productivity growth.

25. The DHS transformation for a variable X is $X_t - X_{t-1}/(1/2(X_t + X_{t-1}))$.

26. In particular, our main TFP estimates from col. 2 of table 1 suggest that a one standard deviation increase in upstream TFP growth variance is associated with TFP growth that is 0.035 percentage points lower.

27. Recall from endnote 25 that the DHS transformation is $X_t - X_{t-1}/(1/2(X_t + X_{t-1}))$. This is undefined when both X_t and X_{t-1} are equal to zero. In the modified DHS, rather than dropping such observations, we set $0/0 = 0$.

28. Specifically, we use the world IO tables to calculate the input share $\alpha_{ik,jl}$ as the share of inputs from industry i in country k that come from industry j in country l. The shares are based only on the nine countries listed earlier.

29. We do not have nominal sales data in our international panel and hence use nominal value-added weights rather than nominal sales weights. All weights are within-country, meaning that they are relative to total GDP of the country.

30. We do not report estimates using the manufacturing sample in this case, both because manufacturing industries are not sufficiently disaggregated in this data set and because doing so would reduce our sample by about two-thirds. Finally, table A10 (http://www.nber.org/data-appendix/c14854/appendix.pdf) shows the robustness of our US results, aggregated to the 30 industries used in table 13.

References

Acemoglu, Daron, Ufuk Akcigit, and William R. Kerr. 2016. "Innovation Network." *Proceedings of the National Academy of Sciences* 113 (41): 11483–88.

Acemoglu, Daron, David Autor, David Dorn, Gordon H. Hanson, and Brendan Price. 2014. "Return of the Solow Paradox? IT, Productivity, and Employment in US Manufacturing." *AER Papers and Proceedings* 104 (5): 394–99.

Acemoglu, Daron, and Pablo D. Azar. 2020. "Endogenous Production Networks." *Econometrica* 88 (1): 33–82.

Acemoglu, Daron, Vasco M. Carvalho, Asuman Ozdaglar, and Alireza Tahbaz-Salehi. 2012. "The Network Origins of Aggregate Fluctuations." *Econometrica* 80 (5): 1977–2016.

Acemoglu, Daron, and Pascual Restrepo. 2019. "Automation and New Tasks: How Technology Displaces and Reinstates Labor." *Journal of Economic Perspectives* 33 (2): 3–30.

Aghion, Philippe, Ufuk Akcigit, Antonin Bergeaud, Richard Blundell, and David Hémous. 2019. "Innovation and Top Income Inequality." *Review of Economic Studies* 86 (1): 1–45.

Aghion, Philippe, and Peter Howitt. 1992. "A Model of Growth through Creative Destruction." *Econometrica* 60 (2): 323–51.

Akcigit, Ufuk, and Sina T. Ates. 2019. "What Happened to US Business Dynamism?" Working Paper no. 25756, NBER, Cambridge, MA.

Andrews, Dan, Chiara Criscuolo, and Peter N. Gal. 2016. "The Best versus the Rest: The Global Productivity Slowdown, Divergence across Firms and the Role of Public Policy." https://www.oecd-ilibrary.org/economics/the-best-versus-the-rest_63629cc9-en.

Atalay, Enghin. 2017. "How Important Are Sectoral Shocks?" *American Economic Journal: Macroeconomics* 9 (4): 254–80.

Autor, David, David Dorn, and Gordon H. Hanson. 2013. "The China Syndrome: Local Labor Market Effects of Import Competition in the United States." *American Economic Review* 103 (6): 2121–68.

Autor, David, David Dorn, Gordon H. Hanson, Gary Pisano, and Pian Shu. 2020. "Foreign Competition and Domestic Innovation: Evidence from US Patents." *AER: Insights* 2 (3): 357–74.

Balsmeier, Benjamin, Mohamad Assaf, Tyler Chesebro, Gabe Fierro, Kevin Johnson, Scott Johnson, Guan-Cheng Li, et al. 2018. "Machine Learning and Natural Language Processing on the Patent Corpus: Data, Tools, and New Measures." *Journal of Economics and Management Strategy* 27 (3): 535–53. https://doi.org/10.1111/jems.12259.

Baqaee, David, and Emmanuel Farhi. 2019. "Networks, Barriers, and Trade." Working Paper no. 26108, NBER, Cambridge, MA.

Bloom, Nicholas, Charles I. Jones, John Van Reenen, and Michael Webb. 2020. "Are Ideas Getting Harder to Find?" *American Economic Review* 110 (4): 1104–44.

Bostrom, Nick. 2014. *Superintelligence: Paths, Dangers, Strategies*. Cambridge: Oxford University Press.

Bresnahan, Timothy F., and Manuel Trajtenberg. 1995. "General Purpose Technologies 'Engines of Growth'?" *Journal of Econometrics* 65 (1): 83–108.

Brynjolfsson, Erik, Daniel Rock, and Chad Syverson. 2021. "The Productivity J-Curve: How Intangibles Complement General Purpose Technologies." *American Economic Journal: Macroeconomics* 13 (1): 333–72.

Byrne, David M., John G. Fernald, and Marshall B. Reinsdorf. 2016. "Does the United States Have a Productivity Slowdown or a Measurement Problem?" *Brookings Papers on Economic Activity* 2016 (1): 109–82.

Cohen, Lauren, Umit G. Gurun, and Scott Duke Kominers. 2016. "The Growing Problem of Patent Trolling." *Science* 352 (6285): 521–22.

Cowen, Tyler. 2011. *The Great Stagnation: How America Ate All the Low-Hanging Fruit of Modern History, Got Sick, and Will (Eventually) Feel Better*. New York: Dutton.

David, Paul A. 1990. "The Dynamo and the Computer: An Historical Perspective on the Modern Productivity Paradox." *American Economic Review* 80 (2): 355–61.

Davis, Steven J., John C. Haltiwanger, and Scott Schuh. 1998. *Job Creation and Destruction*. Cambridge, MA: MIT Press.

Decker, Ryan A., John Haltiwanger, Ron S. Jarmin, and Javier Miranda. 2017. "Declining Dynamism, Allocative Efficiency, and the Productivity Slowdown." *American Economic Review* 107 (5): 322–26.

Diamandis, Peter H., and Steven Kotler. 2012. *Abundance: The Future Is Better Than You Think*. New York: Simon and Schuster.

Gordon, Robert J. 2017. *The Rise and Fall of American Growth: The US Standard of Living Since the Civil War*. Princeton, NJ: Princeton University Press.

Grossman, Gene M., and Elhanan Helpman. 1991. *Innovation and Growth in the Global Economy*. Cambridge, MA: MIT Press.

Gruber, Jonathan, and Simon Johnson. 2019. *Jump-Starting America: How Breakthrough Science Can Revive Economic Growth and the American Dream*. London: Hachette UK.

Helpman, Elhanan, and Manuel Trajtenberg. 1996. "Diffusion of General Purpose Technologies." Working Paper no. 5773, NBER, Cambridge, MA.

Iancu, Andrei. 2019. "Remarks by Director Iancu." Presentation at the International Intellectual Property Conference, Seoul, June 10.

Kurzweil, Ray. 2005. *The Singularity Is Near: When Humans Transcend Biology*. London: Penguin.

Laws, David. 2018. "13 Sextillion & Counting: The Long & Winding Road to the Most Frequently Manufactured Human Artifact in History." https://computerhistory.org/blog/13-sextillion-counting-the-long-winding-road-to-the-most-frequently-manufactured-human-artifact-in-history/.

Liu, Ernest, and Song Ma. 2021. "Innovation Networks and R&D Allocation." Working Paper no. 29607, NBER, Cambridge, MA.

Long, John B., Jr., and Charles I. Plosser. 1983. "Real Business Cycles." *Journal of Political Economy* 91 (1): 39–69.

Park, John N., Robert L. Steigerwald, and Loren H. Walker. 1976. Rectifier Circuits Using Transistors as Rectifying Elements. US Patent 3,940,682, filed November 22, 1974, and issued February 24, 1976.

Sosa, Estanislao N. 2013. "Electron Tube." Encyclopedia Britannica. https://www.britannica.com/technology/electron-tube.

Syverson, Chad. 2017. "Challenges to Mismeasurement Explanations for the US Productivity Slowdown." *Journal of Economic Perspectives* 31 (2): 165–86.

Comment

John G. Fernald, Federal Reserve Bank of San Francisco, United States of America, and INSTEAD, France

Eugenio Piga, INSTEAD, France

I. Introduction

In his influential American Economic Association presidential address in 1998, Arnold Harberger presented a striking mycological metaphor to compare two visions of the growth process: mushrooms versus yeast. As many a lawn owner realizes, mushrooms sprout suddenly, unexpectedly, and unevenly. Yeast, in contrast, causes a loaf of bread to rise smoothly and evenly. Harberger argued that the actual process of productivity growth was inherently uneven and mushroomlike, with selected sectors that grow rapidly and propel the aggregate.

We thought of Harberger's metaphor when we read the intriguing paper by Acemoglu, Autor, and Patterson: "Bottlenecks: Sectoral Imbalances and the US Productivity Slowdown." The authors argue that a key driver of productivity growth is innovation spillovers from upstream suppliers.

But the spillovers, they find empirically, are maximized when upstream suppliers have a relatively balanced pattern of productivity growth. For example, the likelihood of a car manufacturer successfully innovating may be higher if there are upstream innovations not just in semiconductors but also in glass, metals, and plastics. In other words, if Acemoglu et al. were social planners organizing dinner parties, they would serve us bread, not sautéed mushrooms.

The nature of innovation spillovers is a potentially important contribution. But the implications, if they hold, may be even more important.

NBER Macroeconomics Annual, volume 38, 2024.

Focusing on the 1977–2007 time period, Acemoglu et al. find that total factor productivity (TFP) growth among supplying industries has become more mushroomlike over time. This imbalance, they estimate, has led to reduced innovation spillovers, which, in turn, provides a novel explanation for a slowdown in productivity.

This is a thought-provoking paper, full of rich insights about the centrally important issues of what drives productivity and why productivity trends change. Every reader can find something to like, something to wrestle with, something to worry about. The authors have responded to many concerns with copious robustness checks.

In this comment, we first discuss the unusual timing of the productivity slowdown that the authors seek to explain. The paper's executive summary highlights the slowdown after the 1970s. The paper itself restricts itself mainly to data from 1977 to 2007 and seeks to explain an apparent productivity slowdown in US manufacturing in the mid-1990s. This is unusual timing: conventional wisdom as well as a very large existing literature identifies a US productivity speedup in the mid-1990s. After about 2005, however, productivity growth slowed across advanced economies—a slowdown that occurs after the period analyzed in the Acemoglu et al. paper.

As we discuss, the reason the authors focus on an apparent mid-1990s slowdown is that the core data set used in the paper—the National Bureau of Economic Research and Center for Economic Studies (NBER-CES) six-digit industry data set—looks anomalous after 1997.[1] But given the 1977–2007 data window used in the paper's analysis, the results in the paper are, unfortunately, silent on both the 1970s slowdown and the mid-2000s slowdown.

Second, we reestimate Acemoglu et al.'s key equation after making a correction to the factor shares used in the NBER-CES industry data. Our preference would have been for this correction to be the default in the paper; the final version does include this correction in appendix tables. This correction actually appears to strengthen the results in the paper, in that the standard errors are noticeably smaller.

Nevertheless, we remain cautious about putting too much weight on results using the NBER-CES data, given the unusual time-series properties noted earlier. Whatever causes those time-series anomalies, they could affect the underlying industry TFP variances that drive Acemoglu et al.'s results. The factor-share correction, though an improvement, goes only a small way toward resolving the discrepancies.

Thus, our third point is to reestimate Acemoglu et al.'s key equation using an alternative, higher quality, data set. That data set, which is a joint product of the Bureau of Economic Analysis (BEA) and the Bureau of Labor Statistics (BLS), explicitly follows production theory as laid out in Jorgenson and Griliches (1967) and Jorgenson, Gollop, and Fraumeni (1987).[2] A preliminary exploration with these data suggests that, at a three-digit North American Industry Classification System (NAICS) level, mushroomlike (uneven) TFP growth is actually good for spillovers. These results thus run counter to those in Acemoglu et al.

An important caveat is that the BEA-BLS data are much more aggregated, so we lose the granularity of the NBER-CES data. This granularity could be important for the spillovers identified in the paper. Nevertheless, given our concerns about the quality of the NBER-CES data, we view the detrimental effects of unbalanced innovation as an intriguing conjecture, not as a proven fact.

II. The Timing of the Productivity Slowdown

Our first point concerns the anomalous timing of the productivity slowdown addressed by Acemoglu et al. Figure 1 displays the growth of TFP in the market economy from 1947 to 2020, using data from the BEA-BLS Integrated Production Accounts.[3]

The figure highlights a clear productivity slowdown after the late 1960s or early 1970s. Productivity growth picked up again between 1995 and about 2005.[4] There is a second productivity slowdown that became evident after the mid-2000s.

The slowdown period emphasized in Acemoglu et al. focuses on the period from 1997 to 2007, shown with the vertical lines in the figure. From the perspective of figure 1, this dating seems surprising: the 1997–2007 period is close to the fastest 10 years of TFP growth since the 1970s! (This period was only a touch slower than the 1995–2005 period.) The remarkable growth coincided with the emergence of the internet. More broadly, there was a widely documented information-technology-driven transformation across the economy (e.g., Basu et al. 2004; Fernald 2015).

The marked decline in market-sector TFP growth occurred only after 2005. Acemoglu et al. end their analysis in 2007. Hence, for all their intriguing analysis, they are largely silent on the important post-2005 slowdown.[5]

So why do Acemoglu et al. focus on a slowdown from 1997 to 2007? This anomalous timing arises from their core focus on US manufacturing data from the NBER-CES productivity data set. That data set is valuable because it provides input and output data for 462 manufacturing industries.

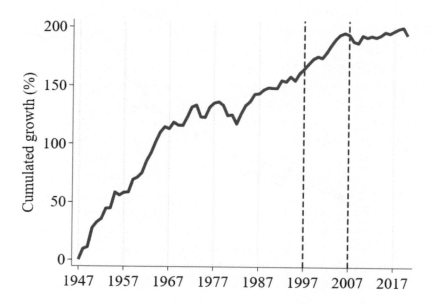

Fig. 1. Market-economy TFP growth, 1947–2020. Bureau of Economic Analysis and Bureau of Labor Statistics Integrated Production Account. Total factor productivity (TFP) is in value-added terms and is constructed by Domar-weighting gross-output TFP growth for market-sector industries. The market economy excludes government, education, health care, and real estate. The figure plots 100 times the cumulated log-change in market-sector TFP since 1947. A color version of this figure is available online.

But it turns out that, after the mid-1990s, the time-series pattern in that data set is completely at odds with other, more standard data sets.

Figure 2 compares manufacturing value-added TFP between our benchmark BEA-BLS data set and the Acemoglu et al. benchmark NBER-CES data set. The thick solid line shows TFP in the BEA-BLS data set. It looks qualitatively similar to figure 1. After the early 1970s, the fastest decade of productivity growth was 1996–2006; there was a very sharp slowdown after 2007. Indeed, the level of manufacturing TFP has edged down slightly since then.

The thick dashed line shows the sharp difference in the time-series pattern that is apparent in the NBER-CES data. The level of TFP roughly tracks the BEA-BLS series up until 1997. But the series diverge during the subsequent decade. The BEA-BLS measure of TFP has its strongest decade of growth since the 1970s. In contrast, the NBER-CES measure stagnates after 1997. Although there is considerable volatility, there appears to be almost no TFP growth over the subsequent 2 decades.

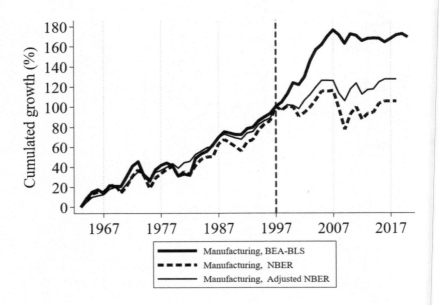

Fig. 2. Manufacturing-economy value-added TFP growth. Bureau of Economic Analysis and Bureau of Labor Statistics Integrated Production Account and National Bureau of Economic Research and Center for Economic Studies (NBER-CES) Manufacturing data set. Total factor productivity (TFP) is constructed by Domar-weighting gross-output TFP growth for manufacturing-sector industries. The figure plots 100 times the cumulated log-change in manufacturing-sector TFP since 1963. The thick solid line shows TFP in the BEA-BLS data set. The thick dashed line and the thin solid line show TFP in the NBER-CES data set before and after correcting factor shares. A color version of this figure is available online.

It is not completely clear what explains the differences in this case. Nevertheless, the NBER-CES data set suffers some well-known shortcomings relative to standard economic theory à la Jorgenson and Griliches (1967) and Jorgenson et al. (1987).

First, nominal factor shares in the NBER-CES data are mismeasured. Labor costs exclude fringe benefits, so labor's share is too low; intermediate services are omitted, so the intermediate share is too low. The low intermediate share also implies that nominal value added is overstated.

As a consequence, labor's share is extremely low in the NBER-CES data; residual capital shares are extremely high. In 1997, for example, labor's share is only 15% of gross output and 31% (!) of value added. In contrast, in the BEA-BLS data set, labor's share is 21% of gross output and 58% of value added.

Second, real factor inputs in the NBER-CES data are crude relative to state-of-the-art growth-accounting conventions. Production-worker hours are available, but for nonproduction and supervisory workers only the number of employees is available. There is no adjustment for the composition of the labor force by experience or education. Capital is a simple stock measure, not a share-weighted capital-input measure. And as noted, intermediate inputs completely omit services, which become more important over time.

A common correction for the first issue, incorrect factor shares, is to adjust the detailed NAICS six-digit NBER-CES factor shares using ratios calculated at a three-digit level (e.g., Bils and Chang 2000). We implemented this correction by calculating the ratio of the BEA-BLS labor and intermediate shares relative to the corresponding shares within each three-digit NBER-CES shares. We then apply the same ratio to rescale labor and intermediate factor shares for all six-digit NBER-CES industries that are part of the same three-digit industry. We then aggregate the series to get an adjusted NBER-CES manufacturing value-added TFP series.

The thin solid line in figure 2 shows the effect of the factor-share adjustment. The adjustment improves the coherence with the BEA-BLS series prior to 1997. The main effect of the adjustment is to give more weight to labor and intermediates relative to capital; this adjustment is particularly important around business cycles, when measured capital is smooth relative to other inputs. After 1997, the adjustment goes in the right direction—it raises mean growth—but not by nearly enough to match growth in the BEA-BLS data set.[6]

Thus, the bulk of the post-1997 discrepancy between the BEA-BLS and NBER-CES data remains unexplained. A preliminary calculation suggests that, when aggregated across industries, the intermediates-price deflator in the NBER data set grows more slowly than in the BEA-BLS data set, so that real intermediate inputs correspondingly grow more quickly. As a result, TFP and real value added grow more slowly. We would emphasize that real value added in the BEA-BLS manufacturing data matches the official national accounts; the NBER-CES data do not.

In sum, the unusual time-series properties of the NBER-CES data leave us somewhat cautious about relying on results using these data. After all, whatever the source of the discrepancy—whether factor shares, deflators, or something else—this discrepancy is built into the underlying industry TFP growth rates and could also affect the variances of industry TFP growth. Those variances are the key input into the Acemoglu et al. empirical specification. We turn to those results now.

III.   Refinements to the Key Empirical Results

Our second point is that correcting factor shares in the NBER-CES data makes surprisingly little difference to the estimation results. This may be because, as noted already, correcting the factor shares only modestly changes the data set's unusual time-series pattern.[7]

The key estimating equation in Acemoglu et al. is as follows:

$$\Delta \text{TFP}_{it} = \beta_{\text{mean}} \sum_{j} \alpha_{ijt-1} \Delta \text{TFP}_{jt} + \beta_{\text{var}} \left(\Delta \text{TFP}_{jt} - \sum_{j} \alpha_{ijt-1} \Delta \text{TFP}_{jt} \right)^{2}$$

$$+ X'_{it-1} + \delta_t + \epsilon_{it}. \tag{1}$$

In this equation, ΔTFP_{it} is the 5-year growth rate of TFP in industry i, the α_{ijt-1} is the shares of nominal revenue purchased by industry i from industry j, X'_{it-1} denotes a vector of other covariates, and δ_t denotes a full set of time dummies. The first term on the right-hand side is the input-weighted TFP average; the second term (in parentheses) is the input-weighted TFP variance. The main estimates in the paper are uninstrumented, though they do present some results with instruments. We focus here on the ordinary least squares results.

The key coefficient is β_{var}, which multiplies the input-TFP variance. A positive coefficient implies that a higher variance of—that is, less balanced—TFP growth among an industry's suppliers is good for growth. That is, mushroomlike supplier TFP growth is good for innovation spillovers. A negative coefficient implies that mushroomlike growth is bad.

A question raised in the previous section is how to measure industry TFP in the NBER-CES data set. There are many potential challenges and pitfalls. For example, nonconstant returns, markups, and unobserved variations in factor utilization all mean that measured TFP growth is an imperfect proxy for technology change (e.g., Basu, Fernald, and Kimball 2006). Time averaging may help—to the extent the nontechnological effects are cyclical—but 5 or even 10 years may not be long enough.

We take a simpler approach here. Given that the factor shares used to calculate TFP in the NBER data set are clearly wrong (underweighting both labor and intermediates), to us the first step—and a natural default—is to correct the shares. Acemoglu et al. instead choose to put those adjustments in appendix tables. This means it is hard for the reader to see all of the implications of adjusting the shares for other findings in the paper.

The first two columns of table 1 show the benchmark regression results from Acemoglu et al. TFP growth at a six-digit industry is taken directly from the NBER-CES data set, without adjusting factor shares. (These correspond to table 1 of the paper, cols. 3 and 7.) In both cases, the coefficient on input-TFP variance is strongly negative: mushroomlike supplier TFP growth is bad for downstream TFP growth.

In the first column, the regression is unweighted. The coefficient on the variance of input-TFP has a t-statistic of around 8. In the second column, we weight industries based on their 1987 shares of nominal gross output. This sensible weighting reduces the coefficient on the variance of input-TFP by about one-third, but the coefficient remains statistically significantly negative.

The third and fourth columns incorporate the factor-share corrections discussed earlier. In the unweighted specification (col. 3), this correction leads to a notable reduction in the magnitude of the coefficient on the input-TFP variance relative to column 1. In the weighted specification, the correction leads to a more modest reduction in the magnitude of

Table 1
Relationship between Industry TFP Growth and Supplier TFP Growth Using the NBER-CES Data Set

			Corrected Factor Shares	
	(1)	(2)	(3)	(4)
Input-TFP average	.65	.53	.26	.31
	(.074)	(.13)	(.089)	(.097)
Input-TFP variance	−.91	−.62	−.66	−.56
	(.12)	(.20)	(.10)	(.11)
Ind. fixed effects	Yes	Yes	Yes	Yes
Industry weighting	None	Sales	None	Sales
Sales Observations	2772	2772	2772	2772
R^2	.37	.60	.36	.61

Note: This table reports estimates of equation (1) (eq. [6] in Acemoglu et al. 2023) for 462 North American Industry Classification System (NAICS) six-digit manufacturing industries 1977–2007. The left-hand-side variable is the nonoverlapping 5-year growth rate of industry total factor productivity (TFP; so six 5-year periods during 1977–2007). The input-TFP average and variance are also calculated over the corresponding 5-year periods. Columns 1 and 2 correspond to columns 3 and 7 of table 1 of the paper; columns 3 and 4 correspond to columns 3 and 7 of table A4 of the paper. Columns 1 and 3 report unweighted ordinary least squares regressions; columns 2 and 4 use the industry's 1987 share of shipments as weights. Time and industry dummies are included in all regressions. Industries are defined using 1997 NAICS codes. Standard errors (shown in parentheses) are clustered at the industry level. NBER-CES = National Bureau of Economic Research and Center for Economic Studies.

the coefficient relative to column 2. (These regressions correspond to table A4 of the paper, cols. 3 and 7.)

Strikingly, the standard error also declines noticeably: the t-statistic actually increases when using the adjusted factor shares. This underscores the resilience of their results when using the NBER-CES data set. It also underscores why we would have preferred to see the factor-share adjusted TFP series taken as the benchmark throughout the paper, because it actually strengthens their empirical findings.

But of course, the magnitude of the coefficient itself is not easily interpretable. Hence, the paper (fig. 5) undertakes a counterfactual exercise to see, if the input-TFP variances did not change from their 1977–87 values, what productivity would have been in the subsequent decades. (The counterfactual holds average supplier-weighted TFP growth fixed at their actual values, so that only the input-TFP variance changes from the actual values.)

The left panel of figure 3 reproduces the results from the paper's figure 5 for manufacturing. Relative to the paper's figure, we present results in terms of annualized percentage changes and show just the bars for actual and counterfactual manufacturing TFP growth. The black bars show the sharp slowdown in (gross-output) manufacturing TFP growth after 1997. The gray counterfactual bars show that, if the variances of input-TFP had been held fixed at their 1977–87 level, there would still have been a slowdown, but it would have been modestly attenuated. In the 1997–2007 period, the results imply that the increase in input-TFP

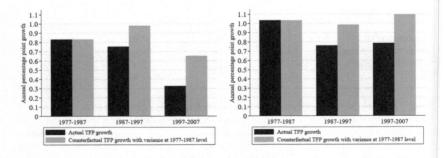

Fig. 3. Magnitude of bottleneck estimates. The left panel reproduces the results from the paper's figure 5 for manufacturing. On the right panel, counterfactual total factor productivity (TFP) (gray bar) is computed from our adjusted (nominal sales-) weighted estimates reported in column 4 of table 1 and represents the TFP growth that would have been observed in the given period if the variance of TFP growth had remained at the same level as during the initial period (1977–87). A color version of this figure is available online.

variance was a drag of about 0.3 percentage points per year to manufacturing TFP growth.

The right panel shows our preferred version of the figure, which incorporates the factor-share adjustments. The biggest difference is that the "actual" bar does not show a slowdown in the 1997–2007 period relative to the preceding decade. That is consistent with figure 2, where adjusting factor shares (modestly) raises TFP after 1997 (though not enough to close the gap with the BEA-BLS or other data sets). It turns out, however, that the gap between the counterfactual and the actual bar is almost identical to that shown in the left panel. Both panels suggest that the increase in input-TFP variance may reduce productivity growth by 0.1 percentage point after 1997. In principle, despite a coefficient that is only modestly attenuated, the gap could have changed more significantly because the underlying industry TFP variances are also affected. But this turns out not to be the case.

IV.   Empirical Analysis Using the Integrated BEA-BLS Data Set

Although the results using conventional TFP with the NBER-CES data do seem robust to correcting factor shares, we started this discussion by raising general concerns about that source of data. Hence, our final point is to see if we can replicate the results in a different, higher-quality data set. It turns out we cannot.

In particular, when we repeat the analysis using the BEA-BLS industry data set, the coefficient on the input-TFP variance is either strongly positive (in manufacturing) or positive but insignificant (in all industries). That is, unbalanced, mushroomlike input-TFP growth appears either positive for spillovers or unimportant.[8]

Table 2 shows these results. For comparability, we focus on the same 1977–2007 period that Acemoglu et al. do. Column 1 restricts the analysis to 19 manufacturing industries; column 2 considers the 55 industries that span the market economy. These results consistently show that higher input-TFP variance is associated with stronger industry TFP growth. This finding contrasts with the evidence from the paper and from table 1, which focused on the NBER-CES data.

It is not clear what explains the difference. The BEA-BLS data set is higher quality, in that it measures inputs and factor shares consistent with economic theory; in addition, the data match the national accounts, which incorporate numerous quality-control checks. At the same time, the data are much more aggregated. The reduced granularity may matter for the results.

Table 2
Relationship between Industry TFP Growth and Suppliers' TFP Growth Using the
BEA-BLS Data Set

	(1)	(2)
Input average	.323	.865
	(.100)	(.145)
Input variance	18.8	3.12
	(7.84)	(5.17)
Ind. fixed effects	Yes	Yes
Industry weighting	Nom. sales	Nom. sales
Observations	114	330
Time period	1977–2007	1977–2007
Methodology	5-year	5-year
Sample	Manufacturing	Market

Note: This table reports estimates of equation (1) (eq. [6] in Acemoglu et al. 2023) 1977–2007
using the Bureau of Economic Analysis and Bureau of Labor Statistics Integrated Production Account. The dependent variable is an industry's total factor productivity (TFP) growth
in a (nonoverlapping) 5-year period, and the two right-hand-side variables are mean and
variance of TFP growth among industry's suppliers, calculated over the same 5-year period.
All columns use the industry's share of shipments as weights. Time and industry dummies
(corresponding to linear industry trends) are included in all regressions. Columns 1 and 2
report ordinary least squares regression for manufacturing and market-sector industries,
respectively. Industries are defined using 1997 North American Industry Classification
System codes. Standard errors are shown in parentheses.

Nevertheless, given the higher quality of the BEA-BLS data as well as
the uncertain quality of the NBER-CES data, these results give us some
pause. Our own take is that the paper's finding in favor of balanced
growth remains a hypothesis rather than a proven fact.

V. Conclusions

The Acemoglu et al. paper proposes a new hypothesis about the nature
of spillovers across firms and industries. They argue that unbalanced,
mushroomlike growth reduces innovation spillovers. And because the
variance of upstream TFP appears to have increased over time, they find
that unbalanced innovation was an increasing drag on TFP growth.

The hypothesis, and the empirical results, are intriguing and thought
provoking. Nevertheless, we remain cautious about this finding. The main
data set that yields this finding—the NBER-CES data set—looks quite different from other, higher-quality data sets. We do not yet know why. That
leaves us hesitant about drawing strong conclusions from these data.
This is especially the case given that a higher-quality, but more aggregated,
data set gives quite different results.

One point we have not addressed is that TFP growth is an imperfect proxy, even after correcting the NBER-CES factor shares. For example, markups, nonconstant returns, shifts in factor utilization, and reallocations within industries or sectors affect TFP growth and the variance of TFP growth. Such effects could easily be correlated through input-output linkages and thereby cause biases in the results. The discussion of Acemoglu et al. by Jennifer La'O and Eugenio Piga in this volume addresses some of these more nuanced and challenging measurement issues.

What this means is that the Acemoglu et al. paper is only a preliminary step in establishing the nature of innovation spillovers through input-output linkages. Subsequent work needs to establish the degree to which the spillovers exist as well as whether the nature of these spillovers can contribute to our understanding of productivity speedups and slowdowns. Hence, our main takeaway is that there is much more work to be done.

Endnotes

Author email address: Fernald (fernaldjg@gmail.com), Piga (eugenio.piga@insead.edu). The views expressed in this comment are our own and do not necessarily represent the views of the Federal Reserve Bank of San Francisco, its staff, or others associated with the Federal Reserve System. For acknowledgments, sources of research support, and disclosure of the authors' material financial relationships, if any, please see https://www.nber.org/books -and-chapters/nber-macroeconomics-annual-2023-volume-38/comment-bottlenecks -sectoral-imbalances-and-us-productivity-slowdown-fernald.

1. The paper brings much more data to bear. Some results add nonmanufacturing industries from BLS data; other results use international Integrated Industry-Level Production Account (KLEMS) data. But the core analysis focuses on the NBER-CES data because it allows considerable granularity.

2. The historical BEA-BLS Integrated Production Accounts are described in Eldridge et al. (2020) and run 1947–2016; the updated data are described in Bureau of Economic Analysis (2022) and run from 1987 to 2020. We merge the data in 1987. See Fernald, Inklaar, and Ruzic (2023) for details.

3. Endnote 2 describes the data. TFP is in value-added terms and is calculated by aggregating TFP growth across market-sector industries using time-varying Domar weights (nominal gross output relative to market-sector nominal value added).

4. See Fernald et al. (2017) for a discussion of the timing of apparent breaks in productivity growth.

5. Fernald et al. (2023) review alternative stories for the advanced-economy TFP slowdown after the mid-2000s, with links to the literature. Their preferred story emphasizes a common trend slowdown in innovation across countries. Such a common trend is consistent with Acemoglu et al.'s argument on declining innovation spillovers. Aghion et al. (2023) provide a quite different story about innovation and trend growth that emphasizes the changing returns to innovation.

6. Mean TFP growth rises more quickly because the corrected shares give less weight to faster-growing capital. Indeed, labor input in manufacturing was falling after 1997 even as capital kept rising.

7. In our comment on the conference paper, we proposed two adjustments: first, to the factor shares, discussed here; and second, weighting the regression (and fig. 5 of their paper) by nominal gross output rather than fixed 1987 single-deflated value added. The joint effect had a major effect on the implications of the regression results. In the final draft of the paper, Acemoglu et al. have adopted our recommended gross-output weighting, which in our view gives more sensible results. (Single-deflated value added deflates nominal value added by the gross-output deflator; it turns out to have odd properties, as our conference discussion highlighted.) They now include the corrected factor shares that we discuss here as robustness exercises in appendix tables.

8. The coefficients are much larger in magnitude than those shown in table 1. The reason is that, in the three-digit BEA-BLS industry data, the input-TFP variances (the right-hand-side regressors) are much smaller. This could be because the data smooth over the sometimes extreme six-digit TFP variances.

References

Aghion, Philippe, Antonin Bergeaud, Timo Boppart, Huiyu Li, and Pete Klenow. 2023. "A Theory of Falling Growth and Rising Rents." *Review of Economic Studies* 90 (6): 2675–702.

Basu, Susanto, John G. Fernald, and Miles S. Kimball. 2006. "Are Technology Improvements Contractionary?" *American Economic Review* 96 (5): 1418–48.

Basu, Susanto, John G. Fernald, Nicholas Oulton, and Sylaja Srinivasan. 2004. "The Case of the Missing Productivity Growth, or Does Information Technology Explain Why Productivity Accelerated in the United States but Not in the United Kingdom?" *NBER Macroeconomics Annual 2003* 18:9–82.

Bils, Mark, and Yongsung Chang. 2000. "Understanding How Price Responds to Costs and Production." *Carnegie-Rochester Conference Series on Public Policy* 52:33–77.

Bureau of Economic Analysis. 2022. "BEA-BLS Integrated Industry-Level Production Accounts (KLEMS)." https://www.bls.gov/productivity/articles-and-research/bea-bls-integrated-production-accounts.htm.

Daron Acemoglu, David Autor, and Christina Patterson. 2023. "Bottlenecks: Sectoral Imbalances and the US Productivity Slowdown," NBER Chapters, in: NBER Macroeconomics Annual 2023, volume 38, National Bureau of Economic Research, Inc.

Eldridge, Lucy P., Corby Garner, Thomas F. Howells, Brian C. Moyer, Matthew Russell, Jon D. Samuels, Erich H. Strassner, and David B. Wasshausen. 2020. "Toward a BEA-BLS Integrated Industry-Level Production Account for 1947–2016." In *Measuring Economic Growth and Productivity*, ed. Barbara Fraumeni, 221–49. Cambridge, MA: Academic Press.

Fernald, John G. 2015. "Productivity and Potential Output Before, During, and After the Great Recession." *NBER Macroeconomics Annual 2014* 29 (1): 1–51.

Fernald, John G., Robert E. Hall, James H. Stock, and Mark W. Watson. 2017. "The Disappointing Recovery of Output after 2009." *Brookings Papers on Economic Activity* 2017 (Spring): 1–58.

Fernald, John G., Robert C. Inklaar, and Dimitrije Ruzic. 2023. "The Productivity Slowdown in Advanced Economies: Common Shocks or Common Trends?" Working Paper Series 2023-07, Federal Reserve Bank of San Francisco. https://doi.org/10.24148/wp2023-07.

Harberger, Arnold C. 1998. "A Vision of the Growth Process." *American Economic Review* 88 (1): 1–32. http://www.jstor.org/stable/116816.

Jorgenson, D. W., and Z. Griliches. 1967. "The Explanation of Productivity Change." *Review of Economic Studies* 34 (3): 249–83. https://doi.org/10.2307/2296675.

Jorgenson, Dale W., Frank M. Gollop, and Barbara M. Fraumeni. 1987. *Productivity and US Economic Growth*. Cambridge, MA: Harvard University Press.

Comment

Jennifer La'O, Columbia University and NBER, United States of America, and *Centre for Economic Policy Research,* United Kingdom
Eugenio Piga, INSEAD, France

I. Introduction

In "Bottlenecks: Sectoral Imbalances and the US Productivity Slowdown," Daron Acemoglu, David Autor, and Christina Patterson document a fascinating and provocative new fact about sectoral total factor productivity (TFP) growth: they find evidence of a strong negative relationship between an industry's own TFP growth and the cross-sectional variance of TFP growth among the industry's intermediate-input suppliers.

In particular, the authors use data from the NBER-CES (National Bureau of Economic Research and Center for Economic Studies) data set on industry-level TFP corresponding to North American Industry Classification System (NAICS) six-digit industries. With these data, they run the following regression:

$$\Delta \text{TFP}_{it} = \beta_m \text{mean}_i\left(\Delta \text{TFP}_{jt}\right) + \beta_v \text{var}_i\left(\Delta \text{TFP}_{jt}\right) + X'_{i,t-1}\beta_{\text{other}} + \delta_t + \varepsilon_{it}, \quad (1)$$

where ΔTFP_{it} is the TFP growth of industry i at time t, δ_t are time fixed effects, and $X'_{i,t-1}$ denotes other (predetermined) covariates. We let mean_i (ΔTFP_{jt}) and $\text{var}_i(\Delta \text{TFP}_{jt})$ denote, respectively, the mean and cross-sectional variance of TFP growth of industry i's intermediate-good suppliers j, weighted by their respective intermediate-input shares.

Although they control for the mean of supplier TFP growth throughout their analysis, the authors' primary coefficient of interest is β_v, the coefficient on supplier TFP growth dispersion. Their main finding is that β_v is negative, significant, and quantitatively large, and they show this to be robust to several specifications.

NBER Macroeconomics Annual, volume 38, 2024.

Acemoglu, Autor, and Patterson (2023) interpret this to mean that an imbalance in TFP growth among an industry's set of suppliers adversely affects the TFP growth of the industry itself. If TFP is measured without error, this is certainly plausible.

However, what if TFP is mismeasured? In this case, the coefficient of interest could instead be capturing Neoclassical effects of changes in supplier productivity. Viewed in this light, the left-hand side of equation (1) would, at least in part, represent movements along an unchanged production possibilities frontier, rather than movements of the frontier itself.

In this comment, we introduce a simple, transparent theoretical framework that illustrates this possibility. We then consider how the proposed Neoclassical channel holds up in the data and leads to a reinterpretation of estimates of β_v.

II. Neoclassical Effects of Supplier TFP Dispersion

We consider a simple, static, partial-equilibrium environment with TFP mismeasurement as in Basu, Fernald, and Kimball (2006) and Burnside, Eichenbaum, and Rebelo (1995). There is a finite set of final-good industries, indexed by $i \in I$. Final-good industries source materials from a unit-mass continuum of intermediate-good industries, indexed by $j \in [0, 1]$. Firms have industry-specific technologies and are perfectly competitive; it follows that there is a representative firm per industry that takes prices as given.

The production function of the representative firm in final-good industry $i \in I$ is given by

$$Y_i = A_i F^i(Z_i K_i, L_i, X_i), \tag{2}$$

where Y_i is the firm's output, A_i is its TFP, and $F^i : \mathbb{R}^3_+ \to \mathbb{R}_+$ is a function homogeneous of degree 1.[1] We let K_i, L_i, X_i denote the firm's capital stock, labor input, and materials, respectively. Capital is fixed, but labor and materials are variable inputs, as well as the utilization of capital, which we denote by Z_i. Note that we can rewrite equation (2) as $Y_i = A_i F^i(\hat{K}_i, L_i, X_i)$, where we let $\hat{K}_i \equiv Z_i K_i$ denote "effective" capital.

We assume that the capital stock, labor, and materials are observable. In contrast, we assume that capital utilization is an unobservable factor of production—it is the unobservability of this factor that gives rise to TFP mismeasurement in our model.

Next, we let materials X_i be a constant elasticity of substitution composite of intermediate inputs sourced from intermediate-good sectors $j \in [0, 1]$. Specifically

$$X_i = \left[\int x_{ij}^{\frac{\rho-1}{\rho}} dj \right]^{\frac{\rho}{\rho-1}}, \tag{3}$$

where x_{ij} denotes the use of intermediate good j in the production of firm i, and $\rho > 0$ denotes the elasticity of substitution across inputs. If $\rho < 1$, then intermediate inputs are complements in production; conversely, if $\rho > 1$, then intermediate inputs are substitutes.

The representative firm of final-good industry $i \in I$ chooses the variable inputs (Z_i, L_i) and intermediate goods $(x_{ij})_{j \in [0,1]}$ to maximize profits given by

$$\Pi_i \equiv P_i Y_i - W L_i - \int p_j x_{ij} dj - W C(Z_i), \tag{4}$$

where P_i is the price of its final good, W is the wage, and p_j is the price of intermediate good j. The last term in equation (4) is the cost of capital utilization; for tractability, we assume that this cost is proportional to the wage, similar to the specification in Basu et al. (2006). One can think of this as workers must be paid overtime to operate machines. We furthermore assume that the cost function $C: \mathbb{R}_+ \to \mathbb{R}_+$ is continuous, twice-differentiable, strictly increasing, and strictly convex.

The representative firm of intermediate-good sector $j \in [0, 1]$ has linear technology $y_j = a_j \ell_j$, where y_j is the firm's output, a_j is its productivity, and ℓ_j is its labor input. This firm maximizes profits $\pi_j \equiv p_j y_j - W \ell_j$; it follows that its price is equal to its marginal cost: $p_j = W/a_j$.

For expositional purposes, we assume that all productivities, $(A_i)_{i \in I}$ and $(a_j)_{j \in [0,1]}$, are exogenous. That is, we completely shut down the effect emphasized in Acemoglu et al. (2023)—in our setup, there is absolutely no effect of suppliers' TFP on own-industry TFP.

We assume that intermediate-good productivities are i.i.d. across industries j and drawn from a log Normal distribution, $\log a_j \sim \mathcal{N}(\mu_a, \sigma_a^2)$, with mean μ_a and variance σ_a^2. Finally, we assume that there is no mismeasurement of intermediate-good supplier TFP, but we explore the implications of final-good TFP mismeasurement when capital utilization is unobservable.

A.   Partial-Equilibrium Characterization

One can split the problem of the representative firm of final-good industry i into an inner cost-minimization problem over intermediate inputs and an outer profit-maximization problem over capital utilization, labor, and materials.

Consider first the inner problem. The firm's cost-minimization problem over intermediate-good purchases is given by $Q_i X_i \equiv \min_{(x_{ij})} \int p_j x_{ij} dj$ subject to equation (3). The solution to this problem yields the following cost-minimizing price Q_i of the intermediate-input bundle X_i:

$$Q_i = \left[\int p_j^{1-\rho} dj\right]^{\frac{1}{1-\rho}}. \tag{5}$$

Combining this expression with equilibrium input prices, and using the fact that supplier TFP is log Normal, we obtain the following exact characterization of the price of materials.[2]

Lemma 1 The price of materials satisfies

$$\log Q_i = \log W - \mu_a + \frac{1}{2}(1-\rho)\sigma_a^2. \tag{6}$$

Therefore, the price of materials is (i) strictly decreasing in μ_a and (ii) strictly increasing in σ_a if and only if $\rho < 1$.

Proof. First, substituting input prices $p_j = W/a_j$ into equation (5) yields

$$Q_i = W\left[\int a_j^{-(1-\rho)} dj\right]^{\frac{1}{1-\rho}}.$$

We may rewrite this in logs as follows:

$$\log Q_i = \log W + \frac{1}{1-\rho}\log\left[\int_{j\in[0,1]} \exp\{-(1-\rho)\log a_j\} dj\right].$$

By log-Normality of a_j, the random variable $-(1-\rho)\log a_j$ is i.i.d. across j and satisfies

$$-(1-\rho)\log a_j \sim \mathcal{N}(-(1-\rho)\mu_a, (1-\rho)^2\sigma_a^2).$$

Finally, by applying the moment-generating function for the Normal distribution, we obtain the expression for $\log Q_i$ provided in equation (6).□

Lemma 1 states that the price of materials is decreasing in μ_A. If intermediate-good producers are more productive on average, this leads to a fall in the average price of intermediate inputs and therefore a fall in the overall price of materials, Q_i.

Lemma 1 furthermore characterizes the impact of σ_a on the cost-minimizing materials price. An increase in the dispersion of intermediate-good productivity translates 1-for-1 to an increase in the dispersion of intermediate-good prices, p_j. How the price of the intermediate-input bundle relates to the cross-sectional variance of input prices depends on whether inputs are substitutes or complements in production. When intermediate inputs are substitutes ($\rho > 1$), the price of the intermediate-good bundle is strictly decreasing in the cross-sectional variance of input prices: if input-price variance increases, the firm can substitute toward lower-cost inputs and, in effect, lower its overall cost of the intermediate-good bundle.

On the other hand, when intermediate inputs are complements ($\rho < 1$), the cost-minimizing price of the intermediate-good bundle is strictly increasing in the cross-sectional variance of input prices. If input-price dispersion increases and inputs are complements, the firm must bear the brunt of more expensive intermediates to achieve the same overall level of materials. It follows that the firm's overall cost of its intermediate-good bundle rises.

Consider next the outer problem of the firm. Recall that capital is fixed; firm i thus solves the following profit-maximization problem:

$$\max_{L_i, X_i, Z_i} P_i A_i F^i(Z_i, K_i, L_i, X_i) - WL_i - Q_i X_i - WC(Z_i),$$

taking prices P_i, Q_i, and W as given. The firm's first-order conditions (FOCs) with respect to labor, materials, and capital utilization, respectively, are given by

$$P_i A_i F_L^i(\cdot) = W, P_i A_i F_X^i(\cdot) = Q_i, \text{ and } P_i A_i K_i F_K^i(\cdot) = WC'(Z_i). \quad (7)$$

That is, at the firm's optimum, the marginal revenue product of any variable input is equal to its respective marginal cost. This brings us to the following result.

Lemma 2   Part (i). If the cross-price elasticity of labor with respect to the price of materials of firm i is strictly negative, then the labor demand of firm i is (a) strictly increasing in μ_A and (b) strictly decreasing in σ_A if and only if $\rho < 1$.

Part (ii). If the cross-price elasticity of capital utilization with respect to the price of materials of firm i is strictly negative, then capital utilization of firm i is (a) strictly increasing in μ_A and (b) strictly decreasing in σ_A if and only if $\rho < 1$.

Proof. Part (i). If the cross-price elasticity of labor with respect to the price of materials is strictly negative, then an increase in Q_i leads to a fall in labor demand. The rest of the statement follows directly from Lemma 1. The proof of part (ii) follows the same logic.□

A negative cross-price elasticity of any variable input with respect to the price of materials indicates that when the price of materials increases, the firm's demand for that input falls. This is simply the definition of complements in production. Lemma 2 therefore states that if labor and effective capital are complements to materials in firm i's production, then the firm's demand for these primary inputs is falling in the cross-sectional variance of intermediate-input suppliers' TFP (provided that $\rho < 1$).

This result follows almost immediately from Lemma 1. If intermediate inputs are complements ($\rho < 1$), then an increase in the dispersion of supplier TFP leads to an increase in the overall price of materials, Q_i. If materials become more expensive, then the firm's demand for materials falls—that is, own-price elasticity is strictly negative. Provided that the relevant cross-price elasticities are also negative, the firm moreover hires fewer workers and uses less capital.

B.   Measured TFP

We now consider how these forces affect measured TFP. We define measured TFP of firm i in our model as the Solow residual of gross output:

$$\log SR_i \equiv \log Y_i - \gamma_{\hat{K}} \log K_i - \gamma_L \log L_i - \gamma_X \log X_i, \qquad (8)$$

where $\gamma_{\hat{K}}, \gamma_L, \gamma_X > 0$ are the factor shares of effective capital, labor, and materials, respectively. The model is static; therefore, one should interpret these levels as deviations from trend. We assume that factor shares are measured correctly, but capital utilization is unobservable. We obtain the following result.

Proposition 1   The Solow residual of firm $i \in I$ defined in equation (8) satisfies

$$\log SR_i = \log A_i + \gamma_{\hat{K}} \log Z_i. \qquad (9)$$

If the cross-price elasticity of capital utilization with respect to the price of materials is strictly negative, then the Solow residual is (i) strictly increasing in μ_A and (ii) strictly decreasing in σ_A if and only if $\rho < 1$.

Proof. We write the production function in equation (2) in logs as follows:

$$\log Y_i = \log A_i + \gamma_{\hat{K}} \log(Z_i K_i) + \gamma_L \log L_i + \gamma_X \log X_i.$$

Substituting this into equation (8) and canceling terms yields equation (9). The rest of the statement follows directly from Lemma 2.□

Proposition 1 states that measured TFP in our model reflects not only the firm's true TFP, A_i, but also its utilization of capital, Z_i, and is in fact strictly increasing in the latter. Combining this observation with Lemma 2, we infer that measured TFP is strictly decreasing in the cross-sectional variance of intermediate-good supplier TFP when $\rho < 1$ and capital utilization and materials are complements.

With this result in mind, we return to the baseline specification of Acemoglu et al. (2023). One could run the following, analogous regression within our framework:[3]

$$\log SR_{it} = \beta_m \mu_{at} + \beta_v \sigma_{at}^2 + \delta_t + \varepsilon_{it}. \tag{10}$$

Provided there is sufficient complementarity among inputs, such a regression run on data generated by the model would result in $\beta_v < 0$. The coefficient of interest would take on this sign not because of any direct effect of supplier innovation on own innovation—recall that we have shut down such channels by assuming exogenous productivities—but instead as the result of standard Neoclassical effects. That is, the coefficient on supplier TFP variance in the above specification would capture movements along the firm's production possibilities frontier, rather than movements of the frontier itself.

The mechanism we highlight in this model is both simple and—we think—reasonable. Provided that intermediate inputs are complements in production, an increase in the dispersion of intermediate-input prices, precipitated by an increase in the dispersion of supplier productivities, puts upward pressure on the cost-minimizing price of the intermediate-good bundle. A more expensive intermediate-good bundle leads to a fall in the firm's capital utilization if effective capital and materials are complements. Finally, provided that capital utilization is difficult to observe and therefore not fully accounted for in the measurement of firm (or sectoral) TFP, such movements in capital utilization would manifest as movements in the firm's Solow residual. The Solow residual therefore falls, not because of any change in the firm's production set, but only because it is an imperfect measure of true TFP.

Our model highlights that a necessary ingredient for this result is the mismeasurement of TFP. If TFP were measured without error (i.e., $\log SR_i = \log A_i$), then the regression in equation (10) would yield $\beta_v = 0$. The way we obtain mismeasurement is by assuming unobservability of a variable factor of production, namely, capital utilization. However, one could accomplish the same objective in a variety of ways, such as assuming observable factors of production but mismeasurement of factor shares. In the latter case, though, whether factor shares are overestimated or underestimated would affect the sign of β_v.

The model itself predicts a negative β_v. Conditional on TFP mismeasurement, a sufficient condition for a negative β_v in our model is complementarity at two levels of aggregation: among intermediate inputs and between the bundle of intermediate goods (materials) and capital. We focus on the case of complementarity, as elasticities less than one are typically borne out in the data (see, e.g., Barrot and Sauvagnat 2016; Atalay 2017; Boehm, Flaaen, and Pandalai-Nayar 2019; Carvalho et al. 2020). On the other hand, the model makes clear that these conditions are sufficient but not necessary: substitutability at both levels of aggregation would also deliver a negative β_v.

III. Controlling for the Neoclassical Channel

The potential for Neoclassical effects due to TFP mismeasurement is a tricky empirical issue. In Subsection IV.E of their paper, Acemoglu, Autor, and Patterson directly address this concern by augmenting their baseline specification with the mean and cross-sectional variance of supplier price growth using industry price data from the KLEMS (Integrated Industry-Level Production Account) data set. This is a clever way of addressing the issue, as it goes directly to the heart of the Neoclassical mechanism.

The Neoclassical channel works purely through prices. To see this, recall that the cost-minimizing price of the intermediate-input bundle, Q_i, satisfies equation (5). It follows that the productivity of supplier j affects the production decisions of firm i only insofar as it alters the intermediate-input price p_j. In other words, the effect of input-price dispersion on the Solow residual is a sufficient statistic for the Neoclassical effect of supplier TFP dispersion.

Translating the model to the data, and abstracting from issues of collinearity, if one were to add the mean and cross-sectional variance of input-price growth to the right-hand side of the baseline regression, the coefficients on these variables would plausibly capture the Neoclassical effects conjectured above.[4]

Acemoglu et al. do exactly this exercise and report their results in table 6 of their paper. We reproduce these results in table 1 of our comment; throughout, we focus exclusively on specifications that include industry fixed effects.[5] Column 1 restates the authors' estimates from their baseline regression without controlling for supplier price growth. This column replicates the paper's main result: a precisely estimated and quantitatively large negative relationship between the variance of supplier TFP growth and own-industry TFP growth. Specifically, the point estimate for the coefficient on the variance of supplier TFP growth, β_v, is equal to -0.912 with a standard error of 0.118.

Table 1
Revisiting Neoclassical Effects

	Baseline TFP Measure			Adjusted TFP Measure		
	(1)	(2)	(3)	(4)	(5)	(6)
Input TFP average	.653	.692	.364	.264	.229	.125
	(.074)	(.083)	(.070)	(.089)	(.101)	(.099)
Input TFP variance	−.912	−.527	−.270	−.657	−.336	−.260
	(.118)	(.243)	(.192)	(.101)	(.203)	(.187)
Input-price average		.077	−.053		−.035	−.089
		(.061)	(.057)		(.062)	(.061)
Input-price variance		−.329	−.368		−.333	−.346
		(.198)	(.165)		(.170)	(.159)
Own-industry employment			.267			.113
			(.018)			(.018)
Ind. fixed effects	Yes	Yes	Yes	Yes	Yes	Yes
Industry weighting	None	None	None	None	None	None
Observations	2,772	2,772	2,772	2,772	2,772	2,772
R^2	.371	.373	.494	.365	.368	.396

Note: This table reports estimates of the baseline equation in Acemoglu et al. (2023) as well as various specifications that control for Neoclassical effects. The dependent variable is an industry's TFP growth in a 5-year period. The right-hand-side variables include the mean and variance of supplier TFP growth, the mean and variance of supplier price growth, and growth in own-industry employment. Columns 1–3 use the authors' preferred baseline TFP series. Columns 4–6 use the adjusted TFP series described at the end of Subsection IV.D of the paper and discussed in Fernald and Piga. All columns report unweighted regressions that include both time and industry fixed effects (corresponding to linear industry trends). Standard errors are clustered at the industry level.

For comparison, column 2 of table 1 reports results for the specification that adds the mean and variance of supplier price growth as controls. Inclusion of these variables results in a point estimate of $\beta_v = -0.527$ for the coefficient of interest with a standard error of 0.243. That is, the magnitude of the supplier TFP variance effect drops to less than 60% of the baseline estimate and is less precisely estimated. On this matter, the authors write: "The alternative specifications . . . indicate that controlling for these Neoclassical channels does not qualitatively change the relationship between supplier TFP variance and industry TFP growth (and that the coefficients on these channel variables are typically insignificant)."

We agree with this assessment when comparing columns 1 and 2. These specifications use the authors' preferred baseline measure of TFP growth for NAICS six-digit industries in the NBER-CES data set. This measure is computed in the typical way, as the residual change in gross output after accounting for labor, capital, energy, and nonenergy materials. However, one issue with the NBER-CES data set is that it omits fringe benefits in labor costs, and its definition of intermediates does not include services. To address this shortcoming, in Subsection IV.D of their paper, Acemoglu et al. consider an adjusted TFP measure using corrected factor shares based on computations by John Fernald and Eugenio Piga—see their discussion of Acemoglu et al. (2023) in this volume for more details on this adjustment.[6]

We find that the authors' conclusion on the role of Neoclassical effects is not as compelling when one uses the adjusted TFP series. Specifically, we run the same specifications described above with adjusted TFP and report our results in columns 4 and 5 of table 1. Column 4 provides estimates of the baseline specification without controlling for supplier price growth; this yields a point estimate of $\beta_v = -0.657$ with a standard error of 0.101.[7] Column 5 reports results for the specification that adds the mean and variance of supplier price growth as controls. Inclusion of these variables results in a point estimate of $\beta_v = -0.336$ with a standard error of 0.203.

Therefore, when using the adjusted TFP measure, the qualitative relationship between industry TFP growth and the variance of supplier TFP growth survives: the point estimate for β_v remains negative. However, after controlling for the Neoclassical channel with supplier price growth, the magnitude of this effect drops to roughly 51% of its baseline estimate and, in particular, becomes insignificant. We thus infer that the inclusion of such controls is not so innocuous.

IV. Another Approach

In the preceding analysis, one primary concern is the potential impact of measurement error in sectoral prices. To the extent that prices are mismeasured, the coefficients on the mean and variance of supplier price growth cannot fully capture the Neoclassical channel they are meant to absorb. To tackle this issue, we consider another approach: including own-industry employment growth as an additional regressor.[8]

To understand why such an empirical approach might be useful, let us briefly return to the theory. Consider again the model presented in Section II, and suppose we make the following functional form assumptions:

$$F^i(Z_i, K_i, L_i, X_i) = G^i((Z_iK_i)^\alpha L_i^{1-\alpha}, X_i), \text{ and } C(Z) = \frac{Z^{1+\xi}}{1+\xi}, \quad (11)$$

with $\alpha \in (0, 1)$ and $\xi > 1$. That is, production exhibits a nested structure with Cobb-Douglas aggregation over effective capital and labor, and the cost of capital utilization is isoelastic. With this specification, we obtain the following theoretical result:

Proposition 2 Let F^i and C satisfy equation (11). A sufficient statistic for variation in the firm's capital utilization is variation in the firm's labor input:

$$\log Z_i = \frac{1}{1+\xi} \log L_i + \frac{1}{1+\xi} \log \frac{\alpha}{1-\alpha}.$$

Proof. We take the ratio of the FOCs with respect to labor and capital utilization in equation (7) and, using the specification for F^i and C in equation (11), we obtain

$$\frac{\alpha}{1-\alpha} \frac{L_i}{Z_i} = C'(Z_i),$$

where $C'(Z) = Z^\xi$. That is, the marginal rate of substitution between capital utilization and labor is equal to their price ratio. This optimality condition yields the following closed-form solution for capital utilization: $Z_i = [\frac{\alpha}{1-\alpha} L_i]^{1/(1+\xi)}.\square$

With these functional form assumptions, the firm's optimal choice of capital utilization is a monotonically increasing, log-linear function of its labor input. It follows that time variation in the firm's labor input serves as a sufficient statistic for time variation in its utilization of capital. This insight is in fact far more general than what is presented here and builds on previous insights found in Basu et al. (2006) and Burnside et al. (1995)—that is, movement in observable factors can contain valuable information about movement in unobservable factors.

With this theoretical result in mind, we return to the empirical analysis presented in table 1. Again setting aside issues of model overspecification, we augment the specifications of columns 2 and 5 with own-industry employment growth as an additional regressor—a proxy for variation in unobservable capital utilization. We report our results in columns 3 and 6, respectively.

Column 3 provides the estimates using the authors' preferred baseline TFP measure. We find that the inclusion of own-industry employment growth reduces the point estimate of the coefficient of interest by more than 70% relative to its baseline estimate: specifically, $\beta_v = -0.270$ (standard error of 0.192). Column 6 reports the results using the adjusted TFP series. This new specification yields a point estimate 60% lower than its baseline measure: specifically, $\beta_v = -0.260$ (standard error of 0.187). Therefore, under both TFP series, when own-industry employment growth is included, β_v becomes insignificant.

Finally, in contrast to the authors' assessment of a weak Neoclassical channel, we find the opposite. In column 3, the point estimate for the coefficient on input-price variance is equal to -0.368 with a standard error of 0.165, and in column 6, the corresponding estimate is -0.346 with a standard error of 0.159. In both cases, the relationship between the variance of input-price growth and measured TFP growth is consistent with the theoretical prediction—that is, negative—and significant. Moreover, in both specifications the estimated coefficient on the variance of supplier price growth is larger in magnitude than the estimated coefficient on the variance of supplier TFP growth.

We thereby conclude that the Neoclassical channel highlighted in this comment is operative in the data in a manner consistent with the theory and quantitatively large.

V.   Conclusion

In this comment, we presented a simple, theoretical framework that illustrates the potential for Neoclassical effects to explain the observed negative relationship between industry TFP growth and the cross-sectional variance of supplier TFP growth. We then reconsidered the empirical analysis and examined whether including controls for the Neoclassical channel—namely, the mean and variance of supplier price growth—alters the point estimate for β_v.

Using both the baseline and the adjusted TFP series, our estimates suggest that the magnitude of the impact of supplier TFP growth variance is highly sensitive to the inclusion of such controls, and, in some cases, the effect becomes insignificant. In contrast, we find empirical support for the Neoclassical channel itself.

Of course, there are caveats to our analysis. First, the specifications that include own-industry employment growth suffer from reverse causality: TFP of industry i should in theory affect its own labor demand. In these specifications, ideally employment growth would be instrumented. Second, throughout the theory we assume that the productivities of the final-good industries i are mismeasured and that the productivities of the intermediate-good industries j are measured with infinite precision. We make this modeling choice to maintain tractability and transparency; a theory that accounts for TFP mismeasurement in all sectors would likely yield richer implications, but this is beyond the scope of our comment.

Finally, we acknowledge that in general TFP mismeasurement is a difficult empirical issue, and admirable work is done by the authors to establish the robustness of their results. Of particular note is their work on patents; the authors turn to patent data and the patent-citation network for more direct evidence on innovation. They document a similar relationship. We conclude that the authors provide a novel and thought-provoking result on sectoral TFP growth, one that leads us to reexamine theories of endogenous technological innovation.

Endnotes

Author email address: La'O (jenlao@columbia.edu), Piga (eugenio.piga@insead.edu). For acknowledgments, sources of research support, and disclosure of the authors' material financial relationships, if any, please see https://www.nber.org/books-and-chapters /nber-macroeconomics-annual-2023-volume-38/comment-bottlenecks-sectoral-imbalances -and-us-productivity-slowdown-2-lao.
1. We furthermore assume that the function $F^i : \mathbb{R}_+^3 \to \mathbb{R}_+$ is continuous and twice-differentiable in all arguments, has positive and diminishing marginal products, and satisfies $F^i(0, 0, 0) = 0$ and the Inada conditions.
2. Due to log-Normality of supplier TFP, the expression for $\log Q_i$ in Lemma 1 is exact. However, it can also be interpreted as a second-order log approximation when the distribution of supplier TFP is not log Normal.
3. Note that the time fixed effects, δ_t, in this specification, would capture aggregate, general-equilibrium effects such as movements in the wage. This implies that the partial-equilibrium characterization of our model is sufficient.
4. Of course, one could break collinearity in the model with demand shocks or measurement error.
5. Specifically, columns 1 and 2 of table 1 in this comment directly correspond to columns 2 and 4 of table 6 in Acemoglu et al. (2023). All columns in table 1 are unweighted regressions with industry fixed effects.
6. Fernald and Piga calculate intermediate and labor-factor shares at the three-digit industry level in both the NBER-CES and the National Income and Product Accounts (NIPA) data. By computing the ratios of these shares, they obtain a panel of conversion factors that are meant to correct for this shortcoming in the NBER-CES data set. Acemoglu et al. (2023) then apply the Fernald-Piga conversion factors to all six-digit industries in the NBER-CES data set that belong to the same three-digit industry. See the accompanying comment by Fernald and Piga for more details on this measure.
7. Specifically, column 5 of table 1 of this comment directly corresponds to column 3 of table A4 in Acemoglu et al. (2023).
8. We thank John Fernald for this excellent suggestion.

References

Acemoglu, Daron, David Autor, and Christina Patterson. 2023. "Bottlenecks: Sectoral Imbalances and the US Productivity Slowdown." NBER Macroeconomics Annual 2023, volume 38, University of Chicago Press, Chicago.
Atalay, Enghin. 2017. "How Important Are Sectoral Shocks?" *American Economic Journal: Macroeconomics* 9 (4): 254–80.
Barrot, Jean-Noel, and Julien Sauvagnat. 2016. "Input Specificity and the Propagation of Idiosyncratic Shocks in Production Networks." *Quarterly Journal of Economics* 131 (3): 1543–92.
Basu, Susanto, John G. Fernald, and Miles S. Kimball. 2006. "Are Technology Improvements Contractionary?" *American Economic Review* 96 (5): 1418–48.

Boehm, Christoph E., Aaron Flaaen, and Nitya Pandalai-Nayar. 2019. "Input Linkages and the Transmission of Shocks: Firm-Level Evidence from the 2011 Tohoku Earthquake." *Review of Economics and Statistics* 101 (1): 60–75.

Burnside, Craig, Martin Eichenbaum, and Sergio Rebelo. 1995. "Capital Utilization and Returns to Scale." *NBER Macroeconomics Annual 1995* 10 (1): 67–124.

Carvalho, Vasco M., Makoto Nirei, Yukiko U. Saito, and Alireza Tahbaz-Salehi. 2020. "Supply Chain Disruptions: Evidence from the Great East Japan Earthquake." *Quarterly Journal of Economics* 136 (2): 1255–321.

Discussion

Christina Patterson opened the discussion by thanking the discussants for their terrific work and useful comments. She agreed with John Fernald that total factor productivity (TFP) is hard to measure and, for this reason, she and her coauthors also used patent data. Furthermore, she added that both the National Bureau of Economic Research and Center for Economic Studies (NBER-CES) and the Bureau of Economic Analysis and Bureau of Labor Statistics (BLS-BEA) data sets have similar levels of TFP but different trends. Hence, the baseline result of the paper that, in the absence of sectorial imbalances, TFP growth would have been higher remains valid. Finally, she explained that most of the specifications in the paper are unweighted because all industries are equally informative about the existence of the mechanism described in the paper.

After Patterson's comment, Erik Hurst asked how to think about the dynamic process of TFP growth. Due to the existence of bottlenecks, do firms adjust their inputs over time so that there will be an increase in TFP with a delay? Following up on this, Valerie Ramey asked whether the bottlenecks are created by a fixed supply of high-quality innovators that are attracted by a small number of large firms. If so, could this create incentives for large firms to integrate vertically to redistribute talent in a more efficient way? Ramey pointed out that, for example, during World War II, the government intervened to avoid bottlenecks. Daron Acemoglu agreed with the point made by Hurst: if bottlenecks are resolved, then the model predicts an acceleration in productivity. However, it is hard to predict when these bottlenecks will be resolved. Indeed, there are many possible stories, including the one suggested by Ramey, and the model does not discuss which distortions are creating these bottlenecks.

Following up, Gabriel Chodorow-Reich commented that in the BLS-BEA data used by Fernald, the manufacturing sector displays a speedup in productivity, but the service sector does not. On the other hand, the NBER-CES data set used by the authors displays a speedup in productivity for both the service and the manufacturing sectors. Furthermore, the rise in concentration in the service sector should have displayed an increase in productivity because smaller and less productive firms exited the market. Hence, the existence of large firms that benefit from upstream inputs makes aggregation very important. However, in the authors' model, only suppliers' productivity dispersion matters, but all of the input-output network should be important in the mechanism proposed by the authors. Chodorow-Reich asked whether the authors could clarify the exercise that they did when holding the variance of one sector fixed, because this implies an increase in productivity for such sectors that has aggregate effects throughout the input-output network. Acemoglu discussed that there is no unambiguous way to solve the issue pointed out by Chodorow-Reich, because changing one variance at a time will change all of them. This is why aggregate variance and supplier variance are kept constant at the level of the 1987–97 period.

The next question was from Ricardo Reis, who asked about reverse causality in the regression using the patent data set. Suppose that there is a fixed cost to file a patent, but that patents are not a particularly accurate measure of TFP. After an increase in demand, the market expands, and firms patent more because the net revenues clear the fixed cost. Mechanically, the number of patent citations of upstream firms rises, possibly more so for larger firms, which raises the variance of supplier patent growth. This is the independent variable of the authors' specification, but it is now being caused by higher demand, rather than causing it. Acemoglu pointed out that this story is plausible, and indeed the authors faced this issue using a fixed-in-time network of citations. Hence, the ideas' supply is not changing over time. Furthermore, the specification with the instrumental variable should assuage Ricardo Reis' concerns.

Acemoglu also thanked Fernald for the insightful discussion. He added that they tried different weighting schemes; however, none of them were able to effectively deal with Fernald's specific issue. The unweighted option seemed the best choice. Finally, Acemoglu added that the BLS-BEA regression is using 90 industries, which are not granular enough to speak about the mechanism discussed in the paper. They chose the NBER-CES data set because it contains around 450 industries, which still may not be granular enough.

Ramey asked Fernald about possible explanations for the divergence of the NBER-CES data set and BEA-BLS data set. Is it possible that TFP has become more difficult to measure, given that the two data sets were similar before but have now diverged? John Fernald pointed out that the two data sets come from different sources. The BEA-BLS is mostly from national accounts, whereas the NBER-CES comes from the census of manufacturing. Furthermore, the NBER-CES data set relies on using the price deflator, and the materials price deflator grows much more slowly in the NBER-CES data set after 1997. This is a possible explanation for the divergence.

Silvana Tenreyro asked whether the data used in the paper also included the international input-output network. Patterson replied that for the TFP specifications, the whole input-output network is used, so the international links are taken into consideration.

Finally, Şebnem Kalemli-Özcan asked whether the authors looked at the motivation of why some sectors experience a sharper increase in the TFP variance than others. Patterson pointed out that this is not the focus of the paper. However, understanding why the variance of the TFP went up is an important step for future work.

4

Aggregate Lending and Modern Financial Intermediation: Why Bank Balance Sheet Models Are Miscalibrated

Greg Buchak, *Stanford University,* United States of America
Gregor Matvos, *Northwestern University and NBER,* United States of America
Tomasz Piskorski, *Columbia University and NBER,* United States of America
Amit Seru, *Stanford University and NBER,* United States of America

I. Introduction

Macroprudential, monetary, and fiscal policies are frequently passed through the financial intermediation sector or implemented directly through financial intermediaries (Kashyap and Stein 2000; Hanson, Kashyap, and Stein 2011).[1] The modern industrial organization of financial intermediation differs from the traditional view of bank balance sheet lending in two dimensions (Buchak et al. 2018, 2024). Specifically, nondepository institutions—that is, shadow banks—now account for a substantial share of lending in many markets, and banks now sell a significant fraction of the loans they originate through securitization. We argue that accounting for the modern industrial organization of financial intermediation is essential in two respects.

First, using bank data to measure lending can lead to erroneous conclusions about how lending responds to economic or policy shocks and the extent to which they are amplified through financial intermediaries. We illustrate this point using micro-level lending data on the largest private credit market in the United States. Second, failing to account for these features of financial intermediation in quantitative macro models can result in inaccurate calibrations of how shocks amplify through financial intermediaries. To study the economics of the problem, we develop and calibrate a parsimonious dynamic quantitative model featuring banks with balance sheet adjustment and shadow banks.

NBER Macroeconomics Annual, volume 38, 2024.

We begin our empirical analysis with the observation that regulators and academics commonly employ three different sources for measuring the extent of lending: the data on bank lending activity from bank balance sheets (e.g., the bank call reports), data on total bank loan origination, or aggregate lending data. We focus our analysis on the US residential mortgage market, the largest private credit market in the United States, with more than $11 trillion of loans outstanding. The advantage of this market is that we observe almost all originated loans and know whether they were (i) originated by a bank or shadow bank and (ii) whether a financial institution retained a loan on its balance sheet or sold it.[2]

We define two empirical multipliers, the "loan-sales multiplier" and the "shadow bank lending multiplier," to capture the mapping between bank balance sheet lending, total bank lending, and total lending. These multipliers measure the significance of two key features of modern financial intermediation described earlier: the extent to which banks sell a significant portion of loans and the involvement of shadow banks in lending. We demonstrate that these multipliers are large and vary over time. For instance, banks on average sell more than half of the mortgages they originate, with this propensity fluctuating between a low of roughly 37% and a high of nearly 80% of annual bank lending. As a result, bank balance sheet lending data, which is frequently used by regulators to gauge lending conditions, accounts for less than half of the variation in the aggregate lending of banks, in terms of both its level and its growth rate. Even perfect bank data are insufficient to assess the evolution of aggregate lending activity; total bank lending accounts for only about 70% of the variation over time in total lending. This is because shadow banks originate a substantial share of loans, and their market share significantly varies over time, from a low of roughly 20% during the Great Recession to a high of 60% in 2021. In fact, the growth in bank balance sheet lending and aggregate lending can occasionally be negatively correlated, especially, as we argue below, in times when bank balance sheets are stressed.

We document a significant correlation between regional income and the composition of financial intermediation, which has a significant impact on the magnitude of both the loan sales multiplier and the shadow bank lending multiplier. Both multipliers are smallest in the highest-income counties, which primarily rely on bank balance sheet lending. Conversely, in lower-income to middle-income regions, which may be of particular interest to regulators due to their typically higher share of risky lending, the multipliers are found to be largest. These results imply that the propagation of shocks in high- and low-income areas differ, as these households are situated in markets with distinct industrial organizations of financial intermediation.

Buchak et al. (2018, 2024) identify three underlying drivers that influence the two margins of substitution: bank balance sheet strength, the relative attractiveness of the loan sale market, and the regulatory burden on banks. First, banks switch away from traditional balance sheet lending and toward selling loans as their capitalization declines. The extent of that switching is determined in equilibrium. Second, the availability and relative attractiveness of the loan sale market affects both margins of substitution. Because shadow banks sell almost all loans they originate, the shadow bank lending margin is crucially affected by the conditions in the secondary loan market.[3] Finally, changes in the regulatory environment also play a role in determining the market share of shadow banks, with Buchak et al. (2018) finding that a substantial part of the increase in shadow bank market share after the Great Recession can be attributed to increased regulatory burden on banks. Our paper provides further evidence of the importance of bank balance sheet strength in shaping the aggregate loan sale multiplier.

To understand whether modifying existing models to account for contemporary financial intermediation frictions is quantitatively important, we develop a parsimonious dynamic quantitative model of financial intermediation. We build on Buchak et al. (2024), in which the loan sales and shadow bank multipliers play a central role in a static setting.[4] Focusing on the dynamics allows us to understand how these margins contribute to the impact and recovery from financial shocks over time. We calibrate the model to the empirical lending multipliers measured in the data. Using the calibrated model, we examine how shocks to bank capital propagate through this augmented model of the financial intermediation sector.

We show that the financial sector is much more resilient to capital shocks ex post than a bank balance sheet model would suggest. The loan sale multiplier and shadow bank multiplier significantly decrease the effect of a capital shock on lending. For example, a large negative shock to bank capital that would lead to a 40% decline in aggregate lending in a model without these multipliers leads to only a 4% decline when these multipliers are present. The accompanying lending rate increase would be 10 basis points instead of 100 basis points. Second, the effect of the capital shock is less prolonged, with a faster recovery of banks. Third, because capitalization shocks are less costly ex post, banks are less prudent with capital ex ante. Intuitively, when the bank has a more difficult time adjusting to shocks, it keeps a larger capital buffer in excess of the statutory capital requirement. In a more complete setting with other margins present, for any given balance sheet capacity, banks originate more loans.

There are two primary features of models that determine how shocks to intermediaries are transmitted to lending and subsequently to real-world outcomes. The first is the responsiveness of lending to a shock to bank capital, and the second is the speed at which banks can rebuild capital after the shock. A traditional bank balance sheet model implies that the impact of reduced bank capital on lending could be substantial because it is the only means through which lending can occur. Banks' inability to extend profitable loans due to inadequate capitalization further implies slow rebuilding of capital and therefore a slow recovery. However, because banks can sell their loans and shadow banks can take over some of the bank lending, the impact of bank capital on lending is much less important. The recovery is faster because undercapitalized banks can instead turn to profitable loan selling, which allows them to rebuild their capital faster.

Finally, we use our setting to illustrate why models based on bank balance sheet lending struggle to quantitatively match data and therefore have important drawbacks as guides to policy responses. Because of the banks' loan sales margin, there is a strong correlation between bank capitalization and bank balance sheet lending but a very weak correlation between bank capital and aggregate lending. A bank balance sheet model forces total lending to depend strongly on bank balance sheet health. It is very difficult for bank balance sheet models to achieve this reconciliation. With the move toward integrating micro data into macro models, it is natural to consider calibrating models to bank-level data instead. With this approach, a researcher can exploit both the cross section in bank capitalization and the time-series changes within a bank. Our results highlight that by using bank balance sheet lending data alone, calibrations overstate the responsiveness of lending to capital shocks. Therefore, neither aggregate lending data nor bank data alone are sufficient to empirically understand the extent of lending responses. Nor can they be used to calibrate macro models of financial intermediation in isolation. Instead, both overall lending and bank balance sheet data must be used in conjunction with the model of modern financial intermediation to fully comprehend the effect of capitalization shocks.

We conclude by discussing the broader implications of our results. There are substantial differences in the industrial organization of the financial sector between countries. The United Kingdom, for example, does not have a large and liquid secondary market for mortgages (Benetton 2021). Our model suggests that the financial intermediation sector propagates shocks to different extents in the United Kingdom and the United States. This casts doubt on regulatory frameworks that propose a uniform treatment of capital requirements across countries, such as the Basel framework.

Our model also implies that policies that target the intermediation sector have distributional consequences. Devoting government resources (subsidies) to recapitalize banks most benefits the highest-income regions. In contrast, policies that operate through secondary markets act across the income distribution. More broadly, regulators who ignore the multipliers we outline may reach inaccurate conclusions about the impact of policies on the credit market and even incorrect assessments about the current health of the lending market. For example, a regulator observing that banks are poorly capitalized would dramatically overstate how aggregate lending would react to further deterioration in bank capital. These biases will vary depending on the ease of loan sales and shadow bank lending in different markets and countries, making it difficult to apply findings from one market to another.

Our paper emphasizes the need to collect data on lending by shadow banks and loans that were not retained on the balance sheets of regulated and closely monitored financial institutions in conjunction with existing approaches, which focus on bank balance sheet data (call report data by traditional banks). In the interim, researchers and policy makers could rely on quantitative lending models, like the one proposed in this paper, to recognize the importance of the modern industrial organization of credit markets and allow more complete inferences from the limited data.

II. Data and Institutional Setting

A. Institutional Setting

The US residential mortgage market is the largest private debt market in the country, comprising more than 50 million properties with an outstanding debt of more than $11 trillion as of 2021. The process of securing a mortgage, called loan origination, involves a borrower submitting a loan application and documentation related to their financial and credit history to the lender. Figure A1 in the appendix shows the annual aggregate mortgage origination volume in the US residential loan market, which varies between a low of $1.4 trillion during the Great Recession and a high of more than $4.7 trillion during the pandemic lending and refinancing boom (2020–21).

There are three main segments of the US residential mortgage market: the conforming loan market, the jumbo loan market, and the Federal Housing Administration (FHA) loan segment. The conforming loan market is the largest, consisting of loans usually extended to borrowers with high credit scores, conservative loan-to-value ratios, and fully documented incomes and assets. Conforming mortgages must be below the conforming loan limit, which increased from $417,000 in 2006 to $548,250 in 2021 for a one-unit, single-family dwelling in a low-cost area. Mortgages that exceed the conforming limit are termed "jumbo" loans.

Conforming loans are eligible for securitization with the participation of government-sponsored enterprises (GSEs), whereas jumbo loans are not. GSEs make securitization of conforming mortgages substantially easier. For example, Fannie Mae and Freddie Mac, the two most prominent GSEs, purchase conforming mortgages and package them into mortgage-backed securities (MBS), insuring default risk. These MBS are particularly attractive to investors interested in relatively safe assets. In 2017, conforming loans packed in MBS guaranteed by Fannie Mae and Freddie Mac made up about 50% of the outstanding residential loans (source: Securities Industry and Financial Markets Association data).

The third market segment consists of FHA loans, mortgages whose risk of default is directly insured by the FHA. They are popular among less creditworthy borrowers and first-time home buyers because they allow down payments as little as 3.5%.

The US residential mortgage market is characterized by the presence of two main groups of originators: banks and shadow banks (nonbank lenders). According to Buchak et al. (2018), traditional bank originations have seen a decline, whereas shadow bank market share grew from less than 30% to more than 50% by 2015. These originators differ in several aspects. First, banks (traditional banks and credit unions) partially fund their lending through insured deposits, whereas shadow banks do not take deposits. Second, they differ in their business models. Banks engage in both portfolio lending and originate-to-distribute models, with portfolio loans making up about 47% of their originations during the sample period. On the other hand, shadow banks almost exclusively use the originate-to-distribute model (Buchak et al. 2024). Third, banks face a substantially higher regulatory burden than shadow banks, including capital requirements, enhanced supervision, and compliance rules.

Furthermore, the presence of a large secondary loan market supported by government guarantees makes the residential lending market unique in comparison with other lending markets. However, the insights gained from this market may be broadly applicable to other credit market segments, such as corporate loans, credit cards, automobile loans, and personal loans, where a similar shift in the industrial organization of financial intermediation has occurred. For example, in the corporate loan market, lenders can sell their loans through collateralized loan obligations (Irani et al. 2021), and in the auto lending market, lenders can sell their loans in the asset-backed commercial paper market (Benmelech, Meisenzahl, and Ramcharan 2017). Similarly, shadow banks have a significant presence in other markets, such as small-business lending, middle-market firm loans, and personal loans.

Shadow banks have also gained a significant presence in other markets. Chen, Hanson, and Stein (2017) indicate that large US banks significantly reduced their small-business lending during the Great Recession and have yet to fully return to this market. Gopal and Schnabl (2022) document a substitution of traditional banks with nonbank lenders in the small-business loan market, resulting in a significant increase in nonbank lending. Irani et al. (2021) observe that shadow banks have entered the corporate loan market as traditional banks increase their capital holdings. Chernenko, Erel, and Prilmeier (2022) report that among middle-market firms over 2010–15, one-third of all loans were directly extended by nonbank financial intermediaries. Furthermore, studies by Tang (2019) and De Roure, Pelizzon, and Thakor (2022) illustrate the significant expansion of nonbank lenders in the personal loan market.

B.   Data

By focusing on residential mortgage lending, we have access to comprehensive micro-level lending data on almost all loans made in this market, regardless of whether the loan was originated by a bank or shadow bank, and whether the financial institution retained or sold the loan. We collect these data from 2005 to 2021 through the Home Mortgage Disclosure Act (HMDA), which requires financial institutions to report detailed information on each loan they originate annually, with limited exceptions. This covers the vast majority of all residential loans in the United States.

We classify a loan as a "balance sheet" loan if the financial institution does not report selling it in the year of origination. We use the HMDA data and Robert Avery's classification to uniquely identify institutions and classify them as "shadow banks" if they are labeled as independent mortgage banks in the HMDA data.[5] Other institutions are classified as banks.[6] To determine the capitalization of each bank, we merge the data with the Uniform Bank Performance Report using a unique RSSD ID number.[7] Most banks insured by the Federal Deposit Insurance Corporation are required to report the composition and elements of their balance sheet each quarter to the Federal Financial Institutions Examination Council (FFIEC), and we use annualized data that averages across quarters. We use each bank's total tier one risk-based capital to risk-weighted assets (code: ubprd487) as the primary measure of bank capital ratio.

We also aggregate the data across US counties and at the national level to study regional and national lending patterns. We use a simple sum for shadow bank volume, total volume, bank volume, bank balance sheet volume, and bank sold volume. We use an annual weighted mean using bank volume as a weight for bank capitalization. We also use several county-level variables, including house price indices from the Federal Housing Finance Agency and unemployment rates from the Bureau of Labor Statistics, to understand the broader economic context.

III. Motivating Facts

We start our analysis by presenting a set of facts that illustrate the importance of recognizing that banks are selling significant share of loans they originate (e.g., by securitizing them) and the increased role of shadow banks in the lending market. To organize our discussion of these two margins, we use the following simple lending accounting framework.

A. Lending Accounting Framework

Balance Sheet Retention and the Loan Sales Multiplier

To analyze the loan sales multiplier, consider an amount of balance sheet lending by bank i at year t, Bank balance sheet lending$_{i,t}$. This information can be inferred from the regulatory bank call reports (regulatory bank balance sheet data) that measure the amount of lending by a bank in terms of loans it retains on its balance sheet. However, if a bank sells some of its loans in year t, its Total bank lending$_{i,t}$ in that year will be larger and given by

$$\text{Total bank lending}_{i,t} = m_{i,t}^{\text{Loan Sale}} \times \text{Bank balance sheet lending}_{i,t} \quad (1)$$

where $m_{i,t}^{\text{Loan Sale}}$ is the lending "multiplier" due to loan sales that equals

$$m_{i,t}^{\text{Loan Sale}} = \frac{1}{1 - \text{Loan Sale Share}_{i,t}}. \quad (2)$$

In equation (2), Loan Sale Share$_{i,t}$ is the fraction of loans that bank i sells at time t. Aggregating across the banks, we get that the total aggregate bank lending at time t is equal to

$$\text{Total bank lending}_t = m_t^{\text{Loan Sale}} \times \text{Bank balance sheet lending}_t \quad (3)$$

where Bank balance sheet lending$_t$ is the aggregate bank lending retained on balance sheet and $m_t^{\text{Loan Sale}}$ is the aggregate lending multiplier due to loan sales.

Shadow Bank Lending Share and the Shadow Bank Lending Multiplier

To account for shadow bank lending outside of the traditional banking sector, we relate the total amount of lending in the economy at time t to total bank lending:

$$\text{Total lending}_t = m_t^{\text{Shadow Bank}} \times \text{Total bank lending}_t, \quad (4)$$

where $m_t^{\text{Shadow Bank}}$ is the shadow bank lending multiplier that equals to

$$m_t^{\text{Shadow Bank}} = \frac{1}{1 - \text{Shadow Bank Share}_{i,t}} \quad (5)$$

and Shadow Bank Share$_{i,t}$ is the fraction of loans originated by shadow banks.

Combining equations (3) and (4), we get the correspondence between the aggregate amount of lending in the economy and the amount of aggregate bank balance sheet lending:

$$\text{Total lending}_t = m_t^{\text{Shadow Bank}} \times m_t^{\text{Loan Sale}} \times \text{Bank balance sheet lending}_t. \quad (6)$$

Consider an example in which bank balance sheets reflect \$300 billion of lending in a given year, but banks sell 50% of their loans and 50% of lending activity is done by shadow banks. In this case, both multipliers are equal to 2, aggregate bank lending is equal to \$600 billion, and overall lending is equal to \$1.2 trillion.

The traditional bank balance sheet lending view corresponds to the case where both lending multipliers are equal to 1:

$$m_t^{\text{Loan Sale}} = m_t^{\text{Shadow Bank}} = 1.$$

In this case, banks retain all their loans on their balance sheets, there are no shadow banks, and the total lending equals the bank balance sheet lending.

In the next section, we document the magnitude of these multipliers, how they evolve over time and regions, and the forces shaping them. In the empirical part, we emphasize the idea that these multipliers imply that measuring lending on bank balance sheets or lending by banks does not accurately represent aggregate lending, and that the inferences differ across regions systematically depending on county income. In the model section, we show that focusing on aggregate lending is insufficient to understand the speed of recovery from shocks or the stability of the banking system. Instead, the composition of financial intermediation and the associated multipliers are critical in determining the overall lending response.

B.   Aggregate Lending: Multipliers Are Large and Time Varying

Balance Sheet Retention and the Loan Sales Multiplier over Time

We begin by showing that the propensity of banks to sell loans is large in magnitude and varies significantly over time. Figure 1A shows the fraction of banks that retain all their loans on their balance sheets and therefore have a loan sale multiplier of 1. Throughout our sample period, close to half of banks in the United States do not sell any residential mortgages they originate. However, these "traditional" banks constitute only about 4% of overall bank loan origination volume (fig. 1B),

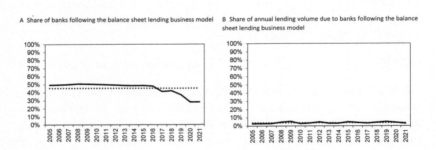

Fig. 1.   Traditional balance sheet lending banks in the residential mortgage market. Panel A shows the percentage of banks among the US mortgage loan originators that do not sell any residential loans in each year, following the traditional bank balance sheet lending model. Panel B shows the percentage of annual bank loan origination volume these traditional balance-sheet-only lending banks account for in each year. Although up to half of all banks do not sell any loans during our sample period depending on the year, they make up on average only around 7% of the loan origination volume. A loan is retained if it is still on the originating institution's balance sheet at the end of the year. Home Mortgage Disclosure Act data.

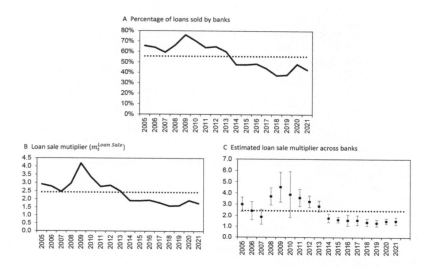

Fig. 2. Bank loan sales propensity and the loan sale lending multiplier. Panel *A* shows the percentage of residential loans sold among the loans originated by banks per year. The dashed line shows the sample mean. Panel *B* shows the implied loan sale multiplier that indicates the ratio of aggregate bank lending to retained on-balance-sheet bank lending. Panel *C* shows the estimated loan sale multiplier in each year based on the estimation of equation (1) with individual bank data with 95% confidence intervals. The coefficient of interest indicates the estimated dollar volume of loans originated by a bank in that year for each dollar of lending retained on the bank balance sheet. Home Mortgage Disclosure Act data.

indicating that most bank lending activity occurs among banks that sell some of their loans.

Figure 2*A* shows that banks on average sell more than half of the loans they originate, with a mean loan sale propensity of 55%. In addition, the loan sale propensity varied widely 2005–21, reaching a peak of 76% during the Great Recession and falling to a low of 38% during the 2018–19 period before the pandemic (fig. A2 shows the banks' loan sale propensity over a longer time period). This results in the loan sales multiplier displaying substantial variation over time that ranges from 1.6 to 4.2 depending on the year (fig. 2*B*). Figure 2*C* illustrates this further by showing the estimated loan sale multiplier in each year based on the estimation of equation (1) with individual bank data along with 95% confidence intervals.

Table 1, column 1 shows that the aggregate bank balance sheet lending data accounts for less than half of the variation in total bank lending, at 46%. Adding bank loan sales in column 2, by definition, results in an R^2 coefficient of 100%. These results highlight the importance of recognizing

Table 1
Variation in the Total Bank Lending Volume Accounted by the Bank Balance Sheet Lending Volume and the Variation in the Total Lending Volume Accounted by the Total Bank Lending Volume

	National Data				County Data					
	Total Bank Lending		Total Lending		Total Bank Lending			Total Lending		
	(1)	(2)	(3)	(4)	(5)	(6)	(7)	(8)	(9)	(10)
Bank balance sheet lending	1.05	1.00			.99	1.11	1.00			
	(.30)	(.00)			(.00)	(.00)	(.00)			
Bank sold lending		1.00					1.00			
		(.00)					(.00)			
Total bank lending			2.27	1.00				1.07	1.05	1.00
			(.40)	(.00)				(.00)	(.00)	(.00)
Shadow bank lending				1.00						1.00
				(.00)						(.00)
County FEs	No	No	No	No	No	Yes	Yes	No	Yes	Yes
Year FEs	No	No	No	No	No	Yes	Yes	No	Yes	Yes
Observations	17	17	17	17	54,829	54,829	54,829	54,840	54,840	54,840
R^2	.44	1.00	.67	1.00	.52	.73	1.00	.53	.86	1.00

Source: Home Mortgage Disclosure Act data.
Note: This table presents the ordinary least squares estimates from the regression of *Total Bank Lending* on *Bank Balance Sheet Lending* (col. 1), *Total Bank Lending* on *Bank Balance Sheet Lending* and *Bank Balance Sheet Sold* (col. 2), *Total Lending* on *Total Bank Lending* (col. 3), and *Total Lending* on *Total Bank Lending* and *Shadow Bank Lending* (col. 4) on the national data. *Total Bank Lending* is defined as annual aggregate residential mortgage origination volume originated by banks. *Bank Balance Sheet Lending* is the annual aggregate residential mortgage origination volume originated by banks that the banks retain on their balance sheet in the year of its origination. *Bank Sold Lending* is the annual aggregate residential mortgage origination volume originated by banks that the banks sell in the year of its origination. *Total Bank Lending* is the annual aggregate residential mortgage origination volume originated by banks and shadow banks. Finally, *Shadow Bank Lending* is the annual aggregate residential mortgage origination volume originated by shadow banks. Columns 5–10 present the corresponding results for the county-level data where we scale the variables by the county-level mean of the dependent variable. Columns 6–7 and 9–10 also include the county and year fixed effects (FE). The estimation sample is 2005–21. Standard errors are reported in parentheses.

that the propensity of banks to sell loans is large in magnitude and varies over time. Figure 3*A* illustrates this in a simple way by showing the extent of inference errors resulting from a failure to recognize that bank loan sale propensity significantly changes over time. This figure plots actual total bank lending volume and inferred total bank lending volume if one erroneously assumes a constant loan sale multiplier equal to its sample mean

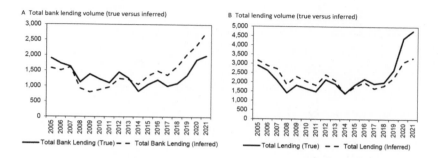

Fig. 3. Errors in inference of total bank lending and total lending volume due to time-varying loan sale and shadow bank multipliers. Panel A shows the total annual bank volume (black) and the inferred total bank volume (dashed) from the aggregate bank balance sheet lending volume (in US$billions) assuming a constant loan sale propensity, resulting in the constant loan sale multiplier equal to 2.42 (the sample mean). Panel B shows the total annual lending volume and the inferred total lending volume from total bank volume assuming a constant shadow bank market share equal, resulting in the constant shadow bank lending multiplier equal to 1.67 (the sample mean). Home Mortgage Disclosure Act data.

to infer the total bank lending from the bank balance sheet lending volume. As we observe, there are significant differences between the inferred and actual aggregate bank lending, ranging from the inferred bank lending underestimating the actual bank lending by close to $600 billion in 2009 to the inferred bank lending overestimating the actual bank lending by close to $800 billion in 2021. In column 1 of table 2A, we illustrate this more formally by regressing the true total bank lending on the inferred total bank lending from bank balance sheet lending assuming a constant loan sale multiplier. As we observe, the inferred bank lending accounts for only about 44% of variation in actual aggregate bank lending. Overall, these results suggest that a simple mapping from bank balance sheet data to aggregate lending outcomes is highly imperfect, and as we later show, depends on economic conditions.

Shadow Bank Lending Share and the Shadow Bank Multiplier

Even perfect bank data are insufficient to evaluate the evolution of lending activity, because the shadow bank multiplier is also large and varies significantly over time. Figure 4A illustrates the proportion of residential mortgages originated by shadow banks along with the shadow bank loan multiplier. As can be seen, shadow banks originate a considerable share of loans, and their inclination to sell loans significantly increases over time,

Table 2
Errors in Inference on Total Bank and Overall Lending Volume

	Total Bank Lending	Total Lending
	(1)	(2)
	Panel A: National Lending	
Inferred total bank lending (constant loan sale multiplier)	.43 (.12)	
Inferred total lending (constant shadow bank multiplier)		1.36 (.24)
Observations	17	17
R^2	.44	.67

	Total Bank Lending				Total Lending			
	(1)	(2)	(3)	(4)	(5)	(6)	(7)	(8)
	Panel B: County-Level Lending							
Inferred total bank lending (constant loan sale multiplier)	.41 (.00)	.48 (.00)						
Inferred total bank lending (time-varying loan sale multiplier)			.39 (.00)	.46 (.00)				
Inferred total lending (constant shadow bank multiplier)					.62 (.00)	.75 (.00)		
Inferred total lending (time-varying shadow bank multiplier)							.58 (.00)	.65 (.00)
County FEs	No	Yes	No	Yes	No	Yes	No	Yes
Observations	55,515	55,515	55,515	55,515	55,527	55,527	55,527	55,527
R^2	.53	.63	.51	.60	.49	.59	.66	.74

Source: Home Mortgage Disclosure Act data.
Note: Panel *A* of this table presents the ordinary least squares (OLS) estimates from the regression of *Total Bank Lending* volume on the *Inferred Total Bank Lending* volume from *Total Bank Balance Sheet Lending* volume (in US$billions) assuming a constant loan sale multiplier equal to the sample mean (col. 1). Panel *B* shows the OLS estimates from the regression of *Total Lending* volume on the *Inferred Total Lending* volume from *Total Bank Lending* volume (in US$billions) assuming a constant shadow bank multiplier equal to the sample mean (col. 2). Panel *B* shows the corresponding results for the county-level data where county-level inference uses the corresponding multipliers at the national level. Columns 1–4 of panel *B* show the OLS estimates of *Total Bank Lending* volume in a county on the *Inferred Total Bank Lending* volume in a county from *Total Bank Balance Sheet Lending* volume in a county. Columns 5–8 of panel *B* show the OLS estimates from the regression of *Total Lending* volume in a county on the *Inferred Total Lending* volume in a county from *Total Bank Lending* volume in a county. In panel *B* in columns 1–2 and 5–6, we infer the county-level lending levels using aggregate loan sale and shadow bank multipliers, respectively, that are based on national data, constant over time, and equal to their sample mean. In panel *B* in columns 3–4 and 7–8, we infer county-level lending patterns using aggregate time-varying loan sale and shadow bank multipliers, respectively, that are based on national and are equal to their sample mean each year. In panel *B*, columns 2, 4, 6, and 8, we also add county state fixed effects (FE). The variables in the county-level regressions are scaled by the sample mean of the dependent variable.

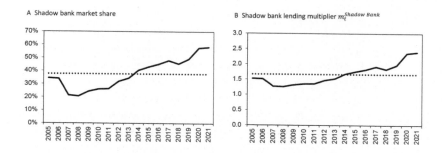

Fig. 4. Shadow bank market share and the shadow bank loan multiplier. Panel *A* shows the percentage of residential mortgage loans originated by the shadow banks in the United States. The dashed line shows the sample mean. Panel *B* shows the implied shadow bank multiplier, with the dashed line again showing the sample mean. Home Mortgage Disclosure Act data.

from about 30% in 2005 to about 60% by 2021 (fig. A2 shows the shadow bank market share over a longer time period). The associated shadow bank multiplier increases from a low of 1.3 in 2007 to 2.4 in 2021, indicating that by 2021, for every dollar of bank-originated loans, there is about $2.40 of total lending, accounting for lending done by both banks and shadow banks (fig. 4*B*). Because shadow bank market share is time varying, bank lending data—including loan sales—account for only about 68% of variation in total lending (col. 3 of table 1).[8] The variability in the shadow bank multiplier makes it difficult to infer aggregate lending from traditional bank information alone. Figure 3*B* illustrates this in a simple way by showing the extent of inference errors on total lending volume if one uses a constant shadow bank lending multiplier (equal to its sample mean) to infer the total lending volume from aggregate bank lending volume (broadly defined, including loan sales). As we observe, there are significant differences between the inferred and the true aggregate total lending levels, ranging from the inferred lending overestimating the actual lending by close to $500 billion in 2009 to the inferred lending underestimating the actual total lending by more than $1.4 trillion in 2021. In column 2 of table 2*A*, we illustrate this more formally by regressing the actual total lending on the lending volume inferred from banks' balance sheets assuming a constant shadow bank lending multiplier. As we observe, inferred total lending accounts for only about 67% of variation in actual total lending. Overall, these results illustrate that a simple mapping from bank data to aggregate lending is highly imperfect and, as we later show, depends on economic conditions.

Aggregate Lending Growth Rates

The variation in the multipliers is also visible in lending growth rates in figure 5, which would be uniform under constant multipliers. For instance, in 2007, bank balance sheet lending increased by 6%, whereas total bank lending and overall lending decreased by 5% and 20%, respectively. In contrast, in 2009, bank balance sheet lending declined by 13%, whereas total bank lending and total lending increased by 22% and 28%, respectively. More systematic analysis in table 3 illustrates that the aggregate bank balance sheet lending growth rate accounts for only about 49% of the variation in the aggregate lending growth rate of banks (col. 1). Including growth in bank loans sold results in an R^2 equal to 97% (col. 2).

Columns 3–4 of table 3 show the similar analysis for the total lending growth rate. Bank lending growth rate, including loan sales, accounts for about 93% of the variation in total lending growth rate. Adding shadow bank lending growth to the regression allows us to explain almost all variation in the total bank lending growth rate, with an R^2 equal to 99% (col. 4).

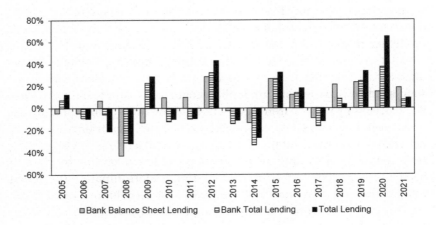

Fig. 5. Growth rates of aggregate bank balance sheet lending, bank lending, and overall lending. This figure shows the annual growth rates of aggregate bank balance sheet lending (gray), aggregate bank lending (horizontal lines), and aggregate total lending (black). The aggregate total lending includes lending by both banks and shadow banks. As we observe, not only are these growth rates different in magnitudes, but in several years they also have opposing signs. Home Mortgage Disclosure Act data.

Table 3
Variation in the Total Bank Lending Growth Rate Accounted by the Bank Balance Sheet Lending Growth Rate and the Variation in the Total Lending Growth Rate Accounted by the Total Bank Lending Growth Rate

| | National Data | | | | County Data | | | | | |
| | Total Bank Lending | Total Lending | | | Total Bank Lending | | | Total Lending | | |
	(1)	(2)	(3)	(4)	(5)	(6)	(7)	(8)	(9)	(10)
Bank Balance Sheet Lending	.82	.41			.34	.36	.34			
	(.21)	(.05)			(.05)	(.03)	(.03)			
Bank Sold Lending		.54					.12			
		(.03)					(.02)			
Total Bank Lending			1.20	.63				.98	.78	.64
			(.08)	(.06)				(.09)	(.04)	(.01)
Shadow Bank Lending				.36						.23
				(.03)						(.01)
County FEs	No	No	No	No	No	Yes	Yes	No	Yes	Yes
Year FEs	No	No	No	No	No	Yes	Yes	No	Yes	Yes
Observations	17	17	17	17	54,446	54,446	54,294	54,596	54,596	54,057
R^2	.49	.97	.92	.99	.29	.76	.81	.78	.92	.97

Source: Home Mortgage Disclosure Act data.
Note: This table presents the ordinary least squares estimates from the same specification as table 1 but estimated on the annual growth rates of these variables. In columns 5–8, the regressions are volume weighted, where the volume is the county-level bank lending volume in dollars in columns 5–7 and the county-level total lending volume in dollars columns 8–10. The estimation sample is 2005–21. Standard errors are reported in parentheses.

C.   The Impact of Bank Loan Sales and Shadow Banks on Regional Lending Patterns

Here we show that there are substantial differences in the bank loan sale propensity and shadow bank market share across US regions. We illustrate that this regional heterogeneity further complicates the use of bank balance sheet data, or even data on bank lending, to learn about overall regional lending patterns. We then show that regions (counties) with different income levels are substantially different in loan sales and shadow bank multipliers. As we argue later, these differences also result in differential shock propagation across regions.

We start by visually illustrating in figure 6 the significant heterogeneity in the bank loan sales propensity and shadow bank market share across US counties. This heterogeneity, together with the time-varying

A Fraction of loans sold by banks

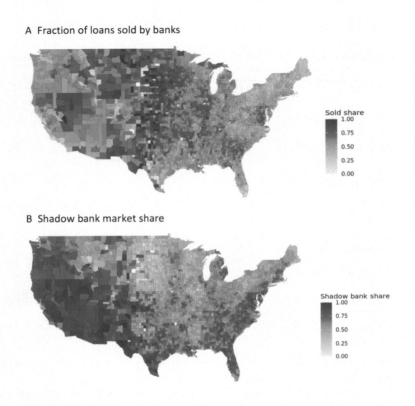

B Shadow bank market share

Fig. 6. Regional heterogeneity—fractions of loans sold by banks and shadow bank share. Panel *A* shows the fraction of loans in a county that banks originate and sell in 2021, the latest year in our data. Panel *B* shows the fraction of loans in a county originated by shadow banks in 2021. Home Mortgage Disclosure Act data. A color version of this figure is available online.

nature of these factors, implies substantial variation in the loan sale and shadow bank multipliers across and within regions. Only about 53% of variation in the county-level lending of banks is explained by bank balance sheet lending (table 1, col. 5). There are also regional differences in how multipliers change over time. Bank balance sheet lending, together with county and year fixed effects, explains only roughly 74% of the variation in county-level bank lending volume (table 1, col. 6). This implies that even after considering level differences in the loan sale multiplier across counties (county fixed effects) and aggregate yearly variation in the loan sale multiplier (year fixed effects), the within-region time variation of the loan sale multiplier is large enough to leave more than a quarter of the variation in total bank lending unexplained. Similarly, shadow bank multipliers also differ substantially across regions: bank lending (balance sheet and loan sales) accounts for about 54% of variation in the county-level total lending volume, which increases to about 86% once we add county and time fixed effects. The latter are a result of an aggregate shift to shadow banks, but even with this aggregate variation accounted for, significant variation in the shadow bank multiplier exists. Variation in the multipliers is also reflected in regional growth rates in lending, which we confirm in table 3 and figure 7. This analysis shows that inferring bank balance sheet lending from a fixed multiplier is insufficient for making precise quantitative statements about the total quantity of lending.

To illustrate this further, in panel B of table 1 we regress the true total bank lending at the county level on the inferred total bank lending from bank balance sheet lending, assuming a constant loan sale multiplier based on its sample mean in the aggregate data. As we observe, the inferred bank lending accounts for only about 53% of variation in the actual aggregate bank lending at the county level (col. 1), and with county fixed effects, it accounts for just 63% of that variation (col. 2). Similarly,

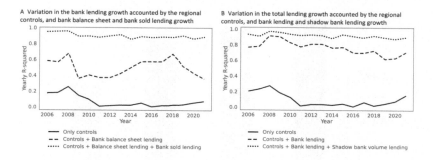

Fig. 7. Accounting for the regional variation in the bank and total lending growth rates over time. This figure shows the R^2 from the county-level regression estimated in each of the plotted years in the cross section of counties. Panel A shows the results for the county-level growth in the bank lending as the dependent variable, and panel B shows the corresponding results for the county-level growth in total lending. In panel A, we show these results from three specifications: (i) one with a set of regional controls including the county-level growth in house prices and unemployment, (ii) one that in addition to controls in the specification (i) adds the growth in the county-level bank balance sheet lending, and (iii) the one that in addition adds the county-level growth in bank sold lending as a control variable. In panel B, we show corresponding results for three specifications: one with a set of regional controls, the second one that in addition adds the growth in the county-level total bank lending, and the one that in addition adds the county-level growth in shadow bank lending as a control variable. Home Mortgage Disclosure Act data. A color version of this figure is available online.

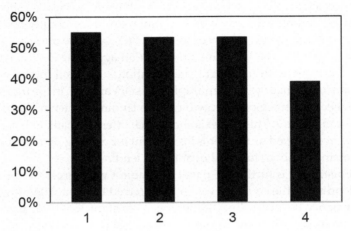

A Bank sold share by county income

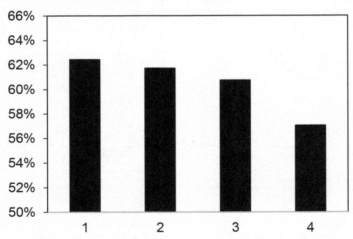

B Shadow bank share by county income

Fig. 8. Regional heterogeneity—fractions of "loans sold by banks" and "shadow bank share" by county income. Panel *A* shows the fraction of loans in a county that banks originate and sell in 2021 sorted by the county income quartile (with 1 being the lowest and 4 being the highest income). Panel *B* shows the fraction of loans in a county originated by shadow banks in 2021 sorted by the county income decile. The means in panels *A* and *B* are weighted by the county-level bank volume and total county-level lending volume. Home Mortgage Disclosure Act data.

as shown in columns 5 and 6, the inferred total lending from bank lending assuming a constant shadow bank multiplier accounts for only about 49% of variation in the total lending at the county level (59% with county fixed effects). Even allowing the multipliers to vary as in the aggregate data and including county fixed effects does not significantly improve the inference on county-level lending patterns. For example, using this method, the inferred total lending accounts for about 74% of variation in actual lending at the county level. This evidence confirms that not only do multipliers vary over time and across regions but also these regional differences evolve over time in a nontrivial way, complicating further the inference of regional lending patterns from just bank balance sheet or bank data.

In figure 8A, we show that banks in counties with the highest income are most likely to keep their loans on their balance sheets. As Buchak et al. (2018) show, this was in part a reflection of tightened regulation on banks after the 2007 crisis that led to banks retreating from lending to low-income households. In addition, because high-income households tend to have jumbo loans (larger loans), the lack of a securitization market for such loans in the post-2007 period implies that in counties with such households, the loan sale and shadow bank multipliers are smallest. Because shadow banks entered in sectors where banks retreated and where the market for securitization existed, the share of shadow bank lending monotonically decreases with income (fig. 8B), resulting in the largest shadow bank multiplier for the poorest counties. As we later discuss, the heterogeneity in multipliers across space implies that recovery from shocks will differ across regions of different incomes.

IV. Bank Capitalization and Secondary Markets Drive the Margins of Adjustment

Buchak et al. (2024) have identified two key drivers behind the loan sales multiplier and shadow bank multiplier. First, banks switch between traditional bank balance sheet lending and selling loans based on their balance sheet strength, and the extent of that switching is determined in equilibrium. Figure 9A shows that the bank loan retention propensity is lower (loan sale propensity is higher) when the aggregate bank capitalization is lower. We show that the relationship between bank capital and share of loans retained on balance sheets holds across banks (fig. 9B) as well as within a bank across time and accounting for loan characteristics (fig. 9C). These results extend the results from Buchak et al. (2024).

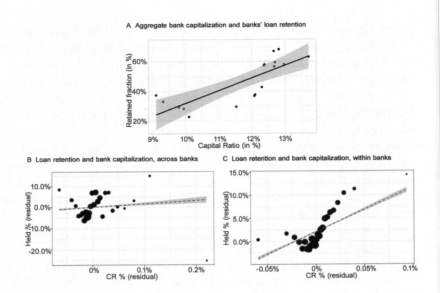

Fig. 9. Bank capitalization and loan retention. Panel *A* plots the relation between average aggregate bank capitalization in a year and the aggregate fraction of loans that banks retain on their balance sheet as a share of all loans they originate in each year 2005–21. The average bank capitalization is weighted by the total volume of the loans they originate. Panels *B* and *C* use bank-level data and show binned scatterplots (25 equal-sized bins) of a bank percentage of loans retained on balance sheet in a given year versus a bank capital ratio (CR) in a given year. Both loan retention and capital ratios are residualized using a set of bank-level controls and year time dummies. "Within" analysis in panel *C* also removes the bank fixed effects. Estimation sample is 2005–21. Home Mortgage Disclosure Act data and Federal Financial Institutions Examination Council Bank Call Reports.

As banks' balance sheet capacity declines, banks shift toward the originate-to-distribute model and then move back toward balance sheet lending as their balance sheet capacity improves.

Second, both multipliers—including the shadow bank multiplier, given that their business model relies on selling loans—also depend on the availability and relative attractiveness of the loan sale market. For example, policies that acquire MBS, such as quantitative easing, can lower the cost of capital for the originate-to-distribute model, resulting in increased loan sale propensity by banks. Because shadow banks do not originate on the balance sheet, the shadow bank lending multiplier is also crucially affected by the conditions in the secondary loan market (Buchak et al. 2024).

Overall, our empirical evidence shows that the shadow bank multiplier and the loan sales multiplier are large and evolve over time as a function of the composition of the financial intermediation system: balance sheet capacity of banks and the presence of shadow banks. These empirical findings have two direct consequences. The first is on measurement. Bank data are frequently used to measure how lending responds to policy, financial, or real shocks and to calibrate models in which lending plays a central role. The time and regional varying multipliers suggest that bank balance sheet lending does not accurately represent bank lending, which in turn does not accurately represent aggregate lending. Importantly, simply grossing up bank balance sheet lending by a fixed, common multiplier across time or regions is insufficient to both measurement and policy making.

In addition, bank capitalization and the presence of shadow banks are major determinants of these multipliers. Because policy frequently affects bank capitalization, these multipliers are therefore not policy invariant. For example, imposing a stricter capital requirement on banks is likely to have a large impact on bank balance sheet lending, but it also simultaneously alters banks' incentives to sell their originated loans and shadow banks' competitiveness with bank lenders. Therefore, understanding only the bank balance sheet lending response to a capital requirement change is insufficient for evaluating its impact on total lending.

The second implication of our empirical exercise is that the severity and recovery from shocks behave differently than predicted by models in which all lending is through bank balance sheets. These heterogeneous responses across the United States are difficult to gauge by looking at just the lending on bank balance sheets.

V.   Model

Our empirical results document that the loan sales and the shadow bank lending multipliers are not only large but also highly variable and endogenous to many relevant policies. Thus, a realistic quantitative policy analysis requires modeling how these multipliers evolve in equilibrium. To illustrate how these multipliers affect policy analysis, we develop a simplified parsimonious dynamic quantitative model of financial intermediation. Our model builds on that in Buchak et al. (2024), which estimates a rich heterogeneous agent demand system for bank and shadow bank loans in which the loan sales and shadow bank multipliers play a central role, but in a static setting. Here, we instead focus on dynamics to understand how these multipliers contribute to the recovery from financial shocks over time and how they affect banks' ex ante incentives to retain capital buffers. This allows us to compare the recovery dynamics

relative to standard bank balance sheet models of financial intermediation, which omit these margins.

We calibrate the model to the empirical loan sales and shadow bank
lending multipliers. Using the calibrated model, we examine how shocks
to bank capital propagate through this augmented model of the financial intermediation sector. Importantly, we counterfactually examine
economies where these margins of adjustment are absent. Our model
highlights the impact of these margins on how shocks to bank capital
propagate, as well as the speed of recovery from shocks to intermediaries. Ex post, these margins ameliorate shocks to bank capital from
both the perspective of the initial impact of the shock and the speed
of recovery from the shock. We then use our model to illustrate where
calibrating a more standard bank balance sheet model leads to incorrect
inferences.

A. Model Specification

We first provide a high-level overview of the model. Banks compete
with nonbanks in imperfect competition to provide loans that mature
in the following period. Banks have capital and are long-lived. Bank
capital gives banks the ability to make on-balance-sheet loans, but regulatory capital requirements impose a severe penalty when bank capital
falls below a statutory minimum. In addition, banks can choose to finance their loans through securitization in a secondary market. Banks
make loan pricing, financing, dividend, and equity-raising decisions
to maximize their discounted present value.

Nonbanks have no capital and cannot make balance sheet loans.
Therefore, they must finance all originations through securitization.
Nonbanks set interest rates to maximize profits. By assumption, lenders
are symmetric within type.

Lenders' loans are imperfect substitutes for one another. This captures
unmodeled horizontal product differentiation such as differences in
lenders' branch networks or other amenities offered to borrowers. This
product differentiation gives individual lenders market power, and consequently there are positive markups and variable profits in equilibrium.
Lenders therefore earn (variable) rents not because of, say, an incentive
compatibility constraint, but because of well-documented imperfect
competition. Loan origination has a fixed per loan "labor" cost, and also
must be financed through balance sheet retention or securitization for
banks, or through securitization for nonbanks. Securitization has a higher

direct marginal cost, but balance sheet financing negatively affects banks' capital ratios.

Loan Demand

Given a vector of economy-wide interest rates $r_t \equiv \{r_{1t}, r_{2t}, \ldots, r_{Nt}\}$ of N lenders at time t, total demand for lender i's loans is given by

$$q_{it} \equiv q_i(r_{it}, r_{-it}; \theta), \qquad (M1)$$

where θ are nonprice characteristics, such as the lender type. Quantities are expressed in units of aggregate bank risk-weighted assets; for example, a quantity of 0.10 means that the bank's flow lending is equal to 10% of its risk-weighted assets.

Nonbank Loan Supply

A fixed number of nonbanks, N_{sb}, compete with a fixed number of banks, N_b.[9] Nonbank loan provision has a labor cost mc_{sb}^l and a cost of securitization mc^s, so that nonbank marginal cost is equal to $mc_{sb} = mc_{sb}^l + mc^s$. Taking other interest rates r_{-j} as given, nonbanks maximize profits as follows:

$$\pi_{sb} = \max_r q_i(r, r_{-it}; \theta)(r - mc_{sb}). \qquad (M2)$$

In equilibrium, because loans are differentiated, the variable markup $(r - mc_{sb})$ will be positive.

The Bank's Problem

A representative long-lived bank's capital ratio is given by c_t. In each period, it decides whether to raise equity I_t (pay dividends), thereby directly increasing (decreasing) its capital ratio. In addition, it sets an interest rate on loans r_{it} and a financing policy $\phi_{it} \in \{0, 1\}$, where $\phi_{it} = 1$ means the bank retains the loan on balance sheet.

Bank investment. The bank can raise equity ($I_t > 0$) or issue dividends ($I_t < 0$); that is, I_t represents net investment. To contribute I_t of equity, the banker must pay an effective cost of $\psi(I_t)$, with $\psi(I_t) > I_t$. That is, the banker pays a cost both when raising equity and when receiving dividends. We assume a convex cost of issuing dividends and a fixed cost of raising equity. Bank investment takes time, so that investment at time t only affects the bank's capital ratio at time $t + 1$.

Bank loan supply. Like nonbanks, each bank offers a differentiated loan to borrowers. Bank loan provision has a marginal labor cost, mc_b^l. If the bank securitizes the loan, it also pays a marginal securitization cost equal to the nonbank's securitization cost, mc^s.

Alternatively, the bank can finance the loan by retaining it on its balance sheet. We capture the fact that the loan is a long-lived asset through the assumption that on-balance-sheet loan origination negatively affects the bank's capital ratio at the time it is originated, and pays out—thus increasing the bank's capital ratio—only in the following period. Loans receive a regulatory risk weight ξ, so that originating quantity q of on-balance-sheet loans reduces regulatory capital by ξq.

Bank profit is as follows:

$$\pi_b(r, \phi) = q_i(r, r_{-it}, \phi; \theta)(r - mc_b^l - (1 - \phi)mc^s). \tag{M3}$$

As with nonbanks, bank variable markups will be positive in equilibrium because loans are differentiated.

Bank capital. We directly model the bank's capital ratio with the following law of motion:

$$c' = \exp(z)c + I + \pi_b(r, \phi), \tag{M4}$$

in which c is the current period capital ratio, c' is next period's capital ratio, z is a shock to bank capital, I is net investment, and π_b is profits from lending, defined earlier. We assume that z follows an exogenous Markov process; for example, an AR(1) with some persistence.

Note that the quantity of on-balance-sheet lending does not appear directly in the law of motion for bank capital, because the one-period loans mature in the following period and become cash, which has a risk weight of zero.

The bank is subject to a regulatory capital requirement, which we model as a severe penalty to flow utility. The penalty is assessed at the end of the period, after the shock z is realized, after the firm has made its investment decision, and after the firm has made its lending rate and financing choice, but importantly before the firm has realized any profits from on-balance-sheet lending. Thus, its effective capital at the time of the regulatory assessment is

$$c^{\mathrm{eff}}(r, \phi) = \exp(z)c - \xi q_b^b(r)\phi. \tag{M5}$$

We denote with $\rho(r, \phi) = f(c^{\mathrm{eff}}(r, \phi))$ the regulatory penalty. Finally, we assume that the bank, when making the decision to retain or securitize its loans, receives an independent utility shock ϵ_{ret} and ϵ_{otd}, which captures heterogeneity in bank capital across banks in reduced form. Thus, its period utility is as follows:

$$u(r, I, \phi) = -\psi(I) + \phi(\rho(r, 1) + \epsilon_{\text{ret}}) + (1 - \phi)(\rho(r, 0) + \epsilon_{\text{otd}}). \quad \text{(M6)}$$

Recall, for positive net investment, $I > 0$, $\psi(I) > 0$; that is, the banker gets disutility from putting more equity into the firm. Conversely, for negative net investment (paying dividends), $I < 0$ and $\psi(I) < 0$; that is, the banker receives utility from dividends.

The bank's problem. With these ingredients defined, we express the bank's problem as follows:

$$v_0 = \max_{\{r, \phi, I\}_t t=0} \sum \beta^t E[u(r, I, \phi)]$$

s.t. $$C_{t+1} = \exp(z_t)c_t + I_t + \pi_b(r_t, \phi_t).$$

Equilibrium and Model Solution

Equilibrium in our model is a set of policy functions $r(c, z)$, $\phi(c, z)$, and $I(c, z)$, which depend on the state variables (c, z) and satisfy these conditions:

1. Banks choose rates, loan retention, and net investment to maximize lifetime utility;
2. Nonbanks choose rates to maximize per-period profits; and
3. Loan demand equals loan supply.

Functional forms and parameters. For quantification, we impose functional form assumptions on the general components of the model. We assume that each lender i faces logistic loan demand:

$$q_i(r_i, r_t; \theta) = m \times \frac{\exp(-\alpha r_i + \delta_i)}{\sum_j \exp(-\alpha r_j + \delta_j)}. \quad \text{(M7)}$$

This form arises naturally out of the standard industrial organization discrete choice framework where a mass m individual borrowers make a discrete choice among N lenders and an outside option of not borrowing. α determines how sensitive borrowers are to interest rates. We assume that nonprice attributes (e.g., amenities or convenience of the lender),

δ_i, are common across lender types, so that banks have nonprice attribute δ_b and nonbank lenders have a nonprice attribute δ_s.[10]

We assume banks have a convex cost adjustment cost for raising equity and issuing dividends, plus a fixed cost when issuing equity, which captures in reduced form both underwriting costs and financing frictions around issuing equity. In particular, we specify $\psi(I)$ as

$$\psi(I) = I + \frac{\gamma}{2}I^2 + \begin{cases} 0 & I \leq 0 \\ C & I > 0 \end{cases}, \quad \text{(M8)}$$

where γ determines the convexity of equity or dividend issuance costs. C determines the fixed cost of raising equity.

We define the regulatory cost function, $\rho(x)$, as

$$\rho(x) = \begin{cases} 0 & x \geq \bar{c} \\ -\exp(-\lambda \times (x - \bar{c})) - \lambda \times (x - \bar{c}) + 1 & \text{when} & x < \bar{c} \end{cases}. \quad \text{(M9)}$$

This formulation imposes no regulatory cost above a threshold, $\bar{c}$, an exponentially increasing cost below the threshold, that is first continuous in level and derivative at the threshold. $\lambda > 0$ controls how quickly regulatory costs rise for an out-of-compliance bank; a lower λ corresponds to a more forbearing regulator.

For the exogenous shocks, we assume that shocks to capital z_t follow an AR(1) process, $z_{t+1} = \theta z_t + \epsilon_t^z, \epsilon_t^z \sim N(0, \sigma_z^2)$. Finally, the securitization and retention shocks ϵ_{otd} and ϵ_{ret} follow a type-1 extreme value distribution with scale parameter σ_{fin}.

Characterizing the solution to the bank's problem. To provide intuition, the bank's problem can be separated into a static problem and a dynamic problem.

The static problem. In the static problem, the bank takes as given its current state, (c, z), and a candidate next-period capital c'. Conditional on its current state and desired next-period capital, the bank chooses interest rates, a financing policy, and an investment policy such that its state transition is feasible and its current period flow utility is maximized. In particular, the bank's intratemporal problem is to maximize

$$u^*(c, z, c') \equiv \max_{r, \phi, I} E[u(r, I, \phi)] \quad \text{(M10)}$$

subject to the law of motion,

$$c' = \exp(z)c + I + \pi_b(r, \phi). \tag{M11}$$

Letting μ be the Lagrange multiplier on the capital law of motion, one has, if the bank securitizes the loan,

$$\psi'(I) = \mu \tag{M12}$$

$$\pi_b'(r, 0) = 0. \tag{M13}$$

Observe that the bank's price-setting decision when originating to distribute does not depend on its capital; it simply aims to maximize profits. In contrast, if the bank retains the loan,

$$\psi'(I) = \mu \tag{M14}$$

$$\xi\left(q_b^b\right)'(r)\rho'(c^{\text{eff}}) + \mu\pi_b'(r, 1) = 0. \tag{M15}$$

That is, the bank's balance sheet pricing decision depends also on how the newly originated loans will affect its regulatory cost. When c^{eff} is far above the regulatory constraint, $\rho'(c^{\text{eff}}) = 0$, and hence this term drops out. In this case, the bank is again setting interest rates to maximize profits. In contrast, when c^{eff} is relatively low, $\rho'(c^{\text{eff}}) > 0$, and the bank will choose higher rates to offset the increased regulatory cost. Observe that for the static plan to be feasible, $I|_{\phi=0} \neq I|_{\phi=1}$, because balance sheet and securitized lending generate different levels of retained profit for the bank, which changes how much investment must be made (dividends paid out).

Finally, given the functional form assumption on the retention shocks, the bank's retention policy takes the following logistic form in expectation, which we interpret as the share of heterogeneous banks following the retention policy:

$$\phi = \frac{\exp(u(r|_{\phi=1}, I|_{\phi=1}, 1) - u(r|_{\phi=0}, I|_{\phi=0}, 0))}{1 + \exp(u(r|_{\phi=1}, I|_{\phi=1}, 1) - u(r|_{\phi=0}, I|_{\phi=0}, 0))}. \tag{M16}$$

The retention policy depends on the difference in flow utilities for retaining versus securitizing the loans. The intuitive trade-off is as follows: Balance sheet lending has lower marginal costs, because the bank does not have to pay the cost of securitization. Thus, profits from balance sheet lending are higher. This means that to maintain a given target level of capital for the next period, the bank can pay out a larger dividend.

When the bank is well capitalized, it will prefer to do this. In contrast, when the bank is poorly capitalized, balance sheet lending leads to a greater regulatory cost, and the value of avoiding this regulatory cost outweighs the benefits of the larger dividend (smaller equity issuance) that balance sheet lending would enable.[11]

The dynamic problem. The static problem produces, for each state (c, z) and candidate next-period capital c', an optimized flow utility $u^*(c, z, c')$. Given this function, the bank's problem can be written as a straightforward dynamic optimization problem where the bank chooses the optimal next-period capital in each state. In recursive form, this is

$$v(c, z) = \max_{c'} u^*(c, z, c') + \beta E[v(c', z')]. \qquad \text{(M17)}$$

Once the optimal dynamic policy function, $c' = g(c, z)$, is solved, the optimal interest rate, retention policy, and investment policy can be recovered directly from the solution to the static problem described earlier.

B. Calibration

The model with specialized functional forms has parameters that we calibrate to produce quantitatively reasonable simulations and counterfactuals. Several of the parameters correspond to values available directly from the literature; others do not. Where possible, we take values directly from the literature or from regulations. We calibrate the remaining parameters via simulated method of moments.

Parameters Calibrated from Existing Literature

We set the subjective discount rate, β, to 0.95. Following Buchak et al. (2024), we set the regulatory risk weight on loans to be $\xi = 0.25$, which corresponds to the statutory requirement for conforming loans. Also following Buchak et al. (2024), we set marginal costs as $mc_b^l = mc_s^l = 3\%$, which incorporates both labor costs and a "baseline" cost of capital averaged over the postcrisis period, and $mc^s = 0.67$. We set $\alpha = 1.65$, which is the average price sensitivity estimated over the US mortgage market. We set $N_b = 25$ and $N_{sb} = 50$, which corresponds roughly to the average number of bank and nonbank lenders in a given metropolitan statistical area.

Parameters Calibrated through the Simulated Method of Moments

There are several remaining parameters to calibrate. Although the calibration is done jointly through the simulated method of moments, it is useful to describe intuitively which moments are most informative about which parameters.

The parameters to be calibrated first concern the capital adjustment cost function: γ, the investment convexity parameter, and C, the fixed cost of raising equity. Next, we calibrate the parameters of the regulatory cost function, $\bar{c}$ and λ, and parameters of the exogenous shock process, θ and σ_z^2. These parameters most directly influence time-series properties of the capital ratio process, and intuitively we exploit various historical moments to inform them. In particular, we use the historical mean, standard deviation, and autocorrelation of levels and changes in the aggregate capital ratio (six moments) to calibrate these six parameters.

Next are parameters of the demand function, m, the market size, and δ_b and δ_{sb}, the nonprice demand characteristics of banks and nonbanks, respectively. These parameters broadly concern aggregate lending quantities as well as means and higher-order moments of bank market shares, or, equivalently, the shadow bank multiplier. In particular, we use four moments to calibrate these three parameters: the historical average flow of lending relative to bank assets (a measure of lending quantities), the mean and standard deviation of the shadow bank multiplier, and the correlation of total lending with bank capitalization.

Finally, the scale parameter of the retention utility shock, σ_{fin}, broadly governs the level and volatility of the loan sales multiplier. We calibrate this parameter using the mean and variance of the loan sales multiplier, together with the correlation of bank balance sheet shocks to lending quantity shocks.

Observe that our calibration is overdetermined, making use of 13 moments to calibrate 10 parameters. Despite this overdetermination, our calibration is able to reasonably match the targeted moments. Table 4, panel A shows the targeted moments used in calibration and the moments produced by the model. Panel B shows the calibrated parameters and summarizes the key moments used in identification. Panel C shows the parameters taken from the literature.

C. Model Discussion

Our model captures the two key multipliers, the loan sales multiplier and the shadow bank multiplier, which we emphasize in our reduced-form

Table 4
Model Calibration

	Target		Model	
	Baseline	Misspecified	Baseline	Misspecified
		Panel A: Targeted Moments		
E[Shadow Bank Multiplier]	2.294	1.000	2.005	1.000
SD[Shadow Bank Multiplier]	.726	.000	.590	.000
E[Loan Sale Multiplier]	2.145	1.000	2.112	1.000
SD[Loan Sale Multiplier]	.459	.000	.101	.000
SD[d Total Lending]	.348	.348	.362	.367
Corr[d Total Lending, d CR]	–	.014	.002	.001
Corr[d Balance Sheet Lending, d CR]	.236	–	.226	.046
Lending Quantity / Assets	.250	.250	.253	.193
E[Capital Ratio]	.109	.109	.162	.099
SD[Capital Ratio]	.013	.013	.098	.037
AR[Capital Ratio]	.985	.985	.939	.895
E[d Capital Ratio]	.000	.000	.000	.000
SD[d Capital Ratio]	.002	.002	.034	.017
AR[d Capital Ratio]	.173	.173	−.045	−.013

Parameter	Description	Baseline	Misspecified	Key Moments
		Panel B: Calibrated Parameters		
γ	Investment cost convexity	43.10	32.46	Capitalization time-series
C	Equity issuance cost	2.08	.59	Capitalization time-series
$\bar{c}$	Regulatory capital requirement	.07	.04	Capitalization time-series
λ	Regulatory intensity	18.39	19.14	Capitalization time-series
θ	Shock AR coefficient	.17	.23	Capitalization time-series
σ_z^2	Shock variance	.31	.36	Capitalization time-series

270

		Value		Source
m	Market size	1.00	1.00	Lending volumes and shares
δ_b	Bank nonprice demand	1.33	1.32	Lending volumes and shares
δ_{sb}	Nonbank nonprice demand	1.42	N/A	Lending volumes and shares
σ_{fin}	Financing shock scale	.01	.04	Balance sheet shares
σ_d^2	Loan demand variance	.13	.13	Lending volumes and shares

Parameter	Description	Value	Source
		Panel C: Externally Calibrated Parameters	
β	Discount factor	.95	Standard
ξ	Asset risk weight	.25	Buchak et al. (2024)
mc_b^d	Bank origination MC	3.00%	Id.
mc_s^d	Nonbank origination MC	3.00%	Id.
mc^s	Securitization cost	.67%	Id.
α	Price sensitivity	1.65	Id.

Note: This table shows key inputs and results from the model calibration. Panel A shows the targeted moments and model simulated moments for the "baseline" model, which has the shadow bank and loan sale multipliers active and aims to target aggregate moments that reflect these, and the "misspecified" model, which runs the calibration with these multipliers shut down and aims to target aggregate moments that do not distinguish bank balance sheet lending from total lending. Panel B shows the calibrated parameters from each calibration and the key set of identifying moments. Panel C shows the externally calibrated parameters: the parameter from the model, its description, the calibrated value, and the source. These parameters are constant across the calibrations. MC = marginal cost.

results. Both margins relate directly to the key state variable, the level of bank capital. To help illustrate these forces, figure 9 plots the bank's policy functions against the level of bank capital. We focus first on the baseline case (solid line) in which both margins are present.

When the bank is well capitalized, the bank's balance sheet provides the lowest-cost source of financing in the economy. Shadow banks, which must finance through more expensive securitization, are at a funding disadvantage relative to banks. Intuitively, banks can replicate the funding of shadow banks, but shadow banks cannot replicate the funding of banks. Although product differentiation and imperfect competition lead shadow banks to have a nontrivial market share, the fraction of loans that shadow banks originate is relatively low because they must pass their higher marginal costs on to borrowers. Banks, facing the choice between low-cost balance sheet financing and higher-cost securitization, tend to choose to retain loans on their balance sheets (fig. 10A). Implicit bank capital cost heterogeneity implies that this fraction is not 100%. In

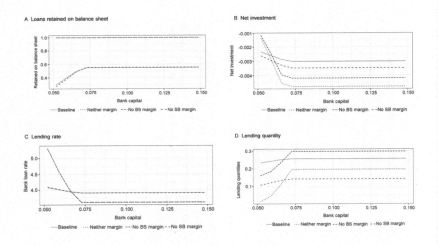

Fig. 10. Policy functions. This figure shows the optimal bank policy functions from the calibrated model for the baseline specification (solid line), the model with no loan sales (BS) margin (narrow-dashed), the model with no shadow bank (SB) margin (wide-dashed), and the model with neither margin (dotted). In each figure, the x-axis is the key state variable, the bank capital ratio. The y-axis shows the bank's optimal policy under each scenario for each value of the capital ratio. Panel A shows the fraction of loans retained on balance sheet. Panel B shows net investment, with a negative number denoting a dividend. Panel C shows the bank's optimal loan rate, and panel D shows the bank's lending quantities. A color version of this figure is available online.

addition, well-capitalized banks can afford to issue dividends (negative net investment, shown in fig. 10B). As low balance sheet funding costs are partially passed on to borrowers, lending rates are relatively low, and lending quantities are relatively high (figs. 10C and 10D).

As bank capital deteriorates, the shadow cost of on-balance-sheet financing increases. Additional on-balance-sheet loan originations reduce bank capital and push the bank closer to the region in which capital regulation imposes significant costs on the bank. As bank balance sheet financing costs rise, the bank endogenously begins to substitute toward an originate-to-distribute model, as shown in figure 10A. Because the bank is forced to substitute toward higher-cost sources of financing and pass these costs on to borrowers, bank lending quantities fall, as shown in figures 10C and 10D. Finally, more poorly capitalized banks lower dividends or even raise equity, as shown in figure 10D.

To quantify the role of the loan sales and shadow bank multipliers, we re-solve our model sequentially turning off these margins, still using the same calibrated parameters. The *No Balance Sheet Margin* counterfactual removes the loan sales margin so banks only originate loans on balance sheet, but it maintains the presence of shadow banks. The *No Shadow Banks Margin* counterfactual removes the shadow bank margin but allows banks to substitute between on-balance-sheet and securitized lending. The *Neither Margin* counterfactual removes both, which corresponds to the pure bank balance sheet model of lending with no loan sales by banks and no shadow bank lending. Figure 9 shows these counterfactual policy functions in narrow-dashed, wide-dashed, and dotted lines, respectively.

First, figure 10A shows that mechanically, under the *No Balance Sheet Margin* and *Neither Margin* scenarios, banks retain 100% of their loan originations, because these counterfactuals assume that banks must retain all their loans. Removing the shadow bank margin in the *No Shadow Banks Margin* scenario does not meaningfully alter the bank's optimal financing decision because that decision is essentially made conditional on having made the loan and does not depend much on the broader competitive environment.

The ability to sell loans lowers bank profits and thus dividends when capital is plentiful, but it also allows them to maintain higher dividends during recapitalization when capital is low. Figure 10B shows the bank's optimal investment (dividend) policy under the counterfactuals. Holding the bank balance sheet margin fixed, shadow banks' presence uniformly decreases dividends that banks pay. Because the lending sector is more competitive and bank profits are lower, banks have less to pay out in steady state. Next, holding shadow bank presence fixed, in the well-capitalized states, dividend payouts are lower in the presence of the loan sales margin. This occurs because of product differentiation: due to bank heterogeneity, even when the sector as a whole is well capitalized, some banks still choose to engage in an originate-to-distribute business model. This model is less profitable than balance sheet lending from a well-capitalized bank, and thus total banking profits, and consequently dividends, are lower. In contrast, in the poorly capitalized states, in the absence of the loan sales margin, banks cut dividends much more sharply and switch to net investment sooner. This occurs for two reasons: First, because banks have no option to switch to loan sales (securitized lending), higher marginal costs reduce their profits, so they are less able to issue dividends. Second, dynamically, because these banks rely more on capital to engage in profitable lending, retained capital is more valuable, so they are quicker to recapitalize.

Giving banks the option to sell loans does not always lead to lower average interest rates, despite the fact that it allows each bank to lower its funding cost. Figures 10C and 10D consider the case of well-capitalized banks. Some banks, even though the sector is well capitalized, choose to engage in securitized lending, which has higher marginal costs. Because of product differentiation, these higher-cost lenders maintain nontrivial market share and raise prices in equilibrium, increasing the average interest rate in the economy. When the banking sector is poorly capitalized, on the other hand, allowing banks to securitize loans decreases average rates. In this scenario, the shadow cost of balance sheet lending increases dramatically. Although the costs of securitized finance are greater than those of balance sheet lending for a well-capitalized bank, they are lower than the costs for a poorly capitalized bank. Some of the cost savings are passed on to consumers, resulting in lower average rates when banks are poorly capitalized.

The largest effects are on quantities of lending, with dramatically different sensitivities of total lending to bank balance sheet capital when these margins are active versus when they are not. When banks cannot sell originated loans, around the point in the state space where bank capital becomes impaired, aggregate lending declines dramatically. In contrast, when banks can sell these loans, the aggregate lending response is much more muted. Thus, a regulator observing a relatively poorly capitalized banking sector thinking only about balance sheet lending would dramatically overstate the impact of further deterioration of bank capital on total lending.

To summarize, the presence of the loan sales and shadow bank margins have the effect of moderating outcomes in the loan market when bank capital deteriorates. When these margins are not present, bank costs rise as capital falls, and these costs are passed through to borrowers, leading to higher prices and lower quantities. When these margins are present, banks shift their financing business model toward securitization. Costs rise, but much less dramatically. In addition, shadow banks provide an important source of lending, particularly when bank capital is low and costs are relatively high.

D.   Capital Shocks under Counterfactual Financing Models

We illustrate the quantitative importance of these margins in the recovery from a negative shock to the intermediation sector. We simulate a negative shock to bank capital in four economies: (1) the *baseline* economy with both margins active, (2) the *No Shadow Banks* economy, with no shadow banks but the loan sales margin still active, (3) the *No Balance Sheet* economy, with no loan sales but shadow banks still present, and (4) the *neither margin* economy, where both margins are shut down. We draw exogenous capital shocks z from the calibrated distribution except at time $t = 0$, for which we impose a large deterministic negative capital shock. We run the simulations 500 times, examine average outcomes across each of the four economies, and plot the implied impulse response functions from these simulations. The results are shown in figure 11, panels *A–E*.

Bank Capital Response

Here we show that the loan sales margin not only substantially increases the resilience of the financial intermediation sector to bank capital shocks ex post but also results in less prudent banks ex ante. We describe the path of bank capital across the four counterfactuals, which is shown in figure 11*A*. The shock at time $t = 0$ dramatically (and mechanically) decreases capital for banks in each counterfactual.

Ignoring the margins of adjustment substantially underestimates the resilience of the financial intermediary sector shock to intermediary capital. When capital falls below the statutory minimum, banks begin to recapitalize through a combination of retained earnings (i.e., decreased dividend payouts) and direct investment. Following the shock, bank capital slowly rebuilds. Our counterfactuals do not incorporate any

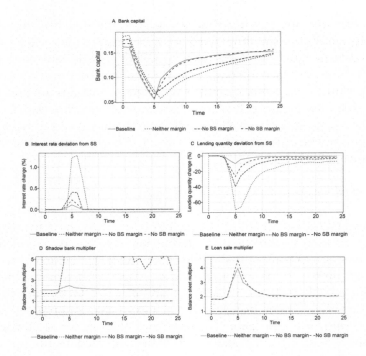

Fig. 11. Counterfactual impulse response. This figure shows the simulated impulse response of a large negative shock to bank capital at time $t = 0$ across the baseline (solid line) and counterfactual scenarios (no loan sales [BS], narrow-dashed; no shadow banks [SB], wide-dashed; neither margin, dotted). The x-axis is the time relative to the shock in quarters. Panel A shows bank capital. Panel B shows the average lending rate in percentage point deviations from the steady-state (SS) value. Panel C shows the percentage change in lending from the steady-state value. Panel D shows the shadow bank multiplier. Panel E shows the loan sale multiplier. A color version of this figure is available online.

regulatory interventions that would increase banks' capital—all capital increases are voluntary given the required capital ratio. When banks can adjust on the balance sheet retention margin, they rebuild capital substantially faster because they can still engage in profitable lending off balance sheet. When banks are restricted in their balance sheet lending, the recovery is slow; although their incentives to rebuild capital are high, their limited capital prevents them from generating substantial retained earnings.[12]

Ex ante, because capitalization stocks are less costly, banks are less prudent with capital and take larger advantage of balance sheet capacity when lending. In other words, when banks have access to securitization, they are willing to lend more on balance sheet for any given level of capital and capital requirements. More formally, without the ability to substitute, banks keep a 3 percentage point larger capital buffer away from the regulatory constraint. One can see this by the higher steady-state level of capital in economies without the loan sales margin (the *No Balance Sheet* economy and the *Neither Margin* economy). Intuitively, when the bank has a more difficult time adjusting to shocks, it keeps a larger capital buffer in excess of the statutory capital requirement. This implies that for a given level of capital requirements and capital, banks' access to securitization allows them to take larger advantage of their balance sheet capacity.

Lending Price and Quantity Response

Figures 11*B* and 11*C* show interest rates and lending quantities relative to the average preshock level in each economy. A common feature across all counterfactuals is that well-capitalized bank balance sheets provide the lowest-cost loan financing. As bank balance sheets are impaired, balance sheet financing becomes costlier, and this is passed through to borrowers in the form of higher rates and consequently lower quantities. Whether these costs are passed through to borrowers through higher prices or lower quantities depends primarily on borrowers' demand elasticity.

Although the direction of the effect is common across each counterfactual, the quantitative magnitude differs dramatically. In the standard bank balance sheet model, there is no margin for adjustment. In this *Neither Margin* counterfactual, the price and quantity response is the largest. Because bank balance sheets are the only source of financing in the economy, the increases in the effective cost of balance sheet financing are unavoidably passed through to borrowers. In our simulations, interest rates increase by more than 100 basis points, and quantities decrease by 60%.

The presence of banks offsets some of banks' inability to lend off balance sheet. Bank lending necessarily becomes more expensive, but some borrowers are able to substitute toward less-expensive shadow bank financing through securitization. Price increases are lower (roughly 35 basis points) and quantity decreases less dramatic (roughly 40%). This counterfactual shows that shadow banks are a partial but imperfect substitute for bank balance sheet lending. Two forces are responsible for this result. First, on the supply side, securitized financing through shadow banks is more expensive than balance sheet financing from a well-capitalized bank. When lending switches to shadow banks, prices must increase to reflect these higher costs. Second, on the demand side, the products that shadow banks offer are not perfect substitutes for the products that banks offer, and thus, even adjusting for the higher price, some would-be bank borrowers would prefer to exit on the extensive margin rather than switching to shadow bank financing on the intensive margin.

When there is no shadow bank margin (but banks can sell loans), as shown in the wide-dashed line in the figure 11 panels, the effects of the capital shock on lending are even more muted. Rates increase by only 25 basis points, and quantities decrease by only 20%. The relatively more important role for the bank securitization margin as compared with the shadow bank margin is consistent with the findings in Buchak et al. (2024). It is explained by the fact that securitized bank lending is a better substitute for bank balance sheet lending than securitized shadow bank lending is. Although costs for securitized financing through banks are higher than costs for balance sheet lending from a well-capitalized bank (a supply-side imperfection), from the perspective of borrowers, both products are still bank loans and thus are closer substitutes on the demand side. For example, some borrowers may prefer the convenience of accessing all bank services in one place. In other words, from the borrower's perspective, a securitized bank loan is almost the same as a bank balance sheet loan, whereas a securitized bank loan is not the same as a securitized shadow bank loan.

Finally, in the baseline scenario where both margins are active, the price and quantity effects are the most muted. Prices increase by roughly 10 basis points and quantities decrease by roughly 10 percentage points. In other words, the two margins of adjustment significantly dampen the effect of capital shocks to the intermediation sector on impact.

Shadow Bank and Loan Sale Multipliers

We next show that the multipliers that we record in the data respond to capital shocks in the intermediary sector. In other words, our model generates large and variable shadow bank and loan sales multipliers (figs. 11D and 11E). Following the capital shock, the loan sales lending multiplier increases from below 2 to nearly 4, meaning that the share of bank lending that is financed through bank balance sheets declines from one-half to one-quarter. The shadow bank multiplier is smaller, increasing from about 2 to 2.5, implying an increase in shadow bank lending share of about 10 percentage points.

To understand how the two margins of adjustment interact, we study the importance of shadow bank lending when we prevent bank loan sales. The shadow bank multiplier becomes volatile, and following the shock increases dramatically to well above 5. Because banks can only originate on balance sheet, nearly all lending migrates to shadow banks following the shock. In contrast, when banks are able to securitize loans, banks continue to originate a large fraction of loans in the economy off balance sheet, and thus the response of the shadow bank multiplier is much more muted on average.

E.   The Consequences of Model Misspecification

Finally, we use our model to illustrate why models based on bank balance sheet lending struggle to quantitatively match data and therefore have important drawbacks as guides to policy responses. To undertake this exercise, we first recalibrate our baseline model but restrict the model to bank balance sheet lending. We use aggregate lending data in the calibration to give the bank balance sheet model the best chance to capture the relationship between bank capital and aggregate lending. We then study the same shock as we did earlier and point to the basic economic tension when bank balance sheet models are confronted with data: that aggregate lending is not very responsive to bank capital.

A Bank Balance Sheet Model Calibration

To highlight the basic economic tension in the bank balance sheet model, we seek to approximate ways in which a researcher would calibrate a model that links bank balance sheet strength to aggregate lending activity without considering the margins we emphasize. This calibration exercise differs from our prior calibration in two concrete ways. First, on the model side, all lending in the economy must be financed on depository institutions' balance sheets. There is no securitization, nor are there shadow banks. This is the sense in which the model is misspecified. Second, on the data side, we overlook the empirical distinction between bank balance sheet lending and total lending, because in the eyes of the model, they are the same. We work from the assumption that aggregate lending is the regulator's main concern. Therefore, to give the model the best chance to perform well on the dimension of aggregate lending, we only match moments concerning total lending. Table 4, panel *A* shows the moments we seek to match in the baseline and bank balance sheet calibrations.

The main economic tension can be seen when the bank balance sheet model targets the correlation between bank capital and aggregate lending, which is empirically very small, at 0.01. On the other hand, the correlation between the change in bank capitalization and balance sheet lending in the data is roughly 0.23. This difference does not arise from the micro-macro data wedge but is instead driven by the two multipliers we describe in the empirical section. The mean shadow bank multiplier and loan sales multiplier are approximately 2.3 and 2.1, respectively, with nontrivial variation over time, which provide discipline for the two margins we study. In particular, a model that recognizes these margins jointly justifies the small bank capital-aggregate lending correlation and the relatively large capital-bank balance sheet lending correlation. It achieves it by allowing bank balance sheet lending to contract with bank capital while aggregate lending does not change much due to substitution of bank balance sheet lending with nonbalance sheet lending by banks and shadow bank lending. However, because the balance sheet-only calibration does not recognize these channels, it is forced to account for a very weak correlation between bank capital and aggregate lending in other way.

One might assume that a misspecified model would simply adjust for the weak correlation by disregarding the significance of bank balance sheets in lending decisions. For instance, it could assign a negligible regulatory cost for violating capital constraints or reduce the costs of equity issuance very substantially. However, such adjustments would contradict the observed positive levels of bank capital in the data that banks endogenously chose. In essence, the data on bank capital imposes constraints on the model, indicating that banks indeed prioritize maintaining positive capital levels above regulatory limits. This presents a dilemma in the mis-specified model: while banks demonstrate a concern for maintaining adequate capital, the level of bank capital appears to have weak correlation with lending in the data.

The bank balance sheet model achieves this difficult reconciliation by finding a set of parameters that minimize the time the bank endogenously spends in the region of the state space where capital is impaired. Table 4, panel B shows the results of the calibration. Broadly, the key difference for the misspecified calibration as compared with the baseline specification are lower but not too low equity issuance costs (both in terms of the fixed cost of issuing equity and the convex adjustment cost) as well as what appears to be a more permissive regulatory regime. Importantly, these parameters mean that the bank spends most of its time outside the region where bank capital impacts bank lending, but when faced with severe enough shocks, the bank will still respond to impaired capitalization by substantially reducing lending.

This exercise thus highlights the basic economic tension in calibrating bank balance sheet models. If they are calibrated to aggregate data, they have to reconcile the low correlation between bank capital and aggregate lending. If, on the other hand, they are calibrated to bank balance sheet data, then they severely overestimate the effect of bank balance sheet shocks.

Policy Consequences of Using Bank Balance Sheet Models

We next show that using bank balance sheet models for policy analysis comes with quantitative drawbacks. We compare the lending response to a negative capital shock in our model with the bank balance sheet model. The nature of the shock is exactly the same as that imposed earlier: a large negative shock to bank capital from the preshock steady state. Figure 12 shows the impulse response.

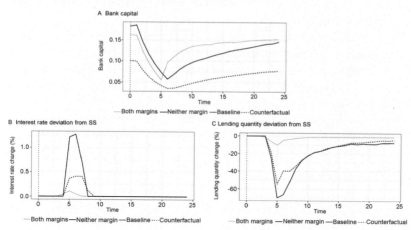

Fig. 12. Misspecified calibrations. This figure shows the simulated impulse response of a large negative shock to bank capital at time $t = 0$ across three scenarios. The solid lines show counterfactuals where both margins are active (gray) and where neither margin is active (black), under the baseline calibration, which matches overall lending, balance sheet lending, and their correlations to bank balance sheet capital under a model where both margins are active. The dotted line shows counterfactuals where neither margin is active under the "misspecified" calibration, which matches overall lending and its correlation to bank balance sheet capital under a model where neither margin is active. The x-axis is the time relative to the shock in quarters. Panel A shows bank capital. Panel B shows the average lending rate in percentage point deviations from the steady-state (SS) value. Panel C shows the percentage change in lending from the steady-state value. A color version of this figure is available online.

Even calibrated to actual data, the bank balance sheet model over-states the increase in interest rates and decrease in lending quantities. In the baseline model with both margins active, the interest rate increase is a modest 10 basis points; in the balance sheet model, rates increase by 50 basis points. Similarly, figure 12C shows that lending quantities de-crease substantially in the bank balance sheet model.[13]

The bank balance sheet model makes two mistakes and tries to thread the needle between them. On the one hand, this model dramatically overstates the impact of bank capital shocks on total lending, in both prices and quantities. This is because the model does not allow for the relevant margins of substitution. On the other hand, the model dramat-ically understates the impact of bank capital shocks on bank balance sheet lending, because a realistic calibration seeks to match the relation-ship between bank capital shocks and total lending needs to match an empirically small correlation. When bank balance sheet lending is the only type of lending in the economy, this necessarily forces the model to generate a counterfactually small correlation between bank balance sheet capital and bank balance sheet lending.

In sum, the bank balance sheet model implies that bank balance sheets are more important for total lending than they really are but less important for bank balance sheet lending than they really are. This is a particularly important distinction, because some sectors of lending have flexible mar-gins of adjustment (e.g., residential mortgage lending) and other sectors lack these margins of adjustment (e.g., business lending).

VI. Discussion and Implications

Several key insights emerge from our analysis. First, we show that the evaluation of any policy that targets credit must incorporate the lenders' ability to sell their loans and the equilibrium interaction of banks and shadow banks. A policy analysis that does not recognize these margins of adjustment will misdirect resources based on faulty perceptions of their effect on aggregate lending as well as where the risk resides in the econ-omy. Shocks to bank capital are neither as severe nor as long lasting as sug-gested by bank balance sheet models. Moreover, the design of policies needs to be mindful that ignoring these margins could have distributional consequences, because the margins of adjustments differ across interme-diaries that serve households across the income distribution.

We also show that bank balance sheet models face a basic economic tension when used in a quantitative setting: they can reconcile either aggregate lending data or bank balance sheet lending data, but not both. Macro financial models that hope to match data in a quantitative sense therefore must account for the industrial organization of the modern financial sector. More broadly, our paper underscores the limitations of bank balance sheets as a source of data on lending (i.e., focusing solely on call report data by traditional banks) and highlights the critical importance of collecting and making available data on overall lending that includes lending done by shadow banks and loans that were not retained on the balance sheets of financial institutions.

Appendix

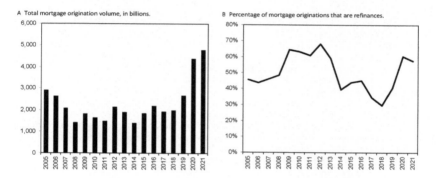

Fig. A1.   Aggregate residential mortgage origination volume and the refinancing share. Panel *A* shows total annual mortgage origination volume in US$billions in the 2005–21 period. Panel *B* shows the percentage of mortgage originations that were refinances in each year. Home Mortgage Disclosure Act data.

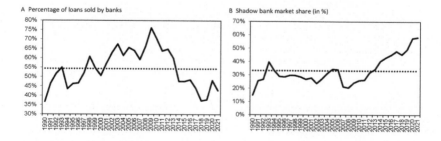

Fig. A2.   Bank loan sale propensity and shadow bank market share over a longer period. Panel *A* shows the percentage of residential loans sold among the loans originated by banks per year 1990–2021. The dashed line shows the sample mean. Panel *B* shows the percentage of residential mortgage loans originated by the shadow banks in the United States. The dashed line shows the sample mean. Home Mortgage Disclosure Act data.

Endnotes

Author email addresses: Buchak (buchak@stanford.edu), Matvos (gregor.matvos@kel logg.northwestern.edu), Piskorski (tp2252@columbia.edu), Seru (aseru@stanford.edu). Buchak is at Stanford Graduate School of Business (GSB) and Stanford Institute for Economic Policy Research (SIEPR), Matvos is at Northwestern University and the National Bureau of Economic Research (NBER), Piskorski is at Columbia GSB and NBER, and Seru is at Stanford GSB, the Hoover Institution, SIEPR, and NBER. We thank our discussants, Itamar Drechsler and Jeremy Stein, as well as Marty Eichenbaum, Erik Hurst, Valerie Ramey, and participants at the 2023 NBER Macro Annual meetings for helpful suggestions. We thank Declan Mirabella and Francesco Spizzuoco for excellent research assistantship. For acknowledgments, sources of research support, and disclosure of the authors' material financial relationships, if any, please see https://www.nber.org/books-and-chapters/nber-macroeconomics -annual-2023-volume-38/aggregate-lending-and-modern-financial-intermediation-why-bank -balance-sheet-models-are.

1. For recent papers on pass-through of macroprudential, monetary, fiscal-policy, and other shocks through financial intermediaries, see He and Krishnamurthy (2013), Brunnermeier and Sannikov (2014), Agarwal et al. (2017), Di Maggio et al. (2017), Drechsler, Savov, and Schnabl (2017), Greenwood et al. (2017), Beraja et al. (2019), Xiao (2020), Cherry et al. (2021, 2022), Corbae and D'Erasmo (2021), Elenev, Landvoigt, and van Nieuwerburgh (2021), Hachem and Song (2021), Begenau and Landgvoit (2022), Bianchi and Bigio (2022), Buchak et al. (2024), Eichenbaum, Rebelo, and Wong (2022), and Wang et al. (2022).

2. Although we focus on the mortgage market, banks now increasingly sell a significant share of their corporate loans, credit cards, auto loans, and personal loans, and shadow banks now account for a substantial amount of intermediation in these markets as well (see Seru 2019; Buchak et al. 2024).

3. There are other forces that can affect the shadow bank sector, such as deposit outflows from the traditional banking sector toward the nonbank sector during times of higher interest rates (see Xiao 2020; Drechsler, Savov, and Schnabl 2022).

4. For other recent models featuring nonbank financial sector, see, among others, Gennaioli, Shleifer, and Vishny (2013), Plantin (2015), Moriera and Savov (2017), Huang (2018), Ordoñez (2018), Jiang (2020), Jiang et al. (2020), Xiao (2020), Hachem and Song (2021), and Begenau and Landgvoit (2022). See also Adrian and Ashcraft (2016).

5. This can be found at https://sites.google.com/site/neilbhutta/data.

6. In our analysis of aggregate and regional lending patterns, we use a broad definition of banks that among others also includes other depository institutions such as credit unions. Our results are very similar if we just focus on commercial banks.

7. Obtained from https://cdr.ffiec.gov/public/PWS/DownloadBulkData.aspx.

8. Table 1, column 4 shows that the addition of shadow bank lending volume mechanically explains 100% of the variation.

9. Our model can easily accommodate nonbank entry, but for simplicity we omit it in the baseline model. The effect of allowing entry is to increase the aggregate elasticity of loan supply, meaning that quantities adjust more and prices adjust less to shocks.

10. In particular, this functional form arises when borrower b chooses among $i = \{0, 1, \dots N\}$ alternatives each with indirect utility $u_i = -\alpha r_i + \delta_i + \epsilon_i$, where ϵ_i is a type-1 extreme value shock. We normalize the indirect utility of the outside option to $u_0 = 0$.

11. For computational tractability, to solve the model, we currently calculate optimal interest rates in an "all balance sheet retention" regime and an "all securitization" regime, and taking these as given and constant across each (c, z, z') tuple, we calculate the necessary investment policy and the optimal choice probability ϕ. Aggregate quantities, rates, and investment are then a weighted average of the all balance sheet retention regime and the all securitization regime, weighted by ϕ. The effect of this simplification is to essentially turn off second-order competitive responses to banks offering higher interest rates when poorly capitalized. That is, in equilibrium, seeing that other banks are offering higher interest rates, competing banks and shadow banks would slightly raise their interest rates. This channel is therefore absent in the currently calibrated version of the model.

12. See Kashyap and Stein (2004) for a discussion of the cyclical implications of bank capital standards.

13. The responses in the calibrated bank balance sheet model are substantially smaller than the declines in the *Neither Margin* counterfactual. This difference arises because the separate calibration of the bank balance sheet model allows it to better match the muted lending responses to bank capital shocks in the data.

References

Adrian, T., and A. B. Ashcraft. 2016. "Shadow Banking: A Review of the Literature." In *Banking Crises*, ed. G. Jones, 282–315. London: Palgrave Macmillan.

Agarwal, S., G. Amromin, I. Ben-David, S. Chomsisengphet, T. Piskorski, and A. Seru. 2017. "Policy Intervention in Debt Renegotiation: Evidence from Home Affordable Modification Program." *Journal of Political Economy* 125:654–712.

Begenau, J., and T. Landgvoit. 2022. "Financial Regulation in a Quantitative Model of the Modern Banking System." *Review of Economic Studies* 89:1748–84.

Benetton, Matteo. 2021. "Leverage Regulation and Market Structure: An Empirical Model of the UK Mortgage Market." *Journal of Finance* 76 (6): 2997–3053.

Benmelech, E., R. R. Meisenzahl, and R. Ramcharan. 2017. "The Real Effects of Liquidity during the Financial Crisis: Evidence from Automobiles." *Quarterly Journal of Economics* 132:317–65.

Beraja, Martin, Andreas Fuster, Erik Hurst, and Joseph Vavra. 2019. "Regional Heterogeneity and the Refinancing Channel of Monetary Policy." *Quarterly Journal of Economics* 134:109–83.

Bianchi, Javier, and Saki Bigio. 2022. "Banks, Liquidity Management and Monetary Policy." *Econometrica* 90:391–454.

Brunnermeier, M. K., and Y. Sannikov. 2014. "A Macroeconomic Model with a Financial Sector." *American Economic Review* 104:379–421.

Buchak, G., G. Matvos, T. Piskorski, and A. Seru. 2018. "Fintech, Regulatory Arbitrage and the Rise of Shadow Banks." *Journal of Financial Economics* 130:453–83.

———. 2024. "Beyond the Balance Sheet Model of Banking: Implications for Bank Regulation and Monetary Policy." *Journal of Political Economy* 132 (2): 616–93.

Chen, B. S., S. G. Hanson, and J. C. Stein. 2017. "The Decline of Big-Bank Lending to Small Business: Dynamic Impacts on Local Credit and Labor Markets." Working Paper no. 23843, NBER, Cambridge, MA.

Chernenko, Sergey, I. Erel, and R. Prilmeier. 2022. "Nonbank Lending." *Review of Financial Studies* 35:4902–47.

Cherry, S., E. Jiang, G. Matvos, T. Piskorski, and A. Seru. 2021. "Government and Household Debt Relief during COVID-19." *Brookings Papers on Economic Activity* 52:1–86.

———. 2022. "Shadow Bank Distress and Household Debt Relief: Evidence from the CARES Act." *AEA Papers and Proceedings* 112:509–15.

Corbae, D., and P. D'Erasmo. 2021. "Capital Buffers in a Quantitative Model of Banking Industry Dynamics." *Econometrica* 89:2975–3023.

De Roure, C., L. Pelizzon, and A. V. Thakor. 2022. "P2P Lenders versus Banks: Cream Skimming or Bottom Fishing?" *Review of Corporate Finance Studies* 11:213–62.

Di Maggio, Marco, Amir Kermani, Benjamin J. Keys, Tomasz Piskorski, Rodney Ramcharan, Amit Seru, and Vincent Yao. 2017. "Interest Pass-Through: Mortgage Rates, Household Consumption and Voluntary Deleveraging." *American Economic Review* 107:3550–88.

Drechsler, I., A. Savov, and P. Schnabl. 2017. "The Deposits Channel of Monetary Policy." *Quarterly Journal of Economics* 132:1819–76.

———. 2022. "How Monetary Policy Shaped the Housing Boom." *Journal of Financial Economics* 144:992–1021.

Eichenbaum, Martin, Sergio Rebelo, and Arlene Wong. 2022. "State Dependent Effects of Monetary Policy: The Refinancing Channel." *American Economic Review* 112:721–61.

Elenev, V., T. Landvoigt, and S. van Nieuwerburgh. 2021. "A Macroeconomic Model with Financially Constrained Producers and Intermediaries." *Econometrica* 89:1361–418.

Gennaioli, N., A. Shleifer, and R. W. Vishny. 2013. "A Model of Shadow Banking." *Journal of Finance* 68:1331–63.

Gopal, M., and P. Schnabl. 2022. "The Rise of Finance Companies and FinTech Lenders in Small Business Lending." *Review of Financial Studies* 35:4859–901.

Greenwood, R., J. C. Stein, S. G. Hanson, and A. Sunderam. 2017. "Strengthening and Streamlining Bank Capital Regulation." *Brookings Papers on Economic Activity* 2017 (2): 479–565.

Hachem, K., and Z. Song. 2021. "Liquidity Rules and Credit Booms." *Journal of Political Economy* 129:2721–65.

Hanson, S. G., A. Kashyap, and Jeremy C. Stein. 2011. "A Macroprudential Approach to Financial Regulation." *Journal of Economic Perspectives* 25:3–28.

He, Zhiguo, and Arvind Krishnamurthy. 2013. "Intermediary Asset Pricing." *American Economic Review* 103:732–70.

Huang, J. 2018. "Banking and Shadow Banking." *Journal of Economic Theory* 178:124–52.

Irani, R. M., R. Iyer, R. R. Meisenzahl, and J. L. Peydro. 2021. "The Rise of Shadow Banking: Evidence from Capital Regulation." *Review of Financial Studies* 34 (5): 2181–235.

Jiang, E. 2020. "Financing Competitors: Shadow Banks' Funding and Mortgage Market Competition." Working paper, University of Southern California Marshall School of Business, Los Angeles.

Jiang, E., G. Matvos, T. Piskorski, and A. Seru. 2020. "Banking without Deposits: Evidence from Shadow Bank Call Reports." Working Paper no. 26903, NBER, Cambridge, MA.

Kashyap, A. K., and J. C. Stein. 2000. "What Do a Million Observations on Banks Say about the Transmission of Monetary Policy?" *American Economic Review* 90:407–28.

———. 2004. "Cyclical Implications of Basel II Capital Standards." *Federal Reserve Bank of Chicago, Economic Perspectives* Q1:18–31.

Moriera, Alan, and Alexi Savov. 2017. "The Macroeconomics of Shadow Banking." *Journal of Finance* 72:2381–432.

Ordoñez, G. 2018. "Sustainable Shadow Banking." *American Economic Journal: Macroeconomics* 10:1–25.

Plantin, Guillaume. 2015. "Shadow Banking and Bank Capital Regulation." *Review of Financial Studies* 28:146–75.

Seru, Amit. 2019. "Regulating Banks in the Era of Fintech Shadow Banks." Andrew Crockett Memorial Lecture, Bank for International Settlements, Basel.

Tang, Huan. 2019. "Peer-to-Peer Lenders versus Banks: Substitutes or Complements?" *Review of Financial Studies* 32:1900–38.

Wang, Yifei, Toni Whited, Yufeng Wu, and Kairong Xiao. 2022. "Bank Market Power and Monetary Policy Transmission: Evidence from a Structural Estimation." *Journal of Finance* 77 (4): 2093–141.

Xiao, Kairong. 2020. "Monetary Transmission through Shadow Banks." *Review of Financial Studies* 33:2379–420.

Comment

Jeremy C. Stein, Harvard University and NBER, United States of America

This excellent and thought-provoking paper by Buchak et al. is motivated by a fundamental observation about the US financial system: a substantial majority of intermediated loans—the authors focus on the specific case of mortgage loans—are originated not by traditional commercial banks but rather by a variety of nonbank lenders, which Buchak et al. dub "shadow banks." They then go on to argue that this observation requires us to re-think existing modeling approaches to the propagation and amplification of economic shocks, which have often focused on bank balance sheets as the key source of friction in the model.

Loosely speaking, one can interpret the authors' story in two ways. A modest interpretation would be that, if nonbank intermediaries do a significant fraction of the lending in the economy, shocks to the capital of just commercial banks narrowly construed will not have as important an impact as they would in an all-bank economy. This statement is almost surely correct and relatively unsurprising: it is analogous to saying that if banks whose names start with letters A through P do a significant fraction of lending in the economy, shocks to the capital of just the minority of banks whose names start with the letters Q through Z will not have as important an impact as would shocks to the capital of the entire banking sector.

A more aggressive, and more interesting, interpretation would be that, if nonbank intermediaries do a significant fraction of the lending in the economy, shocks to the aggregate capital of the entire (bank plus nonbank) intermediary sector will not have as important an impact as they would in an all-bank economy. This interpretation would seem

NBER Macroeconomics Annual, volume 38, 2024.

to reflect an assumption that there is something special about nonbank lending that makes it either less capital reliant or more resilient to capital shocks than bank lending, such that moving market share in origination from banks to nonbanks results in a stabler and less vulnerable financial system overall.

It is a little unclear to me which of these two interpretations the authors have in mind. At least in places, they seem to hint at the latter, more aggressive one. For example, they write: "We show that *the financial sector is much more resilient to capital shocks* ex post than a bank balance sheet model would suggest" (emphasis mine).

Moreover, their modeling framework embodies precisely an assumption of the sort mentioned earlier, consistent with the more aggressive interpretation: they assume that although bank lending requires banks to raise expensive equity capital, nonbanks manage to operate with no equity capital at all and only originate loans for the purposes of selling them in the securitization market. Thus increasing the share of nonbank lending in the economy by assumption reduces the total amount of intermediary capital that is required to generate a given amount of credit creation.

There are two ways that this assumption might go wrong in practice: First, it may be that, as a matter of empirical reality, even nonbanks that primarily originate loans to distribute them do require meaningful amounts of equity capital and are in fact highly vulnerable to shocks to their capital levels. Second, as an increasing fraction of loans are sold off in the securitization market, it becomes all the more important to ask about what type of intermediary (e.g., pension fund, mutual fund, insurance company) is buying these loans and what their capital structures and associated vulnerabilities are. In other words, even if nonbank loan originators are never in any trouble, the lending market can experience sharp contractions if the buyers of securitized loans see their own capacity for intermediation disrupted.

To illustrate the first point, consider the following facts about Rocket Mortgage, one of the leading nonbank mortgage originators in the United States.[1] In 2021, Rocket had a record year, originating $351 billion of mortgage loans, or approximately 9% of all mortgage loans originated in the United States. Although Rocket does in fact rely on an originate-to-distribute model, at year end 2021 they nevertheless held $19 billion of mortgages on their balance sheet, representing approximately 3 weeks' worth of warehouse pipeline that must be inventoried before new loans can be packaged up and resold, in most cases to government-sponsored enterprises (GSEs). At year end 2021, Rocket's equity capital stood at

$9.8 billion, or 2.8% of originations. And their warehouse pipeline also drew on significant lending from banks, in the form of $13 billion in bank funding facilities. These figures suggest that even the nonbank mortgage-origination model requires meaningful amounts of equity capital on the part of the nonbank, as well as an indirect reliance on the health and lending capacity of the banking sector. Indeed, one might think of an intermediary like Rocket Mortgage as a highly leveraged mortgage originator.

Moreover, the vulnerabilities associated with this model can be seen in Rocket's 2022 results. With interest rates rising, its 2022 originations declined sharply, to $133 billion—a drop of about 62%. Moreover, this interest-rate shock resulted in a major hit to Rocket's profits, in part because of losses experienced on its warehouse pipeline: its gain on sale of loans fell from $10.5 billion in 2021 to $3.1 billion in 2022. Notably, this $7.4 billion drop in a key source of profits represented a large proportion—almost 76%—of start-of-year equity capital. Thus it appears that not only are nonbank originators like Rocket dependent on equity capital to run their business, but their capital levels are also highly exposed to the same sorts of shocks as the capital of traditional banks—in this case a shock arising from an unexpected increase in interest rates.

One way to reframe the issues in light of this discussion is to observe that on the one hand, nonbanks like Rocket clearly have a narrower business mix than traditional commercial banks. That is, Rocket focuses exclusively on originating and selling off conforming mortgage loans to the GSEs, whereas banks not only do this but also make on-balance-sheet loans to nonconforming jumbo mortgage borrowers and to a range of other firms and households. At the same time, it may be that within the one segment banks and nonbanks share in common, namely the originate-to-distribute segment for conforming loans, they operate with a similar technology, with similar capital and funding requirements.

This suggests that if one is building a theory of intermediation that encompasses banks and nonbanks, perhaps one should focus not on making distinctions as to the type of intermediary making a given category of loan, but rather on the underlying lending technology, which may differ across loan types but may turn out to be roughly the same for a given loan type, independent of the identity of the intermediary.

Here is a sketch of an exceedingly simple model along these lines. Suppose we have two types of intermediaries, banks and nonbanks. Banks do three things: (i) they make commercial and industrial (C&I) loans L at a rate r_L, with each C&I loan requiring θ units of capital; (ii) they make jumbo mortgage loans J on balance sheet at a rate r_J, with each jumbo loan also requiring θ units of capital; and (iii) they originate and sell conforming mortgage loans C_B at a rate r_C, with each conforming loan requiring $\gamma < \theta$ units of capital for temporary warehousing. Nonbanks only do one thing: they originate and sell conforming mortgage loans C_B at a rate r_C, and as with the banks, each conforming loan requires $\gamma < \theta$ units of capital for temporary warehousing. This formulation thus captures the idea that banks have a broader business mix than nonbanks, but within the conforming-loan segment, the two types of intermediaries have the identical business model.

Suppose that banks in aggregate have equity capital E^B and shadow banks have equity capital E^S. Suppose further that there is downward-sloping demand for all loan types, that markets are perfectly competitive, and that conforming mortgage loans originated by banks and nonbanks are perfect substitutes. In this setting, it is easy to show that in an interior outcome where banks do some originating of conforming loans, all allocations are the same as in a model with only banks that have aggregate capital of $(E^B + E^S)$. Simply put, the existence of shadow banks does not in any way change the vulnerability of the system to capital shocks relative to an all-bank world.

At the same time, the model replicates some of the key empirical facts documented in the paper. For example, when bank capital is impaired (say, due to losses on C&I loans), bank originations decline relative to shadow-bank originations. Conversely, if shadow-bank capital is impaired (say, due to losses on their warehouse portfolio), shadow-bank originations decline relative to bank originations. So there can be substantial movements in the relative market shares of banks and nonbanks, as well as movements in the shares of bank lending that is done on and off balance sheet, that is, in jumbo versus conforming-loan volume.

A numerical example may help drive these points home. Assume that the capital requirement on both C&I loans and jumbo mortgages is 10% and the capital requirement on originate-to-distribute conforming loans is 5%. Initially, the banking sector has total capital of 10 and sets C&I lending to 40, jumbo lending to 40, and conforming originations to 40. The shadow-banking sector has capital of 2 and sets conforming originations to 40.

Now bank capital is hit by an adverse shock, perhaps due to losses in the C&I business, so that bank capital falls to 4, and system-wide intermediary capital is cut in half from 12 to 6. Depending on various elasticities of loan demand, one outcome might be that bank C&I lending drops to 20, bank jumbo lending drops to 20, bank conforming originations fall to 0, and shadow-bank originations remain at 40. Thus in this example, all loan volumes are cut in half with the system-wide capital decline of 50%, which is exactly the same outcome that would have obtained in an all-bank economy with the same starting level of capital and the same adverse shock.

At the same time, the market share in conforming-loan originations swings all the way to the shadow-banking sector, which now does 100% of these originations. But importantly, one cannot conclude from a finding of this sort that the shadow-banking sector in any way buffers aggregate lending outcomes relative to what would have obtained in an all-bank world hit by the same capital shock.

A final observation concerns the impact of financial regulation. In the simple model earlier, there is no reason for shadow banks to secularly take market share in the conforming-loan segment away from traditional commercial banks, given that the originate-to-distribute business has the same economics in both organizational forms. However, in reality, Rocket Mortgage and its nonbank peers have made dramatic inroads into this market in recent years. One plausible explanation is that the heightened bank capital regulation of the post-financial-crisis era may be driving activity to more lightly regulated nonbank originators. If this is in fact the case, and if one thinks of bank capital regulation as having been roughly appropriately calibrated, one may worry that nonbank originators are currently undercapitalized relative to the social planner's optimum, and that this migration actually may be making mortgage lending more vulnerable to shocks, rather than less vulnerable, as in the authors' model. Either way, it is important to bear in mind that even a nonbank originate-to-distribute business relies on adequate capital and is in effect a highly leveraged operation given its thin capital cushion relative to origination volume. If one believes that the economics of the originate-to-distribute model are fundamentally similar across banks and nonbanks, it is hard to escape the conclusion that they ideally ought to be regulated similarly.

Endnotes

Author email address: Stein (jeremy_stein@harvard.edu). For acknowledgments, sources of research support, and disclosure of the author's material financial relationships, if any, please see https://www.nber.org/books-and-chapters/nber-macroeconomics-annual-2023-volume-38/comment-aggregate-lending-and-modern-financial-intermediation-why-bank-balance-sheet-models-are-0.

1. These facts are taken from Rocket Mortgage's 2022 Annual Report, available at https://s25.q4cdn.com/509921419/files/doc_financials/2022/ar/Rocket-Companies-2022-Annual-Report.pdf.

Comment

Itamar Drechsler, *University of Pennsylvania and NBER,* United States
of America

I. Overview

This paper analyzes the origination of residential mortgages in the United
States, highlighting the growth in nonbanks' share of these originations.
Nonbanks, such as Rocket Mortgage and United Wholesale Mortgage,
now originate 60% of residential US mortgages, up from approximately
30% in 2006. The key difference emphasized by the paper between banks
and nonbanks is that nonbanks operate with a very small balance sheet.
This is because they quickly sell all the loans they originate and thus do
not need to hold them on their balance sheet. Combined with nonbanks'
large share of originations, this observation suggests that the importance
of banks' balance sheets has declined markedly, a possibility alluded to by
the paper's original title.[1]

My comment focuses on the question of who are the ultimate end buyers
of the mortgages originated by nonbanks. In my view this question, rather
than who originates the mortgages, is the key to understanding the supply
of mortgage credit. This is because it is the end buyers who supply the capital that ultimately finances the mortgages. Hence, it is their demand for
mortgages (i.e., their willingness and capacity to buy mortgages) that determines the price and quantity of mortgage credit in the market. For this
same reason, regulators who want to influence the supply of credit need to
focus on the factors that affect the ultimate source of that credit.

In other words, although nonbanks have no balance sheet, the mortgages are ultimately held on some entity's balance sheet. These entities

are the ones that raise funds from savers and make investment decisions; therefore, they are substituting for the role traditionally played by depository institutions. Who are they, and how has their composition evolved over time?

I have found that people often assume the mortgage originator is a proxy for the ultimate end buyer of the mortgage. That is, they assume that if the mortgage was originated by a nonbank, then the end buyer must be a nonbank as well. Otherwise a bank should have originated the mortgage. Moreover, nonbanks sell their originations to issuers of mortgage-backed securities (MBS), and MBS are the way nonbank investors (e.g., mutual funds or pension funds) invest in mortgages. Thus, it seems logical that the large increase in nonbank originations corresponds to a similar increase in nonbank holdings of mortgages. Just to be clear, the paper does not say this, but it is an assumption many people make.

I show that this assumption is incorrect. I analyze the composition of mortgage investors over time and show that the share of residential mortgages owned by depository institutions—that is, "traditional" banks—has been between 40% and 50% since around 1990. Their share was at the low end of this range during the mid-'00s boom in "shadow banking" but recovered following the global financial crisis (GFC), rising gradually during the 2010s. With the boom in deposits during 2020–21, banks' share of the mortgage market hits a multidecade peak, returning to its level of 1990. In short, there has been no declining trend in banks' share of residential mortgages.

Why has not the increase in nonbank originations corresponded to an increase in nonbanks' share of mortgage holdings? The reason is that a lot of nonbank mortgage originations are ultimately bought by banks. Nonbanks sell nearly all the mortgages they originate to the government agencies Fannie Mae, Freddie Mac, and Ginnie Mae, also called the GSEs (government-sponsored enterprises). The GSEs package the mortgages into MBS and attach a credit guarantee, with the result that GSE MBS (also referred to as agency MBS) are considered almost as safe and liquid as Treasury bonds. Because investors value the guarantee, effectively all mortgages that conform to the requirements of the agencies on borrower credit score and loan size, referred to as conforming mortgages, are sold to the agencies. This includes many of the conforming mortgages originated by banks. Moreover, since the collapse in nonagency MBS issuance in 2007–8 (discussed below), nearly all new MBS are agency MBS.

Thus, the business of nonbank mortgage originators consists mainly of making conforming applications that they quickly sell to the GSEs. Banks also originate conforming mortgages and sell them to the GSEs. However, unlike nonbanks, they also originate a lot of nonconforming loans. Because these cannot be sold to the GSEs, banks fund them by holding them directly on balance sheet. The majority of these are "jumbo" mortgages, loans that exceed the conforming-loan size limit, typically because they are used to buy large or expensive homes. The fact that jumbo loans are financed almost exclusively by banks points to their continuing centrality as a source of mortgage funding.

Although banks sell many of their conforming loans to the GSEs, they subsequently buy many of them back as agency MBS. Indeed, banks are the largest buyers of agency MBS. As shown below, they currently own (together with credit unions) about 30% of all agency MBS. This is also similar to their share in the early 1990s. Their share decreased between 1990 and 2000 but rebounded during the 2010s and reached a multidecade peak of 38% in 2021. Again, there has been no long-term trend in banks' share of MBS.

Moreover, banks indirectly buy a lot of mortgages originated by nonbanks through their agency MBS purchases, because agency MBS do not distinguish between conforming mortgages originated by banks and nonbanks. This is why nonbanks' increasing share of originations has not corresponded to a decline in banks' share of mortgage holdings.

Why do banks hold so many mortgages, including ones they do not originate? Drechsler, Savov, and Schnabl (2021) argue that banks' deposit franchise makes them natural buyers of long-term fixed-rate assets. As shown in Drechsler, Savov, and Schnabl (2017), the deposit franchise gives banks market power over their deposits, which allows them to pay deposit rates that have a low sensitivity ("beta") to the short rate. This allows banks to hold long-term fixed-rate assets, whose cash flows also have low sensitivity to the short rate, without being exposed to fluctuations in the short rate.

Drechsler et al. (2021) also argue that not only are banks able to own long-term assets, but they also actually need to do so to remain solvent. The reason is that banks incur significant operating expenses to maintain their deposit franchise, and buying long-term fixed-rate assets ensures they have a sufficient stream of income to pay these expenses in case the short rate declines. Thus, the deposit franchise makes banks natural holders of long-term fixed-rate assets, of which residential mortgages are the largest type.

Although there is no trend in banks' share of mortgage holdings, there is a trend in the mortgage ownership of the Federal Reserve and of foreign holders, referred to as the Rest of the World (RoW) by the Financial Accounts, in the past 2 decades. Moreover, within RoW, official holdings, such as by foreign central banks, are a large part.[2] Interestingly, the increased share of the Fed and RoW has come out of the share of nonbank domestic investors (e.g., mutual funds, pension funds, life insurers). As a result, banks have accounted for an increasing share of mortgages owned by domestic private investors (i.e., excluding the Fed and RoW); their share is currently around 66% and was as high as 72% in 2021.

Below, I present the composition of the mortgage market over time and discuss why banks are natural buyers of mortgages. This explains why banks' ownership share of residential mortgages has remained large and steady even as developments in this market have made it easily accessible to other investors.

II.   The Composition of the Mortgage Market

A.   Whole Loans and MBS

Mortgages can be held as either whole loans or as MBS. A whole loan is a single loan held outright, not broken up or packaged into an MBS. Because whole loans are not securitized, most are held by banks. Figure 1 plots whole loans held by banks as a share of all mortgages. The data are from the Financial Accounts of the United States, Z.1 release.[3]

Whole loans held by banks are what people have in mind when they think of "traditional" bank financing of mortgages. Indeed, the figure shows that until about 1980, whole loans held by banks accounted for the bulk of mortgages. However, starting in the late 1970s, their share decreased rapidly with the expansion of agency MBS. By the early 1990s, whole loans held by banks accounted for slightly more than 30% of all mortgages. Since that time, their share has remained stable, with only a slight further decrease.

Figure 2 plots the share of agency MBS of all mortgages over time. Prior to 1970, agency MBS accounted for a negligible fraction of total mortgages. In that year, Freddie Mac was created to offset the contraction in banks' supply of mortgages caused by Regulation Q. As a result, agency MBS expanded rapidly during the 1970s and 1980s. By 1990, it accounted for more than half the mortgage market.

The share of agency MBS dipped during the mid-'00s with the boom in "private-label" securities (PLS). PLS are nonagency MBS, meaning they are issued by private companies and are not guaranteed by the

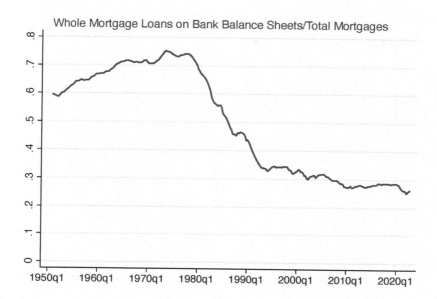

Fig. 1. Whole loan holdings of banks as a share of all mortgages. The figure plots the fraction of all residential mortgages that are whole loans held on bank balance sheets. The sample is quarterly. The data are from the Financial Accounts of the United States Z.1 release, tables L.111 and L.218. A color version of this figure is available online.

GSEs. The mortgages consisted largely of Alt-A and subprime loans, nonconforming mortgages with relatively high-risk profiles. The PLS boom expanded the pool of mortgages and thus lowered the share of agency mortgages. In 2007–8, the PLS market suffered a run that sparked the GFC and virtually ended new issuance for several years. Indeed, PLS issuance has not yet returned in any significant size. Instead, the share of agency MBS recovered and continued rising through the 2010s. Currently, agency MBS accounts for 67% of all mortgages.

B. Who Owns Agency MBS?

Figure 3 plots the share over time of agency MBS held by banks and credit unions. Banks and credit unions have always been significant holders of agency MBS. Again, there is no long-term trend in their share. At the beginning of the 1990s, it was around 30%, similar to its current value. Their share did decrease throughout the 1990s, reaching a low at the end of the '00s. However, it recovered throughout the 2010s and reached a multidecade high of 38% during 2021.

Fig. 2. Agency MBS share of all mortgages. The figure plots the share of all residential mortgages that back mortgage-backed securities (MBS) issued by the government-sponsored entities (GSEs). The sample is quarterly. The data are from the Financial Accounts of the United States Z.1 release, tables L.125, L.126, and L.218. A color version of this figure is available online.

As explained above, banks' large share of agency MBS explains why their share of ownership of all mortgages has remained steady even as agency MBS has grown to be two-thirds of all mortgages. As also noted above, by buying agency MBS, banks are indirectly buying mortgages originated by nonbanks.

Who else buys agency MBS? Figure 4 shows the relative shares over time of the main investors in agency MBS (the shares are normalized to sum to one). The data are from the Financial Accounts of the United States, Z.1 release, as is the case everywhere below unless noted otherwise. Banks have consistently been the largest investors in agency MBS throughout, usually by a large margin. As described above, they currently own about 30% of agency MBS. The monetary authority (the Fed) owns roughly 25%, which it accumulated under quantitative easing. Thus, together banks and the Fed own about 55% of all agency MBS.

The next largest share, with about 15% of agency MBS, belongs to the RoW. More than half of this is held by investors in China, Japan, and Taiwan. Of that, more than 50% is official holdings, which includes these

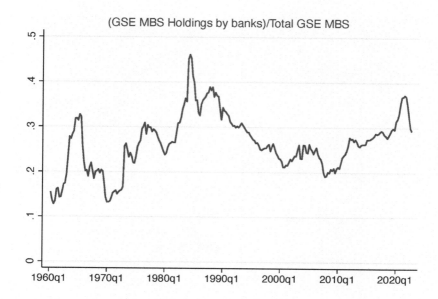

Fig. 3. Agency MBS ownership share of banks and credit unions. The figure plots the share of residential agency mortgage-backed securities (MBS) owned by banks and credit unions. The sample is quarterly. The data are from the Financial Accounts of the United States Z.1 release, tables L.111, L.114, L.125, and L.126. GSE = government-sponsored entity. A color version of this figure is available online.

countries' investment of their substantial dollar reserves. Agency MBS is a major investment of foreign official holders because it is guaranteed by the GSEs and is therefore considered nearly as safe as Treasury bonds.

The next largest category of owners, with a 12.3% share, is "Households." This name is somewhat misleading, because this category includes lightly regulated institutions such as hedge funds and family offices. Other ownership categories are Money Market Funds (6.4%), Mutual Funds (5.8%), Life Insurance Companies (3.1%), and Pension Funds (2.3%). Somewhat surprisingly, the joint share of these various institutions has fallen substantially over the past 2 decades. In the 1980s, life insurers and pensions held a substantial share of agency MBS, but their shares now are very small. More surprisingly, mutual funds' share is at its smallest value since the mid-1980s. I say these shares are surprising because in my experience, there is a popular perception that shadow banks—particularly investment pools such as mutual funds/exchange-traded funds and real estate investment trusts—are displacing banks over time.

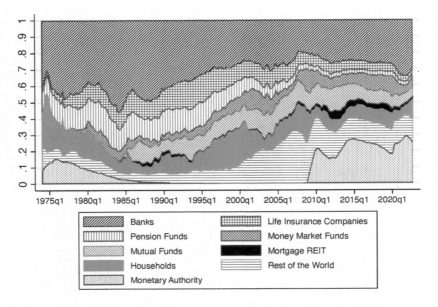

Fig. 4. Agency MBS ownership shares. The figure plots the shares of the largest categories of owners of residential agency mortgage-backed securities (MBS). The sample is
quarterly. The data are from the Financial Accounts of the United States Z.1 release. Residential agency MBS holdings of US chartered depository institutions are from table L.111.
The other holdings are from table L.211. REIT = real estate investment trust. A color version of this figure is available online.

To focus on the relative shares of banks and shadow banks, figure 5
excludes the Fed and RoW and plots the relative shares of domestic private investors in agency MBS. As pointed out earlier, the relative shares
have been fairly stable since around 1990, and there is no decline in
banks' importance in funding agency MBS. To the contrary, during
2021, banks' share of domestic private holdings increased to 59%, a level
not seen since the 1980s.

C.   Why Do Banks Own So Much MBS?

Drechsler et al. (2021) show that banks' deposit franchise allows them to
engage in maturity transformation without being exposed to interest
rate risk. The deposit franchise gives banks market power over retail deposits, which allows them to pay deposit rates that have a low sensitivity to the short rate.

The sensitivity of a deposit's rate to the short rate is called its *beta*. A
fully competitive deposit rate follows the short rate and thus has a beta

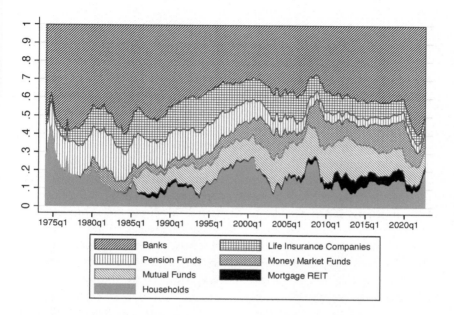

Fig. 5. Agency MBS relative ownership shares of domestic private investors. The figure plots the shares of the largest categories of owners of residential agency mortgage-backed securities (MBS), excluding the US monetary authority (the Federal Reserve) and the Rest of the World. The sample is quarterly. The data are from the Financial Accounts of the United States Z.1 release. Residential agency MBS holdings of US chartered depository institutions are from table L.111. The other holdings are from table L.211. REIT = real estate investment trust. A color version of this figure is available online.

of 1. In practice, banks' average beta across deposit types is far lower, usually between 0.2 and 0.4. This allows banks to invest a significant fraction of deposits in long-term fixed-rate assets without incurring a loss if the short rate rises, as both the cash flows earned from long-term fixed-rate assets and the cash flows paid to depositors have low sensitivity to the short rate. Equivalently, when the short rate increases, the decrease in the value of the long-term assets is offset by an increase in the value of the interest spreads on deposits.

Of course, the deposit franchise is not free. Banks incur large operating costs to maintain their deposit franchise, by providing services in physical branches and online. These operating costs are largely independent of the short rate, which makes them like a fixed-rate liability, so banks must have a constant stream of income to cover them. If banks were to invest only in short-term or floating-rate assets, their income would shrink when the short rate declines, which would put them at risk of failing to cover their operating costs and becoming insolvent. Thus, banks not only can invest in long-term fixed-rate assets but also actually need to do so. Therefore, the deposit franchise makes banks natural owners of long-term fixed-rate assets.

In contrast, the deposit franchise does not provide a hedge for credit risk, and thus banks have no advantage in bearing it. To bear credit risk they need equity, and hence try to limit their exposure to it. The fact that agency MBS is guaranteed and has no credit risk is another reason banks find it attractive. For the same reason, banks are well suited to making other long-term mortgages to low-credit-risk borrowers, such as prime jumbo mortgages.

The second reason banks own such a large quantity of mortgages is that they are very large. More precisely, deposits, which is what they need to fund mortgages, are very large. In June 2023, commercial banks in the United States had $17.3 trillion of deposits (H.8 release of the Federal Reserve for June 21, 2023). At the same time, residential mortgages are one of the two largest types of long-term, fixed-rate, low-credit-risk liabilities, with the other being Treasuries. Hence, it is natural that banks are heavily invested in the mortgage market.

But if banks' share of mortgage buying is steady, why has their share of originations been declining? This is an interesting question. Perhaps nonbank technology companies such as Rocket Mortgage are better at connecting with customers online and through apps than the banks, which are accustomed to using their branch network to sign up customers. Alternatively, some suggest that banks strategically left many originations to the nonbanks to keep an arm's length from the legal and regulatory risks that cost them billions of dollars in fines after 2008.[4]

D. Private-Label MBS and Shadow Banking?

As discussed above, since the collapse in PLS, the overwhelming majority of MBS issuance is agency MBS. For instance, in 2021 private-label MBS accounted for only 4.3% of residential MBS issuance, even though its volume was the largest since 2008 (Housing Finance Policy Center 2023).

Prior to the mid-'00s boom, PLS issuance accounted for around 20% of residential MBS issuance. However, its share increased rapidly from 2003 to 2006 due to demand from issuers of asset-backed securities (ABS), which are investment pools set up to invest in debt instruments such as mortgages. ABS issuers were the main form of shadow banks for mortgages. They were financed mainly by short-term debt securities.

One of the main types of ABS issuers was conduits set up and sponsored by banks to hold PLS. The banks provided the conduits with credit and liquidity guarantees that enabled them to fund themselves with commercial paper. Acharya, Schnabl, and Suarez (2013) show that in sponsoring the conduits, banks were motivated by regulatory arbitrage. By holding the MBS in the conduits rather than on their balance sheets, banks were able to greatly reduce their regulatory capital charges and still earn the risk premium on the MBS.

Figure 6 plots the private-label MBS share of all mortgages over time. There is a sharp increase in 2003. Drechsler, Savov, and Schnabl (2022) provide evidence that this increase was related to the Fed starting to hike rates in mid-2003. They argue that these hikes contracted deposit-funded mortgage supply from banks and that ABS came in to fill the gap. In doing so, the expansion of ABS undid the intended contractionary impact of the Fed's rate hikes.

Ultimately, the expansion in PLS ended badly, as the lack of either a GSE guarantee or financing by insured deposits left ABS issuers vulnerable to a run on their funding, which occurred when credit concerns began to rise in 2007. That episode is an important example of the current paper's warning

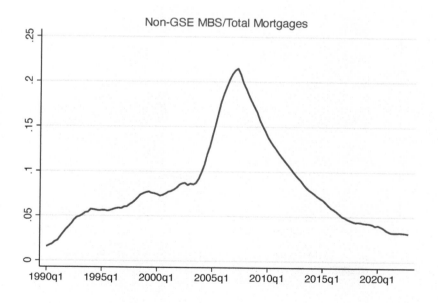

Fig. 6. Nonagency MBS share of residential mortgages. The figure plots the share of all residential mortgages that back nonagency (i.e., private-label) mortgage-backed securities (MBS). The sample is quarterly. The data are from the Financial Accounts of the United States Z.1 release, tables L.127, L.218. GSE = government-sponsored entity. A color version of this figure is available online.

that regulators and central bankers must be aware of nonbanks and the potential for them to substitute for banks in response to restrictive regulations or contractionary monetary policy.

E.   Adding It All Up: How Large Are Banks' Mortgage Holdings?

Figure 7 plots banks' share of all mortgages over time, showing separately the contribution of whole loans (patterned), agency MBS (gray), and PLS (black). The main takeaway is that banks' share of all mortgage holdings has remained fairly steady and close to 50% since about 1990, despite the many changes which took place in the mortgage market. The share did decrease slowly from 1990 until 2008, but recovered throughout the 2010s and reached a multidecade peak in 2021.

Although banks' overall mortgage share has not changed since 1990, the figure shows that there has been a small shift within banks' holdings toward a greater share of agency MBS. As discussed above, agency MBS includes mortgages originated both by banks and by nonbanks, which

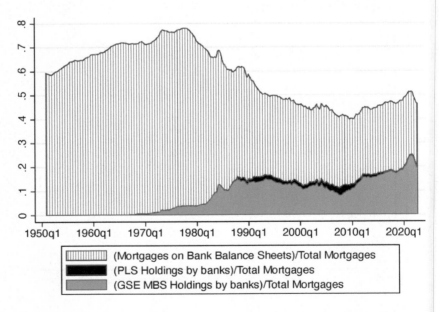

Fig. 7.   Banks' ownership share of all residential mortgages (whole loans + MBS). The figure plots the fraction of all residential mortgages held by banks, either as whole loans or mortgage-backed securities (MBS). The sample is quarterly. The data are from the Financial Accounts of the United States Z.1 release, tables L.111 and L.218. PLS = private-label securities; GSE = government-sponsored entity. A color version of this figure is available online.

explains why banks' holdings share has not declined even as their share of originations has. Finally, the figure shows that banks' share of mortgages declined during the 1980s with the expansion of agency MBS. However, if we go back even further, the figure shows that banks' mortgage share was lower in the 1950s, at around 60%. Compared with this, banks' mortgage share has not changed dramatically over 70 years.

Finally, figure 8 focuses on banks' share relative to private domestic investors (i.e., excluding the holdings of the Fed and the RoW). As discussed above, the main trend in the past 2 decades has been an increase in the Fed's holdings and the holdings of the RoW, a substantial part of which are also official holdings. Taking out these government holdings, we see that banks own 66% of the mortgages held by private domestic investors, similar to their share in the early 1990s. Again, the lowest point for banks was during the PLS boom of the mid-'00s. However, by 2021, banks' share

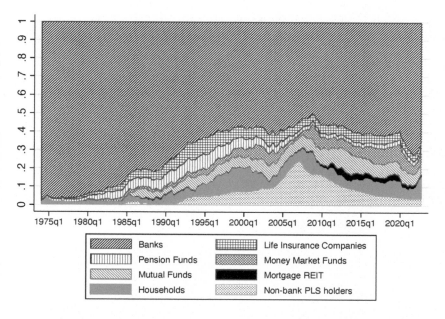

Fig. 8. Domestic private investors' ownership shares of all residential mortgages (whole loans + MBS). The figure plots the shares of the largest categories of owners of residential mortgages, excluding the US monetary authority (the Federal Reserve) and the Rest of the World. The holdings include both whole loans and mortgage-backed securities (MBS). The sample is quarterly. The data are from the Financial Accounts of the United States Z.1 release. Residential whole loan and MBS holdings of US chartered depository institutions are from table L.111. The other holdings are from table L.211. REIT = real estate investment trust; PLS = private-label securities. A color version of this figure is available online.

had increased to a multidecade high of 72%. Thus, banks continue to dominate domestic private funding of residential mortgages.

Endnotes

Author email address: Drechsler (idrechsl@wharton.upenn.edu). For acknowledgments, sources of research support, and disclosure of the author's material financial relationships, if any, please see https://www.nber.org/books-and-chapters/nber-macroeconomics-annual-2023-volume-38/comment-aggregate-lending-and-modern-financial-intermediation-why-bank-balance-sheet-models-are.

1. The original title was "Macropru in the Shadow of Declining Balance Sheet Model of Banking."

2. More than 50% of RoW holdings are due to China, Japan, and Taiwan, of which more than 50% are official holdings.

3. Whole loans are what the accounts label "mortgages" under the "Loans" category. MBS are included under "mortgage pass-through securities" and "CMOs and other structured MBS."

4. See, for example, https://www.wsj.com/articles/banks-no-longer-make-the-bulk-of-u-s-mortgages-1478079004, "Banks No Longer Make the Bulk of U.S. Mortgages," *The Wall Street Journal* (November 2, 2016), and https://www.economist.com/finance-and-economics/2018/12/01/non-bank-firms-are-now-big-players-in-americas-mortgage-market, "Non-bank firms are now big players in America's mortgage market," *The Economist* (December 1, 2018).

References

Acharya, Viral V., Philipp Schnabl, and Gustavo Suarez. 2013. "Securitization without Risk Transfer." *Journal of Financial Economics* 107 (3): 515–36.

Drechsler, Itamar, Alexi Savov, and Philipp Schnabl. 2017. "The Deposits Channel of Monetary Policy." *Quarterly Journal of Economics* 132 (4): 1819–76.

———. 2021. "Banking on Deposits: Maturity Transformation without Interest Rate Risk." *Journal of Finance* 76:1091–143.

———. 2022. "How Monetary Policy Shaped the Housing Boom." *Journal of Financial Economics* 144 (4): 992–1021.

Housing Finance Policy Center. 2023. "Housing Finance at a Glance: A Monthly Chartbook." Urban Institute. https://www.urban.org/tags/housing-finance-glance-monthly-chartbook.

Discussion

Martin Eichenbaum opened the discussion by noting the importance of the topic. He added that when thinking about bank capital, the effective constraint is tied to regulation. For example, in the Common Equity Tier 1 (CET1) ratio, the denominator is risk-weighted assets, so there is a lot of action in terms of shifting the balance-sheet composition to get the right risk weights. If you used microdata on banks that just did a large merger and acquisition transaction, you would see that they immediately sell off assets to reduce risk-weighted assets to get to their target CET1 ratio. He added that accounting also matters. There is a question about whether to hold an asset as available for sale (AFS) or hold to maturity (HTM). If there were losses on AFS assets, this would result in an immediate hit to CET1 capital. He questioned how this applies to Silicon Valley Bank (SVB). Jeremy Stein responded that at the SVB size level, those losses do not flow through regulatory capital regardless of whether the asset is AFS or HTM. Eichenbaum noted the distinction and concluded his comments with a general point: when you get specific about the capital ratio, it opens a lot of issues for regulation and for the risk-weighted composition of assets held.

Greg Buchak thanked the discussants. He pointed out that a common theme from both was the distinction between who produces the security and who holds the security. He added that Stein's discussion focused on the capital structure of who produces the mortgage. He agreed with Stein's comment that banks provide warehouse financing for nonbanks, and so there is some risk. However, he noted that the key question is whether nonbanks are runnable in the same way as banks and, in relation to Eichenbaum's comments, whether Quicken Loans is runnable in the same way as SVB. He stated that although he was not sure of the answer, it was an important question to consider.

Turning to the discussion of Itamar Drechsler, Buchak noted the very interesting data on long-term holders of securities. Although he agreed with Drechsler that banks are important holders, the key question for whether bank balance sheets are quantitatively important for lending prices and quantities of a particular asset is whether that asset can be sold in the secondary market. Although it is true that banks do own a significant share of agency residential mortgage-backed securities, there exist good substitutes for bank balance sheets for owning these assets. He explained that, as their model highlights, shocks to bank capital affect these sellable assets primarily along the margin of who owns them, rather than aggregate prices and quantities of these assets. Whether banks own 30% or 50% of these sellable assets at a particular time is largely (quantitatively and qualitatively) immaterial to this channel in the model. What matters is that sellable assets that happen to be owned by banks should be clearly delineated from unsellable assets that must be held by banks. These include assets like jumbo mortgages, or as Drechsler mentions, other real estate loans for which liquid secondary markets do not exist. Because the sales margin does not exist for these assets, shocks to bank balance sheets transmit directly to prices and quantities of these assets.

Jennifer La'O asked whether there are specific empirical moments that can help distinguish between Stein's model and the authors' model. Jonathan Parker added that a key part of the model is the elasticity of substitution between lending of nonbanks and banks. He felt more transparency on the empirical approach was needed. Buchak responded that they borrow the elasticities from the literature. For example, they can work out the price elasticity by using a bunching estimator to look at what is conforming versus nonconforming; he offered to provide more detail offline.

Parker noted that the mortgage market is quite a specific market that might not be similar to other markets due to the presence of government-sponsored enterprises (GSEs). For example, nonbanks can do a lot on mortgages because mortgages are not information intensive, but nonbanks have not really penetrated markets where banks are "special." Gabriel Chodorow-Reich commented that another area where banks are special is in relation to committed versus uncommitted credit. The former includes term loans or mortgages and is very easy to securitize and subsequently sell off. The latter is very important for commercial and industrial (C&I) lending and is specific to banks, so would likely remain with banks. He asked whether the authors agreed with that assessment. Similarly, Şebnem Kalemli-Özcan commented that big banks provide the majority of C&I lending, and she does not see why this would change and go to nonbanks. She also asked the authors that if we are concerned about nonbanks, should we regulate them more?

Buchak responded that they only focus on the US mortgage market because it is easier to measure. He emphasized that the points they make apply more broadly. He noted that when looking at other countries, mortgage markets typically do not have GSEs, so there is a lot of variation in terms of whether mortgages are deposit financed. He agreed with Stein that the focus here is on the bank balance sheet versus everything else rather than whether it is a bank or nonbank that originates to distribute. Finally, Buchak explained that they are not arguing that nonbanks are great but are making a positive statement that they are important. Normatively, they want to know more about them to think through the issues more carefully.

Tomasz Piskorski reemphasized that we cannot measure total lending from banks' balance-sheet data or bank data alone and assess the responses of the credit market to various policies based solely on such data combined with a traditional balance-sheet model of lending. One overarching insight from their work is that taking into account the endogenous shadow-bank migration margin and the balance-sheet retention margin is critical to understanding the consequences of various policies, including macroprudential ones, in terms of their magnitude, direction, and distributional effects.

Amit Seru further added that in the model of Stein, regulation does not do much. But we know that regulation has a big impact on financing of nonbanks. For example, SoFi and Quicken Loans can make jumbo loans, but they choose not to because they do not wish to take the credit risk. He emphasized that the key message is that for quantitative matters you need to do input-output modeling. For example, if you look at the riskiest part of mortgages related to the Federal Housing Administration, 80%–90% of them are from nonbanks. Banks were regulated aggressively, so they left these markets. Nonbanks could enter because there was a secondary loan-sale market. Although nonbanks can enter the jumbo loan markets, they do not because the associated securitization market essentially disappeared after the global financial crisis. He explained that regulation has had many ripple effects. Therefore, whether nonbanks make the system safer or more fragile is not as simple as highlighted by the discussions of Drechsler and Stein.

Frederic Mishkin asked about the agency problems inherent in the originate-to-distribute model; specifically, whether this moral-hazard issue creates additional vulnerabilities and whether the Dodd-Frank Act has dealt with it. Buchak responded with a technical point that the government-guaranteed mortgages are not riskless from the point of view of the originator. If a mortgagor defaults early, the GSEs will try to put the mortgage back to the originator. This "put-back" risk is one of the main things that nonbanks are worried about.

Seru concluded the discussion by highlighting that although he does not believe that Dodd-Frank has solved the moral-hazard issue, one must look at the system as a whole. Moreover, given that nonbanks have double the capital of banks, one could see this as a sign that the markets are working.

5

Long-Term Expectations and Aggregate Fluctuations

Pedro Bordalo, *University of Oxford,* United Kingdom
Nicola Gennaioli, *Bocconi University,* Italy
Rafael La Porta, *Brown University and NBER,* United States of America
Matthew OBrien, *London School of Economics,* United Kingdom
Andrei Shleifer, *Harvard University and NBER,* United States of America

I. Introduction

The stock market is volatile, as is aggregate economic activity, and the two are connected. At least since Burns and Mitchell (1938), we know that measures of investment and production rise and then fall together across sectors, a phenomenon called the "business cycle." We also know that the aggregate stock market is extremely volatile (LeRoy and Porter 1981; Shiller 1981). Importantly, financial and real volatility are connected: Burns and Mitchell (1938) included the S&P 500 as a leading indicator of gross domestic product (GDP) growth, and subsequent work confirmed that higher stock returns today predict higher future aggregate activity (Merton 1980; Stock and Watson 2003; Backus, Routledge, and Zin 2009).

What drives these patterns? Business cycles are typically traced to the rational response of firms and households to persistent "fundamental" shocks to technology, demand, taxes, and so forth (Ramey 2016). For instance, a positive productivity shock increases current output and rational expectations about future productivity. Households then consume more, and firms hire more labor and invest. An aggregate expansion follows, which gradually reverts as the productivity shock dies out. In principle, such shocks could explain stock market volatility, because stocks are just claims on firms' fluctuating profits. In practice, they do not. Shiller (1981) famously documented an "excess volatility" puzzle: measures of current and rationally expected corporate dividends or earnings are too

NBER Macroeconomics Annual, volume 38, 2024.

stable to account for stock price movements. What drives excess stock price volatility, then? And, going back to the business cycle, does the driver of stock market volatility also affect real activity?

Conventional macro-finance theory addresses these questions by maintaining rational expectations while allowing for variation in investors' required returns, due to changing price or quantity of risk (e.g., Campbell and Cochrane 1999; Barro 2009; Bansal, Kiku, and Yaron 2010). This approach delivers financial and real volatility but is hard to test directly because time-varying risk preferences are difficult to measure. Also, these theories rely on a variation in expected returns that is counterfactual compared with survey measures. In this paper, we follow a different route: we keep required returns constant but allow expectations to be nonrational. Key to our strategy is the use of data on stock analysts' consensus expectations of the earnings growth of S&P 500 firms. One measure turns out to be critical: the analysts' forecast of a firm's long-term earnings growth (LTG), which captures expectations of fundamentals over a 3-to-5-year horizon. Our main variable is the consensus LTG forecast, aggregated across firms in the S&P 500 index.

In the *General Theory* (1936), Keynes stressed the centrality of expectations of long-term profits, also referred to as "animal spirits." Changing business conditions, he argued, could cause excessive changes in these expectations. In good times, the long-term beliefs can be too optimistic, causing a boom in asset prices and real investment, and conversely in bad times. This mechanism can help reconcile excess financial and real volatility, because beliefs about the long term amplify shocks. We use the data on LTG to ask three questions. First, can expectations of earnings growth account for Shiller's excess volatility puzzle and for variation in other business cycle predictors such as interest rates and credit spreads? Second, can such expectations also shed light on the dynamics of real investment, and of other business cycle indicators, including investment shocks? Third, and crucially, what is the role of the nonrationality, measured by analysts' predictable forecast errors?

Starting with Shiller's excess volatility puzzle, in Section II we show that the present value of short- and long-term expected earnings for S&P 500 firms, computed using a constant required return, fully explains observed stock market fluctuations in our sample, 1980–2022. LTG "does the job" because it departs from rationality in a precise way: it is excessively volatile relative to the realized subsequent earnings growth. When LTG is high relative to historical standards, analyst forecasts of short- and long-term profits are systematically disappointed in the future, inconsistent with rationality. High LTG also correlates with higher survey expectations of stock returns, in contrast with standard theories, in which investors expect low returns in good times. High LTG thus proxies for excess optimism: it points to investors being too bullish about future profits and stock returns.

In Section III, we show that the explanatory power of LTG reaches beyond the stock market: higher LTG predicts near-term increases and long-term declines in short- and long-term interest rates, and the reverse pattern for credit spreads. The connection between LTG and the financial cycle is strong: in our local projections (Jorda 2005) we control for, among other things, 12 quarterly lags of the dependent variable, allowing for a very rich pattern of "fundamental" mean reversion. This evidence offers additional support to the hypothesis that boom-bust dynamics in nonrational expectations about the long term act as an important driver of the volatility of key asset prices.

In Section IV, we connect LTG to real activity. Using local projections again, we show that—consistent with Keynes's view—a 1-standard-deviation increase in LTG fuels an investment boom: growth in the investment-to-capital ratio is 3% higher than conventional levels in the following year, corresponding to a 0.4-standard-deviations increase. Crucially, the investment boom sharply reverts 2 years later, and that reversal is fully explained by the predictable disappointment of the initially high LTG. Excess volatility in expectations may thus drive significant investment fluctuations, with overoptimism breeding excessive investment in the short-run and a long-run correction. We confirm this link at the firm level, controlling for any aggregate shocks, including to required returns.

Finally, we connect LTG to conventional business cycle analysis (Sec. V). We show that, in the short term, higher LTG acts like a positive shock: it predicts growth in consumption, employment, and wages. Importantly, though, LTG also predicts a longer-term reversal in these variables. Granger causality tests support the hypothesis that the link goes from LTG to the macroeconomy rather than the other way around. In sum, a directly measured and clearly interpretable variable—changes in the long-term profit expectations of individual firms—predicts aggregate boom-bust comovement among macro variables as well as with financial variables.

As a final exercise, we link LTG to a shock that directly maps to investment volatility, capturing Keynes's notion of the "marginal efficiency of investment" (MEI), the ease with which investment is transformed into capital. Building on Greenwood, Hercowitz, and Huffman (1988), Justiniano, Primiceri, and Tambalotti (2011) estimate shocks to MEI in a dynamic stochastic general equilibrium (DSGE) model and show that they account for 60%–85% of US business cycle fluctuations. We find that higher LTG is positively correlated with contemporaneous MEI shocks, but it predicts negative MEI shocks in the future. This suggests that estimated shocks may partly capture predictable disappointment of excess optimism.

In sum, LTG emerges as a "miracle" variable that, based on a clear theoretical foundation: (i) helps account for the volatility of equities and of safe and risky bonds, (ii) helps explain boom-bust cycles in economic activity, and (iii) does so through predictable disappointment of optimism (as in Minsky 1977). It is challenging to produce business cycle comovement in rational expectations models (Jaimovich and Rebelo 2009). Recent work remedies this problem using shocks that comove with credit spreads or the stock market, such as MEI itself or "risk shocks" (Christiano, Motto, and Rostagno 2014). These shocks, estimated in DSGE models, are engineered to account for large business cycle variation, but they often do not admit a clear economic interpretation. Overreaction in expectations of long-term profits is an intuitive and interpretable source of comovement, and it jointly accounts for changes in the desire to invest and in financial markets' desire to lend. Although we cannot prove that excess volatility in beliefs is the cause of investment cycles, the data indicate that this possibility must be seriously considered, if not adopted as a working hypothesis.

We contribute to two large literatures. The first is recent behavioral work combining expectations and asset price data. Earlier work studied expectations of stock returns and found that they are extrapolative, rather than rational (Bacchetta, Mertens, and Wincoop 2009; Amromin and Sharpe 2014; Greenwood and Shleifer 2014; Barberis et al. 2015, 2018; Giglio et al. 2021). Expectations of bond risk premia also depart from rationality (Greenwood and Hanson 2013; Piazzesi, Salomao, and Schneider 2015; d'Arienzo 2020). Closer to our paper, a line of research studies expectations of future fundamentals, and in particular LTG. La Porta (1996) introduces LTG into finance, showing that its variation across stocks predicts stock returns. Bordalo et al. (2019) account for this fact using a model of diagnostic expectations. The same authors (Bordalo et al. 2024) show, in the aggregate stock market, that LTG jointly predicts forecast errors and returns, and that systematic changes in LTG account for the predictive power of the price-dividend ratio for returns. Here we show that expectations data also resolve Shiller's excess volatility puzzle and link LTG to fluctuations in interest rates, credit spreads, and the business cycle more broadly.

The second body of work studies fluctuations in investment and economic activity. Several papers link the stock market to investment based on Tobin's Q (Fazzari, Hubbard, and Petersen 1988; Barro 1990; Lamont 2000; Morck, Shleifer, and Vishny 1990). They find that stock returns predict firm-level investment better than estimates of Q itself. Gennaioli, Ma, and Shleifer (2016) show that chief financial officer (CFO) optimism about 12-months-ahead profits spurs firm-level investment, dwarfing the role of stock returns. Here we focus on long-term expectations and connect investment to excess stock market volatility. Other papers study the role of expectations and news in the business cycle (e.g., Beaudry and Portier 2006; Lorenzoni 2009). Angeletos, Collard, and Dellas (2018, 2020) argue that the cycle reflects demand shocks unrelated to long-run total factor productivity (TFP), and they conjecture that these are due to expectations of short-run output. Their shock is estimated from a vector autoregression (VAR) and built to maximize explanatory power, but it is not easily interpretable. Our approach is conceptually related to theirs, because departures from rationality also disconnect beliefs from future TFP, but it underscores the importance and promise of using a transparent measure of expectations, LTG, which unveils a new link between nonrational overreacting beliefs and aggregate volatility.

Finally, a growing literature in macro relaxes rationality by assuming either rational inattention/frictions (Angeletos and Lian 2016, 2022, 2023; Gabaix 2019; Angeletos, Huo, and Sastry 2020), overreaction (Bianchi, Ilut, and Saijo 2023; Bordalo et al. 2023; L'Huillier, Singh, and Yoo 2023; Maxted 2023), or learning from extreme events (Kozlowski, Veldkamp, and Venkateswaran 2019, 2020). Bordalo et al. (2023) structurally estimate a real business cycle (RBC) model with diagnostic expectations using data on CFO earnings forecasts. They show that the overreaction of CFO expectations plays a quantitatively important role in driving investment at the firm level by shaping both the demand and the supply of funds. Our innovation here is to explicitly connect financial markets, which are excessively volatile relative to a clear benchmark, to recurrent economic fluctuations.

II.   Shiller's Excess Volatility Puzzle

Campbell and Shiller (1987, 1988) express the price-dividend ratio of a stock with the identity:

$$p_t - d_t = \frac{k}{1 - \alpha} + \sum_{s \geq 0} \alpha^s g_{t+1+s} - \sum_{s \geq 0} \alpha^s r_{t+1+s}, \tag{1}$$

where p_t is the log price at t, d_t is its log dividend, $g_{t+1+s} = d_{t+1+s} - d_{t+s}$ is dividend growth between $t + s$ and $t + s + 1$ and r_{t+1+s} is the realized stock return over the same horizon. Here, k is a constant, and $\alpha = e^{pd}/(1 + e^{pd}) < 1$ depends on the average log price-dividend ratio pd.

In equation (1), variation in the price-dividend ratio is due to variation either in expected future dividend growth, captured by the g_{t+1+s} terms, or in required returns, captured by the r_{t+1+s} terms. Under rationality and a constant required return r, the stock price is given by:

$$p_t^R = d_t + \frac{k - r}{1 - \alpha} + \sum_{s \geq 0} \alpha^s \mathbb{E}_t(g_{t+1+s}). \qquad (2)$$

Price variation comes from changes in the dividend d_t and in expectations of future dividend growth. The intuition for Shiller's puzzle is that the weighted average of dividend growth on the right-hand side of equation (2) should be less volatile than realized dividend growth. But the latter has low volatility itself, so equation (2) cannot account for the large observed volatility of the observed stock price p_t.

To quantify this idea, Shiller constructed a proxy p_t^* for the rational price in equation (2) assuming, at each t, perfect foresight of future dividends and a value for the rational stock price in the last sample period. We replicate the exercise over 1981–2022 using earnings, which matches our expectations data (little changes if we use dividends instead; see app. A, http://www.nber.org/data-appendix/c14860/appendix.pdf). Given the terminal realized earnings per share $D_{2022} = 66.92$, we set the terminal log stock price to $p_{2022}^* = \ln(D_{2022}/(r - g))$. This is the present discounted value of expected earnings at that time, under the assumption of constant average earnings growth g. We set $r = 8.75\%$, which is the average realized return over the sample period, and $g = 5.79\%$, which is also the sample average.

Given the terminal price-dividend ratio $p_{2022}^{RE} - d_{2022}$, the rational proxy p_t^* at earlier dates is computed backward, using at each $t < 2022$ the future realized dividend growth rates:

$$p_t^* = d_t + \frac{1 - \alpha^{T-t}}{1 - \alpha}(k - r) + \sum_{s=t}^{T} a^{s-t}(d_{s+1} - d_s) + \alpha^{T-t}(p_{2022}^* - d_{2022}), \qquad (3)$$

where $\alpha = 0.9981$ (at a monthly frequency) and $k = -\log(\alpha) - (1 - \alpha)\log(1/(\alpha - 1)) = 0.0138$. Figure 1 plots the rational proxy p_t^* (dotted line) against the actual stock price p_t (solid line). Shiller's puzzle is the fact

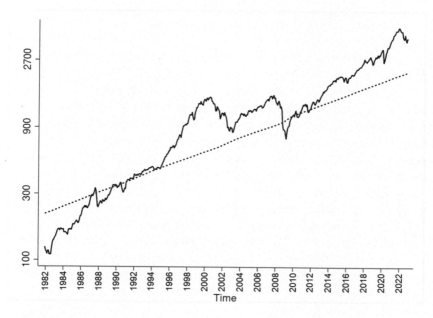

Fig. 1. S&P 500 versus Shiller Index p^*. The figure shows the log scale level of the S&P 500 index (solid line) against the log scale rational benchmark (dotted line) computed according to equation (3). A color version of this figure is available online.

that p_t^* is virtually a straight line, whereas the actual stock price p_t displays large boom-bust patterns, with periods of sustained over-/undervaluation compared with p_t^*.

Most asset pricing research since Shiller (1981) has sought to account for stock price volatility by constructing theories of investor preferences that admit variation in the price and quantity of risk. Behavioral finance has instead mostly focused on extrapolative expected returns (e.g., Barberis et al. 2015, 2018; Hirshleifer, Li, and Yu 2015, building on evidence in Bacchetta et al. 2009 and Greenwood and Shleifer 2014, among others). A smaller body of work has relaxed the assumption of rational expectations of dividends (see, e.g., De Long et al. 1990; Barsky and De Long 1993; Barberis, Shleifer, and Vishny 1998; and more recently Bordalo et al. 2019, 2024). In this approach, which we adopt here, the terms $\mathbb{E}_t(g_{t+1+s})$ in equation (2) are replaced by nonrational expectations $\tilde{\mathbb{E}}_t(g_{t+1+s})$. As long as these expectations display high volatility, stock prices will as well. We next assess this hypothesis using expectations data.

A. Measured Expectations of Future Fundamentals

We gather monthly data on analyst forecasts for firms in the S&P 500 index from the Institutional Brokers' Estimate System (IBES) Unadjusted US Summary Statistics file. Forecasts of dividends per share are only available starting from 2002 and for short horizons. To expand temporal coverage and to have longer-run forecasts, we construct an earnings-based price proxy that uses analyst forecasts of earnings per share. We perform a robustness exercise using forecasted dividends; see appendix A, http://www.nber.org/data-appendix/c14860/appendix.pdf.

We focus on median forecasts of a firm's earnings per share (EPS_{it}) and of its long-term earnings growth (LTG_{it}). IBES defines LTG as the "expected annual increase in operating earnings over the company's next full business cycle. These forecasts refer to a period of between three to five years." LTG_t captures expectations of earnings growth over the business cycle, the other phenomenon of interest here. Data coverage starts in March 1976 for EPS_{it} and December 1981 for LTG_{it}. We fill in missing forecasts by linearly interpolating EPS_{it} at horizons ranging from 1 to 5 years (in 1-year increments). Beyond the second fiscal year, we assume that analysts expect EPS_{it} to grow at the rate LTG_{it} starting with the last nonmissing positive EPS forecast.

Survey expectations refer to the individual firms that analysts follow. Following Bordalo et al. (2024), at each t we aggregate the expected earnings per share of S&P 500 firms into indices of 1- and 2-years-ahead expected earnings, $EPS_{t,t+1}$ and $EPS_{t,t+2}$, respectively. We then aggregate the LTG expectations into an aggregate index LTG_t. Log earnings growth 1 or 2 years ahead are computed based on $EPS_{t,t+s}$. Short- and long-term expectations are volatile, as shown in figure 2. But they capture different kinds of fluctuations. Short-term expectations move mainly due to short-term mean reversion of earnings growth (e.g., these expectations are highest during the crash of 2008). LTG instead captures persistent fluctuations in the estimated growth potential. This will be important for connecting stock market and business fluctuations.

One concern is that analysts may distort their forecasts due to agency. For instance, sell-side analysts may choose to be more optimistic than buy-side ones. Such distortions are arguably stable and hence unlikely to materially affect the time-series variation in forecasts. This is especially true for S&P 500 firms, which are followed by virtually all brokerage houses, so investment banking relationships or analyst sentiment is unlikely to influence the decision to cover firms in the index.[1] Our use of

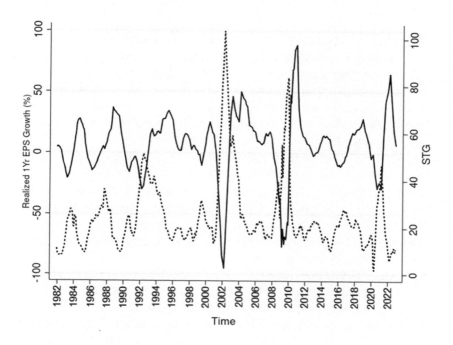

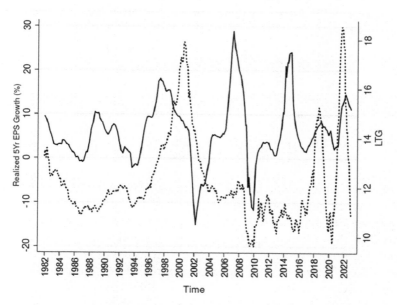

Fig. 2. Volatility of earnings growth and expectations. The figure plots 1-year earnings per share (EPS) growth between $t - 4$ and t against expectations for four-quarter earnings growth between t and $t + 4$ (STG, top panel) and 5-year EPS growth between $t - 20$ and t against expectations for 5-year earnings growth between t and $t + 20$ (LTG, bottom panel). Here, LTG (STG) is calculated by value weighting firm-level forecasts for expected 1-year (5-year) growth in EPS. A color version of this figure is available online.

median forecasts further reduces the impact of outliers. More broadly, strategic analyst distortions should if anything reduce the ability of LTG to capture updating of market beliefs, introducing noise. Contrary to this notion, Bordalo et al. (2019) show that LTG responds to news: firms that obtain a high LTG forecast do so after a sequence of positive surprises over 2–3 years.

Another concern is that analysts estimate expected earnings growth using stock prices themselves, while assuming constant required returns. Bordalo et al. (2024) examine this possibility extensively for their main measure of expectations, LTG, and find strong evidence against it. First, revisions in LTG are more reliably explained by past earnings growth than by past stock returns, at both aggregate and firm levels. Thus, stock price changes are not mechanically incorporated into LTG. Second, LTG predicts future stock returns at both aggregate and firm levels even after controlling for the aggregate- and the firm-level price/ earnings ratio, respectively, and in fact reduces the latter's predictive power. Thus, not only is LTG not mechanically related to stock prices, but it contains genuine variation in beliefs that in turn affects prices themselves. In sum, LTG offers a valuable proxy for market beliefs about future fundamentals.

B. The Expectations-Based Stock Price Index

We build an expectations-based price index $\tilde{p}_t$ by computing the earnings-based ratio:

$$\tilde{p}_t = e_t + \frac{\tilde{k} - r}{1 - \alpha} + \ln\left(\frac{\text{EPS}_{t,t+1}}{\text{EPS}_t}\right) + \alpha \ln\left(\frac{\text{EPS}_{t,t+2}}{\text{EPS}_{t,t+1}}\right) + \sum_{s=2}^{10} \alpha^s \text{LTG}_t + \frac{\alpha^{10}}{1 - \alpha} g. \quad (4)$$

Here, α and r are as before, and $\tilde{k} = k + (1 - \alpha)\text{de} = 0.0123$, where de is the average log payout ratio.

The key difference with Shiller's computation is the use of expectations data. We measure expected growth between t and $t + 2$ using forecasted earnings. We use LTG_t to capture expected earnings growth at business cycle frequencies, specifically between $t + 3$ and $t + 10$. We employ LTG_t up to 10 years ahead because this is the average duration of a business cycle in our data. To compute the price index, we agnostically set the expected growth rate beyond $t + 11$ to be $g = 3.73\%$. This is the value at which the average value of index $\tilde{p}_t$ matches the average stock price p_t in the sample.[2] Obviously, then, success in our exercise is not judged by the extent to which average price levels match but by the extent to which time variation in our index $\tilde{p}_t$ tracks time variation in p_t. We use nominal earnings, but results are robust when accounting for inflation (app. A, http://www.nber.org/data-appendix/c14860/appendix.pdf). Expectations for the very long term may also play a significant role in shaping stock prices, but, unfortunately, we do not have data about them. Imposing constant expected growth after $t + 10$ reduces our ability to account for prices, because arguably expectations of the far future also move.

Figure 3 adds our price index $\tilde{p}_t$ to figure 1 (dashed line). The match is not perfect, but $\tilde{p}_t$ captures low-frequency price movements remarkably well. When the actual price p_t is above the rational benchmark, p_t^*, so is $\tilde{p}_t$; and conversely when p_t is below the benchmark. The index fails to capture the depressed market in the 1980s but does a very good job at capturing the internet bubble of the late 1990s, and the 2008 crisis. Earnings expectations suffer an excessive price drop during COVID-19, when actual earnings tanked, confirming that these beliefs are not mechanically inferred from prices.

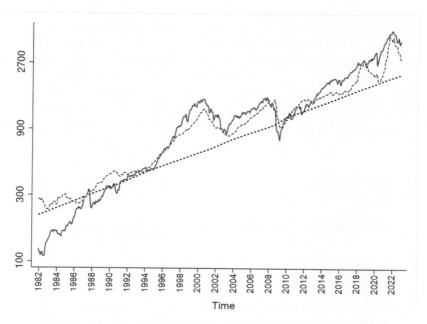

Fig. 3. S&P 500 versus Shiller Index p^* and Expectations-Based Index $\tilde{p}_t$. We plot in log scale the levels of the S&P 500 index (solid line), the rational benchmark index (p_t^*, dotted line, eq. [3]), and the price index based on earnings forecasts ($\tilde{p}_t$, dashed line, eq. [4]). A color version of this figure is available online.

To assess the quantitative ability of beliefs to deliver realistic price volatility, table 1 reports the standard deviations of 1-year changes in our index $\widetilde{p}_t$ and in the actual stock price p_t. We also report the standard deviation of the rational price p_t^*. Our index delivers a realistic amount of price volatility, much higher than that obtained using the rational benchmark.

Overall, measured earnings expectations go a long way toward solving Shiller's excess volatility puzzle. Excess volatility of measured beliefs parsimoniously accounts for excess volatility in the stock market. This finding lines up with recent evidence that short-term earnings growth expectations help account for variation in the price-dividend ratio (De La O and Myers 2021).

Compared with De La O and Myers (2021), our use of LTG proves critical for explaining a large range of anomalies. Although much variation in short-term earnings expectations reflects mechanical mean reversion, LTG captures slow-moving forecasts of long-term growth opportunities. Forming beliefs about the long term is inherently more difficult and, in line with Keynes's argument, may exhibit significant departures from rationality. Because beliefs about the long term are central for investment decisions, this mechanism may help explain market movements.

Consistent with this hypothesis, Bordalo et al. (2024) show that, although short-term expectations are fairly accurate, LTG exhibits a marked departure from rationality that takes the form of overreaction, or excess volatility. That is, high LTG, as well as increases in LTG, predicts disappointment of earnings growth expectations at a 3-to-5-year horizon. This finding contradicts rationality because statistically optimal

Table 1
Volatility of Log Price Changes

	Earnings Index		
	Δp	Δp^*	$\Delta \widetilde{p}$
Variance (%)	15.7	.7	15.3
Conf. interval (%)	14.7–16.7	.6–.7	14.4–16.3

Note: The table reports the standard deviation and 95th confidence interval of a 1-year change in (*a*) the log of the price of the S&P 500 index, Δp, (*b*) the rational benchmark index, Δp^* (eq. [3]), and (*c*) the price index based on earnings forecasts (eq. [4]), $\Delta \widetilde{p}$. The sample period is December 1982 to December 2022.

forecasts should not exhibit predictable errors using a variable, current LTG, which is in the analyst's information set. Bordalo et al. (2024) also find that high current LTG predicts future low stock returns whereas short-term earnings expectations do not, stressing the key role of long-term expectations in explaining market inefficiency.

We next further characterize LTG's nonrationality and its ability to predict financial markets. Starting with nonrationality, we first assess whether high current LTG predicts disappointment at both long and short horizons, controlling also for expectations about the short term. We also assess whether current LTG predicts current and future expectations of 12-months-ahead stock returns. These new rationality tests shed light on the link between excess financial volatility and real activity.

We use the current level of LTG to predict future errors in expectations of earnings growth, where the latter are defined as current forecast minus future realization (so high values indicate excess optimism). We consider errors over several horizons and at several points in time: rows 1–3 of table 2 concern short-term forecasts, that is, about 1-year and 2-year earnings growth, and forecasts about 5-year growth (LTG), respectively. These dependent variables are then measured both contemporaneously with LTG_t and into the future at horizons $t + h$, where $h = 0, \ldots, 10$.

The results support the view that high LTG captures periods of excess aggregate optimism: it systematically predicts positive forecast errors and thus future disappointment of earnings growth expectations. Disappointment persists at least four quarters out, suggesting that LTG is a source of persistent excessive optimism, which eventually reverts. In contrast, expectations about short-term growth do not predict forecast errors (see app. A, http://www.nber.org/data-appendix/c14860/appendix .pdf). This finding strengthens the interpretation of excess stock price volatility as being due to the excess volatility of long-term beliefs. It also suggests that excess volatility of beliefs may drive volatility in real investment, because high LTG captures persistent optimism about the full-term structure of expectations, proxying for times in which the perceived returns to investment are high.

In the fourth row of table 2, we use LTG to predict current and future CFO expectations about 12-months-ahead stock returns. Higher current LTG predicts higher return expectations in the near term.[3] This evidence is also inconsistent with rational models, which predict that in good times rational investors require, and expect, lower returns. It confirms that periods of high LTG exhibit high optimism across the board, and not low required returns as the rational approach postulates.

Table 2
Long-Term Earnings Growth, Forecast Errors, and Expectations of Stock Returns

	Time Horizon (h) of Dependent Variable (Quarters)										
	0	1	2	3	4	5	6	7	8	9	10
	A. Estimates from $y_{t+h} = B_h LTG_t + \varepsilon_{t+h}$										
	Independent Variable: LTG_t										
Dependent Variable											
$y_{t+h} = STG1_{t+h} - \Delta_4 e_{t+h+4}$	9.99**	12.58**	13.82**	13.80**	13.21**	12.25**	11.15**	9.67**	7.47**	5.26*	3.35
	[2.88]	[2.53]	[2.14]	[2.09]	[2.06]	[2.03]	[2.01]	[2.11]	[2.23]	[2.36]	[2.39]
$y_{t+h} = STG2_{t+h} - (\Delta_8 e_{t+h+8}/2)$	5.36**	5.58**	5.53**	5.23**	4.18*	3.42	1.96	.66	-.36	-1.18	-2.12
	[1.40]	[1.50]	[1.71]	[1.95]	[1.97]	[2.15]	[1.93]	[1.67]	[1.68]	[1.69]	[1.46]
$y_{t+h} = LTG_{t+h} - (\Delta_{20} e_{t+h+20}/5)$	3.69**	3.49**	3.04**	2.38**	1.53+	.58	-.33	-1.14	-1.63+	-1.81*	-1.69+
	[.74]	[.74]	[.75]	[.78]	[.82]	[.86]	[.90]	[.90]	[.87]	[.85]	[.87]
	B. Estimates from $y_{t+h} = B_h LTG_t + X_t + \varepsilon_{t+h}$										
	Independent Variable: LTG_t										
Dependent Variable											
y_{t+h} = Expected 1Y S&P 500 return (cfo)$_{t+h}$	.36	.61*	.45	.43	.34	.25	-.38	-.75*	-.61*	-.19	.09
	[.25]	[.25]	[.31]	[.34]	[.37]	[.43]	[.25]	[.28]	[.27]	[.30]	[.27]

Note: The estimates measure the impact of a one-standard-deviation change in LTG$_t$ on the dependent variable. In panel A, forecast errors STG1$_{t+h}$ − $\Delta_4 e_{t+h+4}$ are the percentage point difference in 1-year forecast growth in earnings at time $t + h$ and realized 1-year growth at $t + h + 4$. Forecast errors STG2$_{t+h}$ − $\Delta_8 e_{t+h+8}$ are the percentage point difference in 2-year forecast growth in earnings and realized 2-year growth at $t + h + 8$. Forecast errors LTG$_{t+h}$ − $\Delta_{20} e_{t+h+20}/5$ are the percentage point difference in 5-year forecast growth in earnings at t and realized 5-year earnings growth at $t + h + 20$. Here, LTG$_t$ is aggregate market expectation for 5-year earnings per share growth, calculated by value weighting firm-level forecasts. All regressions in panel A are unconditional. In panel B, Expected 1Y S&P 500 (cfo)$_{t+h}$ is the average expectation of 1-year returns on the S&P 500 of major US chief financial officers (CFOs) from the Richmond Fed's CFO survey. Controls X$_t$ are 12 lags of the dependent variable. Heteroskedasticity-consistent standard errors reported in parentheses are computed according to Huber-White.

+ $p < .10$.
* $p < .05$.
** $p < .01$.

The finding that LTG captures waves of excess optimism and can account for stock price volatility suggests that excess volatility may be caused by nonrational fluctuations in beliefs. The predictable LTG errors in table 2 are in line with overreaction and constitute deeper departures from rationality than rational inattention, noise, or overconfidence (Bordalo et al. 2020, 2024; Bordalo, Gennaioli, and Shleifer 2022). Because belief "frictions" cause sluggish incorporation of public signals into the consensus belief and hence the macroeconomy, they cannot account for excess volatility of prices and beliefs.[4]

The key question is therefore whether the overreaction of LTG can account for macro-financial cycles. Supporting evidence comes from Bordalo et al. (2024). They show that higher LTG optimism, which is associated with high stock prices, predicts lower returns at a horizon of 3–5 years. Expectations of short-term earnings growth instead do not predict returns. In fact, Bordalo et al. (2024) show that the systematic disappointment of LTG accounts for most of the predictability of returns from the aggregate price-dividend ratio. Overreacting long-term beliefs have a strong explanatory power, so that variation in required returns may be less necessary than is commonly assumed, if at all.

We next move beyond stock market efficiency and study whether LTG helps predict movement in other financial markets and in the real economy. The next section studies how changes in LTG affect changes in interest rates and credit spreads, which have also been used to predict economic activity. We then study the role of changes in LTG on fluctuations in real investment (Sec. IV) and other business cycle indicators (Sec. V).

III. LTG and the Financial Cycle

To link LTG to interest rates and spreads, we minimally modify a standard asset pricing model allowing for nonrational, overreacting beliefs about fundamentals. The model is standard in all other respects. This implies that it does not match unconditional phenomena such as the equity premium or the risk-free-rate puzzles. An endowment economy follows an AR(1) autoregressive process for output growth:

$$g_{t+1} = \mu g_t + v_{t+1}. \tag{5}$$

Instead, investors use an incorrect model, in which output growth follows:

$$\tilde{g}_{t+1} = \mu g_t + \omega_t + v_{t+1}, \tag{6}$$

where ω_t summarizes the time-varying belief distortions. When $\omega_t > 0$, beliefs are excessively optimistic about future growth. The belief distortion ω_t—which we refer to as optimism at t—is persistent, and it compounds reactions to present and past news v_{t-s}:

$$\omega_t = \rho \omega_{t-1} + \theta v_t. \tag{7}$$

When $\theta > 0$, beliefs overreact: in equation (6), the current news v_t causes beliefs about growth to shift by $(\mu + \theta)v_t$, which is larger in magnitude than the rational μv_t. If $\theta < 0$, beliefs underreact. If $\theta = 0$, expectations are rational. Equation (7) captures the two key features of LTG_t: its persistence and boom-bust dynamics, with periods of sustained overoptimism followed by disappointment. Bordalo et al. (2024) show that when $\theta > 0$, equations (6) and (7) are a special case of the diagnostic expectations model, in which overreaction to past shocks exhibits a geometric decay, the "distant memory" specification studied in Bianchi et al. (2023).

This formalization captures the minimal features of belief overreaction, so it misses realistic ingredients that are important to quantitatively match overreaction in the data. First, investors overreact only to tangible cash flow news v_t. In reality, investors may also overreact to intangible news about future prospects, such as new technologies. We provide evidence for the latter channel in Bordalo et al. (2024). Second, the model does not feature a production side, which is key for understanding and quantitatively assessing the nexus between belief overreaction and aggregate investment. This aspect is studied in Bordalo, Gennaioli, Shleifer, and Terry (2021), who build and structurally estimate an RBC model using measured CFO forecasts and show the importance of belief overreaction for credit and investment cycles.

The representative consumer has constant absolute risk aversion utility with risk aversion parameter γ. Asset prices are set according to the first-order condition:

$$\tilde{\mathbb{E}}_t[R_{t+1}B(1 + g_{t+1})^{-\gamma}] = 1, \tag{8}$$

where $B < 1$ is the rate of time preference, g_{t+1} is real consumption growth (equal to the exogenous output growth in this endowment economy), and R_{t+1} is the realized asset return. The equilibrium return equalizes the consumer's current and future expected marginal utility of consumption. The key difference with a standard model is that in equation (8) the expectation is taken with respect to the possibly nonrational beliefs in equation (6).

Under rational expectations, time variation in returns is entirely shaped by the intertemporal rate of substitution, $g_{t+1}^{-\gamma}$, also called the stochastic discount factor. When consumption growth g_{t+1} is expected to be higher, the consumer is more affluent in the future compared with the present. Thus, they desire to consume more today, which pushes required returns up, and vice versa when consumption growth is low. Because actual consumption is fairly stable, this theory is a poor description of time variation in asset returns, which goes back to Shiller's excess volatility puzzle for stocks. The conventional fix has been to modify consumer preferences in ways that enhance the volatility in the marginal rate of substitution. Consider instead what happens when, consistent with survey expectations, we relax belief rationality. By exploiting equation (7), we can rewrite equation (8) as

$$\mathbb{E}_t[R_{t+1}B(1 + g_{t+1})^{-\gamma}M(g_{t+1}, g_t, \omega_t)] = 1. \tag{9}$$

The pricing equation under nonrational beliefs can be written as the rational pricing equation in which the new term $M(g_{t+1}, g_t, \omega_t)$ captures the investor's belief distortions. This term replaces nonstandard preferences, but crucially it is not observationally equivalent to them: shifts in beliefs can be disciplined using the expectations data.

Assuming, as is commonly done, joint lognormality of returns and fundamentals, equation (9) pins down the equilibrium risk-free rate and risk premium. These are respectively given by

$$r_{t+1}^f = - \log B - \frac{1}{2}\gamma^2\sigma_g^2 + \gamma(\mu g_t + \omega_t), \tag{10}$$

$$\mathbb{E}_t(r_{t+1}) - r_{t+1}^f = \left(\gamma - \frac{\omega_t}{\sigma_g^2}\right)\sigma_{rg}, \tag{11}$$

where σ_g^2 is the unconditional variance of consumption growth and σ_{rg} is the covariance between the asset return and consumption.

Consider the risk-free rate in equation (10). Here the new term is ω_t: during times of excessive optimism about future growth, the consumer is reluctant to save (they may actually want to borrow against future income). The risk-free rate is then higher. This yields two new predictions. Higher optimism ω_t, proxied by upward revisions of LTG_t, should be associated with: (i) a higher current interest rate r^f_{t+1} and (ii) reversal of interest rates r^f_{t+s} in the future. Interest rate reversals are in part due to fundamental mean reversion in output growth (due to $\mu < 1$), but they can also be due to the disappointment of excess optimism ω_t in the future, because $\rho < 1$. The latter term is responsible for the excess volatility that a rational fundamentals-based approach cannot account for.

Consider next the risk premium in equation (11). Again, the new term here is ω_t: when the consumer becomes more optimistic about future growth, the risk premium is persistently low. This yields two predictions about the time variation in returns, which mirror those for interest rates. Higher current optimism about future fundamentals, captured by upward revisions of LTG, should: (i) be associated with higher contemporaneous realized excess returns on risky assets (because upward belief revisions come with good news) and (ii) predict low average realized excess return $\mathbb{E}_t(r_{t+s}) - r^f_{t+s}$ on the same assets in the future. In Bordalo et al. (2024), we studied these predictions for stock returns, and here we test them for credit spreads: upward LTG revisions should come with low credit spreads in the near term and a predictable increase in future spreads, due to systematic future disappointment in risky bond returns (due, e.g., to higher-than-expected defaults).

We test these predictions by studying the association between the quarterly change in LTG_t and three contemporaneous and future outcomes: the 1- and 10-year interest rates and the Baa credit spread. We perform quarterly local projections (Jorda 2005) using as an independent "shock" the yearly LTG_t change and using as outcomes the year-on-year changes in the variables above. We start from the contemporaneous correlation between the shock and each outcome, $h = 0$, and then predict the outcome variable for future quarters $h = 1, \ldots, 10$.

Following standard practice, we control for 12 lags of the dependent variable. Among other things, this allows us to account for a rich pattern of fundamental mean reversion. We also control for 12 lags in yearly changes in the policy rate, 12 lags of yearly consumer price index (CPI) inflation, and 12 lags of the yearly log change in the S&P 500 index. These controls assuage concerns that our LTG shock may capture fundamental mean reversion, the monetary policy response, and the potentially time-varying required return embodied in stock valuations, resulting in a demanding exercise.

Table 3 reports the estimated coefficients. Consistent with equation (10), an increase in optimism is associated with contemporaneously higher short- and long-term interest rates (panels A and B). This is followed by positive predictability at short horizons $h = 1, 2, 3$ (which is at least in part mechanical due to overlapping quarters). After a period of stability, six-quarters-ahead interest rates revert and decline. This may be due to reversal of optimism about future earnings, which, again consistent with equation (10), reduces demand for funds by consumers and firms, reducing real interest rates.

The evolution of risk premia helps detect the role of systematic forecast errors. Consider panel C, which reports results for the Baa spread. Growing optimism about future earnings growth, due, for instance, to high recent growth, is associated with lower contemporaneous spreads, as captured by the negative coefficient at $h = 0$. Between three and six quarters ahead, the credit spread stabilizes. Consistent with belief overreaction, though, the credit spread eventually reverts: starting from quarter 5, the coefficient turns positive, indicating a predictable tightening of credit markets. In the model, this tightening reflects systematically disappointing future "news."

Since the 2008 financial crisis, a large body of work has used the credit spread as a barometer for financial and real activity. A lower spread is associated with an expansion of output and investment, whereas its widening is predictable and associated with economic and financial reversals (Krishnamurthy and Muir 2017; Lopez-Salido, Stein, and Zakrajsek 2017). Greenwood and Hanson (2013) show that low credit spreads predict negative excess returns on risky bonds, consistent with excess optimism at these times. Our findings offer direct evidence of this channel and underscore the importance of beliefs about LTG.

IV. LTG and Boom-Bust Investment Cycles

The explanatory power of LTG for boom-bust financial dynamics is consistent with Keynes's view that expectations of long-term profits are an important source of volatility in financial markets. Keynes connected the same expectations, which he called animal spirits, to real activity, and in particular to firms' desire to invest. Following this insight, we next assess whether financial and business cycle volatility can be reconciled by studying the connection between LTG and real investment, both in the aggregate and at the firm levels. Relative to Gennaioli et al. (2016), who document the link between CFOs' short-term expectations of earnings growth and investment, we focus on long-term expectations, connecting investment cycles to excess financial volatility.

Table 3
Estimate of $\Delta_4 LTG_t$ on Asset Prices

B_h Estimates from: $\Delta_4 y_{t+h} = B_h \Delta_4 LTG_t + X_t + \varphi_{t+h}$

Time Horizon (h) of Dependent Variable

	0	1	2	3	4	5	6	7	8	9	10
					A. Dependent Variable Δ_4 tbill $1y_{t+h}$						
$\Delta_4 LTG_t$	.21**	.40**	.44**	.39**	.12	−.19	−.37**	−.49**	−.62**	−.74**	−.82**
	[.07]	[.07]	[.09]	[.12]	[.13]	[.13]	[.13]	[.12]	[.13]	[.15]	[.17]
N	151	151	151	151	151	151	151	151	151	151	151
AR^2	.85	.66	.48	.25	.17	.24	.33	.38	.35	.30	.24
					B. Dependent Variable Δ_4 tbill $10y_{t+h}$						
$\Delta_4 LTG_t$	.18*	.35**	.41**	.40**	.16	−.09	−.24*	−.32**	−.32**	−.40**	−.48**
	[.07]	[.08]	[.08]	[.09]	[.12]	[.12]	[.10]	[.11]	[.12]	[.12]	[.13]
N	151	151	151	151	151	151	151	151	151	151	151
AR^2	.77	.60	.49	.37	.25	.27	.30	.29	.24	.20	.16

330

C. Dependent Variable Δ_4 Baa Credit Spread $10y_{t+h}$

$\Delta_4 LTG_t$	−.10	−.13*	−.12+	−.08	.08	.19+	.23*	.22*	.19*	.16+	.12
	[.07]	[.06]	[.06]	[.07]	[.09]	[.11]	[.10]	[.09]	[.09]	[.09]	[.10]
N	151	151	151	151	151	151	151	151	151	151	151
AR^2	.74	.55	.42	.28	.19	.22	.23	.18	.07	−.03	−.06

Note: The estimates measure the impact of a one-standard-deviation change in $\Delta_4 LTG_t$ on the dependent variables. The set of controls X_t include 12 lags of changes in the dependent variable, 12 lags of changes in the policy interest rate, 12 lags of yearly CPI inflation, and 12 lags of the yearly S&P 500 return. Here, Δ_4 tbill $1y_{t+h}$ is the four-quarter percentage point change in the Federal Reserve's 1-year Treasury bond (DGS1). Here, Δ_4 tbill $10y_{t+h}$ is the four-quarter percentage point change in the Federal Reserve's 10-year Treasury bond (DGS10). Here, Δ_4 Baa credit spread $10y_{t+h}$ is the four-quarter percentage point change in the yield spread between Moody's 10-year Baa bond (Baa) and the US 10-year Treasury bond (DGS10). Here, $\Delta_4 LTG_t$ is the four-quarter percentage point change in aggregate market expectation for 5-year earnings per share growth, calculated by value weighting firm-level forecasts. Heteroskedasticity-consistent standard errors reported in parentheses are computed according to Huber-White.

$^+ p < .10.$
$^* p < .05.$
$^{**} p < .01.$

We estimate local projections for aggregate year-on-year change in investment, controlling for 12 lags of the dependent variable, of yearly changes in the policy interest rate, of CPI inflation, and of the yearly S&P 500 return. Our main shock is again the yearly change in LTG_t. The results are reported in table 4, panel A, first row. A 1-standard-deviation increase in LTG_t is associated with an increase in investment that persists until four quarters later, peaking at a 3% increase in the investment-to-capital ratio in the year after the forecast, which corresponds to roughly 0.4 standard deviations of year-on-year investment growth (7.4%). Investment stabilizes for two quarters and then declines by a similar amount.

This behavior is consistent with a mechanism in which excess optimism about LTG fuels a short-run investment boom, which reverts into a bust when beliefs are disappointed and adjust downward. The boom may result from growing demand for capital by firms as well as from an outward shift in the supply of funds. The supply channel is consistent with the reduction in the credit spread documented in table 3, and also with the analysis in Bordalo, Gennaioli, Shleifer, and Terry (2021), who show in an estimated RBC model that shifts in the supply of funds play a quantitatively important role in transmitting changes in expectations to the real economy. In fact, the short-run increase in investment may be predominantly due to a relaxation of capital market "frictions" rather than to new investment plans.[5] The ability of changes in LTG to jointly shift the demand and supply of capital can help account for aggregate comovement, which is otherwise hard to explain based solely on investment shocks or news (Jaimovich and Rebelo 2009; Christiano et al. 2014).

One important question is whether the long-run investment decline estimated in table 4 is connected to the disappointment of optimistic expectations (again, this decline is unlikely to be due to fundamental mean reversion given the 12 investment lags in table 4). We add to the specification of panel A the predictable component of LTG forecast errors estimated in table 2, row 3. The idea here is to check whether times of high excess optimism, in the sense that current LTG is so high that it predictably leads to large future disappointment, predict future investment busts. The estimation results in panel B support this mechanism. Excess LTG optimism, captured by predictable disappointment, accounts for the entire future reversal in aggregate investment growth, which begins to materialize around five quarters ahead. As before, the effects are large in magnitude, with 1-standard-deviation increase in $\widehat{FE}_t$ leading to a

0.27-standard-deviation drop in investment growth 2 years later. Controlling for predictable disappointment, the current LTG shock exerts a much more benign effect: it stimulates investment in the near term, just like a good fundamental shock.

In figure 4, we take this analysis one step further to show that overoptimism at time t, measured by predictable forecast errors, is associated with investment that is cumulatively lower than its initial level. That is, reversals go beyond correcting for initially high investment in a mean reverting way. Instead, they predictably lead to investment 3–5 years ahead that is lower than if no shock to optimism had occurred at time t. This is consistent with excessive optimism at t causing excessive investment in the first year, leading to (i) disappointment in expectations going forward, as well as (ii) a cutback of "inefficient" investment in the subsequent years (assessing the inefficiency of this contraction is, however, beyond the scope of this paper).

One concern in the analysis is that the connection between LTG and investment dynamics may be contaminated by a few large aggregate fundamental shocks such as the collapse of the dotcom bubble or the Great Recession. To assess robustness, we estimate in table 5 the specifications of table 4 at the firm level. In this specification, the shock is the change in firm-level LTG and the proxy for overoptimism is the future forecast error of the firm's earnings growth predicted from the current firm-level LTG. Crucially, in this regression we can introduce time dummies, which control for any aggregate shock, including those potentially affecting required returns. We also add firm fixed effects, which additionally control for firm-level differences in average profitability and risk.

Column 1 shows that, just like at the aggregate level, high firm-level LTG predicts future disappointment in earnings growth. High LTG is thus a proxy for firm-level excess optimism about the long term. Columns 2–6 show that, as in the aggregate investment regressions, an upward LTG revision at the firm level is associated with high year-on-year investment in the near term, but going forward there is also a large and predictable investment decline.[6]

This section delivers a simple yet important message. Expectations of long-term growth can reconcile excess financial volatility with volatility in real investment. This is possible because long-term expectations are excessively volatile and display optimism and predictable disappointment that can jointly account for boom-bust patterns in financial markets and real investment.

Table 4
Estimate of Δ_4LTG and Forecast Errors on Investment-to-Capital

	Time Horizon of Dependent Variable (Quarters)										
	0	1	2	3	4	5	6	7	8	9	10
	A. Estimates from										
	$\Delta_4$investment-to-capital$_{t+h} = B_h \Delta_4$LTG$_t + X_t + \varepsilon_t$										
Δ_4LTG$_t$	.70**	1.83**	2.65**	3.21**	2.45**	.57	-1.27	-2.58**	-2.63**	-1.83**	-.68
	[.20]	[.42]	[.50]	[.53]	[.60]	[.79]	[.81]	[.74]	[.64]	[.63]	[.60]
AR^2	.94	.85	.75	.59	.36	.13	.11	.17	.22	.19	.15
N	150	150	150	150	150	150	150	150	150	150	150
	B. Estimates from $\Delta_4$investment-to-capital$_{t+h} = B_h \Delta_4$LTG$_t + \delta_h \widehat{FE}_t + X_t + \varepsilon_t$										
	First stage: LTG$_t - \Delta_{20}e_{t+20}/5 = \Phi$LTG$_t + \varepsilon_t \rightarrow \widehat{FE}_t$										
Δ_4LTG$_t$	.85**	1.67**	2.20**	2.80**	2.47**	1.47$^+$	.55	-.24	-.84	-.75	-.24
	[.31]	[.49]	[.64]	[.86]	[.89]	[.88]	[.84]	[.76]	[.69]	[.73]	[.82]

334

$\widehat{FE}_t$	.13	.30	.29	.07	−.44	−1.15*	−1.70**	−2.02**	−1.98**	−1.80**	−1.61**
	[.14]	[.24]	[.33]	[.43]	[.46]	[.47]	[.44]	[.39]	[.36]	[.37]	[.42]
AR^2	.95	.87	.75	.57	.37	.17	.15	.20	.25	.25	.20
N	138	138	138	138	138	138	138	138	138	138	138

Note: The estimates measure the impact of a one-standard-deviation change in $\Delta_4 LTG_t$ and $\widehat{FE}_t$ on the four-quarter log growth in investment-to-capital, Δ_4 investment-to-capital. The set of controls include 12 lags of dependent variable, 12 lags of four-quarter percentage point changes in the policy interest rate, 12 lags of yearly CPI inflation, and 12 lags of the log four-quarter S&P 500 return. Here, Δ_4 investment-to-capital is the four-quarter log change in the ratio of nonresidential investment (PNFI) to the previous year's cost of capital (KINTOTL1ES000). Here, $\Delta_4 LTG_t$ is the four-quarter percentage point change in aggregate market expectation for 5-year earnings per share growth, calculated by value weighting firm-level forecasts. Here, FE_t is defined as the difference between (a) aggregate market expectation for 5-year earnings per share growth, LTG_t, and (b) the average annual growth in aggregate earnings per share between quarter t and $t + 20$, $\Delta_{20} e_{t+20}/5$. Here, $\widehat{FE}_t$ are fitted values from the regression of FE_t on LTG_t. Heteroskedasticity-consistent asymptotic standard errors reported in parentheses are computed according to Huber-White.

$^+ p < .10$.
$^* p < .05$.
$^{**} p < .01$.

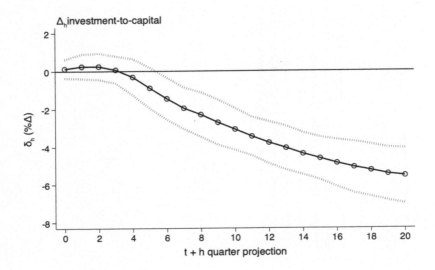

Fig. 4. Impulse response of cumulative investment growth to predictable forecast errors. The figure shows the cumulative impact of a one-standard-deviation change in $\widehat{FE}_t$ on Δ_h investment-to-capital$_{t+h}$. The regression specification is: Δ_h investment-to-capital$_{t+h}$ = $B_h \Delta_4 LTG_t + \delta_h \widehat{FE}_t + X_t + \varepsilon_{t+h}$. The set of controls include 12 lags of yearly growth in investment-to-capital$_t$, 12 lags of changes in the policy interest rate, 12 lags of yearly CPI inflation, and 12 lags of the yearly S&P 500 return. Δ_h investment-to-capital is the h-quarter log change in the ratio of nonresidential investment (PNFI) to the previous year's cost of capital (K1NTOTL1ES000). Here, LTG_t is the aggregate market expectation for 5-year earnings per share growth, calculated by value weighting firm-level forecasts. Here, FE_t is defined as the difference between (*a*) aggregate market expectation for 5-year earnings per share growth, LTG_t, and (*b*) the average annual growth in earnings per share between quarter t and $t + 20$, $\Delta_{20}e_{t+20}/5$. Here, $\widehat{FE}_t$ are fitted values from the regression of FE_t on LTG_t. Heteroskedasticity-consistent asymptotic standard errors reported in parentheses are computed according to Huber-White.

V.   LTG and the Business Cycle

We now extend our previous results to other measures of economic fluctuations. We show that LTG predicts booms and busts in other major business cycle variables, as well as in estimated shocks that are conventionally considered drivers of investment and the business cycle. Figure 5 presents the first exercise: using local projections, it compares the impulse response of investment to a one-standard-deviation upward LTG revision (as given in table 4, panel A) with the predicted responses of year-on-year growth in GDP, aggregate consumption, employment, wages, and inflation (see app. B, http://www.nber.org/data-appendix/c14860/appendix.pdf

Table 5
LTG and Investment at the Firm Level

	(1)	(2)	(3)	(4)	(5)	(6)
		Estimates from: $\Delta_4 i_{i,t+h} = B_h \Delta_4 LTG_{i,t} + \delta_h \widehat{FE}_{i,t} + \varepsilon_{t+h}$				
	$FE_{i,t}$	$h = 0$	$h = 6$	$h = 12$	$h = 18$	$h = 24$
$LTG_{i,t}$	.7770**					
	(.0477)					
$\Delta_4 LTG_{i,t}$		.3134**	.2066**	.0775$^+$	.0544**	.0038
		(.0582)	(.0625)	(.0432)	(.0183)	(.0251)
$\widehat{FE}_{i,t}$		−.1021**	−.1218**	−.1963**	−.2081**	−.1514**
		(.0195)	(.0323)	(.0384)	(.0395)	(.0375)
AR^2	.02	−.03	−.03	−.03	−.03	−.03
N	146,151	133,545	132,166	131,122	130,213	129,461
Firm FE	Y	Y	Y	Y	Y	Y
Time FE	Y	Y	Y	Y	Y	Y

Note: We present firm-level regressions for all US firms in the Institutional Brokers' Estimate System sample. We define firm-level forecast errors as the difference between (a) the expected long-term growth in firm i's earnings, $LTG_{i,t}$, and (b) the average annual growth in firm i's earnings per share between quarters t and $t + 20$, $\Delta_{20} e_{i,t+20}/5$. Here, $\Delta_4 i_{i,t+h}$ is the growth rate in firm i's investment between quarters $t + h - 4$ and $t + h$. We define firm i's investment $i_{i,t}$ as the log of $\Delta_4 K_{i,t+h}/K_{i,t+h-4}$, where firm i's capital stock $K_{i,t}$ includes physical, intangible, and knowledge capital following the methodology of Peters and Taylor (2017). In column 1, we perform an ordinary least squares (OLS) regression of the error in forecasting the firm's 5-year earnings growth on $LTG_{i,t}$. In columns 2–6, we perform an OLS regression of $\Delta_4 i_{i,t+h}$ on (a) the forecast errors fitted in column 1 and (b) the 1-year revision of the forecast of firm i's long-term earnings growth, $\Delta_4 LTG_{i,t}$. Regressions include time and firm fixed effects (FE), which we do not report. The sample period is 1982:4–2018:1. We report Driscoll-Kraay standard errors with autocorrelation of up to 60 lags.
$^+p < .10.$
$^{**}p < .01.$

#page=10 for the corresponding table). The pattern is clear. In the short run, an upward LTG revision acts as a "good shock": it boosts all these variables. A 1-standard-deviation increase in LTG is associated with a 0.31 standard increase for GDP growth, a 0.47 standard increase for consumption, a 0.67 standard increase for employment growth, and a 0.30 standard increase for wages, as well as a 0.43 pp increase for inflation, over the course of the first year. These magnitudes are remarkable given that the impulse response already controls for many current and lagged variables.

The figure also shows that, in the long run, a current increase in LTG is associated with reversals whose magnitude is comparable with that of the initial boom. These dynamics mimic those of real investment and financial

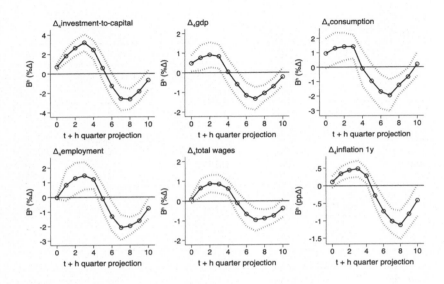

Fig. 5. Impulse projections of business cycle variables. The figure shows the impulse response of business cycle variables to the four-quarter percentage point change in aggregate market expectation for 5-year earnings per share growth, $\Delta_4 LTG_t$, using the local projections (Jorda 2005) method. Here, Δ_4 investment-to-capital is the four-quarter log change in the ratio of nonresidential investment (PNFI) to the previous year's cost of capital (K1NTOTL1ES000). Here, Δ_4 gdp is the four-quarter log change in gdp (GDP). Here, Δ_4 consumption is the four-quarter log change in consumption (PCE). Here, Δ_4 employment is the four-quarter log change in total employment (CE16OV). Here, Δ_4 total wages is the four-quarter log change in total wage and salary disbursements (A576RC1). Here, Δ_4 inflation is the four-quarter percentage point change in yearly CPI inflation (CPIAUCSL). The set of controls include 12 lags of dependent variable, 12 lags of four-quarter percentage point changes in the policy interest rate, 12 lags of yearly CPI inflation, and 12 lags of the log four-quarter S&P 500 return. A 95% confidence interval is shown, computed with Huber-White standard errors.

markets, confirming that expectations of long-term growth can reconcile financial and real volatility. To support this interpretation, and to assess endogeneity concerns, we perform a Granger causality test for each variable and LTG. The results are reported in appendix B, http://www.nber .org/data-appendix/c14860/appendix.pdf#page=10. We find that, in a Granger sense, LTG causes investment growth, GDP growth, consumption growth, employment growth, wage growth, and inflation, whereas the reverse is almost never the case, especially at four and eight quarter lags. Although this evidence is not conclusive, it indicates that LTG does not mechanically adjust to the past. It instead reflects beliefs about the future that are not yet incorporated into economic variables.

A large body of work in macroeconomics traces aggregate comovement to the transmission of shocks. These shocks are typically estimated using DSGE models or VARs with identifying restrictions (Ramey 2016). One shortcoming of this approach is that business cycle variation is often attributed to "black box" drivers, which contain statistical information but are not clearly interpretable. Being directly estimated using business cycle variables, these shocks may statistically outperform LTG. However, LTG has the important advantage of offering a source of comovement that is directly measured at the micro-level of individual firms and is clearly interpretable in terms of economic fundamentals as overreacting expectations of long-term profits. In this sense, LTG offers a useful tool to evaluate the nature of estimated shocks.

To illustrate this idea, we conclude by connecting LTG to estimated shocks to the MEI, which are also viewed as key drivers of investment and business cycle volatility. Justiniano et al. (2011) estimate this shock using a canonical DSGE model and find that it accounts for 60%–85% of US postwar fluctuations in GDP growth, hours, and investment. Keynes coined the term "marginal efficiency of investment" to describe firms' propensity to invest and saw it as driven by two factors: the ease of credit and "the state of long-term expectations" or "animal spirits." In Keynes's view, fluctuations in MEI played a key role in the finance and investment-business cycle nexus. Justiniano et al. (2011) formalize MEI as the productivity with which investment goods are transformed into capital. Remarkably, they show that MEI is high during times in which ease of financing is high, as measured by low credit spreads.

What is the correlation between LTG and contemporaneous macroeconomic shocks typically associated with investment? And can LTG help predict future realizations of these shocks? If beliefs amplify macroeconomic volatility, we would expect that current optimism is associated with good recent shocks. At the same time, because the volatility of expectations is excessive and current optimism predicts future disappointment, optimism may help predict bad shocks in the future. This logic connects shocks to MEI to its long-term expectations component, LTG. Keynes also stressed financial factors, but, due to its explanatory power for financial markets, LTG may also subsume part of that channel. That is, changes in LTG can affect MEI by not only directly increasing entrepreneurs' desire to invest (the demand for credit) but also indirectly, by increasing lenders' optimism (the supply of credit). To assess whether this is the case, we predict current and future MEI shocks using (i) the current LTG revision (a "good news" effect), (ii) current LTG overoptimism (i.e., predictable future disappointment), and (iii) credit spreads, to account for an impact of financial markets on MEI that is independent of LTG.

Table 6 reports the results. As in our previous analysis, upward LTG revisions appear as good shocks: they positively correlate with MEI in the short term. However, high LTG optimism is associated with bad MEI shocks in the future. This is an intriguing finding: it suggests that the estimated MEI shocks do not reflect genuine bad news but rather capture systematic disappointment of excess optimism. Conditional on long-term expectations, the credit spread loses its contemporaneous explanatory power for MEI. This evidence further bolsters the possibility that long-term expectations lie at the core of the nexus between financial and real activity, acting as a driver of excess volatility in both domains, and hence as a source of aggregate comovement.

Christiano et al. (2014) use a DSGE model to estimate "risk shocks," which are shocks increasing the default probability of risky firms in a model with frictional financial markets. The authors show that these shocks, which are estimated to match real and financial volatility (in the credit spread and the stock market), outperform MEI in accounting for business cycle variation. In line with our approach, jointly accounting for real and financial volatility seems to be a key step in accounting for business cycle comovement. Like many estimated shocks, "risk shocks" are hard to directly interpret economically. Perhaps such shocks also capture changes in expectations of future profits, which can drive default risk as perceived by lenders, stock prices, and firms' investment policies, as our empirical analysis shows. In line with this possibility, in appendix B (http://www.nber.org/data-appendix/c14860/appendix .pdf#page=10), we show that a current increase in LTG optimism predicts good news shock informing markets about low risk in the near term (up to eight quarters out), but it also predicts a surprise increase in risk in the future, consistent with the possibility that the combination of anticipated and unanticipated changes in risk may capture overreaction and predictable disappointment of long-term expectations.

In sum, measured expectations of long-term profits can reconcile excess volatility in financial markets and predictable returns with the volatility of investment and the business cycle. This reconciliation is parsimonious and consistent with standard macroeconomic shocks. The key new aspect is the role of overreacting long-term expectations, which are clearly interpretable and have a strong explanatory power. Because expectations move, endogenously, with fundamentals, they act as shock

Table 6
Predicting MEI shocks with LTG and Credit Spreads

	Time Horizon of Dependent Variable (Quarters)										
	0	1	2	3	4	5	6	7	8	9	10
	Estimates from: $\text{mei}_{t+h} = B_h \Delta_4 \text{LTG}_t + \phi_h \text{BaaSpread}_{t+h} + \delta_h \widehat{\text{FE}}_t + \varepsilon_{t+h}$										
	No Controls										
$\Delta_4\text{LTG}_t$	.19**	.22**	.13	.07	.06	.02	.06	-.01	-.03	-.05	-.08
	[.07]	[.07]	[.08]	[.07]	[.06]	[.07]	[.06]	[.07]	[.07]	[.07]	[.09]
BaaSpread_{t+h}	.03	.19+	.14	.06	.10	-.01	.08	.00	-.00	.01	-.03
	[.11]	[.11]	[.09]	[.08]	[.09]	[.09]	[.08]	[.08]	[.07]	[.07]	[.07]
$\widehat{\text{FE}}_t$	-.11*	-.15**	-.15**	-.13**	-.14**	-.11*	-.12**	-.10*	-.08+	-.08+	-.05
	[.05]	[.05]	[.05]	[.05]	[.05]	[.05]	[.05]	[.05]	[.05]	[.04]	[.05]
AR^2	.02	.06	.04	.03	.04	.02	.03	.01	.01	.01	.00
N	95	95	95	95	95	95	95	95	95	95	95

Note: MEI = marginal efficiency of investment; LTG = long-term earnings growth. The estimates measure the impact of a one-standard-deviation change in $\Delta_4\text{LTG}_t$ and $\widehat{\text{FE}}_t$ on mei_{t+h}. The regressions are unconditional (no controls). Here, $\Delta_4\text{LTG}_t$ is the four-quarter percentage point change in aggregate market expectation for 5-year earnings per share growth, calculated by value weighting firm-level forecasts. Here, FE_t is defined as the difference between (a) aggregate market expectation for 5-year earnings per share growth, LTG_t, and (b) the average annual growth in earnings per share between quarter t and $t+20$, $\Delta_{20}e_t - e_{t+20}/5$. Here, $\widehat{\text{FE}}_t$ are fitted values from the regression of FE_t on LTG_t (table 5, col. 1). Here, BaaSpread_{t+h} is the yield spread between Moody's 10-year Baa bond (Baa) and the US 10-year Treasury bond (DGS10). Heteroskedasticity-consistent asymptotic standard errors reported in parentheses are computed according to Huber-White.

+ $p < .10$.
* $p < .05$.
** $p < .01$.

amplifiers. But this also implies that expectations cannot be treated as shocks: seeking innovations orthogonal to available information may capture the rational component of beliefs but risks precluding predictable expectation reversals, the central feature of overreaction. Overreacting long-term expectations, which are clearly interpretable, have a strong explanatory power, and act as shock amplifiers.

VI. Conclusion

Using analyst expectations of LTG for individual US listed firms, we provide some evidence that the well-known connection between financial markets and the macroeconomy is due to the influence of nonrational expectations on both. In line with Keynes's intuition, long-term expectations exhibit excess volatility, which in turn correlates with movements of stock prices and returns, interest rates, and credit spreads, as well as with the cyclical behavior of investment and other real quantities. Belief overreaction arises as an important ingredient that appears both qualitatively and quantitatively important to understand volatility, particularly predictable long-term reversals. Several approaches have tried to account for these facts by changing investor preferences in ways that are hard to measure or test. We highlight the promise of a simple, measurable, and realistic ingredient: overreacting expectations as shock amplifiers.

The analysis presented here only scratches the surface of a daunting task: integrating survey data and realistic models of expectation formation into macroeconomic analysis. One challenge is to explore how, through choices of different agents, nonrational expectations affect the propagation mechanism. Doing so calls for developing theoretical macroeconomic models with overreacting beliefs in which the precise consequences of these links can be assessed. There are several recent attempts in this direction (Ilut and Schneider 2014; Angeletos, Huo, and Sastry 2020; Bordalo, Gennaioli, Shleifer, and Terry 2021; Bianchi et al. 2023; L'Huillier et al. 2023, Maxted 2023) but much remains to be done, for instance in understanding the role of beliefs for consumer demand, labor markets, or price setting.

The second open issue is to measure and study the formation of expectations about the long term. The accumulated evidence shows that expectations about fundamentals are important. But expectations about many other outcomes may play important roles. Examples include perceptions of risks (including financial, political, or climate risks), beliefs about returns to investment (including on savings and on human capital), and also second-order expectations about other investors, which were also discussed by Keynes in the *General Theory*. They have been studied under rationality, but new models of expectations open new avenues. Bordalo, Gennaioli, Kwon, and Shleifer (2021) show how diagnostic expectations about others may help account for asset price bubbles, whereas Bastianello and Fontanier (2023) consider wrong beliefs about the information used by others. Systematically measuring a rich set of expectations (and testing for their departures from rationality) will help to understand the propagation of shocks through the economy.

Finally, there is still much to learn about the formation of expectations. The overreaction in LTG appears delayed and persistent. The sluggish adjustment may come from information frictions, as discussed in Bordalo et al. (2020) and Bordalo, Gennaioli, Kwon, and Shleifer (2021). But what drives overreaction, and why is it more prevalent in expectations about the long term? Keynes (1936) argued that because the long term is so uncertain and hard to imagine, these expectations are likely to be shaped by current events, which are easily accessible. This view is consistent with research in psychology that shows more broadly that beliefs about the future are largely formed from experiences retrieved from memory on the basis of prominent cues (Bordalo, Gennaioli, Shleifer, and Terry 2021). Good times bring strong growth to mind and keep risks out of mind. This effect is stronger for longer-term expectations, where most anything can happen or be believed, whereas imagining the near term is naturally strongly anchored to the present.

The psychology of memory and attention can offer important insights in this enterprise. For instance, even irrelevant personal experiences may matter when forming beliefs about aggregate conditions, because these experiences are salient in a person's mind and can help them imagine an uncertain future. In this respect, memory-based theories of beliefs can jointly shed light on the large observed belief heterogeneity and connect it to systematic biases such as under- or overreaction of consensus expectations to specific shocks. The introduction of realistic departures from rationality in macroeconomics is not like opening Pandora's box where "anything can happen." It is part of a long quest for better microfoundations, deeper "parameters," and the ability to incorporate as well as explain a larger body of data.

Endnotes

Authors email address: Pedro Bordalo (pedro.bordalo@sbs.ox.ac.uk), Nicola Gennaioli (nicola.gennaioli@unibocconi.it), Rafael La Porta (Rafael.Laporta@brown.edu), Matthew

OBrien (m.obrien3@lse.ac.uk), Andrei Shleifer (ashleifer@harvard.edu). We thank our discussants Venky Venkateswaran and George-Marios Angeletos for their very helpful comments, and Lawrence Christiano for providing some data we use in the analysis. We also thank the Chae Family Economics Research Fund at Harvard University for financial support of this research. For acknowledgments, sources of research support, and disclosure of the authors' material financial relationships, if any, please see https://www.nber.org/books-and-chapters/nber-macroeconomics-annual-2023-volume-38/long-term-expectations-and-aggregate-fluctuations.

1. For example, in December of 2018, 19 analysts followed the median S&P 500 firm, and four analysts followed the median firm not in the S&P 500. Analysts are also less likely to rate as "buy" firms in the S&P 500 index.

2. That is, g is the average of g_t, where the latter solves, at each t, the equation $p_t = e_t + (\tilde{k} - r)/(1 - \alpha) + \alpha \ln(\mathbb{E}_t^0 \text{EPS}_{t,t+2}/\text{EPS}_{t,t+1}) + \Sigma_{s=2}^{10} \alpha^s \text{LTG}_t + (\alpha^{10}/(1 - \alpha))g_t$. Results are virtually identical if we let LTG decay as observed cyclically adjusted earnings.

3. Here we focus on expectations of CFOs, which are plausibly more sophisticated than the generic market participant. In the appendix, we show that LTG has a similar impact on other measures of expected returns. Moreover, a Granger causality test supports the view that LTG drives expectations of returns, not the reverse.

4. Bordalo et al. (2020) show, for a broad range of macroeconomic outcomes, that although individual forecasters often overreact, contemporaneous information frictions produce rigidity in consensus forecasts, especially at short-term horizons. Table 2 shows that periods of upward LTG revisions capture times in which overreaction occurs even at the aggregate level, leading to excess volatility in aggregate beliefs and predictable boom-bust patterns in expectations and prices (Bordalo et al. 2024).

5. It may also be the case that firm managers update expectations earlier than analysts.

6. The investment reversal in table 5 is consistent with Bordalo, Gennaioli, Shleifer, and Terry (2021), who show, at the firm level, that excess optimism about short-term growth is associated with predictably higher firm-level credit spreads and lower investment. They stress shifts in credit supply. Here we focus on long-term expectations, not on credit, which may play a role in the effects we document.

References

Amromin, Gene, and Steven Sharpe. 2014. "From the Horse's Mouth: Economic Conditions and Investor Expectations of Risk and Return." *Management Science* 60 (4): 845–66.

Angeletos, George-Marios, Fabrice Collard, and Harris Dellas. 2018. "Quantifying Confidence." *Econometrica* 86 (5): 1689–726.

Angeletos, George-Marios, Fabrice Collard, and Harris Dellas. 2020. "Business-Cycle Anatomy." *American Economic Review* 110 (10): 3030–70.

Angeletos, George-Marios, Zhen Huo, and Karthik Sastry. 2020. "Imperfect Macroeconomic Expectations: Evidence and Theory." *NBER Macroeconomics Annual* 35 (1): 1–86.

Angeletos, George-Marios, and Chen Lian. 2016. "Incomplete Information in Macroeconomics: Accommodating Frictions in Coordination." In *Handbook of Macroeconomics*, ed. John B. Taylor and Harald Uhlig, 1065–240. London: Elsevier. https://www.sciencedirect.com/science/article/pii/S1574004816300118.

———. 2022. "Confidence and the Propagation of Demand Shocks." *Review of Economic Studies* 89 (3): 1085–119.

———. 2023. "Dampening General Equilibrium: Incomplete Information and Bounded Rationality." In *Handbook of Economic Expectations*, ed. Rüdiger Bachmann, Giorgio Topa, and Wilbert van der Klaauw, 613–45. Academic Press. https://www.sciencedirect.com/science/article/abs/pii/B9780128229279000288.

Bacchetta, Philippe, Elmar Mertens, and Eric Van Wincoop. 2009. "Predictability in Financial Markets: What Do Survey Expectations Tell Us?" *Journal of International Money and Finance* 28 (3): 406–26.

Backus, David, Bryan Routledge, and Stanley Zin. 2009. "The Cyclical Component of US Asset Returns." 2009 Meeting Papers, Society for Economic Dynamics. https://pages.stern.nyu.edu/~dbackus/GE_asset_pricing/ms/BRZ%20returns%20latest.pdf.

Bansal, Ravi, Dana Kiku, and Amir Yaron. 2010. "Long Run Risks, the Macroeconomy, and Asset Prices." *American Economic Review* 100 (2): 542–46.

Barberis, Nicholas, Robin Greenwood, Lawrence Jin, and Andrei Shleifer. 2015. "X-CAPM: An Extrapolative Capital Asset Pricing Model." *Journal of Financial Economics* 115 (1): 1–24.

———. 2018. "Extrapolation and Bubbles." *Journal of Financial Economics* 129 (2): 203–27.

Barberis, Nicholas, Andrei Shleifer, and Robert Vishny. 1998. "A Model of Investor Sentiment." *Journal of Financial Economics* 49 (3): 307–43.

Barro, Robert. 1990. "The Stock Market and Investment." *Review of Financial Studies* 3 (1): 115–31.

———. 2009. "Rare Disasters, Asset Prices, and Welfare Costs." *American Economic Review* 99 (1): 243–64.

Barsky, Robert, and J. Bradford De Long. 1993. "Why Does the Stock Market Fluctuate?" *Quarterly Journal of Economics* 108 (2): 291–311.

Bastianello, Francesca, and Fontanier, Paul. 2023. "Partial Equilibrium Thinking, Extrapolation, and Bubbles." December 15. https://ssrn.com/abstract=4666338.

Beaudry, Paul, and Franck Portier. 2006. "Stock Prices, News, and Economic Fluctuations." *American Economic Review* 96 (4): 1293–307.

Bianchi, Francesco, Cosmin Ilut, and Hikaru Saijo. 2023. "Diagnostic Business Cycles." *Review of Economic Studies* 91 (1): 129–62.

Bordalo, Pedro, John Conlon, Nicola Gennaioli, Spencer Kwon, and Andrei Shleifer. 2023. "Memory and Probability." *Quarterly Journal of Economics* 138 (1): 265–311.

Bordalo, Pedro, Nicola Gennaioli, Spencer Yongwook Kwon, and Andrei Shleifer. 2021. "Diagnostic Bubbles." *Journal of Financial Economics* 141 (3): 1060–77.

Bordalo, Pedro, Nicola Gennaioli, Rafael La Porta, and Andrei Shleifer. 2019. "Diagnostic Expectations and Stock Returns." *Journal of Finance* 74 (6): 2839–74.

———. 2024. "Belief Overreaction and Stock Market Puzzles." *Journal of Political Economy* (forthcoming).

Bordalo, Pedro, Nicola Gennaioli, Yueran Ma, and Andrei Shleifer. 2020. "Overreaction in Macroeconomic Expectations." *American Economic Review* 110 (9): 2748–82.

Bordalo, Pedro, Nicola Gennaioli, and Andrei Shleifer. 2022. "Overreaction and Diagnostic Expectations in Macroeconomics." *Journal of Economic Perspectives* 36 (3): 223–44.

Bordalo, Pedro, Nicola Gennaioli, Andrei Shleifer, and Stephen Terry. 2021. "Real Credit Cycles." Working Paper no. 28416, NBER, Cambridge, MA.

Burns, Arthur F., and Wesley Clair Mitchell. 1938. "Statistical Indicators of Cyclical Revivals." National Bureau of Economic Research. https://www.nber.org/system/files/chapters/c4251/c4251.pdf.

Campbell, John, and John Cochrane. 1999. "By Force of Habit: A Consumption-Based Explanation of Aggregate Stock Market Behavior." *Journal of Political Economy* 107 (2): 205–51.

Campbell, John, and Robert Shiller. 1987. "Cointegration and Tests of Present Value Models." *Journal of Political Economy* 95 (5): 1062–88.

———. 1988. "The Dividend-Price Ratio and Expectations of Future Dividends and Discount Factors." *Review of Financial Studies* 1 (3): 195–228.

Christiano, Lawrence, Roberto Motto, and Massimo Rostagno. 2014. "Risk Shocks." *American Economic Review* 104 (1): 27–65.

d'Arienzo, Daniele. 2020. "Maturity Increasing Overreaction and Bond Market Puzzles." https://papers.ssrn.com/sol3/papers.cfm?abstract_id=3733056.

De La O, Ricardo, and Sean Myers. 2021. "Subjective Cash Flow and Discount Rate Expectations." *Journal of Finance* 76 (3): 1339–87.

De Long, J. Bradford, Andrei Shleifer, Lawrence Summers, and Robert Waldmann. 1990. "Noise Trader Risk in Financial Markets." *Journal of Political Economy* 98 (4): 703–38.

Fazzari, Steven, R. Glenn Hubbard, and Bruce Petersen. 1988. "Investment, Financing Decisions, and Tax Policy." *American Economic Review* 78 (2): 200–205.

Gabaix, Xavier. 2019. "Behavioral Inattention." In *Handbook of Behavioral Economics—Foundations and Applications* 2, ed. B. Douglas Bernheim, Stefano DellaVigna, and David Laibson, 2:261–343. Amsterdam: North-Holland. https://www.sciencedirect.com/handbook/handbook-of-behavioral-economics-applications-and-foundations-1/vol/2.

Gennaioli, Nicola, Yueran Ma, and Andrei Shleifer. 2016. "Expectations and Investment." *NBER Macroeconomics Annual* 30 (1): 379–431.

Giglio, Stefano, Matteo Maggiori, Johannes Stroebel, and Stephen Utkus. 2021. "Five Facts about Beliefs and Portfolios." *American Economic Review* 111 (5): 1481–522.

Greenwood, Jeremy, Zvi Hercowitz, and Gregory Huffman. 1988. "Investment, Capacity Utilization, and the Real Business Cycle." *American Economic Review* 78 (3): 402–17.

Greenwood, Robin, and Samuel Hanson. 2013. "Issuer Quality and Corporate Bond Returns." *Review of Financial Studies* 26 (6): 1483–525.

Greenwood, Robin, and Andrei Shleifer. 2014. "Expectations of Returns and Expected Returns." *Review of Financial Studies* 27 (3): 714–46.

Hirshleifer, David, Jun Li, and Jianfeng Yu. 2015. "Asset Pricing in Production Economies with Extrapolative Expectations." *Journal of Monetary Economics* 76:87–106.

Ilut, Cosmin, and Martin Schneider. 2014. "Ambiguous Business Cycles." *American Economic Review* 104 (8): 2368–99.

Jaimovich, Nir, and Sergio Rebelo. 2009. "Can News about the Future Drive the Business Cycle?" *American Economic Review* 99 (4): 1097–118.

Jorda, Oscar. 2005. "Estimation and Inference of Impulse Responses by Local Projections." *American Economic Review* 95 (1): 161–82.

Justiniano, Alejandro, Giorgio Primiceri, and Andrea Tambalotti. 2011. "Investment Shocks and the Relative Price of Investment." *Review of Economic Dynamics* 14 (1): 102–21.

Keynes, John Maynard. 1936. *The General Theory of Employment, Interest and Money*. London: Macmillan.

Kozlowski, Julian, Laura Veldkamp, and Venky Venkateswaran. 2019. "The Tail That Keeps the Riskless Rate Low." *NBER Macroeconomics Annual* 33 (1): 253–83.

————. 2020. "The Tail That Wags the Economy: Beliefs and Persistent Stagnation." *Journal of Political Economy* 128 (8): 2839–79.

Krishnamurthy, Arvind, and Tyler Muir. 2017. "How Credit Cycles across a Financial Crisis." Working Paper no. 23850, NBER, Cambridge, MA.

La Porta, Rafael. 1996. "Expectations and the Cross-Section of Stock Returns." *Journal of Finance* 51 (5): 1715–42.

Lamont, Owen. 2000. "Investment Plans and Stock Returns." *Journal of Finance* 55 (6): 2719–45.

LeRoy, Stephen, and Richard Porter. 1981. "The Present-Value Relation: Tests Based on Implied Variance Bounds." *Econometrica* 49 (3): 555–74.

L'Huillier, Jean-Paul, Sanjay R Singh, and Donghoon Yoo. 2023. "Incorporating Diagnostic Expectations into the New Keynesian Framework." *Review of Economic Studies*. https://doi.org/10.1093/restud/rdad101.

Lopez-Salido, David, Jeremy Stein, and Egon Zakrajsek. 2017. "Credit-Market Sentiment and the Business Cycle." *Quarterly Journal of Economics* 132 (3): 1373–426.

Lorenzoni, Guido. 2009. "A Theory of Demand Shocks." *American Economic Review* 99 (5): 2050–84.

Maxted, Peter. 2023. "A Macro-Finance Model with Sentiment." *Review of Economic Studies* 91 (1): 438–75.

Merton, Robert. 1980. "On Estimating the Expected Return on the Market: An Exploratory Investigation." *Journal of Financial Economics* 8 (1): 323–61.

Minsky, Hyman. 1977. "The Financial Instability Hypothesis: An Interpretation of Keynes and an Alternative to 'Standard' Theory." *Nebraska Journal of Economics and Business* 16 (1): 5–16.

Morck, Randall, Andrei Shleifer, Robert Vishny. 1990. "The Stock Market and Investment: Is the Market a Sideshow?" *Brookings Papers on Economic Activity* 2 (1): 157–215.

Peters, Ryan, and Lucian Taylor. 2017. "Intangible Capital and the Investment-q Relation." *Journal of Financial Economics* 123 (2): 251–72.

Piazzesi, Monika, Juliana Salomao, and Martin Schneider. 2015. "Trend and Cycle in Bond Premia." Working paper, Stanford University.

Ramey, Valerie. 2016. "Macroeconomic Shocks and Their Propagation." Working Paper no. 21978, NBER, Cambridge, MA.

Shiller, Robert. 1981. "The Determinants of the Variability of Stock Market Prices." *American Economic Review* 71 (2): 222–27.

Stock, James, and Mark Watson. 2003. "Forecasting Output and Inflation: The Role of Asset Prices." *Journal of Economic Literature* 41 (3): 788–829.

Comment

George-Marios Angeletos, Northwestern University and NBER, United States of America

I. Introduction

The paper by Bordalo, Gennaioli, La Porta, O'Brien, and Shleifer offers intriguing new evidence on how expectations of future earnings growth drive, or at least correlate with, asset prices and investment. In particular, the authors argue that the observed variation in expectations of long-term growth (LTG) in earnings—their preferred survey measure of subjective expectations—can account for Shiller's excess volatility puzzle, for time variation in financial predictors of the business cycle, and for boom-bust cycles in real investment. These findings not only provide support for theories that emphasize the importance of departures from full rationality or full information but also indicate that LTG is a useful measure for quantifying these departures.

I start my discussion with a simple asset-pricing model to help clarify what the paper does vis-à-vis the theory (at least from my perspective). The route I take is somewhat different from, but also complementary to, the route taken in the paper. The latter is based on the Campbell-Shiller decomposition, which is a pure accounting exercise. My approach is more structural but offers a sharper mapping between the key empirical variables in the paper and their theoretical counterparts in a wide set of models.

Once this backdrop is clear, I summarize some of the key findings regarding asset prices. I next zero in on the authors' preferred structural interpretation and identify a few challenges with this interpretation.

NBER Macroeconomics Annual, volume 38, 2024.
© 2024 National Bureau of Economic Research. All rights reserved. Published by The University of Chicago Press for the National Bureau of Economic Research. https://doi.org/10.1086/729207

In particular, I question how much of the evidence speaks in favor of overextrapolation from past earnings as opposed to pure "animal spirits." Finally, I reassess the connection between LTG and the business cycles, using a different empirical prism than that in the paper.

All in all, I will qualify somewhat the authors' narrative about overextrapolation, especially in the business-cycle context. But this is meant to be a complement to the authors' paper, not a critique. The paper is making three important contributions at once: it provides a quantitatively potent proxy for subjective expectations, it identifies a rich set of novel empirical regularities, and it advances the authors' agenda about diagnostic expectations and overextrapolation. Even if my discussion "succeeds" in qualifying the last contribution, this only reinforces the other two contributions.

II. Theoretical Backdrop: A Simple Asset-Pricing Model

Consider a simple CARA-normal asset-pricing model along the lines of Singleton (1987). There are overlapping generations of traders, who live two periods, have constant absolute risk aversion (CARA) preferences, and may or may not have rational expectations or complete (homogeneous) information. These agents trade two assets: a risk-free bond, whose return is fixed at r, and a risky asset, whose period-t price is denoted by p_t. In this context, the period-t equilibrium price satisfies the following restriction:

$$p_t = \frac{1}{1 + r}\bar{E}_t[e_{t+1} + p_{t+1}] + u_t, \tag{1}$$

where e_{t+1} denotes the realized dividend, or earnings, in period $t + 1$, $\bar{E}_t$ denotes the period-t average expectation in the cross section of traders, and u_t is a "residual" that encapsulates the effects of time-varying risk, liquidity shocks, and noise traders on period-t asset demand.[1]

Momentarily disregard this residual, assume that the average expectation satisfies the law of iterated expectations, and finally impose $\lim_{k \to \infty} \beta^k \bar{E}_t[p_{t+k}] = 0$. Then, iterating the above equation gives the asset price as the average subjective expectation of the discounted present value of earning:

$$p_t = \tilde{p}_t \equiv \bar{E}_t\left[\sum_{k=1}^{\infty} \beta^k e_{t+k}\right]. \tag{2}$$

The full-information rational-expectations (FIRE) counterpart is given by

$$p_t^* \equiv \mathbb{E}_t\left[\sum_{k=1}^{\infty}\beta^k e_{t+k}\right],$$

where $\mathbb{E}_t$ stands for the rational information conditional on full information about the economy's history about to, and inclusive of, period t. The paper's contribution is to provide an empirical proxy for $\tilde{p}_t$, to contrast it to an empirical proxy for p_t^*, and to document how the former helps account for a number of empirical regularities that appear as puzzles under the FIRE prism.[2]

Before I elaborate on this contribution, let me clarify what this angle misses. To obtain equation (2) from equation (1), I made three simplifying assumptions: I disregarded the role of time-varying risk, liquidity, and noise traders; I assumed the law of iterated expectations, which holds when expectations are both rational and homogeneous but not more generally; and finally I imposed a no-bubble condition. Relaxing these assumptions yields the following generalized asset-pricing equation:

$$p_t = \underbrace{\bar{E}_t\left[\sum_{k=1}^{\infty}\beta^k e_{t+k}\right]}_{\tilde{p}_t} + \mathcal{U}_t + \mathcal{B}_t, \tag{3}$$

where

$$\mathcal{U}_t \equiv \bar{E}_t\left[\sum_{k=0}^{\infty}\beta^k u_{t+k}\right]$$

embeds news about future risk, liquidity needs, and noise traders, and

$$\mathcal{B}_t \equiv \sum_{k=1}^{\infty}\beta^k\left\{\bar{E}_t^k[e_{t+k}] - \bar{E}_t^1[e_{t+k}]\right\} + \lim_{k\to\infty}\beta^k\bar{E}_t^k[p_{t+k}]$$

captures the roles of speculation and bubbles. More precisely, $\mathcal{B}_t$ combines the traditional form of explosive bubbles in the sense of $\lim_{k\to\infty}\beta^k\bar{E}_t^k[p_{t+k}] \neq 0$ with finite bubbles, or speculation more generally, in the sense of a nonzero wedge between first- and higher-order beliefs.

Equation (3) helps position the authors' paper to the broader asset-pricing literature. This paper is all about $\tilde{p}_t$ and its difference from p_t^{FIRE}; the literature on long-term risk is all about $\mathcal{U}_t$; and the literature on speculation and higher-order beliefs is all about $\mathcal{B}_t$. The paper's focus on $\tilde{p}_t$ is easily motivated, but the following important qualification must be kept in mind. In principle, $\tilde{p}_t - p_t^*$ could be correlated with $\mathcal{U}_t$ and $\mathcal{B}_t$. For instance, a "wave of optimism" may represent periods in which people do all the following at once: they overestimate earnings (which maps to a high $\tilde{p}_t$ relative to p_t^*); they underestimate risks (which maps to a high $\mathcal{U}_t$); and they overestimate their ability to beat the market (which maps to high $\tilde{\mathcal{B}}_t$). It follows that the offered empirical proxy, LTG, could confound variation in $\tilde{p}_t$ with variation in $\mathcal{U}_t$ and $\mathcal{B}_t$, even after controlling for fundamentals (or for p_t^*).

More succinctly, if overoptimism about earnings correlates with overoptimism about the ability to beat the market, is it the former or the latter that drives the Shiller puzzle? The evidence provided in the paper does not allow an answer to this question. Notwithstanding this limitation, I share the authors' prior that LTG is likely to be more tightly connected to subjective expectations of earnings than to any of the other, omitted, forces—and I adopt this prior in interpreting their evidence below.

III. Theory Meets Evidence

In the preceding analysis, I defined two key theoretical objects: the average subjective expectation of the discounted present value of earnings, denoted by $\tilde{p}_t$; and its FIRE counterpart, denoted by p_t^*. If one wishes to quantify how important deviations from rationality (or, more precisely, from FIRE) are in driving actual asset prices, one may therefore proceed as follows: construct empirical proxies for $\tilde{p}_t$ and p_t^*, and check which one of the two accounts is better for the observed fluctuations in actual prices.

From this perspective, we can read the paper as follows. First, let me clearly distinguish the theoretical objects defined above from the empirical counterparts found in the authors' paper: the variables $\tilde{p}_t$ and p_t^* defined above are henceforth denoted by $\tilde{p}_t^{\text{theory}}$ and $p_t^{*,\text{theory}}$, respectively, whereas the corresponding empirical proxies in the paper are denoted by $\tilde{p}_t^{\text{data}}$ and $p_t^{*,\text{data}}$, respectively.

Next, let us zero in on how $\tilde{p}_t^{\text{data}}$ and $p_t^{*,\text{data}}$ are defined and whether they are valid proxies for their theoretical counterparts. Start with $\tilde{p}_t^{\text{data}}$, which is the heart of the authors' contribution. The authors use surveys of analysts to calculate both short-term forecasts of earnings over the next 2 years, measured by $\text{EPS}_{t,t+1}$ and $\text{EPS}_{t,t+2}$, and longer-term forecasts of earnings over the next 10 years, measured by LTG_t. The details of these measures can be found in the paper.[3] For the purposes of my discussion, it suffices to note the following. If we treat these survey-based forecast measures as empirical proxies for $\bar{E}_t[e_{t+k}]$ over $k \in \{1, 2, \ldots, 10\}$, and if we proxy e_{t+k} for $k \geq 11$ with the unconditional mean of e_t, then we reach the following empirical counterpart for $\tilde{p}_t^{\text{theory}}$:

$$\tilde{p}_t^{\text{data}} \equiv \text{EPS}_{t,t+1} + \beta\text{EPS}_{t,t+2} + \left(\sum_{k=2}^{10}\beta^k\right)\text{LTG}_t + \left(\sum_{k=11}^{\infty}\beta^k\right)\bar{e}. \qquad (4)$$

Let us now turn to the FIRE benchmark, $p_t^{*,\text{theory}}$, and its empirical counterpart, $p_t^{*,\text{data}}$. One possibility is to define the latter as the realized discounted present value of earnings, namely to let

$$p_t^{*,\text{data}} \equiv \sum_{k=1}^{\infty}\beta^{k-1}e_{t+k}. \qquad (5)$$

This is a valid empirical proxy for $p_t^{*,\text{theory}}$ because the difference between realized earnings and their FIRE forecasts is necessarily unpredictable under the FIRE hypothesis; in other words, $p_t^{*,\text{data}}$ equals $p_t^{*,\text{theory}}$ plus measurement error. But there is an obvious problem with the above definition: we, as econometricians, cannot observe realized earnings up to infinity. Given this constraint, let us redefine the relevant empirical proxy as

$$p_t^{*,\text{data}} \equiv \sum_{k=1}^{T-t}\beta^{k-1}e_{t+k} + \beta^{T-t}p_T,$$

where T is the end period in our (the authors') data.

Note that $p_t^{*,\text{data}}$ has at least two theoretical interpretations. The one used by the authors, and self-evident in equation (5), is that it coincides with the equilibrium price under perfect foresight. I instead have interpreted $p_t^{*,\text{data}}$ as an empirical proxy for the equilibrium price that obtains under FIRE, which is a weaker assumption than perfect foresight. The two interpretations are mutually consistent for the reason already explained: under FIRE, the difference between perfect- and imperfect-foresight outcomes is unpredictable. This basic observation closes the gap between what the paper does (which, as mentioned in the beginning, is based on the Campbell-Shiller decomposition) and the theoretical backdrop I introduced above.

Finally, note that everything I have done here is in terms of levels, because I have implicitly assumed a stationary environment. The actual implementation in the paper allows for unit roots and trends, following the traditional approach of analyzing price-earnings ratios and growth rates. This is necessary given that earnings and asset prices in the data are not stationary, but the essence is the same.

We are now ready to inspect how $\tilde{p}_t$ and p_t^* look in the data and how they relate to actual asset-price movements. This is done in figure 1, which is a reproduction of that found in the paper. Three facts are evident here:

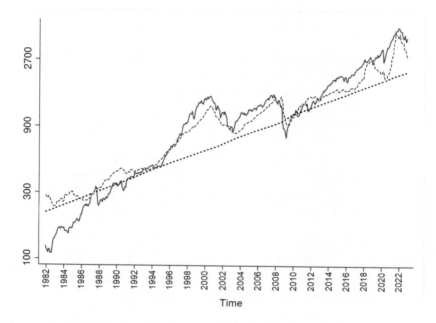

Fig. 1. Taken from the paper, the figure plots in log scale the levels of the S&P 500 index (solid line), the rational benchmark index (p_t^*, dotted line), and the price index based on earnings forecasts ($\tilde{p}_t$, dashed line). A color version of this figure is available online.

1. p_t is almost entirely disconnected from p_t^*, and the former's variance is multiple times larger than the latter's.

2. $\tilde{p}_t$ is also disconnected from p_t^*.

3. There appears to be significant comovement between p_t and $\tilde{p}_t$, especially at the business-cycle frequencies, and the two variables have commensurate volatility at these frequencies.

Fact 1 is familiar. The key lesson here is facts 2 and, especially, 3: Shiller's puzzle and the apparent disconnect between asset prices and fundamentals largely disappear once we measure "fundamentals" by the subjective expectations of earnings.

Clearly, this is a valuable lesson: if we take the variation in the subjective expectations of future earnings growth for granted, we have made a significant progress in accounting for the observed cycles in asset prices. But the puzzle is not really gone. Instead, it takes a new form: Why are subjective expectations so disconnected from the rational ones? And what drives their variation in the first place?

IV.   Structural Interpretation: Some Challenges

Toward answering the above questions, the authors propose to replace the rational expectations hypothesis with an alternative model of how expectations are formed. Here, I review this model and identify a key limitation of it.

The authors' main idea, consistent with their broader agenda on "Diagnostic Expectations" (e.g., Bordalo, Gennaioli, and Shleifer 2017; Bordalo, Gennaioli, La Porta, Shleifer 2020, Bordalo, Gennaioli, Ma, Shleifer 2020), is that people tend to overextrapolate from recent innovation in earnings. This idea can be operationalized as follows. First, suppose that the true, objective, process for earnings growth is an AR(1) process:

$$e_{t+1} = \mu e_t + v_{t+1}, \tag{6}$$

where e_t is earnings at time t, v_t is an i.i.d. innovation, and $\mu \in (0, 1)$ is the actual persistence in earning. Next, suppose that the agents believe, incorrectly, that earnings obey the following process:

$$e_{t+1} = \mu e_t + \omega_t + v_{t+1}, \tag{7}$$

where ω_t is itself an AR(1) process with the same innovation,

$$\omega_t = \rho \omega_{t-1} + \theta v_t, \tag{8}$$

with $\rho \in (0, 1)$ and $\theta > 0$. By equations (6) and (7), ω_t identifies the excess optimism/pessimism about future earnings:

$$\omega_t = \mathbb{E}_t^{\text{subjectve}}[e_{t+1}] - \mathbb{E}_t^{\text{rational}}[e_{t+1}].$$

By equation (6), such excess optimism/pessimism is itself persistent (because $\rho > 0$), and the innovations in it are positively correlated with the actual innovations in earnings (because $\theta > 0$). Putting everything together, we have that the following is true: whenever there is a positive innovation in earnings, people become excessively optimistic about future earnings, and their optimism outlasts the actual increase in earnings.

In short, there is overreaction in expectations, particularly at medium horizons. Clearly, this is going in the right direction: the evidence demands that subjective expectations are more volatile than rational ones. But how close can we get to the data with this simple model? Why not estimate the parameters ρ and θ, which regulate the gap between subjective and rational beliefs, on some key moments, and then evaluate the model's quantitative performance on other relevant moments?

For instance, suppose we calibrate ρ and θ so as to match the persistence and the volatility of the difference between $\tilde{p}_t$ and p_t^*. This would "solve" the volatility puzzle by construction. But I suspect that this success would come at two obvious costs: first, it would require an incredibly large value for θ, and second, it would predict, counterfactually, that the variation in long-term forecasts far exceeds that in short-term forecasts; that is,

$$\text{Var}(\text{LTG}_t) > \text{Var}(\text{EPS}_t).$$

The first point is obvious: that is what it takes, according to the authors' model, to make $\tilde{p}_t$ multiple times more volatile than p_t^*. The second point stems from the more substantial loading of these mistakes in medium-term forecasts.

Alternatively, suppose we estimate an AR(1) process for earnings growth, obtain estimates for the earning innovations v_t, and proceed to estimate θ and ρ by regressing LTG_t (or $\tilde{p}_t$) on these estimated innovations. I suspect that this exercise, which takes the author's model of expectations "seriously," would deliver a much smaller estimate for θ than the previous exercise and would fail to account for the excess volatility puzzle. Instead, I suspect that most of the volatility LTG_t and $\tilde{p}_t$, and most of their covariation with actual stock prices, is accounted from a persistent residual that is itself orthogonal to earnings. That is, I guess a "better" model of subjective expectations seems to be one where (i) the gap between subjective and rational expectations is given by

$$\omega_t = \rho\omega_{t-1} + \theta v_t + u_t, \tag{9}$$

where the new term, u_t, is a pure "noise," orthogonal to current, past, and future earnings; and (ii) this noise accounts for a much larger fraction of the variation in ω_t than the actual innovation in earnings.

Assuming that my guess is correct, what have we really learned? Are the fluctuations in LTG_t and asset prices the product of significant over-extrapolation from past earnings? Or are they merely the manifestation of large, persistent waves of optimism and pessimism that have little connection to actual earnings?

A similar point applies to the authors' narrative about business cycles. In previous work (Angeletos, Collard, and Dellas 2018), I have argued that, within the class of business-cycle model customarily used in theoretical and quantitative work, one can make large gains in accounting for the data by augmenting these models with large, persistent waves of optimism and pessimism that have little connection to fundamentals such as TFP and monetary or fiscal policy. I suspect that this lesson survives the inclusion of LTG_t as part of the data that the model must fit. Therefore, although I am fully on board with the authors' idea of using LTG_t as a measure of subjective expectation and of disciplining theory with it, I am not sure yet what the take-home lesson is about the "origins" of the fluctuations in either asset prices or macroeconomic quantities.

Let me use a concrete episode to illustrate what I mean. During the "dot-com bubble," the stock market, aggregate investment, and the expectations measure LTG_t all surged together. But we know that this had little, if anything, to do with positive innovation in actual earnings. The authors may want to interpret this episode as overextrapolation of some kind of "news." But if such news is completely orthogonal to actual fundamentals, what is the gain from calling them "news" as opposed to pure random mistakes in expectations and is overextrapolation different from the persistence of such mistakes? In my view, it would be desirable to disentangle more precisely whether the aggregate data require overextrapolation for past earnings or just persistent animal spirits.

To be fair, the paper offers a battery of evidence at the micro level (cross section of assets) that is extremely informative but that I will not review here. This evidence points, quite persuasively, in the direction of persistent mistakes in expectations and of predictable boom-busts in asset prices and investment. But it remains unclear how much of this predictability is due to overextrapolation from past earnings and how much of it is due to persistent animal spirits. In summary, I think a natural next step would be to quantify the relative contribution of overextrapolation and animal spirits at both the macro and the micro levels. And although there is no reason to expect this contribution to be the same at the two levels, the micro evidence may of course help discipline the answer to the macro question.

V. What about Macro Impact?

Let me now zero in on how useful the observed fluctuations in LTG are for understanding business cycles in real macroeconomic quantities. Toward this goal, I conduce the following exercise. First, I take a macro VAR with the "usual suspects" (unemployment, gross domestic product, investment, hours worked, consumption, utilization-adjusted TFP, inflation, and interest rates) and augment with three key variables from the authors' paper: the subjective expectations measure LTG, the actual 1-year earnings growth, and stock prices. Next, I identify various semistructural shocks, each one of which accounts, by construction, for the bulk of the business-cycle variation in a targeted variable (say, unemployment or LTG). Finally, I inspect the comovements generated by these shocks and use these comovements to inform theory (i.e., to detect what kind of models have a good chance to account for the data).

This exercise builds on my prior "anatomy" of US business cycles (Angeletos, Collard, and Dellas 2020). There, I argued that the business cycle can be accounted by a single shock called the Main Business Cycle Shock (MBC), which exhibits the following key empirical properties. First, it accounts for more than 50% of the fluctuations in unemployment, output, investment, and hours worked at business-cycle frequencies. Second, it looks the same—in terms of both variance contributions and dynamic comovements/impulse response functions (IRFs)—whether it is identified by targeting unemployment (my preferred specification) or by targeting any other of the aforementioned quantities. Third, it is orthogonal to measured TFP at all horizons, which suggests this shock is neither a conventional TFP shock nor a news shock about future TFP. Fourth, it explains little of the fluctuations in inflation, which challenges its interpretation as a demand shock moving the economy along a (nonflat) Phillips curve. Finally, this shock appears to capture waves of optimism and pessimism that are uncorrelated to measured fundamentals; see also the complementary structural findings in Angeletos et al. (2018).

Table 1 repeats the empirical exercise from my previous work after the inclusion of earnings, LTG, and stock prices. The first row, in particular, revisits the original MBC shock (namely the shock that targets unemployment). Evidently, the main lesson from my earlier work survives: this shock continues to account for the bulk of the fluctuations in all the key macroeconomic quantities (but not of TFP or inflation). But a new lesson also emerges: although this shock accounts for a sizable component of the

Table 1
Variance Contributions of the MBC and Other Shocks to Different Variables

Target	u	Y	h	I	TFP	π	e	LTG	p
Unemployment (u)	61.6	41.3	44.0	43.8	6.0	5.6	24.9	12.3	31.0
Forecasts (LTG)	6.2	7.8	4.5	8.0	4.2	4.6	8.7	70.2	27.2
Earnings growth (e)	17.4	11.5	18.0	10.1	5.1	19.2	81.5	8.6	7.1
Stock prices (p)	32.9	30.7	20.1	30.0	7.7	4.2	6.4	36.2	83.5

Note: MBC = Main Business Cycle; TFP = total factor productivity; LTG = long-term growth in earnings.

fluctuations in asset prices, it does not appear to account for much of the fluctuations in LTG.

The second row shows the flip side: the "LTG shock," namely the shock identified by maximizing its contribution to LTG, accounts for 70% of the variation in LTG itself and for nearly 30% of the variation in stock prices, but only for 5%–10% of the variation in employment, output, hours, and investment. The last two rows complete the picture by considering the shocks that target, respectively, the actual earnings growth and stock prices. Two more lessons obtain. First, the shock that accounts for most of the fluctuations in actual earnings accounts for little of the fluctuations in the key macroeconomic variable and for even less of the fluctuations in LTG and stock prices. And second, the shock that accounts for most of the fluctuations in stock prices accounts for about 30% of the fluctuations in other macro quantities or LTG.

I am unsure how to reconcile these findings with those in the paper. The exercises in the paper emphasize statistical significance at the micro level, whereas my exercise here focuses on variance contributions at the macro level. But when I look at the above table, I am led to a different structural interpretation than that advocated by the authors: although the ups and downs in LTG help account for a significant portion of the boom and busts in asset prices (consistent with fig. 1), they are less useful for accounting for the business cycles, and they also do not appear to be triggered by fluctuations in actual earnings. Put differently, I see again more evidence in favor of "animal spirits" than in favor of "overextrapolation."

Let me dig a bit further by inspecting the dynamic patterns induced by the first two of the four identified shocks in table 1. The remaining two are omitted because they add little to the overall picture.

Figure 2 zeroes in on the IRFs of the economy with respect to the MBC shock.[4] Clearly, the shock generates the kind of joint dynamics in unemployment and other macro quantities that one naturally associates with real-world business cycles: large comovements in all these variables that last for a few years. This echoes my earlier work. What is novel in this figure is how the MBC shock propagates in actual and expected earnings. On the one hand, we see that a sizable boom in real economic activity triggers a boom-bust in actual earnings growth. On the other hand, we see that this comes together with a modest but persistent boom in subjective expectations. This picture seems consistent with the authors' overextrapolation hypothesis, except that the value of θ needed to account for this evidence is likely to be much smaller than that needed to account for the excess volatility puzzle.

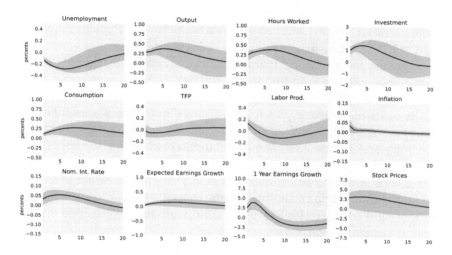

Fig. 2. The Main Business Cycle shock

Figure 3 shifts the focus to the LTG shock, namely the shock that accounts for the bulk of the fluctuations in subjective expectation of earnings. Evidently, positive innovations in LTG trigger sizable and relatively persistent fluctuations in LTG itself, together with a boom-bust in actual earnings growth. They also predict a rather persistent movement in investment, but they do not seem to trigger significant movements in unemployment or

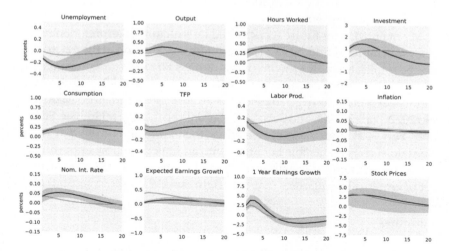

Fig. 3. The long-term growth shock (gray lines) versus the Main Business Cycle shock (black lines). A color version of this figure is available online.

hours worked. Finally, and perhaps more surprisingly, a positive innovation in LTG appears to contains news about future TFP.

Together, these findings paint a more complex—and arguably more intriguing—picture than that in the authors' paper. It seems that LTG is a proxy for at least three different forces: (i) overextrapolation of innovations in actual earning, which is the authors' main hypothesis; (ii) news about future TFP, which is the focus of another important literature (Beaudry and Portier 2006; Jaimovich and Rebelo 2009; Lorenzoni 2009; Barsky and Sims 2011); and extrinsic sentiments, as in some of my work (Angeletos and La'O 2013; Angeletos et al. 2018) or the earlier literature on multiple equilibria and animal spirits. I hope that future work will shed further light on the relative importance of these three forces and on the "right" structural interpretation of the data.

VI. Conclusion

In conclusion, this is an impressive paper, full of interesting, informative, and novel facts. It provides compelling evidence that fluctuations in subjective expectations, as measured by LTG, helps account for fluctuations in asset prices and investment both in the aggregate and in the cross section. And although I have quibbled about both the right structural interpretation and the significance of these findings for business cycles, it should be clear that my own explorations are only a natural follow-up to the authors' own contribution.

My main wish for future work would be structural interpretation of the relevant empirical findings and a quantitative evaluation of the macroeconomic implications. A growing literature has already started evaluating the quantitative performance of fully fledged macro models without fully rational expectations (e.g., Angeletos et al. 2018; Bhandari, Borovička, and Ho 2022; Bianchi, Ilut, and Saijo 2021; Bordalo et al. 2021; L'Huillier, Singh, and Yoo 2021 and various references therein). The current paper by Bordalo et al. presents this literature with an important new opportunity, by providing both a compelling measure for subjective expectations and a set of empirical regularities that the "right" model ought to account for.

Endnotes

Author email address: Angeletos (angeletos@northwestern.edu). I am grateful to Fabrice Collard for his help in generating the results of Section V and to Dalton Rongxuan Zhang for his help in drafting this comment. For acknowledgments, sources of research support, and disclosure of the author's material financial relationships, if any, please

see https://www.nber.org/books-and-chapters/nber-macroeconomics-annual-2023-volume
-38/comment-long-term-expectations-and-aggregate-fluctuations-2-angeletos.

1. To ease the exposition, I abstract from any difference between earnings and dividends so that e_t stands interchangeably for dividends and earnings. Also note that the assumption of CARA preferences and Gaussian uncertainty.

2. The authors of this paper use, as does much of the literature, *rational expectations* (RE) as synonymous to "rational expectations with a representative agent." The latter assumes not only rational expectations (i.e., coincidence of subjective beliefs and objective distributions) but also complete information (i.e., that all agents share the same information and that they have common knowledge of everything, including one another's rationality). A large theoretical literature has highlighted how the relaxation of the latter assumption can help rationalize a number of phenomena that prima facie look like failures of rationality. With this in mind, I am careful to refer to the relevant benchmark as FIRE instead of merely RE.

3. We should note a terminological discrepancy between finance and macro here. The term *long-term* is not the same as that typically understood in macroeconomics. In this context, it pertains more to business-cycle frequencies or the short-to-medium term—the LTG measure is defined under the business-cycle frequency. A point to bear in mind is that the measure is an average of analysts' expectations for individual firm earnings. This can be likened to each person predicting their income and then these expectations being aggregated. It is important to note that the mean expectation of personal income may not equate to the mean expectation of aggregate income. Similarly, the average expectations of individual firm earnings may not necessarily align with the average expectations of aggregate earnings. Thus, there might be a discrepancy between what we believe is priced in the centralized market and this measure. Although it is important to note this potential difference, its significance remains uncertain, and I will abstract from it.

4. Keep in mind that this shock looks the same, in terms of both variance contributions and IRFs, whether it is identified by targeting unemployment (the specification used here) or any other of the aforementioned macro quantities. See Angeletos et al. (2020) for further details and a battery of robustness checks.

References

Angeletos, G.-M., F. Collard, and H. Dellas. 2018. "Quantifying Confidence." *Econometrica* 86:1689–726.

———. 2020. "Business-Cycle Anatomy." *American Economic Review* 110: 3030–70.

Angeletos, G.-M., and J. La'O. 2013. "Sentiments." *Econometrica* 81:739–79.

Barsky, R. B., and E. R. Sims. 2011. "News Shocks and Business Cycles." *Journal of Monetary Economics* 58:273–89.

Beaudry, P., and F. Portier. 2006. "Stock Prices, News, and Economic Fluctuations." *American Economic Review* 96 (4): 1293–307.

Bhandari, A., J. Borovička, and P. Ho. 2022. "Survey Data and Subjective Beliefs in Business Cycle Models." Mimeo, New York.

Bianchi, F., C. L. Ilut, and H. Saijo. 2021. "Diagnostic Business Cycles." Working Paper no. 28604, NBER, Cambridge, MA.

Bordalo, P., N. Gennaioli, R. La Porta, and A. Shleifer. 2020. "Belief Overreaction and Stock Market Puzzles." Working Paper no. 27283, NBER, Cambridge, MA.

Bordalo, P., N. Gennaioli, Y. Ma, and A. Shleifer. 2020. "Overreaction in Macroeconomic Expectations." *American Economic Review* 110 (9): 2748–82.

Bordalo, P., N. Gennaioli, and A. Shleifer. 2017. "Diagnostic Expectations and Credit Cycles." *Journal of Finance* 73:199–227.

Bordalo, P., N. Gennaioli, A. Shleifer, and S. J. Terry. 2021. "Real Credit Cycles." Working Paper no. 28416, NBER, Cambridge, MA.

Jaimovich, N., and S. Rebelo. 2009. "Can News about the Future Drive the Business Cycle?" *American Economic Review* 99:1097–118.

L'Huillier, J.-P., S. R. Singh, and D. Yoo. 2021. "Incorporating Diagnostic Expectations into the New Keynesian Framework." https://ssrn.com/abstract=3910318.

Lorenzoni, G. 2009. "A Theory of Demand Shocks." *American Economic Review* 99:2050–84.

Singleton, K. J. 1987. "Asset Prices in a Time-Series Model with Disparately Informed, Competitive Traders." In *New Approaches to Monetary Economics*, ed. W. A. Barnett and K. J. Singleton, 249–72. Cambridge: Cambridge University Press.

Comment

Venky Venkateswaran, *New York University and NBER,* United States of America

This paper, Bordalo et al. (2023), is the latest in a series of interesting and thought-provoking papers by the authors (along with other coauthors) using survey data to help explain/understand classic questions in macro and finance: What are the fundamental drivers—and the associated mechanisms—of fluctuations in aggregate economic activity and asset prices? What is the role of behavioral biases in these phenomena?

The primary contribution here is to make the case that forecasts by equity analysts of long-term earnings growth rates (LTG) are key to understanding movements in financial-market variables and macro aggregates. The forecast data come from the Institutional Brokers' Estimate System (IBES), which asks respondents to report the expected operating earnings growth "over the company's next full business cycle," defined as a period of 3–5 years.[1] In addition, respondents also report forecasts of earnings (in levels, usually on a per share basis) at short horizons (usually a couple of years from the reporting date).

A few comments about the coverage of the data on this dimension are in order. Most stocks (more than 75%) in the S&P 500 index have LTG entries in any given year, with an average number of analysts reporting LTG around 2. Both these metrics show a declining trend over the past 2 decades. For comparison, coverage for short-horizon forecasts has been relatively more stable, with almost all firms in the S&P 500 reporting forecasts in a given year and an average of 15–20 reporting analysts. Despite the lower coverage for the LTG forecasts, the composition of analysts making those forecasts is tilted, if only slightly, toward the more prolific and accurate analysts, a reassuring pattern.[2] Finally, a number of LTG

NBER Macroeconomics Annual, volume 38, 2024.

forecasts are accompanied by a price target, which lines up reasonably well with the value implied by the LTG forecast.

An important concern is whether analysts are adapting their forecasts in response to changes in stock prices—or, more generally, learning from market prices as in Grossman and Stiglitz (1980). In a recent paper, Chaudhry (2023) tests exactly this hypothesis exploiting plausibly exogenous mutual fund flow-induced trading. He finds that exogenous price increases raise both LTG and short-term forecasts. The magnitudes are consistent with the interpretation that analysts are revising their forecasts to rationalize observed price changes. This concern also gains some steam from the observation that other long-term forecasts (such as the 10-year gross domestic product [GDP] growth forecasts from the Survey of Professional Forecasters) seem to be much more stable. In other words, if LTG movements do indeed reflect beliefs about long-run fundamentals, they seem to be predominantly those of equity-market participants.

The authors try to address this concern in a companion paper, Bordalo et al. (2022). Specifically, in that paper, the authors report that (i) about a third of the variation in revisions to LTG are explained by past LTG and sustained earnings growth, and past returns do not add much explanatory power, and (ii) LTG predicts future stock returns even after controlling for price-earnings ratios. They interpret these findings as evidence that LTG is not simply the result of analysts mechanically reverse-engineering market prices (and are consistent with a model of extrapolative behavior). These are reassuring findings, but only modestly so. Although they do point to a component of LTG that is distinct from the information contained in prices, the extent to which that component drives the excess volatility and the investment effects—the objects of interest in this paper—is less clear. More work is needed, perhaps incorporating implied volatility, to isolate the effects of extrapolative biases.

A related concern stems from agency frictions. It is well known that sell-side equity analysts' forecasts show significant evidence of positive bias (i.e., analysts are systematically overoptimistic about earnings). This is often attributed to the fact that sell-side equity analysts are effectively paid by investment banking or trading businesses—see, for example, Michaely and Womack (1999) and Jackson (2005). The positive bias is apparent in the LTG data as well—the average LTG is significantly higher than realized earnings growth. Bordalo et al. (2023) effectively assume that this is likely to be a time-invariant bias and so can be ignored when studying fluctuations. They also argue that this is especially likely to be the case for large stocks. It would be nice to see evidence, even if suggestive or anecdotal, supporting these claims. It is not unreasonable to conjecture that the incentives for equity analysts to distort fluctuate with conditions in the investment banking business. One strategy would be to use proxies for these conditions (e.g., deal flows) as controls.

The first set of results emphasized in the paper relates to the well-known excess volatility puzzle in Shiller (1981). Shiller showed that, if we assume rational expectations and a constant required rate of return, the observed variability of dividend growth implies an upper bound for the volatility of the price-dividend ratio. Because dividend growth in the data is quite stable, the bound is also quite low, far below the observed volatility in that ratio. This striking finding has sparked a large literature that tries to resolve this puzzle. This body of work is too voluminous to survey here, so I will confine myself to mentioning a couple of the better-known resolutions here. One influential approach is based on time-variation in discount rates (more precisely, in risk premia)—for example, as in Campbell and Cochrane (1999), Bansal and Yaron (2004), or Wachter (2013). Another approach departs from rational expectations, for example, by introducing learning, as in Barsky and De Long (1993).

The authors perform a simple experiment to demonstrate an alternate resolution using survey evidence on LTG. They construct an expectations-based index of stock prices over time using a time-invariant discount rate and the observed LTG forecast at each t (suitably aggregated from stock-level forecasts) for the expected earnings growth for years $t + 2$ through $t + 10$. Short-run forecasts and current earnings are used for horizons shorter than 2 years, and the terminal growth rate (beyond year 10) is set to match the average level of stock prices in the sample:

$$\tilde{p}_t = e_t + g_{t,t+1} + \alpha g_{t+1,t+2} + \sum_{s=2}^{10} \alpha^s LTG_t + \frac{\alpha^{10}}{1 - \alpha} g. \tag{1}$$

This price series displays considerably higher variability relative to Shiller's rational expectations benchmark and does remarkably well in matching the observed price fluctuations, especially at the low frequency. The paper then makes the case that this volatility is the result, at least partly, of systematic departures from rationality. It does so by showing that LTG systematically predicts future forecast errors at both long and short horizons: a high LTG forecast today is associated with positive forecast errors in the future. There is also a positive, albeit weak, relationship between LTG and expected returns from the Richmond Fed's CFO Survey. In other words, high LTG (and arguably, therefore, high equity valuations) is associated with high expected returns, which is contrary to the predictions of models with time-varying discount rates. In those models, high valuations are associated with low risk premia and, therefore, low expected returns.

The next set of results examines the ability of LTG revisions to predict changes in interest rates, credit spreads, and investment. They show that an upward revision to LTG is associated with higher short- and long-term interest rates, both contemporaneously and over the following three quarters. Further out, the relationship turns negative, arguably due to reversal of the initial uptick in LTG. The opposite pattern is observed in credit spreads (tightening at short horizons followed by widening), though the relationship is weaker.

The investment results show a striking pattern: an upward revision to LTG sparks an almost immediate investment boom with the investment-capital ratio rising by about 3% over a horizon of 3 quarters and then reversing these gains at a horizon of 7–10 quarters. To tie the reversal to the predictable reversal in "optimism," a fitted value for future forecast errors (obtained by regressing observed forecast errors on the level of LTG) is added to the regression and shown to account for the entire future reversal.[3] These patterns hold at both the aggregate and the firm levels.

These findings are very interesting but also somewhat puzzling. In a simple neoclassical setting, an upward revision in long-run productivity growth tends to cause an investment slump in the short run. This is a well-known issue (often referred to as the comovement puzzle) in the literature on news shocks—see, for example, Jaimovich and Rebelo (2009). A possible resolution acts through a financial accelerator channel, among other ingredients (see Christiano and Motto 2014). A natural direction for future research is to evaluate this hypothesis with a full-fledged quantitative model, but independently, it might be useful to look for reduced-form evidence supporting this financial channel. The results on interest rates and spreads are suggestive but can be strengthened further by looking at quantity variables as well. For example, is the investment boom sparked by an LTG revision accompanied by firms raising capital, whether in the form of debt or equity? As with the investment regressions, this exercise can be made more convincing by running them at both the aggregate and the firm levels.[4]

The last set of results extends the analysis to other macro variables—GDP, consumption, employment, wages, and inflation. The patterns are similar to those for investment—an upward revision to LTG acts like a "positive" business-cycle shock in the short run (3–4 quarters), which largely reverses itself over a longer horizon (6–10 quarters ahead).[5] The

LTG is also shown to be correlated with the marginal efficiency of investment (MEI) shock, which Justiniano, Primiceri, and Tambalotti (2011) argue plays a dominant role in US business-cycle fluctuations.

Interpreting these results as the discovery of a new factor (a "miracle" variable, as the authors term it in the introduction) driving volatility in economic activity and financial markets might be premature. At the very least, it remains to be shown that LTG fluctuations can quantitatively account for the business-cycle data. Second, it is not clear how we can distinguish LTG from other contenders for that title, especially if LTG partly reflects (to the extent analysts are changing their forecasts in response to stock market valuations) those factors.[6]

In summary, Bordalo et al. (2023) is a valuable addition to an influential agenda and contains a wealth of results spanning many important topics in macroeconomics and finance. It also raises interesting questions about belief formation and mechanisms through which it affects the economy—questions which will spark and guide future work in this important area.

Endnotes

Author email address: Venkateswaran (vvenkate@stern.nyu.edu). For acknowledgments, sources of research support, and disclosure of the author's material financial relationships, if any, please see https://www.nber.org/books-and-chapters/nber-macroeconomics-annual-2023-volume-38/comment-long-term-expectations-and-aggregate-fluctuations-venkateswaran.

1. The use of earnings growth—as opposed to say, dividend growth—is common practice in the literature, because data on the latter are available only for more recent time periods.

2. For this purpose, *prolific* and *accurate* are defined as being above median in terms of the number of forecasts and below median in terms of mean-squared error.

3. It might be helpful to use the fitted forecast error specification for the other results in the paper as well, for example, the interest rate and credit spread effects.

4. In the absence of financial frictions, it is not clear that firms should raise investment in response to overoptimism in stock markets (unless, of course, the firm is also subject to the same bias).

5. Again, here it would be helpful to see the extent to which the reversal can be explained by the predictable component of future forecast errors.

6. To cite a few, in addition to the MEI shock of Justiniano et al. (2011), we also have risk shocks from Christiano and Motto (2014) and the confidence shock in Angeletos, Collard, and Dellas (2018).

References

Angeletos, George-Marios, Fabrice Collard, and Harris Dellas. 2018. "Quantifying Confidence." *Econometrica* 86 (5): 1689–726.

Bansal, Ravi, and Amir Yaron. 2004. "Risks for the Long Run: A Potential Resolution of Asset Pricing Puzzles." *Journal of Finance* 59 (4): 1481–509.

Barsky, Robert B., and J. Bradford De Long. 1993. "Why Does the Stock Market Fluctuate?" *Quarterly Journal of Economics* 108 (2): 291–311.

Bordalo, Pedro, Nicola Gennaioli, Rafael La Porta, Matthew OBrien, and Andrei Shleifer. 2023. "Long-Term Expectations and Aggregate Fluctuations." *NBER Macroeconomics Annual* 38 (1): 311–347.

Bordalo, Pedro, Nicola Gennaioli, Rafael La Porta, and Andrei Shleifer. 2022. "Belief Overreaction and Stock Market Puzzles." Working Paper no. 27283, NBER, Cambridge, MA.

Campbell, John Y., and John H. Cochrane. 1999. "By Force of Habit: A Consumption-Based Explanation of Aggregate Stock Market Behavior." *Journal of Political Economy* 107 (2): 205–51.

Chaudhry, Aditya. 2023. "The Impact of Prices on Analyst Cash Flow Expectations." https://ssrn.com/abstract=4443349.

Christiano, Lawrence J., and Roberto Motto. 2014. "Risk Shocks." *American Economic Review* 104 (1): 27–65.

Grossman, Sanford J., and Joseph E. Stiglitz. 1980. "On the Impossibility of Informationally Efficient Markets." *American Economic Review* 70 (3): 393–408.

Jackson, Andrew R. 2005. "Trade Generation, Reputation, and Sell-Side Analysts." *Journal of Finance* 60 (2): 673–717.

Jaimovich, Nir, and Sergio Rebelo. 2009. "Can News about the Future Drive the Business Cycle?" *American Economic Review* 99 (4): 1097–118.

Justiniano, Alejandro, Giorgio E. Primiceri, and Andrea Tambalotti. 2011. "Investment Shocks and the Relative Price of Investment." *Review of Economic Dynamics* 14 (1): 102–21.

Michaely, Roni, and Kent L. Womack. 1999. "Conflict of Interest and the Credibility of Underwriter Analyst Recommendations." *Review of Financial Studies* 12 (4): 653–86.

Shiller, Robert J. 1981. "Do Stock Prices Move Too Much to Be Justified by Subsequent Changes in Dividends?" *American Economic Review* 71 (3): 421–36.

Wachter, Jessica A. 2013. "Can Time-Varying Risk of Rare Disasters Explain Aggregate Stock Market Volatility?" *Journal of Finance* 68 (3): 987–1035.

Discussion

Gianluca Violante opened the discussion, commenting that the paper of Ricardo De la O and Sean Myers shows that cash-flow growth expectations explain most movements in the S&P 500 price-dividend and price-earnings ratios. In the De la O and Myers paper, short-run expectations have a more important role than long-run expectations. Instead, the authors have the opposite result: long-run expectations are more important. How can these two different views be reconciled? Is it possible that the definition of *long run* is different in these two works? Şebnem Kalemli-Özcan followed up with a similar comment. In the international literature, the relationship between exchange rate expectations and uncovered interest rate parity deviations is better captured by expectations of 12–18 months. Nicola Gennaioli explained that the two views can be reconciled because short-term expectations are very volatile and comove with earnings and dividends. This is why short-term expectations comove with the price-dividend ratio. However, although long-term earnings growth expectations predict market returns, short-term earnings growth expectations do not. Furthermore, long-term earnings growth expectations dampen the predictive power of the price-dividend ratio for returns. Thus, long-term expectations, not short-term ones, are key to understanding market inefficiency. Finally, replying to the discussants, Gennaioli explained that long-term earnings growth expectations are a valid proxy for nonrational beliefs because they exhibit significant independent variation from market prices. Long-term earnings growth expectations are partly revised by past earnings performance and partly by news about the future. However,

NBER Macroeconomics Annual, volume 38, 2024.

recent returns in the stock market cannot instead predict the revision of long-term earnings growth expectations.

Jennifer La'O pointed out that the predictability of forecast errors rules out full information rational expectation models but does not immediately imply irrationality. Indeed, predictability of the forecast errors can also be explained by a rational agents model with incomplete information. For example, if agents learn over time about a latent variable, it is possible to have predictability of forecast errors. Gennaioli replied that La'O is right. In this paper, the authors do not try to tease out the mechanism of expectation formation, which they do elsewhere but to show new empirical facts on the connection between measured expectations, the predictability of the error, and the macro-financial system. Understanding the scope of learning and irrationality is an interesting and open question for future work.

Ricardo Reis asked for a clarification of how the aggregate long-term growth forecast is constructed, because whether one weights by stock market value, book value, or amount of investment would make a big difference to how one interprets the results. Furthermore, he suggested that the authors estimate the investment regressions at the firm level instead of at the aggregate level, because authors could match the firm's earnings forecast with their respective balance sheet. It should be the case that when a firm's earnings forecasts are optimistic, then that firm invests more. Gennaioli explained that the long-term growth forecast is constructed as the value-weighted average of the median forecast of each firm. Furthermore, Gennaioli added that forecast error can be predicted at the firm level without relying on any weighting scheme. Furthermore, the investment regressions were also estimated at the firm level. These results were not shown in the presentation but are in the paper.

Daron Acemoglu pointed out that analysts' forecasts influence the market through the behavior of investors. However, if incentives of the analysts are changed, for example with an increase in their wage by 10% when they report more positive news, then it could be that investors, and thus the market, react less to analysts' information. To believe that analysts' forecasts are informative of market behavior, it must be assumed that investors' behavior is independent of analysts' incentives. To what extent can analysts' forecasts be a good proxy for market behavior? Gennaioli pointed out that there is no obvious reason to believe that the incentives of analysts should be unstable, due to incentives, in a way that induces them to be excessively optimistic in good times and pessimistic in bad times. Most importantly, this feature of expectations emerges when one looks at data from market participants that may have very different incentives from analysts. Other work with his coauthors shows that a chief financial officer's growth expectations of their own company were in line with analysts' expectations. Furthermore, a CFO's expectation predicted firm investment better than market variables, such as the Tobin's Q. Therefore, expectations data, including those of analysts, seem good proxies for beliefs about the future growth of firms.

Martin Eichenbaum commented that the comovement of news shocks and the business cycle cannot be explained by the real business-cycle model. However, nominal rigidities and credit market frictions can explain this comovement. Gennaioli agreed with this point and added that financial market frictions are an important complement to excessively volatile expectations, because the empirical results indeed show that financing investment when expectations are optimistic is relatively easier, potentially leading to a subsequent bust in investment when excess optimism is corrected.